THE GLOBAL
CONNECTION

by the same author

The Police
A Radical Future (ed.)
Crime and Society
Parks for People
The Fourth World (ed.)
The Foundations
The Police in Society
Minorities: A Question of Human Rights (ed.)
A Bridge of People

THE GLOBAL CONNECTION:

The Crisis of Drug Addiction

Ben Whitaker

JONATHAN CAPE
THIRTY-TWO BEDFORD SQUARE LONDON

First published 1987
Copyright © by Ben Whitaker 1987

Jonathan Cape Ltd, 32 Bedford Square, London WC1B 3EL

British Library Cataloguing in Publication Data

Whitaker, Ben
    The global connection: the crisis of drug addiction.
    1. Drug abuse
    I. Title
    362.2'93   HV5801

    ISBN 0-224-02224-5

The quotation from T. S. Eliot's *The Wasteland* on p. 414
appears by kind permission of Faber & Faber Ltd.

Photoset by Rowland Phototypesetting Ltd
Bury St Edmunds, Suffolk
Printed in Great Britain by Ebenezer Baylis & Son Ltd
The Trinity Press, Worcester and London

'I have drugged their Possets, that Death and
Nature do contend about them.'

Macbeth, II.ii.7

'That lies should be necessary to life is part and
parcel of the terrible and questionable character
of existence.'

Nietzsche, *The Will to Power*

'One does what one is; one becomes what one
does.'

Robert Musil

Contents

TABLES

Author's Note

I wish to thank, besides many who have asked to remain anonymous, the following for their help in discussing issues in this book: H. Bing Spear, B. Bubbear, Neville Nagler and others at the Home Office; Peter Lowes; Jasper Woodcock; Dr Michael Gossop; Dr Black and others at the DHSS; Roger Lewis; Michael Davies and Marian Bennett among others at the UN Narcotics Control Division, Vienna; Francis Huxley; Dr Philip Connell; Dr A. H. Ghodse; Mervyn Manby; Dr Victoria Blackstone; Dr Martin Mitcheson; Dr Jean Curtis-Raleigh; many individual members of Narcotics Anonymous, Parents Anonymous and Alcoholics Anonymous; Brian Moser; Bernard Simon; Prof. Alan Maynard; Steve Abrams; Dr Fish; Eleanor Sutter; Brian Inglis; Michael Schofield; Jenny and Dr Michael Barraclough; Malise Ruthven; Lady Barbara Wootton; Bill Rice of TACADE; the Rt Hon. Tim Raison MP and several colleagues at the Overseas Development Administration; Dr Davis amongst others at the Health Education Council; Dr Peter Bourne; Sir Bernard Braine MP; Jim McCulloch in Bangkok; James Walston in Rome; Brian Arbery and his colleagues at Turning Point; Lyn Perry and her colleagues at Release; Jane Christian and her colleagues at the Hungerford Project; John Calder; the Rev. Gordon Moody; Stanley Mitchell amongst others at the Scottish Health Education Group; Prof. Anthony Clare; Martin Short; Dr Brian Wilson; Dr Mitchell Rosenthal and Dr George de Leon of Phoenix House, New York; Frank Dobson MP; Michael Meacher MP; Dr Alfred McCoy of the University of New South Wales; Dr Lord David Pitt; Peter Cutting and others at HM Customs and Excise; Dr I. Khan and others at the World Health Organization; Mr Peter Imbert, Mr R. K. Broome, Chief Superintendent Penrose, Detective Inspector Lavery of the Royal Ulster Constabulary and many other police officers; the South Wales Association for the Prevention of Addiction; Professor and Mrs Schlesinger in New York; Robert Morgenthau (New York City District Attorney) and Charles Hefferhan; Bruce Jensen, Andrew Pucher and other members of the US Drug Enforcement Administration; Don des Jarlais and Bruce Johnson of the New York State Division of Substance Abuse Services; Brian Pratt of Oxfam, formerly in Lima; Diane Hayter and Roy Johnson of Alcohol Concern; David and April Gladstone in Marseilles; Jonathan Benthall; Dr David Weissbrodt; Dr Frances d'Souza; Mr L. Weerackody of the Sri Lankan Dangerous Drugs Control Board in Colombo; Lisa Appignanesi; Brian Lapping; Prof. Hugh Tinker; George and Diana Melly; Sally Belfrage; David Tomlinson of Phoenix House UK; Dr Alberto Sabatino of Rome; Giorgio Verrecchia and Ellen Farquharson for help with translations; Faith Clark; Dr E. Engelsman of the Dutch Ministry of Health; Dr M. Kooyman of the Jellinek Clinic, Amsterdam; John Margetson and colleagues at the British Embassy, The Hague; Prof. Sir Martin Roth; Nina Walder in Geneva; Mike Ashton and others at the Institute for the Study of Drug Dependence; Charles Medawar; David Turner, Lorraine Hewitt and colleagues at the Standing Conference on Drug Abuse; Sarah Daniels; Nell Dunn; Brian Freemantle; Ann Mavroleon; Dr Dannie Abse; Tim Rathbone MP; Dee Wells; Jeanne Henny; Tim Renton MP; Mr V. Sofinsky; the Rt Hon. Bill Deedes; Ruth Runciman; David Simpson; Michael Ratner; Richard Emery of the New York Civil Liberties Union; Robert Kilroy-Silk; and Brer Ruthven. I am especially grateful to my wife Janet, to Liz Calder and Sarah-Jane Forder of Jonathan Cape, Xandra Hardie, and Michael Sissons of A. D. Peters for their encouragement; and Philippa Price, Pam Roberts, Peggy Roberts and Kathy Hubbard for deciphering as well as typing.

This book is dedicated to my children and their generation, with my hope it may help a more rational and honest understanding about drugs and their implications.

B.C.G.W.

London, 1986

Introduction:
The Crisis Today

What does the present increase in the use of drugs teach us about our society? Psychotropic chemicals which alter perception or mood are many people's solution to the problem of existence: an attempt to change and transcend, if not to elude and escape, our human condition. Law officers estimate that illegal drug sales in the United States are now running at $110 billion a year: a tax-free figure that exceeds the combined profits of the USA's 500 largest industrial corporations, and surpasses the budget of most members of the United Nations. The challenge this onrush of drugs presents to the world can be regarded as a mirror. Hedonist, moralist or puritan, each person – including those who write about it – sees in the phenomenon a different image (just as every user's experience of narcotics is unique). Society tends to recognize in drug issues whatever pattern it desires to find.

For many members of the public the whole subject arouses fear, and hence loathing: a demonic nightmare they attempt to exorcize by refusing even to think about it. An addict said: 'Most people would rather forget about people like us.' Yet ostracizing those who misuse drugs is likely to increase the feeling of isolation or rebellion that induced the users to begin taking them. The majority of citizens see the non-medical use of drugs as moral depravity – a vice to be extirpated, ruthlessly stamped on like a disturbing snake. Others feel pity for such 'victims', regarding them not as fiends deserving their nemesis, but as people suffering from a weakness or sickness requiring help and treatment. Governments throughout the world assume not only the right but the responsibility to control them. Yet a number of individual citizens consider, as J. S. Mill did, that the right to use drugs is an issue of personal liberty which, while children must be protected, adults are entitled to decide without interference. This freedom extends even to the point of self-destruction, since the law in most countries allows alcoholism, chain-smoking or suicide in any other way. The *laissez-faire* view appeals equally to those who hold opinions such as: 'If some people are stupid enough to take drugs, so be it' (or more brutally, 'That is their funeral') or 'Why should the rest of us spend large sums of our money on police or doctors to stop them?'

The majority of us at one time have taken some form of medical or other chemical to shield us from a reality that we are reluctant to confront. Does the recreational use of drugs require public intervention, or is it a matter of private individual choice, like the freedom to overeat, smoke or follow one's religion? Does drug misuse affect only the user-victim, or does it inevitably impinge on other people, even serving to undermine the well-being and perhaps the survival of society itself? The debate focuses on whether, in the knot linking individuals to the community, the net result of drugs is to enhance human existence by expanding experience, or to confuse and pollute civilization. Are narcotics and hallucinogenics merely a means of evading human responsibility, an abdication and avoidance of life; or do they offer a gap in the curtain, part of mankind's continuing quest for Burne-Jones's 'land no one can define or remember, only desire'? The contemporary expansion of drug use is a warning signal of weaknesses and faults in our society, besides loneliness and despair: why otherwise should a significant number of talented and privileged people prefer drugs to the reality of the present day? Drug-taking is no recent invention: it has long been debated whether attempting to escape from the immediate world of materiality is part of human nature – not to be criticized any more than the search for religion – or whether such a journey is yet another illusion. Might the modern spread of drug abuse and dependency be generated by the restrictions of our internalized culture? Even if this be the case, can mandatory control, prohibition and punishment ever be morally justified, or is this, as some allege, a middle-class tactic to stigmatize dissidence as depravity? Many people in any event strongly disagree whether criminal sanctions are the right way to deal with drug abuse (and who is to define when indulgence becomes 'abuse'?). Should it be seen as a social problem, or as an illness requiring treatment – perhaps even mandatory – for those who, following De Quincey, try to extend their consciousness at the risk of their health? An addict is both violator and victim. However, by what principle should, or can, any person be forced to conform or be healthy: to whom does one owe a duty to live 'normally'?

Part of our worry derives from the political dangers implicit in drugs which have been prophesied in the warnings of Aldous Huxley, Orwell and others. Huxley, taking the name for his drug of the future from the religious intoxicant used by the Aryan invaders of India, described in *Brave New World Revisited*[1] a society where Soma had become 'the people's religion'. Like religion, the drug gave the power to manage and compensate – to control through pleasure. A dictator could use it to ensure against 'maladjustment', social unrest or dissent. By such means he could dispense happiness or illusion, sedating, stimulating or hallucinating the population as required (at times of crisis, pharmacists would be ordered to dispense stimulants; during other periods, tranquillizers and hallucinogens). In our own era, thiopentone (Pentothal) and sodium amytal have already been employed to achieve extraordinary results at totalitarian show-trials in Europe.

Weakness or vice, crime, disease, sin, psychiatric symptom or social problem, the use and misuse of drugs involves crucial issues for any society. The subject, however, is not (as frequently presented) gothic horror, mystery, or a whodunnit – although it is habitually mythicized by both addicts and opponents. Discussions about drugs are not infrequently deeply emotive, replete with ignorance, value-judgments, ambiguities, ironies, scapegoats, myths and stereotypes culled from selective evidence. Few issues tend to arouse more anxiety, irrationality, passion, fascination or outrage. (Kipling pointed out that words themselves are the most powerful drug known to mankind.) History is full of this confused reaction by humankind towards fellow-beings hooked on drugs, typified by the ambivalent feelings we show today towards alcoholics. The media's fascination with the subject feeds an appetite not unlike that which our ancestors displayed towards illicit magic or the trials of witches. But alarm in the Press can fuel moralistic panic (not reassured by a minority of drug-users' ostentatiously rejecting conventional society), while ignoring the much greater damage wrought by tobacco and alcohol, which are causing over a hundred times more premature deaths than do hard drugs, but upon whose fiscal revenue governments have become dependent.

In society today, a wholly non-drug-taking individual has become statistically the exception, a deviant; we consume ever-increasing quantities of tranquillizers, sleeping pills, pain killers and stimulants. Why do humans, whose proclivity for the Faustian bargain of harmful drugs distinguishes them from other animals, vent a complex Caliban-like rage at the reflection they see? Is the emotion against drugs an instinctive wish to save society from self-destruction – or is it panic due to ignorance? Fear has become so strong that several countries have surrendered more civil liberties in measures against drugs than they have been prepared to forgo to counter murder or terrorism. Could it be that this reaction might be the reflex of puritans who feel, in their crusades against sinful pleasures and their determination that others shall not enjoy different routes to happiness, a powerful need to suppress something in themselves? Perhaps the virulence of some of the feelings engendered should at least caution us that psychotropic drugs are not the attribute of a dehumanized race apart, but – especially in the continuum of contemporary reliance on alcohol and an ever-growing number of prescribed drugs – one more human activity susceptible to misuse as most others. The world would be simpler without illegal drugs or nuclear fission, but neither can now be wished away or disinvented; nor does it serve any purpose to make either a scapegoat for the real problem, which is the use human beings make of them.

Policy towards drugs is an issue which cuts across traditional political attitudes, evoking ironic contradictions to customary dogma. Most people on the left feel compelled in this field to place an exceptional limit on civil liberties, while right-wing people are driven to abandon their private enterprise creed of free-flow market economics in favour of swingeing state intervention, or even to advocate a public monopoly. One Conservative commented, 'The illicit drug trade is just a bit too naked – and too successful – an example of capitalism.' But a government minister also argued, 'The amount of crimes committed by people to pay for their supplies is worse than the physical harm drugs cause; but since this is a result of making them illegal, would the situation be any worse if they were decriminalized and controlled?'

Society, on any interpretation of the current situation, cannot avoid some difficult decisions to meet this challenge. Anybody advocating a quick or simple solution is a victim of myopia or sees the facts only as he would wish them to be. Until the Second World War the problem could be viewed as an alien matter that might affect China or the USA, but could be discounted in Europe when drug-use seemed to be limited to a stable minority of social casualties and so appeared to be under control. Today, however, every government in the world is feeling alarm at the accelerating threat from drugs' pervasion of urban and rural communities alike. From being an indulgent escape route for certain adults, they have become a spreading fashion for young people, many of whom find too late that they are out of their depth. Like a plant whose roots spread wildfire underground, drug offshoots now appear rife across the social spectrum. When not just the unemployed, but the children of MPs, Congressmen, at least one Prime Minister, an Emperor and several Presidents become addicts, official minds concentrate wonderfully and actions previously thought impossible are declared imperative.

Today, however, many authorities privately express pessimism or impotent defeatism. Experts in the USA fear that present policies on drugs echo the earlier doomed attempt to prohibit alcohol, and are producing only a combination of undesirables: illegal drug sales are increasing; supplies from criminal sources are causing death and injuries through being adulterated; and the law on the issue seems incapable of enforcement, so that respect for the law in general is being undermined as otherwise law-abiding people are driven into the hands of organized crime to obtain their drugs. As one official involved with the problem warns: 'I'm afraid Europe is certain to follow the USA's path of escalating nightmare, but the Americans have no clue what lessons to pass on to us.'

Internationally, another paradox has surfaced. The West used to blame the problem on the growers in poor countries – 'The Third World's revenge upon the Rich World for its economic exploitation,' as Maurice Strong once described it: a retribution upon the West for having ignored the poverty of peasants in Asia and Latin America. Now the developing nations equally are finding themselves victims of their own rising production of heroin and cocaine – as well as of a reverse flow of unsafeguarded medical drugs being sold to them by the richer nations. Developing countries complain in international discussions that they are asked to sacrifice and destroy their peasant farmers' coca and opium crops because of faults in Western societies, while these same rich nations are profitably trafficking in synthetic drugs such as amphetamines and barbiturates – as well as alcohol and cigarettes – that are being dumped on people of the developing world. An abundance of heroin and cocaine supplies has resulted in traffickers developing new markets along the transit routes and in the producer nations. In 1972 heroin traffic was reported in thirty-four countries; by 1982 this had become fifty-one. Cocaine trafficking also has spread from twenty-nine to forty-six countries in ten years. The international illegal heroin trade is now estimated to gross more than $225,000,000,000 annually. Disrupting economies as it corrodes the integrity of producer nations, the illegal drug industry is now their biggest export and has – as described in Chapter 14 below – become so powerful in several countries that it threatens the government itself.

Globally, illegal drugs are estimated to have overtaken oil and are now the world's second biggest trade next to armaments, so that in value they amount to some 9 per cent of all international merchandise. They attract the most enterprising talent of organized crime, since they are the most lucrative of all underworld activities. Twenty years after the 'war against drugs' was made a top priority in the USA, a recent State Department survey admits the failure of virtually every strategy tried: the worldwide production of coca has increased by more than two-fifths, and that of opium poppies has expanded by over half since 1980. During 1985, the US government spent $1.5 billion in its efforts to stem the expansion, largely in vain. In the USA itself, marijuana has become the country's second biggest cash crop – a fact which effectively undermines Washington's efforts to persuade poorer nations to police their own farmers for the USA's sake. The USA does not have full diplomatic relations with several of the major drug-producing countries, including Afghanistan, Iran and Laos; but even in countries such as Mexico, Pakistan, Peru, Colombia, Bolivia and Thailand with which it has close ties, the drug trade flourishes. The potential list of additional countries capable of growing supplies is infinite: 'It's like trying to nail a blob of mercury,' in the words of one American diplomat attempting to cope with narcotics. Western Europe's illegal heroin problem in 1982 overtook that of the USA. Moreover, the British police informed a court recently that heroin was being imported on virtually every flight from Pakistan concealed inside aircraft and in the diplomatic bag. When an occasional consignment is detected, the consequent temporary price rise only helps to increase the traffickers' profits. It is a measure of the failure that, despite all the American efforts to gain control, the North American price of heroin actually fell from $2.25 a milligram in 1979 to $1.66 in 1982, and the wholesale price of cocaine has dropped even faster – by more than half between 1983 and 1986. Most worrying of all may be the advent of 'designer' drugs, now spreading from California to Australia and Europe, which are artificial variants of heroin, LSD and cocaine that can be made in kitchens and college laboratories.

The only hopeful sign in the USA is a levelling-off in the number of young people using cannabis, but against this has to be set a disturbing rise in amphetamines. The size and value of the illegal market in cocaine has now overtaken that of heroin. Over 25 million people in the USA have used cocaine at some stage; more than one in five snort a line regularly; and an estimated 5,000 new people try cocaine each day. By contrast with only a few years ago, when it was considered relatively innocuous, cocaine has now been proved a destructive drug which induces powerful psychological dependency and can be lethal, especially when taken as 'crack' or by freebasing. At least 1 million Americans now need professional help with problems from this drug: a telephone help-line recently set up by New Jersey doctors for cocaine users was inundated with thirty times the number of calls expected. The various implications are sobering. In 1980 – the last year for which figures are available – of the 5,324 US servicemen transferred from nuclear weapons duty,

1,726 were guilty of using drugs, including LSD, heroin and cocaine.

The World Health Organization (WHO) stated in 1985 that the total number of people seriously affected by the abuse of drugs (excluding cannabis) was at least 18 million and continues to increase in nearly every country across the world. Less widely reported was WHO's finding that cigarette smoking is responsible for the premature deaths of 1 million people a year (100,000 in Britain alone): culpably, almost all discussion of 'the drug problem' fails to remember that nicotine and alcohol damage far greater numbers than do heroin or cocaine. Europe's official total of heroin addicts is now 290,000, although experts believe the real figure is at least half a million more. Health experts in West Germany estimate that in that country several hundred thousand children between the ages of eleven and sixteen are regularly taking various forms of drugs. Malaysia has well over 100,000 opiate addicts; Pakistan at least 300,000, and Thailand 600,000; Iran is believed to have more than 1 million. Efforts to counter the problem are becoming correspondingly desperate. Paraquat herbicide is being sprayed on drug-growing farms, while in Peru surgeons perform operations to remove the cingulum part of the brain in an attempt to stop cocaine addiction. Despite every effort, areas of Peru – like Colombia and Bolivia – are now beyond civil control because of the power of drug barons and the wealth they command: a single recent Colombian consignment of cocaine had a street value of $1,200,000,000 (£827,586,000) – a sum exceeding the total budget of the government resources trying to counter the traffic. One illegal laboratory alone in the Amazon jungle employs 1,000 people and can supply the USA's needs four times over. Roberto Suarez, a Bolivian narco-millionaire, offered a deal to the US State Department: he would settle his country's $4,000,000,000 foreign debt, which the national government was incapable of doing, in exchange for the release of his son who had been arrested in the USA.

Western Europe, and the United Kingdom in particular, has been targeted by drug-trafficking syndicates as ripe for expanded exploitation of the markets in cocaine and heroin. By 1986, heroin seizures in Britain were three times those of 1982, and over tenfold the annual amount seized in the late 1970s. Whereas in 1978 more than three-quarters of the heroin discovered in Britain was in transit, three years later over 80 per cent was for consumption in the UK itself. By 1984 the quantity of heroin being seized in Britain exceeded the total amount seized that year in the USA. David Alton, a Liverpool MP, was telling the House of Commons: 'The number of addicts has risen from 3,000 in the so-called drug-crazed 1960s to probably 100,000 in the heroin-hooked 1980s . . . For as little as £5, two young people can buy sufficient heroin for a night. It is cheaper than watching a film at the cinema or spending a night at the local pub. But the price that the user can pay is often the ultimate one.' Since 'smoking the dragon' makes needles no longer necessary – though, deceptively, it is equally potent – heroin addiction has spread from inner cities to penetrate rural Wales, conventional market-towns such as Marlborough and farms in Lincolnshire, as well as to Edinburgh housing estates and Merseyside primary schools. Clinics estimate that over 10,000 more people in Britain are likely to become addicted in 1986 and 1987, with their average age falling steadily; the Chief Inspector of Constabulary has warned that some quarter of a million people in Britain may be addicted to opium derivatives by the end of the decade if the spread of drug-abuse continues at its present rate. Whether or not such fears are realized, there is a danger that civil liberties will be eroded as a result of panic; but unless a better strategy is adopted, the hysteria is likely to grow. Sir Patrick Hamill, head of the Glasgow area's police, describes the drug situation throughout the country as the 'worst scourge probably of this century'; Dr Kay Carmichael, who lives there, reports that drug addiction is 'spreading in Glasgow like a plague. The dealers organize weekends when drugs are handed out free in pubs. It is rife in housing schemes where alcohol used to be the only escape.' The House of Commons Home Affairs Select Committee warned in 1985 that Britain faces the most serious peacetime threat to its national well-being as a result of hard drugs. Assessing the government's response to this, the Commons Select Committee on the Misuse of Drugs reported: 'Existing services are woefully inadequate . . . Treatment facilities are few, underfunded, often inaccessible, and always with long waiting lists . . . There is still little sense of direction in the government's preventive efforts.'[2] Even among the minority of addicts lucky enough to receive treatment, some 70 per cent revert to the drug. As a worried probation officer in Holyhead (where the number of heroin addicts has risen from two to 150 in two years) says, 'If we can't even cure the handful of addicts we've had for years, how are we going to cure thousands?'

All statistics about illegal activity as regards drugs obviously have to be treated with particular caution and reserve. The exact dimensions will never be known accurately. No statistic, however, can record the anguish of a family trying to cope with an addict. But if, as the evidence indicates, the strongest causes of the spread of drug abuse are social contact and cheaper availability, the future is going to see the problem increase at a compound rate – especially if the research finding is correct that most heroin addicts are liable to convert several others to the drug. And, as dependency multiplies, the huge profits of the expanding demand inevitably attract the involvement of more producers, traffickers and professional criminals in an ascending spiral.

If not checked, such a change is likely to transform – if not devastate – societies both rich and poor. Previous sensationalism may have lulled many people into not confronting the reality of the threat. The one certainty is that there is no escape in adopting an ostrich position. Time has almost run out in which to construct a sensible solution. The official tactic of playing down the crisis, in the hope that it will go away, is no longer tenable. Since future generations are likely to take an ever-increasing amount of drugs, we should learn and understand the reasons – as well as the consequences. This is as true for those who take a libertarian attitude as for those who hold with restriction and control. Too often, however, views are based on an emotive fear of what is not understood. Drugs have always been surrounded by myths. Up until now, the only clear response to the subject has been confusion. We must now re-assess our present ideas and adopt a new and coherent strategy. What are needed are practical solutions, not moral panic. Policies that are not directed to the causes of the problem may do more harm than good. 'At present', says one involved senior official, 'we're only attempting to deal with the symptoms, and we're losing that battle all along the line. Now it's up to society.'

This book's aim is to set out the facts and options as objectively as possible, and then offer suggestions for future policy. The first chapters trace the genesis of the situation throughout the world; Part Two looks at the character of the drugs themselves; Part Three examines the reasons for drug use, and the efforts to cope with them by both treatment and control, before advancing some forecasts and recommendations. Inevitably much of the total picture takes the form of a mosaic, because every drug-taker is unique. The text attempts to trace each of the relevant related facets of the global connection. This is because we should examine the interlocking pieces which make up the whole puzzle – including the commercial and political ramifications lying behind the moral and the medical issues – in order to have any hope of confronting the problem cohesively. Before we prescribe any answer, we should first diagnose correctly.

Part One

The Rise of the Problem

I

A Mazy Road:
The Historical Perspective

'The gods are just, and of our pleasant vices
Make instruments to plague us.'

King Lear, V.iii

The history of drug use has occasional elements of ironic comedy, but more often is unnecessary tragedy. Drugs are not a recent phenomenon: as long as records have been kept, individuals from virtually every society have used or misused substances – at first natural and later synthesized – in attempts to enhance their feelings, performance or health. People of successive cultures have ingested chemicals into their bodies by varied routes: eating, drinking, smoking, sniffing, inhaling, popping pills or injecting. Whether or not we call such chemicals drugs is a matter of cultural chance, but one that can greatly affect our attitudes. A judge drinking glasses of port, a chain-smoking saloon-bar politician, a journalist relying on coffee to work – each believes that drug addiction is something that happens to others.

Apart from what is perhaps the earliest reference to an intoxicant – Noah's drunkenness in the Book of Genesis [1] – the mescal bean has been prized by Amerindians for at least 10,000 years. The value of the juice of the oriental white poppy, *Papaver somniferum*, for inducing sleep and eluding pain is recorded on Sumerian tablets more than 6,000 years old. Remains of its seeds have been found in the lake huts of the late Stone Age in Switzerland; and traces of opium were discovered in a late Bronze Age Cypriot vase, shaped like a poppy head, which was unearthed in Syria in 1986. Homer in the ninth century BC wrote that Helen offered Telemachus nepenthe containing opium 'to lull all pain and anger and bring forgetfulness of every sorrow'.[2] Assyrian medical inscriptions from the seventh century BC describe how 'early in the morning old women, boys and girls collect the juice by scraping it off the wounds [in the poppies] with a small iron scoop and depositing the whole in an earthen pot': exactly the same process that can be seen in the fields of Asia today. Cannabis has been recently discovered aboard a very early Punic longboat excavated, appropriately, in western Sicily; opium poppies are mentioned by Hippocrates, Aristotle, Virgil in his *Aeneid*,[3] Livy, Ovid and the elder Pliny – as well as in ancient writings from Egypt, Mesopotamia, Persia and China where they were used medicinally more than nine centuries ago. Galen recommended poppy juice, 'for it resists poison and venomous bites, cures deafness, epilepsy, fevers . . . the trouble to which women are subject, melancholy and all pestilence'. But a warning occurred in 1037 when Avicenna, the famous Persian physician, died from opiate intoxication. Thirty-one centuries earlier an Egyptian priest had written in vain: 'I, thy superior, forbid thee to go to the taverns. Thou art degraded like the beasts.'

Columbus, on his voyage to Hispaniola and Cuba in 1492, found people smoking tobacco cigars. His followers discovered being used in America some eighty different hallucinogenic and narcotic plants as yet unknown in Europe. They included Datura (Jimson-weed – *yerba del diablo*) and Morning Glory, as well as coca and the peyote cactus – which the Aztecs ate as a 'divine messenger' to put them in touch with their gods. In the same way South Sea islanders drank kava to communicate with the supernatural, and bhang (a drink made from cannabis, referred to in Sanskrit literature as the 'food of the gods' and 'the heavenly guide') was a favourite of Shiva in the Hindu pantheon. Almost invariably drug consumption in early days was a group activity – in the way our sacramental taking of communion wine and ceremonial toasts is today. The connection between drugs and religion recurs all over the world. The Aztecs felt they must become intoxicated at major sacred ceremonies, if they were not to displease their gods. In 1600 BC the Aryan invaders of India worshipped Soma, whose source is now identified as the halluci-nogenic mushroom fly agaric. Most early communities had their priests or shamans, sorcerers, medicine men or witch doctors, revered for their ability to communicate with visions and spirits, often in a drug-induced fit or trance. The shaman and his congrega-tion shared hallucinogens – like rock stars and their fans at festivals today. A number of visions in early times are now thought likely to have been caused by ergot or other hallucinogenic agents.[4] Before he took mescalin Aldous Huxley wrote:

> From poppy to curare, from Andean coca to Indian hemp and Siberian agaric, every plant or bush or fungus capable when ingested of stupefying or exciting or evoking visions has long since been discovered and systematically employed. The fact is strangely significant; for it seems to prove that always and everywhere Human Beings have felt the radical inadequacy of their personal existence, the mystery of being insulated selves and not something else, something wider . . .

Why did drugs fall from religious and medical veneration to widespread condemnation? Their links with earlier religions under-lay some of the Christian Church's opposition; medicine men and witches were primitive competitors for the health service provided by missionaries and monasteries, as they later were for early physicians. European arrivals in the New World, however, rapidly made good the omission of one major drug of which the Amer-indians were ignorant. This was 'fire-water': alcohol's introduction caused the demoralization a new drug wreaks on a social milieu unused to it. Alcohol soon became internationally the most widely used drug of all, being able to be produced from the fermentation of different plants growing in virtually every climate in the world. In the tenth century, Rhazes's discovery of how to distil spirit alcohol was hailed as the creation of aqua vitae – a new wonder drug. Yet alcohol has inflicted more havoc among Australian aborigines and Amerindians than any other drug throughout history. The Rastafarians, who use ganja cannabis as the sacrament of their religion, despise communion wine as harmful as well as heretical.

Glue sniffing, often thought of as a modern aberration, also has

5

roots in the practice throughout history of inhaling different chemical fumes for pleasure or intoxication. At the Delphic oracle in ancient Greece, the Pythia priestess inhaled a vapour that came from burning henbane seeds or else was carbon dioxide escaping from a rock fissure in order to facilitate her visions. Incense has played a role in several religions' ritual since time immemorial. Snuff was encountered by Columbus in the West Indies and its commercial revival is being attempted again today. From the end of the eighteenth century in Britain and the USA it was fashionable to sniff ether, chloroform or nitrous oxide for euphoric amusement (hence the latter's name of laughing gas) before these came to be used as anaesthetics. Coleridge described the recreational use of nitrous oxide – which was also inhaled by Humphry Davy, Josiah Wedgwood and William James – as 'the most unmingled pleasure' he had ever experienced. Legendary Victorian nannies used whiffs of coal-gas to quieten crying babies. Once the vogue for a drug wanes, it rarely recurs; though ether, used as a cheap inebriant in Ulster and by Harvard students a century ago, reappeared in some soft drinks in the USA during Prohibition.

Drugs have been chewed, as a gentler alternative to direct introduction into the bloodstream, for millennia: opium-eating has long been practised in Iran and India. The use of kat and coca leaves as stimulants antedates that of coffee or tea. Kat (*Catha edulis*, a shrub with a mildly amphetamine-like effect) was listed in an Arabian medical book more than seven centuries ago; today several million people in East Africa and the Arabian Peninsula are still habitual kat chewers, and imports of it are now reaching Europe. In South America, paintings depicting coca chewers have been found on Mochican pottery from the Classic epoch of AD 500. The coca shrub – the basis of cocaine – enjoyed a key position in the Inca Empire. It was regarded as the sacred, living manifestation of divinity, being buried with the dead to help them on their journey to another world. The aristocracy restricted the privilege of its use to themselves; a *chuspa* coca pouch was the insignia of the crown. The Spanish identified the plant with indigenous resistance, and Catholic missionaries tried to stamp out its reputation as dangerous idolatry. By 1616 the Inquisition was recorded to be seeking to ban women in Mexico taking 'certain drinks of herbs and roots with which they enrapture and stupefy the senses. The hallucinations they have, they regard as revelation.' None the less many *Conquis-*

tadores and church officials themselves did not scruple to make fortunes out of coca estates. They also learnt that it was possible to wring longer working hours out of the Indians with less food if they gave them coca leaves, which enabled the conquered labourers to endure the misery of their situation. Bolivian tin miners today still chew coca to help them through their exhausting work underground, being paid a daily allowance of leaf as part of their wages. In the Andes, Aymara and Quecha Indians three times a day suck balls of coca leaves which contain 1 per cent of cocaine. This not only increases their physical endurance against tiredness and hunger, but also makes breathing easier in the thin oxygen at the extreme altitudes where the Amerindians live, in some of the highest inhabited areas of the world. Even today the local people in the Altiplano measure time and distances in *cocada*: how far a man can travel while chewing one wad of coca. These Indian users do not appear to become addicted: on moving down to lower altitudes most give up their coca without apparent hardship. 'Mama Coca' was also used as an anaesthetic by Inca surgeons when they performed their precocious trepanning operations, just as it is still used in local anaesthetics throughout the world today. According to Amerindian tradition, coca was a gift from heaven to better the lives of people on earth: 'For the Indian, coca leaves provide the same benefits that aspirin, coffee, tea, stimulants, sedatives and numerous other medicaments supply in our society,' according to the botanist Richard Martin. He goes on:

> Coca is an integral part of the Indian's way of life, deeply involved with his traditions, his religion, his work and his medicine. To deny the use of coca to the Indians is as serious a disregard for human rights as would be an attempt to outlaw beer in Germany, coffee in the Near East or betel chewing in India. The recent attempts to suppress and control the use of coca can be interpreted only as the latest step in the white man's attempt to exterminate the Indian way of life and make him completely dependent on the alien society and economy which has gradually surrounded him.[5]

The consumption of coca, however, never caught on in Europe – nlike the products of two other New World plants, tobacco and ~colate. (Nicotine, a highly toxic alkaloid, was used by Amer- ~ns as a pesticide.) The first European known to have smoked

7

tobacco was Columbus's colleague, Rodrigo de Jerez, who on his return (almost a century before Raleigh) so alarmed his fellow Spaniards by breathing smoke that they believed the Devil had entered him, and as a consequence in 1493 the Inquisition cast him into prison for consorting with Satan. Ironically during his years of incarceration the weed became fashionable at Court: Jean Nicot – the young French ambassador to Lisbon who was to give his name to the word nicotine – sent a plant from Virginia to the French Queen Mother, Catherine de Medici, who became Europe's earliest recorded tobacco addict. Nicot was the first man to realize the financial potential of this traffic, and set up a trade in tobacco which made his fortune. By the seventeenth century, however, King James I of England and the Chinese Emperors were denouncing the weed, the Tsar of Russia was executing subjects found in possession of it, while the Mogul Emperor merely ordered that smokers' lips should be slit. Nor were these the only drug-users to suffer early persecution. A century earlier a German prince gave financial rewards for information leading to the conviction of coffee drinkers; and the anaesthetic chloroform was condemned as irreligious on the grounds that since man is born to pain as he is to sin, he should bear his sufferings with penitent lack of complaint.[6] (Even the humble potato, upon its introduction to Scotland, was sternly ostracized as unholy because it was not mentioned in the Bible.) Both coffee and tea have, in their time, been castigated by governments as malignant poisons. When coffee, which had originated in Ethiopia, became popular the official reaction was much the same as that towards cannabis today: its sale in sixteenth-century Egypt was banned, stocks of it were burned, and those people who ignored warnings about its insidious nature were arrested.[7] In the next century coffee houses were similarly suspect in the eyes of the British government, being regarded as dens of sedition; and to add to the drink's problems English women petitioned against it on the grounds that it caused impotence and sterility.[8] England, however, was swept in the eighteenth century by what the Press today would call an epidemic plague of tea addiction. Its consumption rose by a factor of more than twenty, despite its denunciation by William Cobbett as possessing 'corrosive, gnawing and poisonous powers. I[ ]was the destroyer of health, an enfeebler of the frame, an engende[ ]er of effeminacy and laziness, a debaucher of youth and a make[ ]misery in old age.'[9]

Ironically, opiates had been popular in Europe for far longer, being praised by Chaucer as well as Shakespeare. The Crusaders had learnt of the value Arabs placed on opium in battle to lend courage as well as heal wounds. Sir Thomas Sydenham, who gave his patients Syrup of Poppies or the highly opiated Venice Treacle, declared in 1680 that 'Among the remedies which it has pleased Almighty God to give man to relieve his sufferings, none is so universal and so efficacious as opium . . . without opium there would be no medicine.' As early as the middle of the seventeenth century, the famous *Herbal* of Nicholas Culpeper had recorded: 'Of the flowers and seed is made a syrup, which is frequently, and to good effect, used to procure rest and sleep in the sick and weak . . . and to ease pain in the head as well as in other parts. It is also used to cool inflammations, agues or frenzies, or to stay defluctions which cause a cough, or consumption.' The Pilgrim Fathers carried lauda-num linctus (alcohol combined with 2 per cent of opium) to America on the *Mayflower*. Though *Cannabis sativa* (which North Amer-icans call by its Mexican name of 'marijuana') had been brought to Europe with opium by the Moorish invaders of Spain and employed from early times as a pain-killer and tranquillizer, it was not generally popular until much later.

To our ancestors, as in tribal societies today, magicians and witches were known as medicine men and women, who consumed and prescribed narcotic or hallucinogenic plants – such as thorn-apple, certain mushrooms, mandrake, belladonna (deadly night-shade) or henbane – to induce states ranging from giddiness, frenzied convulsions or visions, to stupor, trance or death. Medieval midwives and witches, whose early alternative medicine was to attract the male establishment's aggression, administered ergot and atrophine (from belladonna) during labour at childbirth. Some of them anointed their own bodies, including internally, with halluci-nogenic ointments derived from henbane and mandrake; the legend of witches flying on broomsticks has been traced to belladonna, which can give those who ingest it an illusion of flying through air.[10] Besides their medical and religious roles, such substances were valued by people as a means of exploring new mental and spiritual dimensions, and were used like alcohol in an attempt to escape the worries and responsibilities of a hard existence. In eighteenth-century England gin offered 'oblivion for a penny': by 1750 in St Giles's every fourth house was a gin-shop. Hogarth's Gin Lane engravings showed the children of gin-soaked mothers looking 'shrivel'd and old as though they numbered many years'. Profiteering from drugs is not a modern development – witness Dr Johnson's words on the sale of a brewery: 'We are not here to sell a parcel of boilers and vats, but the potentiality of growing rich beyond the dreams of avarice.'

Le Mort, a Leyden chemistry professor at the beginning of the eighteenth century, was the first man to combine opium with camphor and produce paregoric, which was soon widely used to control diarrhoea, deaden toothache – or to 'soothe' fretful babies. There were few alternative pain-killers to opiates even in the nineteenth century. Laudanum – first used by Paracelsus in early fifteenth-century Basle – was sold for a penny by post or from pubs, market stalls, travelling salesmen and quacks. Just as cigarettes can be bought today in almost any corner grocery or sweet-shop, so only a little over a century ago could opium be widely purchased. Far from being thought of as a dangerous drug, it was taken as a general palliative much as aspirin (which was unknown before 1899) is nowadays, and it was welcomed as a cheap therapeutic means of self-medication which avoided the expense and pain of being bled or blistered by a doctor. Its effectiveness in suppressing symptoms led it to be mistaken as a cure in all kinds of cases. Mothers and nurses dosed restless babies with 'Godfrey's Cordial', 'Mother's Quietness', or 'Soothing Syrup', all containing laudanum; the opium-based 'Infant's Preservative' was advertised as 'laying the foundations for a good constitution'. Not surprisingly, a number of young children became addicted, and 'some babies were so susceptible to opium that they died of narcotic poisoning after doses containing no more than two drops of laudanum'.[11] These cases were exposed in an early example of investigative journalism by Angus Bethune Reach in the *Morning Chronicle* in 1849:

> First the child is drugged until it sleeps, and then too often it is drugged until it dies . . . in process of time, as the child gets accustomed to the drug, the dose must be made stronger still . . . if the quantity of laudanum comes expensive, they use crude opium instead . . . In Manchester, in the course of seven years, there perished 13,362 children 'over and above the mortality natural to mankind'.

'Pate de Jujubes' was the name given to opium lozenges, commended by former East India Company medical men; opium pills, plasters and enemas were also widely sold. Dr Collis Browne's famous chlorodyne mixture – a brown syrup of morphia, chloral, cannabis and alcohol that was first used in India – continued to be sold in Britain without a prescription until very recently. Gee's Linctus, also still popular, similarly contains camphorated opium tincture. Moulded opium was used as a contraceptive cap, preferred as an alternative to Casanova's half of a squeezed lemon. Opiate 'Sleepy beer' was drunk in the country round Crickhowell; 'poppy-head tea' and opium beer had their devotees, especially among the inhabitants of depressed areas such as the Fen district. In 1827 the annual opium consumption in Britain was 17,000 lb. (600 mg. a head of the population); by 1859 this had risen to 61,000 lb.[12] Britain also re-exported opium all over the world, some half of it to North America. Most of this was imported from Turkey, though some was grown successfully in certain areas of Britain. In 1830, a Mr Young, an Edinburgh surgeon, succeeded in obtaining 56 lb. of opium from one acre of poppies, which he sold at thirty-six shillings a lb. Opium which has been grown in England and elsewhere in Europe is as rich in morphia as that grown in the East; examples of French-grown opium have been found to yield 22.8 per cent of morphia, the highest percentage known anywhere.

'Most men and women lead lives at the worst so painful, at the best so monotonous, poor, and limited that the urge to escape, the longing to transcend themselves if only for a few moments, is and has always been one of the principal appetites of the soul. Art and religion, carnivals and saturnalia, dancing and listening to oratory – all these have served, in H. G. Wells's phrase, as "Doors in the Wall",' wrote Aldous Huxley, adding: 'Most of these modifiers of consciousness cannot now be taken except under doctor's orders, or else illegally and at considerable risk. For unrestricted use the West has permitted only alcohol and tobacco. All the other chemical Doors in the Wall are labelled Dope, and their unauthorized takers are Fiends.'[13] Thomas De Quincey had described in 1822:

> Some years ago, on passing through Manchester, I was informed by several cotton-manufacturers, that their work-people were rapidly getting into the practice of opium-eating; so much so, that on a Saturday afternoon the counters of the

druggists were strewed with pills of one, two, or three grains, in preparation for the known demand of the evening. The immediate occasion of this practice was the lowness of wages, which at that time would not allow them to indulge in ale or spirits: and wages rising, it may be thought that this practice would cease: but I do not believe that any man, having once tasted the divine luxuries of opium, will afterwards descend to the gross and mortal enjoyments of alcohol.[14]

Ironically, European people used opiates because they regarded them as sedative, whereas in the East they were valued as a stimulant. In the Mogul Empire they had been an intoxicant reserved for the Court; Turkish soldiers were feared because of their custom of taking them before battle. At the time when Marx claimed that religion was the opium of the people, much of Europe's population had little alternative to using opiates because expensive doctors were beyond their reach. It is very striking how little abuse was recorded, compared to today, of a narcotic so cheap and widely available. Some people became iatrogenically addicted after using opiates during an illness; others took them recreationally because they were cheaper than gin or beer. Why then did they lose popularity? Up to De Quincey's time, people had remained largely silent about opium's addictive property; its consumption was considered like drunkenness to be a matter for private rather than public morality. But the publication of De Quincey's *Confessions* brought the subject into open public debate. He wrote, 'Happiness might now be bought for a penny and carried in the waistcoat pocket.' Several deaths from opium overdoses were blamed on the influence of this book, though Carlyle, who had been thinking of experimenting, was deterred by De Quincey's description, and said, 'A thousand times better to die than have anything to do with such a Devil's own drug.' Among those, however, who besides De Quincey are known to have consumed opiates – including morphine – are Clive of India (who, an addict for twenty years, died in a fit after a double dose of opium), Crabbe, Elizabeth Barrett Browning, King George IV (given opiates to counteract alcoholism), Henry Addington, Florence Nightingale, J. M. W. Turner, Shelley, Keats, Southey, Berlioz, Lamb, Scott, Darwin, Lord Erskine, Sir James Stephen (who drafted the criminal code used throughout much of the British Empire), Branwell Brontë, Ruskin, Rossetti, Isaac

Milner, Coleridge, Francis Thompson, Dickens (who described an opium den in *Edwin Drood*), Poe (who, like Baudelaire, was fascinated by De Quincey's *Confessions*), William Wilberforce (who took opium three times a day for thirty years) and Byron – a fair pantheon of late eighteenth- and nineteenth-century talent. Disraeli made a record-breaking five-hour budget speech in Parliament on a mixture of brandy and opium pills; Gladstone preferred to be fortified in the Commons by a volatile cocktail of ether, sherry and eggs. Among modern British victims has been the promising painter Christopher Wood who at the age of twenty-nine in 1930 fell beneath a train, befuddled by the opium habit he had learnt from Jean Cocteau.

How much contribution – negative or positive – drugs make to the work of any writer or artist is extremely difficult to determine. Do they unlock or do they muddy the creative imagination? Samuel Taylor Coleridge, first given laudanum at school in 1791 for his rheumatic fever, wrote to his brother seven years later: 'Laudanum gives me repose, not sleep; but you, I believe, knew how divine that repose is, what a spot of enchantment . . .' He had already written 'The Rime of the Ancient Mariner', and was soon to write the fragment, 'Kubla Khan': although the latter may have been born in an opium-induced dream, the sources of the imagery of both poems were very likely found in the happiness he discovered with Wordsworth and his sister in the magical Quantocks.[15]

> The poet's eye in his tipsy hour
> Has a magnifying power
> Or rather the soul emancipates the eye
> Of the accidents of size.

Thomas De Quincey's expert opinion – based on, in his own words, 'seventeen years' use and eight years' abuse of its powers' – was that opium is unlikely to create anything new. He concluded: 'If a man whose talk is of oxen should become an opium-eater, the probability is that (if he is not too dull to dream at all) he will dream about oxen.' Its effect, he said, was on feeling and energy: 'Opium gives and takes away. It defeats the steady habit of exertion, but it creates spasms of irregular exertion.' De Quincey further described an opium eater as one who feels 'that the Divine part of his nature is paramount; that is, the moral affections are in a state of cloudless serenity; and over all is the great light of the majestic intellect', but he testified that opium took away the central creative 'nexus' and gave writers a 'disgust' for their work. Arthur Rimbaud (1854–91), who was taking opiates in Paris when he was seventeen and wrote all his poems and prose before he was twenty, recorded his ambivalence with the words: '"You will always be a hyena . . ." protests the devil who crowned me with such pleasant poppies.'[16] Other writers' experiences varied. Robert Louis Stevenson, given cocaine for his respiratory illness, wrote *Dr Jekyll and Mr Hyde* about, as well as with the help of, the drug within a mere six days. Alexandre Dumas and Jules Verne were among other devotees of cocaine. Wilkie Collins, who produced *The Moonstone* under the influence of opium taken to escape the pain of his rheumatism, wrote in 1865: 'Who was the man who invented laudanum? I thank him from the bottom of my heart . . . I have had six delicious hours of oblivion; I have woken up with my mind composed; I have written a perfect little letter . . . '

'What is it tonight, morphine, or cocaine?' Dr Watson was to ask; Conan Doyle's most famous creation's testimonial to the '7 per cent solution' (cocaine) he injected was that it is 'transcendingly stimulating and clarifying to the mind'. Sherlock Holmes remained a hero of the establishment in Britain without any sign of parents feeling the need to warn children against the corruption of his drug abuse. Baudelaire, Dumas, de Nerval and Gautier – like Sir Richard Burton – preferred hashish (cannabis), which had been introduced to France by Napoleon's Army of the Nile. The Romantic writers of the Club des Haschischins in Paris – Bohemian precursors of modern-day hippies – experimented with drugs to find short-cuts to visionary inspiration. 'Reality', Baudelaire said, 'lies only in dreams.' Although in 1844 his friend Dr Moreau found that hashish produced irresistible laughter, Baudelaire declared it arrested time, but regretted that it made a man 'incapable of action, good only for dreaming'. Gautier and Baudelaire both came to renounce cannabis. Baudelaire – although also an alcoholic – declared: 'These poisonous stimulants seem to me not only one of the most terrible and certain means used by the Spirit of Darkness to recruit and enslave this wretched humanity, but even as one of his most perfect embodiments.' His final verdict was that 'There is a fatal danger in such habits: one who has recourse to poison in order to think, will soon be unable to think without poison.' (Nevertheless, in 1983 the police in Britain seized copies of his book, *Hashish, Wine and Opium*, first published 133 years earlier, together with copies of Aldous Huxley's *Doors of Perception*.) D. G. Rossetti was addicted to chloral; W. B. Yeats took both hashish and mescalin; Aldous Huxley argued for the religious potential of LSD; but Arthur Koestler was to have a bad experience with psilocybin, which revived memories of his time as a political prisoner. The work of most creative addicts has been more undermined than enhanced by their lifestyle. (Some have even used drugs as a means of coming down out of the high excitement of creation.) None of the plays of Tennessee Williams's last twenty years, when he was injecting speed (amphetamine) and other drugs, had any success: critics complained he was an author lost in an unreal world of his own. When the magazine *Ambit* held a competition for writers who claimed that LSD helped them to write, the results were embarrassing. Most creativity demands a hard discipline: a drug-taker often isolates himself in his own world and cuts lines of communication. It is true that Malcolm Lowry was able (like Scott Fitzgerald and O'Neill) to write his masterpiece about alcoholism despite its effects, but the majority of authors, as Dylan Thomas discovered, have found they can only be creative when free of intoxication.

Cocaine never became popular in Britain in the nineteenth century (apart from being used as a dental anaesthetic), although until 1868 opium continued to be sold widely without any legal restrictions. At the start of the nineteenth century, however, Frederich Serturner, a twenty-year-old German apprentice pharmacist who was experimenting with crude opium, had succeeded in extracting some white alkaloid crystals that put animals to sleep. He named the resulting potent pain-killer 'morphine', after Morpheus, the Greek god of dreams. It soon became known as 'God's own medicine', and was hailed as a 'wonder' cure for everything from nymphomania to insanity. Other opiate alkaloids, such as the now well-known codeine, were also formulated; but it was the use of morphine that grew dramatically, especially after Alexander Wood's development of the hypodermic syringe needle fifty years later. Morphine and heroin taking tended to be a solitary activity, compared with cocaine and opium users' social gregariousness. Legal controversy about opiate addiction was first aroused in 1828 when the Earl of Mar died, two years after taking out insurance on his life and having consumed 2,940 mg. of opium and an ounce of laudanum daily, which the contesting insurance company contended had been responsible for shortening his existence. Although the Restoration poet Thomas Shadwell had earlier been known to be an opium addict, attitudes had since changed. The eighteenth-century toleration of regular drug use as a 'habit' of conscious choice had gradually given way to the view of it as sick dependency produced by a 'disease of the will'. Drug-taking, particularly amongst the lower orders, was increasingly seen as violating middle-class concepts of normality, and began to be defined as unacceptable deviancy: throughout history, the habit repeatedly becomes a matter of public concern only when its indulgence is perceived as being shared by *hoi polloi*. In 1851 the Arsenic Act became the first law to regulate the sale of a drug in Britain, giving chemists a professional monopoly in its dispensation as a result of lobbying by the Pharmaceutical Society. The 1868 Pharmacy Act extended the restriction to morphine, though not to paregoric. Doctors, pursuing professional status, condemned self-medication – especially amongst the working classes – and urged that drugs should only be available on prescription. Controls on drugs were advocated from a combination of professional medical self-interest and a developing concern for public health reform. There were also those who voiced fears about degeneracy amongst working-men – fermented by waves of xenophobic public fear about the handful of Chinese opium 'dens' in the Limehouse docklands of London. The first use of the term opium 'fiend' can be traced to 1889. By 1908 opium was included in the Poisons Schedule, requiring pharmacists who sold it to have personal knowledge of their customers, who had to sign a poisons book. Habitual drug use came to be viewed as a disease or even a form of insanity, especially by the Temperance Movement who equated it with alcoholism. Moralists preferred to condemn addiction – then as now – as a failure of self-control. Another current of opinion, originating in the USA, began to see addiction as a vice manifesting not just self-indulgence, but a contagious social problem – which therefore necessitated control by penal laws as well as by international action.[17]

Britain's ambivalence towards action about opiates during the nineteenth century contrasted with the attitudes of other countries such as the USA or China. Britain's stance was not unconnected with the fact that throughout this period the British Empire was the world's largest grower, processor and highly profitable trafficker of opium. China was the principal market for – and victim of – this trade: indeed, the British fostered addiction there, obtaining and jealously guarding a virtual monopoly of the drug, and fought the 1839–42 'Opium' War largely to defend these profits against an Emperor who was struggling to cure the problem and stamp out the trade.[18]

It was an extraordinary and shaming episode, which is still not adequately dealt with in British history teaching today. Opium – a shiny brown-black solid gum which is soft when new and possesses a bitter smell and taste – had originally been brought to India by Arab traders in the eighth century AD. There is no word for it in Sanskrit or Hindi, but by the fifteenth century, under the Mogul Emperor Akbar, poppy fields were being widely cultivated throughout Bengal. In China poppies had first been grown as ornamental plants or for the medical value of their opium, especially in combating cholera; it was only when tobacco had spread to the Old World and Asia that a few Chinese copied tobacco smokers and began to inhale opium fumes by burning it over a candle. Classically, opium is smoked in a long pipe – producing 'pipedream' fantasies, though it can also be eaten. (Daniel Defoe's Robinson Crusoe sailed from the Straits to China in a ship that was carrying the drug because he had 'heard that it bears a great price among the Chinese'.) In 1788 Warren Hastings delivered his famous opinion that opium was 'a pernicious article of luxury, which ought not to be permitted but for the purposes of foreign commerce': the East India Company consequently exported the local stocks to China. Most Chinese and their leaders did not use opium and resisted this incursion, however, as a result of increasing addiction despite opium being officially forbidden, the Deputy Governor of Canton was by 1799 reporting that: 'The weak and infirm perish gradually from want and hunger, while the strong and violent become thieves and robbers, the ultimate ruin of all being thus equally certain and inevitable.' A decree the next year sought to ban all trade in opium. The British traders, however, ignored this with impunity; and formed the first large-scale 'trafficking ring': the total quantity of Indian opium imported into China rose from 4,000 chests in 1811 to 35,455 chests (2,250 tons) in 1839 – shipped aboard heavily-armed contraband clippers from Calcutta, before being smuggled ashore in 'scrambling dragons' or 'fast crabs'.

Mahatma Gandhi was later to comment: 'It is no defence to urge that the vice has existed in India from time immemorial. No one organized the vice as the present government has for revenue purposes.' Indeed the East India Company, having first established a monopoly over poppy farming in Bengal, 'pushed to the utmost the sale of the poppy, and the manufacture and sale of the drug, for the sake of revenue. It licensed the ships with their captains and their crews. It provided that they should be absolutely controlled by its officers in China. It fixed its own stamp to the drug and took pains that it should be manufactured expressly to suit the tastes of the Chinese. Yet because the trade was illegal it disclaimed and instructed its officers at the receiving post to disclaim all knowledge of the drug.'[19] Although the 1833 reform Parliament in Britain terminated the East India Company's monopoly, the Chinese faced a worse situation thereafter through having to deal with the government of 'the barbarians' itself. The Imperial Qing court very nearly accepted a policy of legalizing opium, but finally determined to try to eradicate it. In 1839 the Emperor sent the scholar-poet Commissioner Lin to Canton (now called Guangzhou) to enforce the law requiring that all opium should be handed over for destruction: this move, however, was seized upon by Palmerston as a pretext to declare war so that he could force opium and trade on China, and De Quincey was among those who applauded. In vain *The Times* protested that Britain was 'sitting on an international crime'. In vain Lin wrote to Queen Victoria in an eloquent letter (which was never delivered):

I am told that in your own country opium smoking is forbidden under severe penalties. This means that you are aware how harmful it is. But better than to forbid the smoking of it would be to forbid the sale of it and, better still, to forbid the production of it, which is the only way of cleansing the contamination at its source. So long as you do not take it yourselves, but continue to make it and tempt the people of China to buy it, you will be showing yourselves careful of your own lives, but careless of the lives of other people, indifferent in your greed for gain to the harm you do to others; such conduct is repugnant to human feelings and at variance with the Way of Heaven . . .

The superior European gun-power ensured that the Opium War ended in 1842 with the Chinese not only being insultingly forced to pay reparations of $6 million for the illegal opium that Lin had seized, but also to cede to 'the barbarians' Hong Kong – at the suggestion of one William Jardine, an opium trader in Canton – as well as to open five treaty ports. (It is this treaty which the present Chinese government in 1984 insisted on renegotiating, now enjoying a reverse position of *force majeure* over the British.) When the firm of Jardine Matheson transferred its head office to Hong Kong in 1844, little business there was being conducted other than opium: the fortune of the company was founded during the next thirty years on what *The Cambridge History of China* calls 'the world's most valuable single commodity trade of the nineteenth century'. During this period India's opium exports trebled, though the British government deflected moral criticism by ostensibly deploring the trade whilst its navy secretly protected the smugglers.

In many parts of southern and eastern Asia, poppies became such a commercially tempting crop to grow that good agricultural land was diverted from the production of essential food. Addicts who could not afford both food and opium deprived themselves of the former, so that they and their families starved. For the richer classes, opium smoking was a social grace as well as pleasure; for the poor, addiction offered escape from unhappiness – although the cost of their craving added to the cycle of their poverty and despair. An increasing number ended their lives by swallowing an opium overdose. In 1850 the young Chinese Emperor Hienfang once again attempted to implement his father's and grandfather's measures to eliminate the scourge: smokers were given five months to abandon the habit, after which they risked decapitation; and to assist reform, every ten families were organized into a self-guaranteeing unit, while physicians prescribed a range of anti-opium remedies. Unfortunately, as these remedies usually contained opium in another form (often morphine), they tended to perpetuate where they did not exacerbate the problem: the ban on opium smoking in fact resulted in a rapid spread in the use of morphine pills and injections.[20] (This substitution for one drug of a newer and stronger one, which is at first hailed as an antidote, is one of the recurrent patterns in the history of drug use.) In 1906, by which time over 14 million people in China, some one-third of the population, had become opiate users, the government drew up a new and more realistic ten-year plan for reform: poppy cultivation was to be licensed and eliminated by 10 per cent a year, with other crops being substituted; opium dens were prohibited; smokers were to be licensed, with those aged sixty or over being treated leniently, in a policy leading to the habit's progressive elimination over a decade; and negotiations were to be opened once more with the British and other traffickers. This time, however, the situation was different because the Chinese had new and powerful allies on their side.

For years, Americans amongst others had been pointing out the hypocritical contrast in the attitude towards opium of the sanctimonious and wealthy nation which lost few opportunities to remind the world about its abolition of the slave trade. In vain did the leaders of the nation of shopkeepers attempt to reply that, whereas Adam Smith's and Ricardo's argument that there must be no interference with supply and demand applied to the slave trade (since slavery took away a person's right to dispose of his labour in the open market for the highest price), no such moral problem arose with the trade in opium. The concern of American diplomats and traders was practical as well as moral, because the opium traffic threatened the Open Door policy they desired for the expansion of other trade into China. Meanwhile, British and American missionaries, who believed that opium hampered the spread of the Gospel,[21] appealed to public opinion in Britain (the tactic which had been effective in the anti-slavery campaign) to press the government to change its policy. But the opposition's motion in the House of Commons to condemn the Opium War, despite the support of Peel and the youthful Gladstone (who characterized it as 'a war more unjust in its origin, a war more calculated to cover this country with permanent disgrace, I do not know') was defeated by nine votes. Palmerston's principal argument – used for the next seventy years, only reluctantly abandoned in the case of the slave trade, and heard yet again recently in the debate as to whether the United Kingdom should continue to export leg-irons – was that even if the British were to stop their trade, its place would only be taken by opium from Turkey and Persia. When the government lost a further censure motion on the *Arrow* incident which sparked the second Opium War in 1857 (as a result of a campaign led by Cobden, Gladstone and Disraeli), Palmerston promptly appealed to the country and won a jingoistic victory. In the House of Lords, the Earl of Albemarle deployed on behalf of the government the pro-traffickers' second line of prevarication:

> It was the abuse, not the use, of opium which was pernicious. In this respect, it differed not at all from other narcotics with which we were more familiar in England (namely, ardent spirits, wine, beer or cider). Drunkenness was the great source of crime in England, yet no one seriously thought of suppress-ing the use of intoxicating drinks by legislative enactment . . . If the Chinese could not get the opium they would take to ardent spirits and the crisis resulting would increase ten to one hundredfold.[22]

Jardine Matheson reassured the Governor of Hong Kong in a letter dated 28 November 1867: 'Since 1860 it has been rendered abundantly clear that the use of opium is not a curse, but a comfort and a benefit to the hardworking Chinese.' None the less on the platform at an anti-opium meeting at the Mansion House in 1881 attended by delegates from thirty countries there were ranged Cardinal Manning, the Archbishop of Canterbury and Lord Shaftesbury – termed by *The Times* 'a triumvirate which might well overawe evil itself', though evidently it did not awe Her Majesty's government. A public petition of 205,000 signatures followed in a campaign led by the Quakers; a mere ten years later the government agreed to buy further time by the appointment of a Royal Commis-sion under Lord Brassey. The witnesses and report of the Commission proved bafflingly contradictory. In the Commons Dr Furquharson, MP, had praised opium as a valuable prophylactic against fever, stating it was taken for that purpose as freely in the Fen district as in the Orient. The Commission's finding with regard to China was (in words which were to echo in other official reports over the next century): 'We conclude that the habit is generally practised in moderation, and that when so practised, the injurious effects are not apparent; but that when the habit is carried to excess, disastrous consequences, both moral and physical, inevitably fol-low.' Although one of the Commissioners, Henry Wilson, MP, wrote a vigorous minority dissent – 'The report adopted by my colleagues appears to me to partake more of the character of an elaborate defence of the opium trade of the East Indian Company and of the present Government of India than of a judicial pronouncement' – the administration in India was relieved to have obtained a stay of execution, since it derived a large part of its revenue from the drug's trade. Nor was the British official condonation of narcotic dependency confined to India. As late as 1904, opium sales accounted for 59 per cent of all government revenue in the British Malayan Straits Settlements.[23] Because opium smoking is a social custom practised in groups, it is easily contagious. Chinese overseas labourers, retaining their habit with the help of opium dens supplied by the state-regulated opium monopolies, gradually infected in turn the indigenous populations of Thailand, Indo-China, Burma and Malaysia.

Reform, however, eventually won – impelled as much by employers' reports on the deleterious effects of opium on the efficiency of their Chinese labour, as by the popular pressure for anti-opium laws which spread across the world. The most influential campaign came from the USA, which, following a 1904 Commission that condemned the effects of opium after the annexation of the Philippines, abolished its former Spanish colonial predecessors' franchise of the drug there – thus demonstrating to the British that it was perfectly feasible to do likewise. In the USA and Britain, as well as in China, emotion against drugs was exacerbated by xenophobia against foreign pollution, which was felt to be somehow more evil and intrinsically worse than indigenous poisons. (Capt. Hobson, an American crusader described as being of 'virtually unlimited moral indignation', declared: 'Like the invasions and plagues of history, the scourge of narcotic drug addiction came out of Asia': another theme repeatedly to be woven into the pattern of most national attitudes to drugs.)[24] Nevertheless, China's subsequent eradication of its massive opiate problem was to become one of the very few significant encouraging events in the history of drugs in the twentieth century.

US concern had been prompted by its own increasing experience of the two main illicit drugs today: heroin and cocaine. The diamorphine alkaloid, later to be given the seductive brand name 'Heroin' (from the German word *heroisch*: of supernatural power), had first been synthesized by the British chemist C. R. Alder Wright by heating morphine and acetic anhydride at St Mary's Hospital, London in 1874.[25] Initially marketed as a cough remedy, it was soon hailed as another 'miracle drug', and was found to be three times as effective a pain-killer as morphine. Introduced into the USA and Britain under its striking new name by the German pharmaceutical company Bayer in 1898, it was welcomed as a means of treating morphine dependency – until the addiction of those treated with it was noticed. (Morphia was used by Dr Halstead to treat his own cocaine dependency, while Dr Bentley recommended cocaine to cure morphine addiction.) In America panaceas of opiates and cocaine became highly popular as alternatives to the previous painful remedy of bleeding (sometimes three-quarters of a patient's blood supply being drained) or drastic prescriptions based on mercury. Medical followers of Benjamin Rush, one of the signatories of the Declaration of Independence, used to administer as much as 10 grams of mercury an hour, with the consequence that the patient lost his teeth and jawbone, soon followed by his life.

The USA first acquired a significant problem of opiate dependency from the profligate dispensation of morphine to wounded soldiers during the Civil War in the 1860s, so that addiction was called the 'soldier's disease'. Army officers as well as doctors even poured morphine on to their hands, and allowed their soldiers to lick it off.[26] Opium was also used until the end of the nineteenth century to pacify violent criminals.[27] Others succumbed iatrogenically: Eugene O'Neill's mother became addicted to morphine after complications at his birth in 1888.[28]

By 1895 at least 3 per cent of the US population (predominantly in the upper and middle social classes) were dependent on narcotics – although newspapers did not then campaign against the problem, possibly because advertisements for patent opiate preparations were a major source of their revenue. The twentieth century therefore started with more opiate addicts per head of the population in the USA than there are today. The burgeoning patent-medicine industry blamed the rise in addiction on over-prescribing doctors; the doctors blamed it on the consumption of opiate-based patent cures. Adamson's Botanic Cough Balsam was one of many containing the magical new elixir, heroin. At least 600 patent American nostrums contained significant amounts of opiates, in addition to the large number of other preparations based on cocaine or cannabis (such as Tilden's Extract and the highly successful Robinson's Life Extract) – not to mention the many hundreds more fortified with America's favourite drug, alcohol. Following the rise of the Prohibition movement after Maine first outlawed the sale of alcoholic beverages in 1851, sales of patent medicines such as Hostetter's Bitters (78 per cent proof, but under the law not an alcoholic beverage) rose sharply. By 1915, the recreational abuse of heroin had led to the admission of 425 cases of heroin dependency to Bellevue Hospital in New York; three years later the New York Health Commissioner estimated that there were at least 150,000 addicts in the City, the majority of them dependent on heroin and many from the armed forces. Furthermore, a clandestine American criminal traffic in drugs was emerging, following the 1909 law passed by Congress which laid down that thenceforward opium could only be imported for medical purposes, with the result that many opium dependants turned to heroin as a ready substitute.

The complications caused by cocaine were slower to be recognized. In 1885 the American pharmaceutical company Parke-Davis promoted cocaine as a wonder drug that would 'supply the place of food, make the coward brave, the silent eloquent, and free the victims of alcohol and opium habit from their bondage'. In the USA, pharmacological remedies openly boasting a base of cocaine became widely popular as a means of dealing with every form of complaint from melancholy and flu to impotence. By 1896 the *New York Herald* reported 'The Whole Town Mad for Cocaine'. Bartenders served cocaine with whisky. Cocaine parlours burgeoned for polite clienteles. It was a universal panacea, sold in chewing-gum, in cigarettes, and – significantly – in nose-sprays: catarrh powders (some virtually pure cocaine) for headaches and sinus ailments presaged 'snorting'. Cocaine's seemingly miraculous potency and easy availability threatened physicians' traditional privilege to grant and withhold medicines. Celery-coca tonic was helpfully advertised as being capable of curing both sexual apathy and sexual excess. (Any positive effect of drugs on sexual performance seems highly subjective, with placebos enjoying a suspiciously high rate of success. Virtually every drug – besides an amazing range of other foods and drinks – has been claimed to be aphrodisiac (see Chapter 4), but has also at other times been blamed for spoiling desire.)

The popularity of cheap shot-in-the-arm drinks led drug-stores to develop their role as soda-fountains. In 1886, the year after Atlanta went 'dry', an impecunious pharmacist called John Pemberton cooked up in his backyard a coca-laced 'brain-tonic' elixir aimed at the temperance market which he first named 'Coca Kola' – soon changed to Coca Cola, although it became popularly known as 'dope' as well as 'coke'. The cola part derives from the West African Kola tree, whose nuts contain caffeine, and had an aphrodisiac reputation. Pemberton added sugar, caramel, colouring, phosphoric acid and carbonated water in a 'secret formula'. Although the cocaine component had to be discontinued in 1903 when a presidential commission – pressured by Southern politicians fearful of what it would do to black Americans – criticized 'the baneful effect of the powerful habit-forming drugs' in many soft drinks, it is still flavoured with coca leaves and contains caffeine. Pemberton sold his Coke title for $2,300; astutely promoted for the relief of 'headache and exhaustion', it proved so popular that more than sixty other varieties competed for the public's thirst, and in 1919 it was resold for $25 million. (Today it is also used as a contraceptive douche in a number of developing countries.) Meanwhile, a shrewd Corsican called Angelo Mariani was having a spectacular success advertising with Cheret posters his 'French Coca Wine' produced from Peruvian coca leaves, which was backed by the personal endorsements of Thomas Edison, Sarah Bernhardt, Ibsen, H. G. Wells, Zola, Dumas, Gounod, Verne, sporting teams and 8,000 doctors, not to speak of three popes and sixteen heads of state, including Queen Victoria, four kings and the two US presidents Grant and McKinley.

An even more influential testimonial for cocaine had been provided by Sigmund Freud, the Viennese father of psychoanalysis. Intrigued by reports of its use by the army, he tried it both orally and by injection to counter his own nervous depression at the age of twenty-eight in 1884. It was, he immediately told his fiancée, 'a magical drug'. He described its effects as:

exhilaration and lasting euphoria, which in no way differs from the normal euphoria of the healthy person . . . You perceive an increase of self-control and possess more vitality and capacity for work . . . Long intensive mental or physical work is performed without any fatigue [or] . . . the unpleasant after-effects that follow exhilaration brought about by alcohol. Absolutely no craving for the further use of cocaine appears after the first, or even after repeated taking of the drug; one feels rather a curious aversion to it.[29]

For three years Freud pressed cocaine on his family, friends and colleagues. However, he sharply realized the illusion he had been under about the drug's effects when his patient, Dr von Fleischl-Marxow, to whom he had mistakenly given what he called 'frightful' doses to wean him from morphine, escalated his cocaine intake to 1 gram daily (twenty times the dose Freud himself took from time to time) – and furthermore began to develop a paranoid psychosis in which he believed that there were white snakes crawling over his skin. Unlike Fleischl-Marxow, Freud, himself a twenty-cigars-a-day smoker, was able to give up cocaine without effort – by contrast with his tobacco habit, on which he continued to be dependent until he developed a cancer of the mouth that was to kill him. Freud later had to defend himself against charges by Dr Erlenmeyer that he had loosed 'the third scourge of the race', worse than the earlier two of alcohol and morphine, upon the world, and abandoned further research into cocaine to his colleague Carl Köller, who found it to be an effective local anaesthetic for use in eye surgery.

By the turn of the century, although William Gillette in 1901 was still elegantly inserting the needle on stage during his performances in the title role of *Sherlock Holmes*, cocaine's benevolent reputation was becoming increasingly clouded. It was further tarnished the next year by the publication of a Chicago woman's memoirs entitled *Eight Years in Cocaine Hell*. The Press hastened to launch its first sensational campaign against the drug, publishing lurid accounts of young women being seduced by it into white slavery, innuendoes about its energizing effect upon the black population, and graphic stories of criminals so high on coke that they had become immune to police gunshots. The crusade was underway to demand penal laws against the 'fallen magic'.

2

The Struggle to Control

'The principal task of civilization, its actual *raison d'être*, is to defend us against nature.'
Sigmund Freud, *The Future of an Illusion* (1927)

The first American attempt to regulate drugs by law did not – like many subsequent efforts – produce the consequences intended. The Pure Foods and Drugs Act passed by Congress in 1906 required 'dangerous drugs' to be listed on the label of any preparations containing them. The then president of the Proprietary Association, however, reassured his members that 'people generally will reason . . . that preparations which come up to the requirements of a congressional enactment must be all right, or certainly, that they are not harmful or dangerous'. He was right: the Act did indeed boost rather than weaken sales of patent medicines, because the public believed that the new law guaranteed their safety. Arsenic beauty aids continued their popularity. During this period, the annual consumption of opium was thirty-six grains a head in America, compared with three grains in France and two in Germany. Eight years later, after a hard campaign, the medical profession won the exclusive right to prescribe opiates and cocaine; but even though such prescriptions now account for 75 per cent of drug sales, the annual total of over-the-counter drug sales has also mushroomed from $150 million prior to regulation to well over $7.3 billion today.

Until the beginning of the twentieth century, there was little or no moral stigma attached to drug use. The long pursuit of international drug control started on 1 February 1909 at the Palace Hotel in Shanghai, when the American Episcopal bishop of the Philippines was elected President at the inaugural meeting of the first International Opium Commission. It was marred by the fact that one key producing country, Turkey, refused to attend at all; Britain came reluctantly and only as a result of American insistence. The British government, as Peter Lowes points out, was at the time trying to bury with as little publicity as possible the skeleton of the India–China opium trade, which, having proved a domestic embarrassment, now threatened to become an international scandal. Three years earlier the House of Commons under a new Liberal government had passed without a division a resolution 'reaffirming its conviction that the Indo-Chinese opium trade was morally indefensible', and requesting the government to take such steps as 'may be necessary to bring it to a speedy close'. The background to this apparent sea change of policy was that Indian exports of opium to China were anyway in decline, having been eclipsed by China's own domestic production. Pressed by backbenchers, the British government offered to reduce opium exports to China progressively each year, provided the Chinese also cut their own home output and did not import from other countries. The Chinese agreed; an Imperial Decree was issued in Peking phasing out – once again – opium's production or use over a period of ten years. Britain, nevertheless, remained the world's main manufacturer and exporter of opium until as late as the 1930s.

The USA's alarm at opium's popularity at home (there were 118,000 Americans of Chinese origin living in the US at the time, almost half of whom were allegedly opium smokers) was redoubled by the spectacle of addiction it had found on annexing the Philippines in 1898, as a result of which Theodore Roosevelt invited representatives of the thirteen nations involved in the Far East to convene the 1909 Commission in Shanghai. Three years later, the International Opium Conference (the Commission's offspring with plenipotentiary powers) adopted the 1912 Hague Convention – the first multilateral instrument to be aimed at the suppression of narcotics. The Turkish and Persian governments, however, refused to ratify the Convention; and, in the absence of any international staff to back it, supervisory responsibility was passed to the Dutch government, from whom it was to be inherited by the League of Nations.

The Hague Convention failed because of a fatal flaw: being based only on a voluntary compliance, it left each nation to establish its own laws for the control of drug abuse. The futility of this was exposed by the British not only continuing but actually stepping up their monopoly production in India; when Gandhi started his 1921 campaign against what he called 'that other oppressor', his followers were arrested for 'undermining the revenue'. So much for the moral weight of the House of Commons; two years later, at least 1,280 tons of opium were still being officially produced in British India, despite less than one-tenth of this quantity being needed for medical and scientific use. In the face of Chinese and American protests, the British continued to insist on growing opium for what they termed other 'legitimate' purposes – which they interpreted to include trafficking profit for the government of India, whose net revenue from opium as late as 1929–30 was £1,758,500.[1] The great moralist writer George Orwell – Eric Blair – was in fact the son of a British 'opium-wallah' in India, his father being a government assistant sub-deputy opium agent in Bihar and Bengal.

The country which enacted the most effective controls was the USA, which ratified the Hague Convention within less than twelve months and passed the 1914 Harrison Narcotics Bill the next year. Woodrow Wilson joined Teddy Roosevelt in an alliance on the issue. The appearance of Sax Rohmer's *The Insidious Dr Fu Manchu* – a best-selling novel in which an oriental tries to take over the white world through drug addiction – helped to link emotive racism with panic about narcotics.[2] Dr Koch of Philadelphia warned that attacks upon white Southern women were the 'direct result of the cocaine-crazed Negro brain'. The American Press reported in the First World War that Germany was lacing cosmetics with heroin powder in order to addict all American womanhood. (Similar rumours that 'subversion through drug addiction is an established aim of Communist China' circulated, without any evidence, during the Korean War in 1950.)

Initially the Harrison Act was ostensibly a tax measure – which resulted in the anomaly that the enforcement of American narcotics policy was a duty of the Treasury until 1968. It did not ban 'maintenance' doses, but restricted opium and its derivatives to a medical prescription by a doctor 'acting in good faith in the legitimate practice of his profession', and any such treatment had to be recorded. Two years after prohibition, however, the Supreme Court interpreted this phrase as excluding heroin maintenance for addicts, and any doctor or owner of a clinic who provided such a prescription faced arrest and professional ruin, if not jail as well.[3] Finally, heroin was totally banned by the courts for any medical use at all, as a result of warnings like that from Dr Alexander Lambert of New York's Bellevue Hospital:

> Heroin destroys the sense of responsibility to the herd . . . the herd instincts are the ones which control the moral sense . . . Heroin obliterates responsibility the same as cocaine, and it makes much quicker the muscular reaction, and therefore is used by criminals to inflate them, because they are not only more daring, but their muscular reflexes are quicker.[4]

In vain from across the Atlantic the British Conservative MP Capt. Walter Elliot in the House of Commons attacked Americans for 'their extraordinary savage idea of stamping out all people who happen to disagree with their social theories [concerning narcotics and alcohol] . . . and their recent treatment of socialists'. Both Houses of the US Congress – impressed by Dr Dana Hubbard's testimony asserting that 'heroin is the drug used by addicts of over 95 per cent of New York's underworld' – unanimously passed in 1924 a one-sentence amendment to the Harrison Act which prohibited the importation of opium for the purpose of making heroin.

Professor Arnold Trebach, together with some other American authorities, argues that this policy was tragically ill-advised, and that there has never been any evidence that heroin causes organic damage or should not be used as an effective pain-killer.[5] Following world-wide US pressure, however, the total illicit annual production of heroin fell from 9,000 kg. in 1926 to less than 1,000 in 1935; by 1979 it was down to 101 kg. – of which 96 kg. were used in the United Kingdom, where public policy took a markedly divergent course from that in the USA. Unlike in the USA, where judges had pronounced what medical policy should be in this field, in Britain such decisions were kept as the prerogative of medical opinion. At first the British government had started to follow the American model of the Harrison Act. During the First World War, possession of cocaine had been banned for the armed forces in the 1916 Defence of the Realm Act (DORA) under regulation 40B. Drug control became one more of the many disparate 'no win' responsibilities of the Home Office – where it has remained ever since. Public opinion was agitated by the death of a young actress called Billie Carleton, supposedly from a cocaine overdose after the Victory Ball at the Albert Hall: the furore caused by this society scandal enabled the Home Office to comply with international pressure, and as a result the Dangerous Drugs Act was passed in 1920, making it illegal to possess opium, morphine and heroin as well as cocaine unless prescribed or supplied by a doctor.

The first major charge came with the report of the Rolleston Committee in January 1926. The Committee's recommendations were to set the distinctive nature of British addictive drug policy for the next four decades.[6] Its character was crucially determined by the fact that it was appointed not by the Home Office but by the Ministry of Health (itself established only seven years earlier), with a membership drawn from the medical profession and a chairman who was the President of the Royal College of Physicians. The Committee's terms of reference were 'to consider and advise as to the circumstances, if any, in which the supply of morphia and heroin (including preparations containing morphia and heroin) to persons suffering from addiction to those drugs may be regarded as medically advisable, and as to the precautions which it is desirable that medical practitioners administering or prescribing morphia or heroin should adopt for the avoidance of abuse'. Virtually every witness heard by the Committee testified that heroin was essential for certain kinds of medical cases and should on no account be banned. Members of the Committee visited the USA and disliked the policy and results they saw there. The Committee reported without any hesitation that addiction was a problem, not of sin, but for medical treatment: 'a manifestation of disease and not a mere form of vicious indulgence. In other words, the drug is taken in such cases not for the purpose of obtaining positive pleasure, but in order to relieve a morbid and overpowering craving.'[7] The Committee's concern was less with hedonistic users, than with cases who had become addicted when undergoing medical treatment or through professional access to drugs. An 'addict' the Committee defined as 'a person who, not requiring the continued use of the drug for relief of the symptoms of organic disease, has acquired, as a result of repeated administration, an overpowering desire for its continuance, and in whom withdrawal of the drug leads to definite symptoms of mental or physical distress or disorder.' It concluded that their drugs should be gradually reduced, but could not always be entirely withdrawn: not only for 'the relief of pain due to organic disease such as an inoperable cancer', but controversially also:

> When every effort possible in the circumstances has been made, and made unsuccessfully, to bring the patient to a condition in which he is independent of the drug, it may become justifiable in certain cases to order regularly the minimum dose which has been found necessary, either in order to avoid serious withdrawal symptoms, or to keep the patient in a condition in which he can lead a useful life . . . in one class, such attempted complete withdrawal produced severe distress or even risk of life; in the other, experience showed that a certain minimum dose of the drug was necessary to enable the patients to lead useful and relatively normal lives, and that if deprived of this non-progressive dose, they become incapable of work . . .

The Committee's report – humanely insisting in the face of a strongly prohibitionist climate that doctors should care for, as well as try to cure, addicts – was completely accepted by the British government. Although control of strategy for dealing with drug addiction remained with the Home Office, this department is in no position to pronounce on what is bona fide medical practice, and so an uneasy dichotomy grew up between it and medical authorities over evolving an overall drugs policy – a problem which has persisted ever since. Rolleston recommended – in accordance with the distrust the medical profession has for lawyers and judges – that any doctor who recklessly overprescribed should have his case considered not in a criminal court, but by a special medical tribunal composed primarily of doctors. Although this was made law in 1928 no such tribunal ever in fact convened for forty-five years. The Committee also rejected, as a violation of the confidential doctor–patient relationship, the idea that addicts should be compulsorily entered on a register, even to monitor those who might be obtaining multiple prescriptions. This too the government accepted until 1968, although the Rolleston recommendations other than the one for tribunals were never enacted into legislation. The Home Office did, however, develop its own unofficial index of addicts from 1936 onwards: this initially showed a national total of 616, almost equally male and female, who included 147 'professional' addicts (doctors, dentists, pharmacists or nurses, who had become addicted through their working access to dangerous drugs). A significant number of the other cases were of iatrogenic or therapeutic origin: people who had become addicted through being prescribed an opiate as treatment for an illness. The users controlled their habit without publicity or deterioration, many retaining both their jobs and their families. Amongst their number were politicians, businessmen, barristers, professors, naval and military officers, an explorer and a few artists, besides doctors and nurses; many were aged at least sixty, and morphine was the main drug of addiction. The British government reported to the League of Nations that its country's tiny opium consumption was now almost entirely limited to some of its few Chinese inhabitants. Recreational drug use was largely confined to cocaine, taken by a few Bohemians, as described in the *Diary of a Drug Fiend* of Aleister Crowley (who himself was to die a heroin addict). A vogue for cocaine, as well as morphia from silver syringes, hit the decadent white settlers in Kenya between the wars. Morphia at that date continued to be more popular than heroin; it was morphia that Virginia Woolf carried in her pocket when a German invasion looked likely in 1940.

The Home Office did not even consider it necessary to have a separate Drugs Branch until 1934: the Branch's staff today still remains very limited in numbers, though not in quality. By 1953 the total number of addicts known to the Home Office was down to 290, of whom seventy-one were 'professional' cases. In 1958 a British MP reported to the UN that there were fifty-two registered addicts in England and Wales and two in Scotland, and that they were all over forty years old. H. B. Spear, for many years the highly-respected Chief Inspector of Drugs at the Home Office, says that prior to the Second World War the number of addicts in Britain used to be so few and law-abiding that the Home Office was able to maintain personal contact and give them helpful advice; although he also considers that the Rolleston Committee displayed 'astounding naivety' in its belief that addicts were unlikely to be capable of obtaining illegal sources of drugs if doctors controlled the legal supply.[8] Neither was the problem of doctors who were themselves addicts tackled.

To liberals in America, Canada and elsewhere, this British policy seemed astounding in its compassion when contrasted with their own countries' criminalization of addiction. The so-called 'British system' (although there was in fact no one system, since doctors were free to prescribe differently) aimed at humane containment rather than treatment. It derived from the fact of how small a drug problem Britain had until the 1960s, and that it was also believed to be diminishing. There were only two prosecutions for cocaine in the UK in 1927, and twenty-seven for opiates; by 1938 the annual number of opiate convictions had fallen to six, and even in 1958 there were still only eight. Prescribed supplies of opiates were seen as the best way to avoid the development of a criminal market and addict crime. It is, however, crucial to remember a fact which is often overlooked: that the Rolleston Committee distinguished between drugs being taken 'to relieve a morbid and overpowering craving', and when they were 'for the purpose of obtaining positive pleasure'; their recommendation of medical prescription of opiates applied only to the former cases, where addiction was 'a manifestation of disease and not a mere form of vicious indulgence'. None the less, even this approach was anathema to the US authorities, who thought that the British were living in a soft-headed cloud-cuckoo-land.

At the 1930 meeting of the Southern Sheriffs and Policemen's Association, it was proposed that police officers must be issued with heavier calibre weapons since it was seriously contended that black skin had become impervious to the standard calibre bullets because 'virtually every Negro was addicted to cocaine'. The addict stereotype of Mrs Dubose, the elderly upper-class morphia dependant of Harper Lee's *To Kill a Mockingbird*, or as portrayed in Eugene O'Neill's autobiographical *Long Day's Journey into Night*, gave way to the tough heroin junkie of Nelson Algren's *Man with the Golden Arm* – one of several books and films which did a disservice by sensationalizing the trauma of withdrawal.[9] Henry Anslinger, the Director of the new US Federal Bureau of Narcotics from 1930 until 1962, was a former Assistant Commissioner of Prohibition who was driven by messianic ambition. In comparison with Britain, whose enforcement agency consisted of four men directed by one part-time Home Office civil servant, the new US Bureau was given over 150 full-time and frequently armed agents with an annual budget of more than 1 million dollars.[10] Some of the statements of Anslinger's staff echoed the sexual and xenophobic myths and innuendoes of Capt. Hobson's *Drug Addiction – A Malignant Racial Cancer*, painting lurid pictures of orientals using drugs to seduce 'women from good families' to work in brothels. An English woman living in Vancouver told me she remembers panic rumours that girls were being forcibly injected in crowded dance-halls so they could be kidnapped and made to succumb to addiction. Opium was popularly associated with prostitutes who were reputed to use it in the belief that it reduced their menstrual cycles. Heroin was blamed for causing violent assaults, even though medical evidence indicates that opiates – unlike alcohol – far from resulting in aggression, decrease any violent response to provocation as well as individuals' sex and hunger drives. Despite all his rhetoric, Anslinger himself supplied the addicted Senator Joe McCarthy with morphine as a favour.

Anslinger nursed an equally incandescent detestation of mari-juana (cannabis). Without adducing any reliable evidence he blamed it also for violent crime – especially amongst Mexicans and blacks – and eventually succeeded in having it bracketed with heroin and prohibited by being added to the Harrison Act in 1937. The Press took up his denunciation of 'reefer madness' as an invisible hydra-headed threat to the nation. The state of Missouri prescribed life imprisonment for a first offence of selling cannabis or a second offence of possessing it; Massachusetts enacted that anybody found in a place where marijuana was kept, or in the company of anybody possessing it, could be jailed for five years; although in 1961 the Supreme Court struck down a Californian statute that made addic-tion a criminal offence, as being contrary to the Eighth Amendment of the Constitution. Peyote alone is now partly exempt from the ban on drugs in the USA so that it can be used sacramentally by the 225,000 adherents of the syncretist Native American Church. In 1960 there were 169 federal arrests in the USA for marijuana offences; by 1966 the number had risen to 15,000. Profound changes were transforming drug use in the USA as they were in Europe. Hitherto, heroin had been considered to be the drug mainly of some poor and black people, to relieve the grind of physical labour and depressing conditions of the ghetto. (James Baldwin charged that narcotics became common in Harlem after 1944 because they 'had been dumped in the ghetto deliberately to destroy the black population'.) Billie Holiday, the great jazz singer, was one of those sentenced to life imprisonment for heroin addiction, before she died from an overdose. Cocaine, the retail price of which rose sharply as a result of the Harrison Act, was the drug of choice among the glamorous and rich: then, as now, it was a vogue in Hollywood as well as with blues singers and musicians. According to the *Journal of the American Medical Association* in 1923 the secret behind the dreamy faraway look in cinematic close-ups of many stars at the time was cocaine; and it was white 'nose powder' which endowed Charlie Chaplin with superman strength in *Modern Times*.

The Second World War witnessed a hiatus in the illegal drug trade, with the Mediterranean heroin laboratories unable to operate and traffic world-wide halted by naval and military patrols. Following the Allied victory, Anslinger's policy was adopted in the wake of the occupying American armies by Germany and Japan. In the post-war USA, however, rock and roll took up the drug culture of Tin Pan Alley, climaxing in the 1960s with Jimi Hendrix, the Byrds' 'Eight Miles High', the Rolling Stones' 'Get Off My Cloud' and 'Sister Morphine', the Beatles' 'Yellow Submarine', 'Golden Brown', the Grateful Dead, 'Mr Tambourine Man' and Steppenwolf's 'Snowblind Friend'. Hippies in caftans were fazed by Sergeant Pepper; on Ibiza signs read 'Don't walk on grass – smoke it'. Head-shops did a brisk trade in coke spoons fashioned of ivory and silver for $199; the richest pop-stars flaunted a golden coke straw. It was the era when The Old Dope Peddler in Tom Lehrer's bitter-sweet song was believed to be 'doing well by doing good', and the ideas of first Aldous Huxley and then Timothy Leary, Ken Kesey and his Pranksters, Carlos Castaneda and Alexander Trocchi messianically swept campus audiences. In 1954 *The Doors of Perception* more than any other single work fermented the new post-war drug interest: Huxley gave drug culture intellectual respectability, while other writers such as Allen Ginsberg and William Burroughs connected it to anti-materialist protest. Peyote offered the urbanized young a promise of the illusion of reverting to ancient Indian roots. Leary preached the 'Politics of ecstasy' – 'Tune in, turn on and drop out': 'We saw ourselves', he said afterwards, 'as anthropologists from the twenty-first century inhabiting a time

module set somewhere in the dark ages of the 1960s', being persecuted like many disturbing innovators, such as Galileo or Stopes,
had been throughout history. Eager pilgrims to India, Mexico or
Nepal absorbed drugs as well as gurus. Cannabis became the
currency of the 'Make Love Not War' movement. Possession of
LSD was first made a crime in 1966, despite its disciples' protest that
it was a religion. Allen Ginsberg was to write in *Howl*: 'I saw the
best minds of my generation destroyed by madness . . . at dawn
looking for an angry fix.'

However, by the time the two anti-heroes snorted in the 1969 cult
film *Easy Rider*, the hippiesque idealism of San Francisco's Haight-
Ashbury drug culture was starting to be riven by darker, anarchic
tension, as pot (marijuana or cannabis) and acid (LSD) gave way to
speed (methamphetamine) and smack (heroin). Some of the early
LSD prophets unfortunately seemed to have scrambled their brains
in acid. The black leader, Eldridge Cleaver, attacked Leary's
advocacy of drugs in 1971 as counter-revolutionary. The original
hedonistic drop-outs – idealistic, anarchic or naïve – had embraced
spiritual or pleasure-principle life-styles as alternatives to the
straight ones of the squares (or 'sordids', 'crumblies' or 'Son et
Lumière', as teenagers called oldies). Now this movement found
itself challenged and threatened by junkies who were being manipulated by violent dealers. Altamount succeeded Woodstock. Across
the mood of Bob Dylan fell the shadow of Charles Manson. The
California 'Brotherhood of Eternal Love' was transmogrified from
the Jekyll of a registered religion proselytizing emancipation
through pot and acid, to the Hyde of an international conglomerate
which syndicated drugs for vast profits. Hell's Angel bikers operated a network across North America delivering speed, heroin and
cocaine. Organized crime muscled in to take over the trade, and the
profits persuaded the Mafia to reverse its previous policy of eschewing involvement. When the children of Congressmen began to be
counted amongst the hooked, the politicians began to take the issue
very seriously indeed.

Public panic was fuelled by the USA's view of addiction as a
psychopathic condition, coupled with a fear that each heroin addict
converts an average of some six others to the drug, by contact,
recommendation or in order to trade. If this theory is correct the
exponential growth of future heroin users in the population becomes disturbing in the extreme; even allowing for the likelihood

that at least two of the six may only use intermittently, another two will give up, and that (as many American soldiers showed) drug use does not stop many people leading approximately normal lives. Edward Jay Epstein, in his brilliant if ultimately not wholly persuasive polemic *Agency of Fear*,[11] forcefully argues that ambitious Republican political leaders exaggerated the situation so as to exploit the public's phobia. Governor Nelson Rockefeller – whose great-grandfather William Avery Rockefeller had founded the family fortune by dealing in bottled nostrums – after his 1964 defeat, adopted a hard line against drugs in order to make him appear less of a liberal beside Senator Goldwater and his other hard-line rivals. Declaring – not the first or the last to do so – that the 'epidemic' of addiction in New York State had attained the gravity of a 'plague', he called for 'all-out war' against it. He pressed laws through the legislature first for 'civil commitment' (the compulsory incarceration of even unconvicted addicts for up to five years), and then for mandatory life sentences for even sixteen-year-olds who possessed small quantities of amphetamines, LSD or heroin. It was a stance which certainly played well in Peoria. Panic about drugs led to the peace-time abrogation of civil rights on a scale not even permitted for murder inquiries. Rockefeller's staff prepared further plans to declare a 'drug emergency' and to ask President Nixon and Mayor John Lindsay for emergency concentration camps to quarantine all of New York City's addicts. Nixon, not to be outdone, upped the bidding on the rhetoric and made a war on drugs the central plank of his 1968 election campaign. By 1971 he was warning that this 'national emergency' could 'surely in time destroy us', and determined to jail Leary, its symbol. A few months later he rashly claimed: 'We have turned the corner on drug addiction.'

Despite the crusade, over a hundred heroin shooting-galleries flourished in the north-west part of Washington DC – the area that is the heart of America's establishment, hard by the White House and the Capitol. Within the next decade, there were estimated to be more people receiving heroin treatment in the federal capital itself than in the whole of Britain. By 1970 a greater number of US soldiers were being evacuated from Vietnam as a consequence of drug problems than because of war wounds: several thousand veterans returned home addicted to heroin, though most of them were to kick the habit when away from the stress of war. Drug abuse was denounced no longer as a plague, which implied involuntary sickness, but in terms of wilful moral depravity and terminal degeneracy. It was raised to the top of the political agenda because the US administration took fright at the nexus between drugs, dissent over Vietnam and the anarchic young's new counter-culture. Even some philanthropists seriously proposed that it might be necessary to shoot addicts. In vain an expert federal committee on narcotics and drug abuse cautioned that: 'Hasty and ill-considered policies may not only be ineffective, but they may generate different types of casualties and adverse consequences of medical, social and legal nature, such as loss of respect for the law, extensive arrest records (for youthful violations) . . . '[12]

There were at that date more than 9 million known alcoholics in the USA, compared to less than 100,000 identified narcotics addicts – although the drinkers, having more votes, were less amenable to being made easy political scapegoats.

Meanwhile Britain entered the 1960s in a state of familiar com-placency, not to say smugness, about its drug situation. American experts continued to visit it from a country where addiction was worsening despite draconian laws, to view the paradox of how the liberal 'British system' kept addicts to a contented total of below 500. But the British drug scene was changing. One impetus was the number of North American addicts who crossed the Atlantic to seek asylum from the Federal Bureau of Narcotics and also from the new penal drug code that Canada had enacted in 1958: in the next three years seventy Canadian addicts fled to Britain, including some with records for trafficking. The new drug-users were not self-effacing like the middle-aged addicts on the Home Office's list, but often youthful non-conformists who attracted publicity. Now that white Anglo-Saxon Protestant society had reluctantly come to admit the public existence of sex, young people found that drugs were the challenge with which they could most easily shock conven-tional opinion; and the Press obligingly rose to the bait again and again.

There were other new developments: in 1951 Smith, Kline and French had started to manufacture Drinamyl (a mixture of the stimulant dexamphetamine and the barbiturate hypnotic, amylo-barbitone), known during its 1960s vogue as 'Purple Hearts' or 'French Blue'. The popularity of amphetamine pep pills such as

39

Methedrine, Dexedrine and Benzedrine as boosters was nothing new. When in 1947 the socially-aspirant Tory MP 'Chips' Channon hosted a dinner-party that Somerset Maugham, one of his guests, told him was the 'apogee of his career' (the guests included two female queens), he proudly recorded in his diary how he had laced the cocktails with Benzedrine 'which I find always makes a party go'. Yet it was the adoption of such stimulants by young people which began to terrify that same establishment, oblivious to the argument that speed users were seeking greater energy and awareness, rather than the nihilist escape of opiates or alcohol. Meanwhile, convictions for cannabis offences in the UK, which had risen from fifty-one in 1957 to 588 in 1962, increased from 1,191 in 1966 to 3,071 in 1968. In 1961 the UK ratified the United Nations International Single Convention consolidating a number of previous treaties which committed it to control a range of drugs that included opiates, cocaine and cannabis; a similar UN Convention on Psychotropic Drugs that covered stimulants and sedatives as well as hallucinogens was to follow ten years later. However, the new Interdepartmental Committee of Inquiry that also reported to the British government in 1961 and was the first since the Rolleston Committee of 1926, seemed oblivious to the transformation taking place in drug use. The Committee, chaired by Sir Russell (later Lord) Brain, a neurologist and former President of the Royal College of Physicians, was described by a knowledgeable Home Office official as being 'a typical establishment body, which consulted old sources, and wasn't told what was really happening'. It did indeed reaffirm the Rolleston doctrine that addiction should be regarded as an illness – 'an expression of mental disorder rather than criminal behaviour'; but it reported that specialist clinics to treat such illness were not necessary, averring that cases could be dealt with in the psychiatric wards of general hospitals. Since it also endorsed that many addicts were respectable citizens 'often leading reasonably satisfactory lives' and claimed there was minimal evidence of drugs 'procured by illicit means', the Brain Committee stated that there was still no need for any of the tribunals recommended by Rolleston more than three and a half decades earlier.

This cosy myopia was immediately overwhelmed by evidence from all sides. Table 1 shows the unmistakably significant signs of inflation in the number of known new heroin addicts in the UK:

Table 1: **Number of known new heroin addicts in the UK, 1959–1968**

Year	No.	Year	No.
1959	11	1964	162
1960	24	1965	259
1961	56	1966	522
1962	72	1967	745
1963	90	1968	1,306

In the face of these figures, the Brain Committee was hastily reconvened and asked to think again and harder. Politicians were becoming worried: the Press was full of drug shock-horror stories. The public's attitude towards drug-users had altered sharply, from pity for an invisible handful of harmless ageing victims, to resentment at challenge from unrepentant youthful subcultures. Harsher laws were swiftly enacted: 1964 saw both a new Dangerous Drugs Act that outlawed the growing, or allowing premises to be used for the smoking, of cannabis (extended two years later to include LSD and mescalin); and a hastily-drafted Drugs (Prevention of Misuse) Act which made the unauthorized possession of amphetamines a criminal offence.

The next year saw the number of known heroin addicts (although starting from a low base) more than five times what it had been five years earlier. Scapegoats were rapidly identified, and a media witch-hunt started for six over-prescribing 'junkies' doctors' who were treating cases ostracized by the majority of their colleagues. They provided generous prescriptions from a variety of motives: some were unscrupulously venal, others naïvely kind, senile or pliable in the face of drug-users' manipulation and wheedling. One doctor alone was later found to be issuing 600,000 tablets of heroin a year, giving scripts of 1,000 tablets a time which inevitably provided a lucrative surplus to be sold. The two best known of these doctors were Dr Isabella Lady Frankau, who in 1962 prescribed 6 kg. of heroin but whom many patients describe as compassionate and caring; and Dr John Petro who prescribed heroin and cocaine in Piccadilly lavatories, or from a parked car or the tea buffet at Baker Street underground station. Petro was a surgeon of some talent, regarded by colleagues as muddled and over-generous rather than criminal, but he unfortunately acted as a link between two types of drug abuse by prescribing speed or injectable Methedrine as an alternative to cocaine. The prescribing doctors' defence was that by giving addicts their drug supply at cost price, they cut out criminal traffickers, and enabled them to lead stable, law-abiding lives. Several doctors, like Lady Frankau, used to deal with addicts on a Robin Hood basis, charging the rich ones heavily but treating the poor ones free. They argued that the drug problem would die out with the existing addicts, and meanwhile crime would be prevented since addicts would not – as they did in the USA – need to steal so as to pay criminal suppliers.

Dr Griffith Edwards recently described the ideal system aimed at in Britain as giving the addict neither too little nor too much, so 'that the illegal market will neither be economically encouraged, nor fed by the surplus'.[13] In the 1960s and 1970s, however, this did not allow for pharmacy break-ins or addicts who forged and multiplied prescriptions, ruthlessly playing off some doctors against others. The nightly queues lengthened at all-night chemists like Boots in Piccadilly Circus as addicts waited to get the next day's supply at one minute past midnight. The drug clientele had changed significantly: although their number was still not large, the majority no longer were innocent therapeutic victims, but hedonistic younger users of illegally-obtained drugs, who were unwilling to co-operate with officialdom. The disease concept of addiction advocated by Rolleston, and accepted when the addicts were middle class, came under increasing criticism; most of the new users refused to see themselves as sick but openly asserted their desire for opiates to experience euphoric 'highs'. At least forty of them were reported to be teenagers; working-class addicts only began to be identified in any number in the late 1960s. Known cocaine users had also risen in five years – from thirty to 311 – a majority of whom were also using heroin.

The Brain Committee, shaken and stirred, made another attempt in 1965 and recommended for the first time that the sacrosanct discretion of British doctors should be circumscribed.[14] Although addicts were still to be treated as sick rather than criminal, only certain doctors, mainly in special treatment clinics, should have the right to prescribe them cocaine or heroin. By 1972 the number of doctors allowed to prescribe to addicts had been cut from 85,000 to 150, all of them drug-addiction specialists. The Committee, drawing an analogy with infectious diseases, also recommended that addicts must now be notified to the Home Office. The Dangerous Drugs Act of 1967 implemented these recommendations; but drug users

denounced Brain II as being 'reactionary' and 'hysterically vindic-
tive', and the Home Office itself had argued to the Committee in
favour of tribunals to curb the over-prescribing few, rather than the
introduction of a ban and treatment centres.

The hope was that the clinics would contain the problem by
removing addicts from the black market. Dr Margaret Tripp said:
'Our purpose was to seduce them into the clinics . . . No small part
of the British toleration of legal addiction is due to the clinics'
success in getting addicts out of sight.' None the less, the movement
to 'kick the habit, not the addict' did not succeed. Drugs continued
to exercise – sometimes fatal – attraction for all social classes, from
rock stars to the grandson of a former Prime Minister: in 1965
the twenty-year-old Joshua Macmillan died from an overdose at
Oxford. The new treatment centres, when they belatedly became
available in 1968, dispensed heroin on a much restricted scale:
although this prevented surplus heroin from being resold, a black
market with street gangs of suppliers rapidly arose to fill the gap. An
unknown 'iceberg' of at least three-quarters of the total number of
addicts refused to go near the clinics or even to desire withdrawal.
The number of heroin addicts known to the Home Office continued
to rise from sixty-eight in 1959 to 521 in 1965, 899 in 1966, 1,299 in
1967, and 2,240 in 1968. Unlike the USA's treatment that is tightly
restricted to methadone (a synthetic opiate developed by the Germans during the Second World War when they could no longer get
British opium, but which has proved to be as dangerously addictive
as earlier substitutes: in the 1970s more people in New York died
from methadone poisoning than from heroin), the British policy is
to leave the choice of drug and dosage to the individual clinician.
His crude earliest rule-of-thumb was often, at the end of an
exhausting horse-trading session, to halve the addict's request –
until word of this went round the addicts and they raised their
bids accordingly. The problem of 'competitive prescribing' was
described in two UK Hospital Memoranda at the time:

'Some addicts will not accept withdrawal treatment, at any rate
to start with, and complete refusal of supplies will not cure their
addiction – it will merely throw them on the black market and
encourage the development of an organized illicit traffic on a
scale unknown in this country. The aim is to contain the spread
of drug addiction by continuing to supply this drug in minimum

quantities, where this is necessary in the opinion of the doctor, and where possible to persuade addicts to accept withdrawal treatment.' (*Memorandum 1967/16*)

'It is most important that hospitals in the National Health Service should deal with all addicts who come to them, so as to reduce the danger of setting up a new illicit market.' (*Memorandum 1968/11*)

Drug abuse in Britain, according to Piers Brendon, 'was invented in 1965, a couple of years after sexual intercourse . . . ' Illegality was by then more piquant than immorality as a way of revolting against the never-had-it-so-good materialism of the 1950s. Illicit dealing and abuse continued to be still mainly focused in the centre of London. Young people exchanged cult codes – such as spelling out LSD's initials in the title of 'Lucy in the Sky with Diamonds' – about which most parents remained innocently ignorant; for the susceptible, stories in the Press added a tragi-glamorous notoriety. However, it was one thing for the *jeunesse dorée* to enjoy orgies, but quite different if ordinary people began to acquire such habits. The establishment became uneasy. In 1967 Mick Jagger was sentenced to three months' imprisonment for illegally possessing four amphetamine tablets; the Appeal Court, however, quashed the sentence after *The Times* asked in a leading article 'Who breaks a butterfly upon a wheel?' Acid, hash, love-hearts and speed were sold openly to rolling and stoned hippies at flower-power pop festivals. As a message to the Wootton Committee *The Times* carried an advertisement, organized by Steve Abrams with finance from some of the Beatles, and signed by a number of well-known figures, advocating the legalization of cannabis. It asserted that pot's dangers were exaggerated and that the law outlawing it was not only damaging but unworkable – although elsewhere the same newspaper was seriously warning that cannabis was a danger to white girls 'since a principal motive of the coloured man smoking hemp is to stimulate his sexual desires', and a former policeman was given a seven-year jail sentence for possessing a tiny amount of cannabis. The next year the Report of the Wootton Committee, set up by Roy Jenkins, recommended that the penalties for the possession of cannabis should be reduced (see Chapter 11 below); and although the Report did not find favour with his successor as Home Secretary, James

Callaghan, the penalty for possession was in fact lowered under the following Conservative government in 1971.

In September 1967 the Metropolitan Drugs Squad discovered in London the first known supply of the new and purer 'Chinese No. 3' heroin powder, which had been smuggled from south-east Asia via Hong Kong, and was intended for intravenous injection. The taste for injecting drugs had developed from a habit at that time in west-central London for taking both speed (Methedrine) and barbiturates intravenously. From 1969 onwards the Gerrard Street area of Soho became a centre of heroin traffic, initially organized by Hong Kong Triads: the first warning about this was written in *The Times* by a young reporter called Norman Fowler, fifteen years later to be the cabinet minister responsible for health and social security. Drugs often go in unpredictable waves of fashion. The Rev. Kenneth Leech, who was then working in Soho, recalls: 'It was Methedrine use which provided the bridge between the needle culture and the kids in the clubs. It provided the "escalator" role which is often, wrongly, attributed to cannabis. It was Methedrine which made the process of "fixing" an integral part of the West End drug culture.'[15]

The 1971 Misuse of Drugs Act codified the previous drug law and divided prescribed drugs into three categories, specifying penalties for their production, importation, sale or possession according to the degree of damage they were held to cause.

Class A   includes heroin, opium, morphine, methadone, cocaine, LSD and mescalin, PCP ('Angel Dust') and dipipanone (Diconal).

Class B   includes cannabis, codeine, the more potent amphetamines such as Benzedrine and Drinamyl, and now methaqualone and barbiturates.

Class C   includes the less strong amphetamine-like drugs.

Further measures came with the 1972 Poisons Act which made it an offence to sell barbiturates such as Seconal or Nembutal without a prescription. (Doctors now also need a Home Office licence to prescribe heroin or Diconal.) Since 1968 doctors have been required to supply the Chief Medical Officer at the Home Office with details of anybody they believe or suspect to be dependent on opiates or cocaine – but not LSD, cannabis or barbiturates; this information is kept confidential and has no legal consequence for the addict – though one of the reasons for the low rate of return is because of hesitation to inform the government department that is most connected with the police. By the late 1970s, the treatment centres had become stricter, refusing to prescribe injectable drugs for new patients and usually providing only oral methadone. Addicts turned instead to independent doctors who would prescribe Diconal ('Dike', in which dipipanone provides a heroin-like 'buzz'). In 1982, two doctors prescribed 197,000 Diconal tablets, worth £1 million on the black market, in only six months. In that year dipipanone caused more overdose deaths than heroin, and, as Kenneth Leech commented: 'Irresponsible prescribing has not been reduced, simply transferred to other drugs.'

During the 1970s the 'drug problem' did not diminish in either Europe or America, although the public perception of it became less panicky as the media coverage was less alarmist than in the decade before or after. The UK Home Office hoped that, as drugs had previously had cycles of fashion, heroin might retreat of its own accord in the way LSD seemed to have done. Prior to 1967 virtually no illegal heroin trade had been known in Britain – but in the meantime the world supply position was altering radically (see Chapter 14 below). Following the restriction which meant that prescriptions were obtainable only from treatment clinics, by 1969 the street price of a 10 mg. heroin tablet had risen from 15p to £1, and the profits generated a flourishing black market network. The watershed was in 1978–9, when Britain changed from being a transit point for heroin to becoming itself a major market. The police believe that the initial suppliers of heroin to Britain were Iranian exiles, using the drug to transfer assets out of Iran: seventy-one Iranian nationals were convicted of heroin offences between 1977 and 1979. The heroin originated from Asia, where, however, the 'Golden Crescent' of south-west Asia was starting to overtake the 'Golden Triangle' of Thailand and Indo-China as the major source of supply: the amount of illegal heroin coming from Pakistan rose by a factor of twenty in the five years following 1973, and multiplied again after the upheaval in Afghanistan. Before long addiction in the supply and transit countries was following in the wake of that in the traditional demand nations: the 'global connection' became multi-directional.

In the Western world heroin increasingly registered on the barometer of pop music, from punk to New Wave; Sid Vicious, Keith Moon, and two of The Pretenders were among musicians who died of an overdose. For the first time since the 1920s, cocaine too has become a fashion among rich trend-setters who snort a line through rolled-up bank notes – so much so that a London doctor not long ago asked the Home Office if he was required to give official notification of all the cocaine addicts he met socially. By contrast with heroin's Circean ability to charm human beings into passive self-absorption, cocaine deludes active users into a belief that they can harness and control its power. However, the practice of 'freebasing' cocaine and, most recently, the epidemic of smoking it as 'crack' have led to addiction and injury – as seen in Chapter 8. Wealthy users became drug gourmets, discussing supplies like wine connoisseurs reviewing vintages: one extremely rich 33-year-old peer told the Editor of the *Tatler* that 'the way to tell an English gentleman is by the quality of his drugs'. After appearing to stabilize in the mid-1970s, the statistics have since risen inexorably, as Table 2 demonstrates:

Table 2: **Increase of heroin and cocaine use in the UK, 1975–1985**

	No. of notified narcotic drug addicts at end of year	Heroin seizures (in kg.)	Cocaine seizures (in kg.)
1975	3,425	6.9	7.1
1976	3,474	20.2	9.9
1977	3,605	26.6	13.7
1978	4,116	60.8	16.1
1979	4,787	44.9	24.0
1980	5,107	38.2	40.2
1981	6,157	93.4	21.1
1982	8,144	195.5	18.8
1983	10,235	236.2	80.0
1984	12,489	361.6	65.5
1985	16,112	366.4	85.4

These cases are notified to the Home Office by the doctors who treat them, but since the majority of addicts never go near a doctor, no one knows the true figure. The real total is considered by experts to be between five and ten times higher; adding the number of occasional users, the figure for heroin takers is at least double again.

(Out of 450 drug abusers admitted to Scottish prisons in 1983, only three were found to be on the Home Office's list.) Nine-tenths of the new addicts recently notified are on heroin, which, with the drop in drug prices, has now spread throughout all areas and social groups.

The 1980s found Britain quite unprepared for the crisis. Even were most addicts willing to embark on withdrawal at clinics – which they are not – sufficient treatment facilities would not be available. Such hospital drug treatment centres as there are were planned for a mere 1,200 addicts, with almost all of them situated solely in the London area. Waiting-lists of several weeks deterred new cases. It is probable that less than one in ten of Britain's addicts attend any clinic; many of the remainder see no need to seek treatment, because they view their drug habit not as an illness, but as a style of life. Among the few who do attend clinics, subsequent relapse is unfortunately more often the rule than the exception. The tiny size of Britain's previous drug population, together with the earlier tradition of treatment by maintenance, means that few clinics have much experience of how to induce cures. Many GP doctors loathe dealing with drug cases, whom they regard in the main as disruptive, manipulative and suffering only from a self-inflicted complaint.

Facilitated by the easier new habit of smoking rather than inject-ing, heroin has spread among young people in the limbo of unem-ployment, in rural areas as well as cities; but it was not until 1984 that district health authorities were asked to investigate and draw up means of tackling heroin addiction. Multiple drug use habits have also become common: if heroin addicts are unable to get their supply, many of them prefer to try poly-drug experiments rather than face withdrawal. H. B. Spear concludes: 'Clearly some com-plex social processes had occurred to create a demand for heroin where none had existed for the previous thirty years. Whereas the alternative society of the 1960s, while favouring the use of cannabis, drew the line at the use of heroin, there is now a disturbing acceptance by a wide section of society of heroin as a recreational drug.'[16] A fair amount of rock music has always flirted with drugs, but smack and coke came to replace acid and pot in its argot. Roger Lewis comments, 'Whereas LSD was the drug of the 1960s, sup-posed to expand minds to new horizons, heroin is the drug of the 1980s, blocking out bleakness and despair.' Leech confirms this and points out: 'The easy availability of heroin could not have happened at a worse time for Britain's youth, when so many face unemployment and hopelessness and when whole communities are in despair. For heroin is classically the drug of despair: it is a cynical irony that it is virtually the only addictive substance to decrease in price since the present government took office.'[17] By 1986, Scotland Yard estimated that UK organized crime syndicates were making more than £500 million a year from drug trafficking. The legacy of Britain's nineteenth-century greed in forcing opium upon China has come full circle as a *damnosa hereditas*. A 1986 report from the European Parliament announced that there are as many as 1.5 million heroin addicts in the EEC countries, and that drug-related offences account for half of all arrests in Western Europe.

Neither has the USA's policy succeeded. In New York City there are officially admitted to be at least 1,000 heroin shooting-galleries, which through their shared needles are prime centres for spreading AIDS. Heroin and cocaine arrests there doubled between 1979 and 1982, but drug-dependent deaths increased twice as fast. New black heroin which is strong and cheap has spread from Los Angeles to Boston, Detroit, Denver and Phoenix. *High Times* ('The magazine of high society: free to prison libraries'), a glossy $2, 140-page monthly with a readership of 4 million, circulates the prices of drugs in various countries like Stock Exchange listings. Especially on the West Coast, 'script mills' masquerading as clinics sell unlimited drug prescriptions in league with compliant pharmacies. A glut of increasingly pure and inexpensive cocaine 'crack' is on easy offer across the country: aspirant executives offer clients coke in place of Martinis; and the prospect of a flood of new 'designer' drugs (described later) is causing serious concern.

Kevin McEneany of Phoenix House, New York, reflects, 'There is an explosion of new chemicals: why are human beings spending fortunes to get high for forty-five minutes? There must be a great void, a spiritual emptiness in their lives.' Any solution to the problem – whether in the UK or elsewhere – has outgrown the capacity of the police to stop or clinics to treat, and is now a challenge facing the whole community.

3

International Solidarity: The Present Situation Across the World

'The most terrible reality brings us, at the same time as suffering, the joy of a great discovery, because it merely gives a new and clear form to what we have long been ruminating without suspecting it.'

Marcel Proust, *Cities of the Plain*

North America and Britain are far from unique in facing an escalating drug problem. Traffic and abuse observe no frontier; today no country, rich or poor, is immune. In **Eire**, which had been untouched by the drug fashions of the 1960s, Dublin's heroin crisis is now proportionately more serious than New York's, with more than 7,000 addicts in a population of half a million, compared with virtually none in the 1970s. The number of beds available for in-patient treatment is just nine. Until very recently the heroin market throughout Dublin was a monopoly nurtured by the brothers of one entrepreneurial family, who carved up between them the capital's demand for exploitation. Their system was to employ prostitutes as couriers to import supplies from Amsterdam, and a network of small boys to distribute within the city. Possessing as it does the fastest-growing young population and youth un- employment in Europe, the Irish market was an overripe target, and addiction is now spreading from Dublin to Cork and Galway. Having witnessed free packets of heroin being given away outside schools, Tony Gregory, a Dublin teacher who has become an independent member of the Irish parliament, resolved to mobilize the local community against the threat. The most efficient and ruthless counter-action against drug-pushers, however, has been mounted by the IRA, in a campaign calculated to pre-empt the police by winning public support, which is described in Chapter 15 below. Ironically, Northern Ireland, despite its other difficulties, has virtually no drug problem because both the IRA and Protestant paramilitary puritans maintain an iron control in their communities.

In **France** the national supply of heroin paradoxically increased after the break up in 1973 of the 'French Connection' laboratories in Marseilles, since these had been organized to export to America. It is now at a record level: the total of French drug addicts is estimated to be 120,000, with another 800,000 users, of whom 85 per cent ominously are aged under twenty-five. Despite frequent raids by the *Brigade des Stups* (the French drugs squad), in Paris the Chalon area near the Gare de Lyon has, like Belleville and Montmartre, become an open drug market with Senegalese sellers and Arab residents driven to violence in consequence. **Switzerland** is also witnessing a disturbing expansion of heroin use, particularly in the cities of Geneva and Zurich. Some 4,000 addicts are reported in Geneva alone, which has become a major new entrepôt for drug traffic as a result of its wealthy international links and the large number of foreign residents able to import by means of the diplomatic bag. Whereas in 1974 there were thirteen drug-related deaths in Switzerland, the number had risen to 102 five years later. Neighbouring **Austria** is now estimated to have a heroin addict population of 10,000. The US government has become seriously concerned at the vulnerability of its forces in Europe – and especially in **Western Germany** – to having their operational ability incapacitated by drugs. In 1978, 8 per cent of the US Army's Berlin Brigade admitted to using heroin; American sailors at the Holy Loch nuclear submarine base have been found using LSD as well as other illegal drugs. By 1983 as many as one in four American servicemen were admitting to having used drugs during a single period of one month. Congressman Lester Wolff believes that drugs are now crippling the US army in Western Europe for the same reasons that they had undermined its troops in Vietnam: 'They have the same spare free time, no idea of their mission, and availability.' The other NATO countries likewise are worried at the exposure of their five-days-a-week servicemen who, frequently bored when away from their own country, are able to visit for weekends places like Amsterdam and Frankfurt where drugs are easily available. John Mortimer observes with regard to the frustration of these soldiers' lives and duties: 'They are involved in an endless game of "let's pretend", like actors forever rehearsing for a play which can't be performed, because the first night would mean the ending of the world.'

It is **Italy**, however, with an abuser population of around a quarter of a million, which today has the highest incidence of drug use of any country in Western Europe. This is partly an offspin of the Mafia's involvement (described in Chapter 14 below): their heroin industry is valued at £500 million a year, and by 1980 the Italian Health Minister was driven to suggesting that heroin might have to be provided free to addicts in an attempt to destroy the Mafia's hold. At present, by a delicate compromise under Italian law (as in the UK), the use of drugs is not punishable, but being in possession of them is.[1] Private cannabis smoking is ignored, as it largely is in post-Franco Spain too. The initial impetus of drugs in Italy began from 1970 onwards amongst the younger generation of the northern cities. To start with it was a fashionable symbol of protest, a statement against the mass-culture and materialism of adult society. At first few illicit drugs were seen in the south of the country, or in politicized sectors of the community who boycotted them on the grounds that narcotic passivity would undermine political commitment. A second and deeper wave of addiction arrived with the mid-1970s in the wake of political despair following the failure of the 'youth revolt', and promoted by professional suppliers who were exploiting the disillusion caused by rising unemployment. Young people, as in Germany, reacted against the authority of the older generation, whom they criticized as being 'apathetic, indifferent and lost', and they pronounced that their parents had forfeited any right to transmit moral values because of their preoccupation with consumer ambition. By the next decade the drug culture had spread to embrace even twelve-year-olds in poor slum areas, and female/male or south/north differentials in drug-taking were being eroded. Drug-dependent children are used, especially in Naples, as pushers and couriers, since as minors they cannot be prosecuted on arrest. Supplies have become available throughout Italy, particularly in places that teenagers frequent, such as bars, discos, squares, parks and schools.[2] One 25-year-old addict was arrested for forcing his mother into prostitution to pay for his heroin habit. Today the *per capita* incidence of opiates is highest in Milan and Florence, followed by Genoa, Bologna, Turin and Rome.[3] The principal source of supply, for not only Italy but most of Europe, is Western Sicily, where Asian opium is regularly imported from Lebanese and Turkish ports and then converted into heroin with French chemicals in Mafia-controlled laboratories in and around Palermo. From there it is distributed throughout Italy – in cigarette cartons, briefcases, shoe-boxes, musical instruments or cassettes – and the lucrative profits are laundered by the Mafia and their accomplice politicians into respectable companies and property spreading far beyond Sicily and Calabria. The Naples-based Camorra in its turn concentrates on developing the cocaine market, with striking success: Italian consumption of cocaine is now some three times the average for the continent.

Spain is the major gateway for the entry into Europe of Latin American cocaine as well as Moroccan hashish. Since the liberalization of the Spanish Criminal Code in 1983, the possession of drugs is no longer a punishable offence unless the quantity involved greatly exceeds the normal requirements for a person's own use. Several thousand people were freed from jail as a result of this new ruling. Drugs became, according to Dr Enrique Pedro Munoz of Madrid, fashionable as a way of expressing personal freedom after the repressive years under Franco. But in 1984 the government responded to public outcry and a disturbing rise in crime by deciding to increase prison penalties for trafficking and also to ban the use of heroin. Today Barcelona has some 5,000 heroin dependants, and Madrid 11,000 – out of a population of 4.7 million (compared with 8,500 out of 1.85 million in West Berlin, and 10,000 out of 700,000 in Amsterdam).

The most controversial contemporary drugs policy, by far, is that in the **Netherlands**. Its results are worth considering particularly carefully, because at least it represents (especially by the City Council of Amsterdam) a new approach. Despite its puritan history, the Netherlands has for many years been linked to the international drug culture by its trading position and traditional tolerance. For much of the post-war period Amsterdam became the centre of Europe's drug trade. The legal position in the Netherlands is that the use of drugs is officially banned and punishable by a fine, though in practice few fines are imposed. The smoking of cannabis is widely tolerated as a matter of policy, in a deliberate attempt to stop young people resorting to black-market dealers who might also offer them hard drugs. Pictures of cannabis leaves are a common sign outside many cafés and bars in Amsterdam, especially in the Zeedijk and old port areas. Cannabis plants placidly ripen on houseboats opposite one of the police stations; though when five radical Kabouter members were elected to the City's Council in 1970, they raised even Dutch eyebrows by 'turning on' with cannabis during a council session. Opium dens amongst the Far Eastern community are also countenanced. In the early 1970s the Chinese 14K Triad organization gained control of Amsterdam's opiate market; rival gangs of its members feuded over the lucrative heroin monopoly, a struggle which was won by Yong Fatt Tong, an underworld syndicate leader who made Amsterdam a place of pilgrimage for drug smugglers before he was shot dead in 1975 – a similar fate subsequently being shared by three of his successors. Many of the customers for heroin are not Dutch but Surinamese, Americans, Moluccans, Germans or Britons. When the municipal council of Enschede, a small Dutch town five miles from the German border, authorized the sale of cannabis at one of its youth centres in October 1982, so many Germans poured over the frontier to buy supplies that the policy had to be reversed within less than a month. The episode is yet one more illustration of the fact that if drug policies are to have any hope of success, they must be agreed internationally. For the Dutch themselves, the legalization of cannabis has not resulted in the Sodom and Gomorrah predicted: whereas a 1976 survey throughout the Netherlands showed that 15 per cent of those aged between thirteen and twenty-five were using cannabis, by the end of 1983, after the controlled distribution of cannabis had been implemented, the figures for the same group had dropped to below 2 per cent.

Stronger even than its Calvinist puritanism, the Dutch ethos elevates common sense and the value of the individual's personal freedom. 'The Dutch drug policy', as a government official explains, 'is characterized by pragmatism. Its central aim and the basis of legislation is to prevent and lessen the risk to the community and the individual that are associated with the use of drugs. It must be emphasized that the Dutch policy's objective is not the combat of drug-taking itself.'[4] The stance towards heroin is consistent: 'the starting-point is not to prosecute drug-users but to reduce the dangers . . . Legislation which criminalizes drug use can on the individual's level have the consequence of social isolation, pauperization and bad health,' Dr Engelsman, the Secretary of the Dutch Interministerial Steering Group on Alcohol and Drug Policy, told me.[5] He went on:

> A lot of addicts have no contact with any clinic – they wouldn't go near any drug-free therapeutic agency. Hence the purpose of the buses dispensing free methadone: to increase all possible contacts and try to persuade them to start treatment. Detoxification should be the long-term aim, but in the short term it is necessary first to improve the life of addicts so that they don't disintegrate and die, and second to make their lives less criminal. But now the Minister is asking, what are we doing for all the addicts who are using the system? We can't accept so much permanent addiction in our society.[6]

The problem facing the Dutch government is certainly far from easy. The Netherlands has an estimated 20,000 heroin users, spending more than 650 million guilders on the drug each year. A survey showed that 42 per cent of these heroin users steal to pay for their supply and 19 per cent deal in the drug.[7] Most of the new addicts are not hippies, but depressed and poor people, many of them immigrant or unemployed. Despite the fact that in 1977 the head of the Dutch drug squad was appointed the overall commander of the entire police to emphasize the government's belief that heroin was the Netherlands's main criminal problem, five years later the number of murders – many of them drug related – in Amsterdam per head of population exceeded that of any other city in the world.[8]

The initial policy in the early 1970s had been to offer methadone at treatment centres, in order to attract addicts into making contact with professional help. Success was underwhelming. The numbers of addicts and street crimes rose, and in 1978 the policy changed to dispensing methadone free to any Dutch person over sixteen years old who wanted it, in an effort to cut down on illegal dealing and crime. Heroin, several Amsterdam councillors are convinced, becomes an epidemic precisely because of its illegality: users turn into small dealers to support their habit, and sell to new users who in turn have to find more consumer-customers. The City Council therefore decided that the only way to sever the growing identity of interest linking criminals and drug-users was to legitimate the source of supply. It established four official fixed dispensing posts, together with two buses which make a regular circuit of five one-hour stops round the city to distribute methadone. The result has been 2,500 people a day availing themselves: Amsterdam has attracted at least half the country's addicts (there are another 3,000 in Rotterdam and 2,500 in The Hague). Uneasy about the effect on the tourist trade in its uniquely beautiful city, the Amsterdam Council next provided a houseboat centre for addicts – followed by another one for Surinamese addicts; the Moluccans too now want their own centre – to keep them away from the city's public places. Certainly the Dam Square and Vondel Park are not now the rendezvous for pushers and spaced-out junkies which they were formerly. The intention was not only to regulate and study the addicts, but to put them in touch with treatment centres, but this has not succeeded: very few of those on maintenance show any inclination to go near a therapeutic agency. Because their methadone is free, many users now have money to buy other drugs, especially cocaine, from criminal sources. Some have therefore suggested that cocaine too should be distributed free – whereupon alcoholics have protested, where is the justice in not giving them free alcohol? Another recent radical proposal by the Amsterdam mayor, Ed Van Thijn, to distribute heroin free to 300 resident addicts as a one-year experiment has been vehemently opposed by the Press and the central Dutch government, who argue that this would, *inter alia*, violate international treaties. Dr Martien Kooyman, the highly-respected Director of the Jellinek Centrum (the main drug-free therapeutic community which also caters for alcoholics in Amsterdam), believes that on balance the disadvantages of maintenance (which **Sweden** abandoned in 1967) outweigh its benefits, and it is a dead-end policy. He argues that the city should develop community health centres which would help other people in addition to drug-users, and offer methadone only to those addicts prepared to commit themselves to a course of withdrawal. He is also a strong advocate of family therapy – especially for teenage drug-users, whose symptomatic habit often can be a cause or effect of personal problems. Counselling with siblings, parents or sexual partners can succeed in getting some addicts to realize the drastic consequences their habit is having on others:[9]

Many of the adolescents I see feel unwanted and that they lack a basic right to exist: insecure, they manipulate their family or friends to find out the boundaries of love or concern. The aim of the treatment should be to try to increase their self-esteem. But a number of them are also unable to accept success – through their feeling of unworthiness – and struggle to disrupt the treatment.[10]

By contrast, the **Soviet Union** claims it has no real drug problem ('except for occasional thefts from chemists' shops,' a diplomat from the Ukraine qualified). 'The data of the past few years comes to approximately 2,500 and 3,500 people suffering from various forms of addiction,' declares Edward Babayan, the former Head of Detoxification Services in the USSR. 'All addicts are registered. Of course I cannot say that these statistics are absolutely accurate, because it is not at all simple . . . though in the past thirty years the Soviet Union has not had a single case of heroin addiction.'[11] Any use of or trade in heroin, LSD and cocaine is strictly banned. Prior to the 1917 Revolution, narcotics had been widely used by many inhabitants of Central Asia as well as certain other regions of Russia such as Georgia, and opium retains its devotees today in the traditional Muslim areas of the Uzbek and Turkman Soviet Socialist Republics. In addition the inhabitants of Afghanistan (a major opium-growing country) have lately succeeded in hooking a number of Soviet soldiers on heroin as well as opium – tactics identical with those that the Vietnamese employed against American troops a decade earlier. The young Soviet soldiers are vulnerable for the same reasons American conscripts were susceptible in Vietnam: because they are cut off from home constraints, bored, frightened, and under harsh pressure to prove themselves as men. Hashish also retains a covert popularity in Muslim areas of Soviet Central Asia and the Caucasus where relatively little alcohol is consumed, despite the central government's ban on any form of cannabis intoxication. Nevertheless throughout the Soviet Union peer-group attitudes towards drugs are much sterner than they are towards alcohol. The contention that drug taking is only a problem for Western nations has been abandoned. Any magazine like *High Times* or films that romanticize the use of drugs is unthinkable, but recently the Soviet Press, now more frank under Mr Gorbachev, has carried an increasing number of teenage drug reports as warnings for its readers. Whereas traffickers are given a minimum of five years in prison – doubled for a second offence – drug-users are not jailed but sent to work-farms. 'My colleagues and I treat addiction like an infectious disease,' explained Dr Lilian Kirillova. 'Addicts try to draw more and more people into their group. Therefore, they should be isolated from the healthy public and given medical treatment. When they are cured, they can go back to a normal life.'

The most serious drug problem in Russia, as its new leadership has belatedly recognized, is chronic alcoholism. Vodka first became a state monopoly in Russia in the fifteenth century,[12] and its sales since then have produced enormous profits for both Tsarist and Soviet governments (except during ten years of prohibition that ended in 1924). The tax on alcohol currently raises some 40 per cent of all direct and indirect taxes paid by Soviet citizens; but the price paid in absenteeism, crime, accidents and family breakdowns is heavier: more than half of Soviet divorces, for example, have been attributed to drink-related problems,[13] and the number of deaths recorded due to acute alcoholic poisoning rose from 12,500 in 1965 to 51,000 in 1978. Overall, alcohol is estimated to be responsible for costing the Soviet Union as much as 7 per cent of its gross national product. Recently factory foremen have been warned that they are held responsible for their workmates, and that if they fail to report drinkers they likewise will suffer punishment. All government functions have now been declared dry, with official toasts ordered to be in mineral water. The once-derided American Cola soft drinks are now welcomed, and Mikhail Gorbachev has ordered the minimum drinking age for alcohol to be raised from eighteen to twenty-one. He has also decreed that no wine or vodka shall be sold in Moscow shops or restaurants before 2 p.m. – though he has not as yet gone so far as Peter the Great, who executed those of his subjects who drank vodka at breakfast. The new restrictions have resulted in a sharp rise in the sales of eau de Cologne, and even thefts of de-icing fluid by pilots.

In **Hungary** similarly, few drugs are seen apart from occasional cannabis cigarettes (not least because international suppliers decline to accumulate unconvertible currencies like the forint), but the country's alcoholism increases in line with its prosperity: as many as 300,000 out of the population of 10 million have been categorized as alcoholics. **Bulgaria** is an established route for drugs from Lebanon and the Near East, rather than a consumer itself; **Yugoslavia** has some 20,000 addicts; although **Albania** has succeeded in preserving its isolation from drugs as well as from other Western habits. The worst drug problem in Eastern Europe has taken root in **Poland**. Polish estimates of their opiate users range from 200,000 to more than twice that number. International trafficking syndicates spurn smuggling drugs into the country because they do not want zlotys, but this makes little difference: Poland's farmers have a long tradition of growing legal crops of opium poppies for seeds and oil, from which many of them also produce home-made morphine and heroin. In rural areas peasants customarily drink morphine tea, but since 1980 many young Poles have also acquired a habit of boiling ground poppy seeds to produce a powerful injectable mash called 'Kompott',[14] from which a number of them have died. The police give a higher priority to repressing politics than drug use, and the incidence of drugs and drunkenness is increasing (as in Eire) as an antidote to *anomie* and despair. In the centre of Warsaw, street-dealers offer syringes ready primed with Kompott (even unsterilized syringes, being scarce, are regularly recycled). For several years addicts from all over Europe have visited Poland to buy cheap heroin.

By contrast, although alcoholism is a major problem amongst **Canada**'s Indian people, as it is for Australian aborigines, the illegal drugs in Canada – which is estimated to have some 20,000 heroin addicts plus a quarter of a million people using cocaine[15] – are smuggled in from abroad. Heroin reaches its west coast from the Golden Triangle of south-east Asia, and the eastern Canadian provinces from the Golden Crescent of south-west Asia. In addition Mexican heroin and South American cocaine and methaqualone are transported over the US border by Mafia-linked syndicates employing motorcycle gangs. Separate criminal organizations control the sale and distribution of heroin and cocaine in Toronto, Montreal and Vancouver. It is significant that the Canadian price of cocaine has dropped steadily over recent years[16] – indicating that the expansion of imports continues to outstrip the rising demand.

Other major arteries for the North American market flow through islands in the Caribbean (described in Chapter 14 below), whose politics have as a result been corrupted to the very top in addition to their own inhabitants being permeated by drugs. More than one in ten of the population of the **Bahamas** is reported to have become addicted to freebased cocaine. An officially-sponsored report in July 1984 stated that a 'severe drug problem exists in government corporations, hospitals, major hotels, a number of banks, restaurants, industrial corporations at Grand Bahama, government ministries, fast-food businesses and night clubs.' The report added that on Bimini, as many as 80 per cent of people aged between fifteen and twenty are using drugs. During a recent conference in Nassau, seven out of thirty-five schoolchildren volunteered 'drug-dealer' as their preferred career. Cocaine is now estimated to contribute at least 10 per cent of the Bahamian gross national product. Whereas drug-dealing has provided new fortunes for some very senior Bahamians, cannabis has long been a popular tradition in **Jamaica**. Today, although frowned on by middle-class adults, it remains deeply embedded in working-class culture, with its own built-in controls and *rite de passage*. Originally introduced by East Indians to ease their labour when they were imported to work on sugar plantations following the emancipation of the slaves in 1838, it is locally known as 'ganja' and is the sacramental herb for the Rastafarian religion. The unlicensed cannabis trade is now worth over \$1.5 billion annually and exceeds twice the value of all Jamaica's legitimate exports combined. Besides using more than eighty unofficial airstrips on the island, smugglers' planes land on the broad sandy beaches and empty roads in rural areas. While cannabis – especially the potent *sinsemilla* (Spanish for 'without seeds') brand much in demand in the USA – despite being technically illegal, provides Jamaica's biggest source of badly-needed foreign exchange, local officials are more worried at the increase of hard drugs amongst young people in Kingston.[17] The Prime Minister, Edward Seaga, has admitted:

> The ganja trade in the last month was virtually what was keeping the economy alive. It supplied black-market dollars . . . The question of legalizing it so as to bring the flow of the several hundred million dollars in this parallel market through the official channels . . . would mean an extremely big boost to our foreign exchange earnings . . . Regardless of whether we want it or not, the industry as such is here to stay. It is just not possible for it to be wiped out.[18]

The Jamaican government successfully employs the drug trade as a bargaining counter to extract an increase in economic assistance from the USA. The CIA also alleges that **Cuba** plays a political role in drug-smuggling, but certainly in its internal society Castro enforces a vehement puritanism, with only a few writers and artists having enough temerity to deviate by smoking cannabis in private. By contrast, the *houngan* voodoo priests in **Haiti** are reputed to use the nerve drug tetradotoxin (obtained from puffer fish) to create zombies.

Throughout Latin America, a massive influx of rural populations to the sprawling cities has resulted in the traditional cultural and religious patterns of using coca and mescal being replaced by chaotic commercial drug habits that lack any social traditions to act as a safeguard. A number of South American governments only began to take their countries' drug production and trade seriously when in recent years their own schoolchildren began to succumb to cocaine. In **Colombia**, on Bogota street corners teenagers addicted to 'bazuka' (a cocaine base capable of causing neurological damage) are the latest market for *narcotraficantes* who are so powerful that they command a state-within-a-state, richer than the police and owning their own congressman, armies and planes as well as popular sports teams and well-organized factories. Illegal drugs account for more than 35 per cent of Colombia's gross national product. Until recently the $500 million annual trade in refining and exporting cocaine to North America was regarded with more than a little national pride. A degree of doubt, and certainly a turning point in the government's attitude, arrived on 30 April 1984 when the nation's Justice Minister Lara Bonilla – who almost alone had warned how great a threat the *narcos'* trade had become to the country – was himself killed by assassins hired by the *narco* tycoons of Medellin.

Lara Bonilla had denounced facts such as that money from narcotics was financing half of the nation's fourteen professional soccer teams, and that in the elections the month before his murder millions of traffickers' dollars had swollen the campaign purses of both the Conservative and Liberal parties. To increase their profits even further, the Colombian narco-millionaires recently started new coca plantations covering several thousands of hectares inside their own country; however, when the quality of these indigenous plants' leaves proved inferior to the traditional supplies imported from Bolivia and Peru, they turned to selling them as basuka base for the expanding market in Colombia itself.[19] There are now estimated to be 3 million drug-addicts in Colombia out of a population of 28 million. The Pope on his visit to the country in 1986 described the drug trade as 'a new and more subtle form of slavery'. It is money from narcotics which fuels the chronic insurgency in this tenuous democracy, financing both right-wing death-squads and left-wing guerrilla groups in order to destabilize any government that attempts to police the drug industry: little surprise was aroused by the recent discovery of the corpses of a hundred peasants shot by *narcos* in a cave in Cesar province, an area which used to be a centre for marijuana ranching before being replanted with coca because so much marijuana is now being cultivated in the USA itself. That the endemic violence is being exported along with cocaine, is shown by the increasing number of massacres carried out by rival Colombian trafficking gangs in the USA.

The same pattern – of rising addiction amongst youths in the urban ghettos coupled with *narco* fortunes being made up-country in pragmatic alliances with armed guerrillas – is to be seen emerging in the neighbouring democracy of **Peru**. Over one-third of the world's total supply of cocaine paste is estimated to originate from the Upper Huallaga Valley there; but in 1984, in order to concentrate on the Shining Path guerrillas, the authorities had to virtually cease troubling the drug-growers of that area for fear of increasing peasant support for the guerrillas if they did so. Bankers calculate that the (ostensibly illegal) export of cocaine paste in that year was probably worth £1,000 million to Peru's balance of payments. The traditional inhabitants of the eastern slopes of the Peruvian Andes are now trapped in an unhappy squeeze between the Scylla of new entrepreneurs seizing their land for drug profits, and the Charybdis of the military and guerrillas' retaliatory massacres.[20] Meanwhile, Peru's own addict population is estimated to have grown to 150,000. In **Bolivia** the drug industry described in Chapter 14 has long been central to the country's whole economic system, as it is also in certain parts of **Mexico** where the resulting corruption has proved to permeate deep into the police force. In **Belize**, a slump in sugar prices has driven several estates to grow marijuana instead of sugar for the US market. Throughout the north of Latin America, more and more farmers are turning from growing food crops to producing coca and marijuana, from which they are able to make several times as much profit.

There is scarcely a country in the world which now claims with any conviction that its drug situation is solved; most governments, in every continent, privately concede that it is worsening. In Africa, the problem may be at an earlier stage, but the pattern is ominously familiar. Crops of opium poppies have recently been discovered being secretly grown in the **Sudan** as well as in **Egypt** – where the heroin and cocaine trade is now estimated to exceed £800 million annually, and addiction has caused a crisis amongst Cairo university students. Cocaine is sold in Cairo and Alexandria mixed with ground human bones to increase its bulk. Meanwhile, hashish remains a staple of the Egyptian working class, though since its traditional source of supply is Lebanon, prices reflect the vicissitudes of the political situation there. Under President Mubarak's rule it is no longer marketed openly in the centre of Cairo, as it used to be in front of the police's glazed eyes; many Egyptians have lately turned to cheap pharmaceuticals, since in Egypt anybody can purchase drugs without needing a prescription. One of the few encouraging developments is that the Abu El Azayem Mosque in Cairo has pioneered a drug-treatment project designed to educate the public as well as treat individuals, which could provide a model to be followed by mosques and churches everywhere. In many parts of the Middle East, an addict is looked upon in much the same way as a local drunkard may be regarded in Europe, with an amused if contemptuous tolerance. The inhabitants of those Islamic countries which respect the ban on alcohol often instead chew the leaves of the amphetamine-like alkaloid shrub kat (khat or qat)[21] to achieve intoxication. This description of a group of men enjoying kat in **Yemen** (with its close echoes of cocktail or cannabis parties in the West) will be recognizable in several countries throughout the area of the Horn of Africa:

> Many houses have a special room for the purpose. It is given a special name, such as 'peace room', or 'mercy room'. In this colourful and scented setting members of the party arrive, everyone bringing his share of kat. The segregation of the sexes in kat parties is faithfully observed, female parties being less frequent and not so formal. Shortly after the beginning of the session, a sense of well-being dominates the atmosphere. The mind becomes very active, and the stream of talk flows easily and passionately. After about three hours the group reaches a

63

stage when a sense of 'wisdom' and self-content generally prevails. This, however, does not continue long, and in about another hour the mood changes and personal problems and difficulties emerge. Some men then become restless and irritable and they may erratically and impulsively leave the party. Those who stay behind tend to become more intimate.[22]

When in 1983 the **Somali** government – under pressure from its more purist financiers in Saudi Arabia – banned kat, there were violent protests; 2,082 people were arrested for kat offences in the following twelve months. It is widely popular in Djibouti, Yemen and Ethiopia as well as in Somalia, where many consumers spend more than half their income on this drug. Saudi Arabia banned it totally in 1956, but in North Yemen crops of it are replacing essential food growing. Despite being prohibited in **Djibouti** by the French in 1957, five tons a day are now regularly imported into there by air – at considerable cost to the fragile economy – from Ethiopia (in whose hilly climate it grows easily). In 1982 I saw a police car delivering supplies of kat in rural Djibouti; many government and commercial offices there do not function after lunch due to the effects of the drug.

For most other African countries, however, it is alcoholism that is increasingly more serious as a social problem. A recent survey of one crowded slum area of Nairobi, the capital of **Kenya**, found that 46 per cent of the males and 24 per cent of the females could be categorized as alcoholics. What is responsible for this striking incidence? Cultural roots are disintegrating fast in most African societies. Family influence and traditions are crumbling: the extended family which sheltered so many people has become too costly to preserve. Neither the authority of traditional religion nor the fear of witchcraft now deters the young from defying codes of behaviour. The rapidity of socio-economic changes bewilders people and, as happened during the Industrial Revolution in Europe and North America, causes stress leading to a desire for escape or oblivion through alcohol. The hundreds of thousands of new rural migrants to cities, where there are no recreational facilities but where alcohol is readily available and seductively marketed, are particularly vulnerable.[23] Meanwhile, drug-smuggling – especially of methaqualone and barbiturates – is expanding throughout both East and West Africa, as the quickest way to acquire hard currency on top of high profits. Mandrax tablets, which in large doses have a heroin-like effect, are carried in bulk from Bombay to South Africa via Zambia. Whereas during the 1968 civil war in Nigeria the government supplied cannabis to its soldiers before battle, by 1984 its successors were forced by the rise in crime to announce that drug-traffickers would in future face a firing-squad. Despite this, Lagos has become a major transit point for heroin en route to Europe from Pakistan and India.

It is nevertheless in Asia that the drug problem reveals its most evolved complexity. Opium has always originated from there, but now over 60 per cent of the world's heroin is also consumed in that continent. In 1975, Thailand had 350,000 opiate addicts; by 1978 this figure had grown to 500,000 – more than all the addicts of Europe put together. Bangkok's incidence of heroin addiction exceeds that of New York: in all some 7 per cent of the city's 6 million population are addicted to hard drugs, according to Dr Kachit, the director of drug rehabilitation there.

The genesis of the problem lies in the fact that many farming communities in the uplands of south-east and south-west Asia still rely upon growing opium for their survival. Its oil is a staple for cooking, while its leaves and seeds can be eaten and its pods used for feeding cattle. Opium gum itself represents a cash crop at least six times more valuable than any comparable alternatives. Although amongst Thai hill people – such as the Hmong and Yao – opium continues to be smoked, mainly by male adults, it is heroin that is now causing catastrophe in urban communities. Of the 33,533 admissions to Thai drug-treatment centres in 1980 (compared with a total of 6,632 in 1972, and 18,452 in 1976) heroin cases accounted for an overwhelming 29,782 – while opium caused only 2,216, cannabis 481 and morphine 47. Glue and petrol sniffing has also become common at a number of schools. Young people are well aware that drugs are only too easy to obtain from pharmacies.[24] Less scrupulous employers in Bangkok have a practice of administering 'horse pill' amphetamines to their workers to boost productivity; one woman in a knitting factory recounted: 'The boss gives us each one of the pills, at about 10 o'clock at night. Then after that my hands shake, my head becomes very awake. I work all night, fast. If you take too much they burn out your brains.'[25]

In neighbouring Laos, heroin was unknown before 1972, despite the fact that the means for its production had been available since the beginning of the century. However, in 1971 the Royal Lao government, under strong US pressure, introduced the first-ever law against opium in order to stem the flow of Lao opium to the American troops in Vietnam. The effect of this ban on the availability of narcotics in Vietnam was nugatory, but in Laos itself the result was to develop a market in heroin (which was found to be more profitable to trade than opium), accompanied by a wave of corruption among the police.[26] **Burma** is authoritatively believed to have 48,000 addicts, mainly now similarly on heroin. Cannabis is grown in **Indonesia**; and east Asia's first plantation of cocaine has recently been discovered in the **Philippines**, with its production earmarked for Hong Kong. **Singapore**'s 2,000 heroin addicts in 1975 rose more than five-fold (aged between twelve and thirty and spanning the social spectrum) by March 1977 – despite the government's introduction of the death penalty for drug-trafficking, under which twenty people have been hanged. Today, as a result of an intensive campaign to cure and then rehabilitate addicts, the official total has been reined back to 6,000. A number fled across the border into **Malaysia**, where according to one Malay authority, drug abuse has 'spread with the speed and characteristics of a contagious disease, and there has been neither time, experience nor the opportunity for the individual to build up resistance'. Malaysia admits to 104,000 addicts among its 14 million people, although the actual total is reliably thought to be closer to half a million. Belatedly its government too has stirred into action. The police are now empowered to keep suspected drug-users in preventive detention without trial for up to two years – a period that on review can be renewed indefinitely. Such measures have their dangers: one Malay youth was recently released after seven years in jail on what turned out to be false suspicion of possessing heroin. Because of the incidence of drug abuse amongst officials, civil servants have been offered rehabilitation on half pay if they volunteer for treatment – and urine tests ordered for all who do not. Even the transportation of corpses from across the Thai border has been banned, because of the number of sachets being smuggled in cadavers. The death penalty is mandatory for anyone convicted of carrying more than 15 g. (half an ounce) of heroin or related substances (collectively known as *dadah*): thirty-six drug offenders have been judicially executed, and many nationalities are among those currently in the death cell. Concern that drugs may be planted by smugglers on innocent people is heightened when only a balance of probability is required for conviction, and not a standard of proof beyond reasonable doubt. Nevertheless, heroin remains easily available today in Kuala Lumpur. It was not until 1983 that the government began to take any real action against drugs, after two complacent decades when Malaysia was a major conduit for exports coming from the Golden Triangle. And the sole treatment in Malay detoxification centres – which have space for only 2,000 addicts – is still 'cold turkey' withdrawal, so that two-thirds revert to their habit following release.[27]

The experience of **Vietnam**, which on its independence inherited a quarter of a million heroin addicts, is more hopeful. Australian doctors report that, despite the economy's poverty, the 100,000 addicts in Ho Chi Minh City (the former Saigon) have been reduced to 5,000, through a firm policy including acupuncture treatment to release the body's natural opiates as a substitute.[28] The Vietnamese assert that the heroin trade throughout their country had been encouraged for political reasons by first French Intelligence and then the CIA, prior to being spread less wittingly by the US forces' own addicts. Today some opium still enters from the Lao-Thai border, and a few Vietnamese inject opium ash ('to have peaceful dreams, to forget . . .' as one said) since heroin is extremely difficult to obtain. In the Drug Rehabilitation Centre in Ho Chi Minh City, the inmates are mostly aged between twenty and thirty-five and three-quarters of them have committed some crime: they are not volunteers, but have been brought in by the police. All but three members of the Centre's controlling committee are, as in a number of European treatment centres, themselves former drug-addicts. The programme, which each day starts with vigorous exercises (many of the staff were formerly in the South Vietnamese army), is regimented but loud Western rock music is also allowed. Treatment comprises herbal medicines in addition to acupuncture: no substitute drug such as methadone is given – through calculated policy, as well as necessity, because supplies are very short. A success rate of 70 per cent is claimed; jobs are found for as many former addicts as possible – often on agricultural communes many kilometres distant from the previous sources of addiction. It is the Centre's committee which decides when each inmate shall be allowed to leave. Preservation of family links is encouraged, but two out of three addicts' families feel shame and reject them, and a few inmates never leave the Centre because they have nowhere else to go for shelter or food. A United Nations expert concluded: 'The element of compulsion is controversial. But if such a very poor nation can take this trouble to rehabilitate its addicts, what excuse have richer societies for not being bothered?'

Hong Kong's rate of addiction proportionately exceeds even that of Thailand. By 1975 the colony was estimated to have 900,000 opium and heroin users out of a population of 4.3 million, though cocaine, LSD or cannabis are virtually unknown. Formerly, it was possible to contend that the overall incidence of opium addiction in Hong Kong was less than the rate of alcoholism amongst the Europeans there; but following the ban on opium in 1946 the use of heroin spread apace. Heroin chemists exploited a lucrative market amongst the opium smokers, including thousands of refugees from China, who were deprived of their drug. Chasing the dragon of heroin is simpler – and less pungent, and therefore less detectable – than smoking the opium from which it is derived. Hong Kong Chinese syndicates, possessing a fierce loyalty and clan secretiveness that rivals the Mafia's, control much of the organized traffic of heroin from the Golden Triangle area. There are now at least fifty Triad societies active in Hong Kong, with a total membership of more than 90,000; the largest which is involved in drug-trafficking, the 14K society, has at least 10,000 secret members. Thai trawlers bring bales of opium and, now, refined morphine and heroin to rendezvous just outside the colony's waters, from where they are collected by motorboats or some of the numerous local fishing junks. Many of Hong Kong's commercial and banking experts are adept at laundering the trafficking's profits, and, certainly at least until very recently, the colony's police were deeply penetrated by corruption. Four separate retailing syndicates – dominated by Chiu Chan Chinese from Swatow – distribute local sales, especially in the Kowloon area, and illegal immigrants are often blackmailed into acting as 'snakehead' couriers. Recently Hong Kong has begun some belated efforts at drug education, and community rehabilitation houses have been started by SARDA (the Society for the Aid and Rehabilitation of Drug Addicts), which prefer Chinese traditions of harmony and co-operation rather than American confrontational techniques. Despite this, the overall drug situation in Hong Kong contrasts discreditably with that in Singapore, China or

Vietnam. When the colony reverts to Chinese rule, it will be interesting to see where its trafficking organizations transfer their bases to. **Taiwan** is one popular candidate: Taiwanese heroin traffickers, like the Yakuza gangs of Japan, are now operating as far afield as New York's drug market.[29]

In 1973 **South Korea** decreed a minimum sentence of seven years' imprisonment – with capital punishment for profiteers or habitual offenders – for even the possession of hemp, LSD or other hallucinogens. **China** itself has never forgotten the experience of its Opium Wars. According to M. Heikal, when Chou En-lai was Prime Minister he told President Nasser: 'Some of them [the US troops in Vietnam] are trying opium. And we are helping them . . . Do you remember when the West imposed opium on us? They fought us with opium. And we are going to fight them with their own weapons . . . The effect this demoralization is going to have on the US will be far greater than anyone realizes.'[30] A World Health Organization team that visited China in 1982, however, found that since the 1948 revolution China has effectively eradicated its own opium addiction by means of a combination of firm prevention, treatment and rehabilitation. Villagers not only nag any drug-taker into reforming, but help to find him or her a job. There is now no illicit opium farming, and the country's own medical needs of 20 tons a year are grown under strict supervision. The WHO team reported: 'There were very few people with narcotic dependence and none with heroin. No evidence of illicit traffic in narcotics or psychotropic drugs has been reported.'[31] Though a little opium was reported in late 1985 to have been smuggled into the southern province of Yunnan from Burma, and a number of students enjoy cannabis, China's success in dealing with an inherited drug problem of such a scale is impressive. It eloquently shows what can be achieved when firm measures are backed by wide community support for the rehabilitation of ex-addicts – in contrast to countries like Britain, where any proposal for a new drug-treatment centre almost inevitably arouses a howl of protest from the neighbourhood. Draconian methods have also been deployed in **Japan** to deal with a different drug problem. During the Second World War, Japanese airmen and soldiers were officially given amphetamines to stimulate their fighting capacity; subsequent to 1945, pharmaceutical companies unloaded their vast stockpiles of these drugs on to the general public, advertising them as being good both to provide energy and to restore a sense of well-being after the demoralization of defeat. There was a surge in the habitual use of methamphetamine capsules, but it was not until 1955, when there were over half a million abusers, that legislative action was taken. The police aggressively rounded up users of the drug, who were sentenced to prison or committed to mental hospitals. From 1963 onwards similar methods were adopted against the 50,000 heroin users who were being supplied by the Yakuza gangs; by 1970 the authorities claimed that there was no active heroin addict left in Japan.[32] However, criminal gangs (of which the biggest is the Yamaguchi-guni) continue selling amphetamines – including to students who are under pressure in Japan's highly competitive society.

In large parts of **India**, opium taking is historically as deeply rooted as it was in China. The Mogul Emperor Humayun himself was addicted, and in some areas today opium is still traditionally a rich man's pleasure, whereas cannabis (drunk or chewed as bhang, or smoked as hashish at festivals) is widely grown as the drug for poorer people. Nevertheless, some rural areas, such as West Rajasthan, as many as a third of the adult male population are addicted to opium, although several hundred have recently been weaned by mobile 'de-addiction camps' like those organized by Narayan Singh, each of which concentrates upon the inhabitants of a particular village or community so that afterwards they will give each other mutual support. India has recently become a significant source of illegal drugs for export. It is now virtually the only country in the world where private opium production for medical purposes remains legal, but lately an increasing amount of this is being smuggled abroad or converted into heroin.[33] India's internal addiction rate has also risen to a record level: Arnard Nadkarni of Bombay's General Hospital describes heroin addiction as spreading like a 'guerrilla movement'. Delhi was by 1986 estimated to contain 90,000 heroin addicts, mainly among middle-class youths whose parents are now pressing the authorities to take action. Over 1,000 addicts seeking treatment in Delhi hospitals in 1985 had to be turned away because of lack of beds. Half-ounce packets of heroin can be bought at Delhi University for £1. In January 1986 a record 1,200 lb. of heroin was seized at a farmhouse north of Bombay. India's importance on the map of the world's heroin routes has increased because the Iranian revolution and the Soviet invasion of Afghanistan have impelled the traffickers who buy the Golden Crescent's opium crops to seek new outlets southwards. Smuggling over Pakistan's vast 1,400-mile border with India is difficult, if not impossible, to prevent. Migrant workers provide a pool of impoverished and readily bribed couriers, and their absence while they are abroad has contributed to the breakdown of family ties and been blamed as part of the reason for the rise in drug abuse on the subcontinent itself. Heroin was first introduced to **Sri Lanka** by Western tourists to pay for cheap holidays in the late 1970s; drug arrests in Colombo have recently risen from eight in 1981 to more than 2,000 in 1985. A succession of bumper poppy crops has caused the increasingly sophisticated traffickers to develop new markets throughout South Asia as well as abroad: dealers – by contrast with the traditional users – now find it more profitable to convert opium locally into heroin, which is easier to conceal and transport than the bulkier raw material.

Not a single heroin addict was reported anywhere in **Pakistan** before 1979. Today the country has at least 300,000 cases, despite heroin addiction being a criminal offence, with 75,000 in Karachi, and Quetta, Lahore and Peshawar also being badly affected. A 1985 government survey found that 1.7 million of the country's 84.5 million population are addicted to drugs of one type or another. In the past, Pakistan supplied enormous amounts of opium for Iran, but when that market closed after the fundamentalist revolution in 1979, Pakistanis processed their opium into heroin in bathtub laboratories on the North-West Frontier, and that area became the main source of supply for Europe and the USA as well as for increasing sales in Pakistan itself. General Zia's sudden ban in the same year on opium – which several million Pakistanis were accustomed to buying from government-licensed vendors – exacerbated the problem. Dr Zaheer Khan, who runs a treatment centre for addicts in a Karachi slum, says: 'In other drug-ridden societies, the majority of addicts are deviants or social rejects. Here it's the white-and blue-collar workers, the professionals, students and children who are involved.' The problem is aggravated by the fact that the poppy is the only profitable cash crop available to the refugees from Afghanistan. This puts the US government in an embarrassing political dilemma, since heroin is a principal source of finance for the anti-Soviet guerrillas. It is also true that Pakistani control is not assisted by some key customs officials and police officers being addicted as well as corrupt. At the Sohrab Goth market in Karachi heroin is sold openly in the presence of policemen. A certain degree of throat-clearing takes place whenever this situation is put to Pakistani drug officials. One gram of 60 per cent pure heroin can be bought in Pakistan for only 40 rupees (less than £2) – compared to $3,000 (£2,000) in the USA – and Peshawar students smoke 4 rupee-heroin cigarettes. The majority of Pakistan's heroin addicts are male, middle class, aged under twenty-five and live in cities. Dr I. Tareen, the director of the drug abuse treatment centre at Lahore's Mayo Hospital, says he believes an important impetus for addiction in young people is that 'they cannot adjust to our inhuman social conditions which openly disregard what they consider the minimum standards of social justice'. The solution of the drug problem, he adds, 'lies in a basic change in our social values. We should have a society which is more concerned with man than with materialism, a society in which people are respected for themselves and not for their money or status . . . Detoxification alone is not sufficient. It must be linked with broader-based measures, including treatment, rehabilitation, after-care and social reintegration. Such measures can only be successful with the active co-operation of families and the community.'

In several Islamic countries, cannabis and narcotic users attempt to argue that these drugs are nowhere expressly forbidden in the Koran. Alcohol alone was singled out for prohibition by the prophet Muhammad, because it was the main dependence-producing drug in his era – as it is now – being brewed from sorghum, dates and honey as well as grapes. Although there is no mention of other drugs in Muslim holy books or in Muhammad's sayings, strict Islamic authorities today ban any addictive drug, classing them as analogous to *Khamr* (wine).[34] In **Afghanistan**, however, a tradition of administering opium to prisoners persists as a way of keeping them passive and to prevent them from escaping. Drug-trading convoys range freely between Afghanistan and Pakistan, armed with Kalashnikov rifles, and describing themselves as assorted guerrillas. In **Lebanon**, struggles for the huge profits from the drugs trade underlie a much greater proportion of the present fighting than is generally recognized: hashish is the country's major export crop, but heroin is catching up fast. High quality opium as well as hashish is transported in bulk from the Bekaa Valley by heavily armed Syrian and other syndicates. The profits provide both foreign exchange for Syria and weapons for warring Christian Phalangists and Palestinian groups alike. Tanks and patrolling sentries protect plantations of hashish in the Hermil Hills near the border with Syria. Throughout the Middle East and North Africa hashish remains a cultural crutch for many poor working men (as kava is in the South Pacific), lending them the temporary relief of dreaming about a less miserable existence.[35] A blind eye continues to be turned towards its use, despite ostensible official disapproval in Lebanon, Egypt and Morocco. The area's most serious opiate problem remains that of **Iran**. Restrictions were repeatedly postponed because of the large revenue generated by the government-run opium monopoly. By the time the Shah banned opium production in 1955, 7 per cent of the population – at least 600,000 people – were addicted, and substitute supplies arriving from Afghanistan, Turkey and Pakistan continued to find a ready market. In the initial aftermath of the Islamic revolution, Ayatollah Khomeini concentrated on stamping out alcohol, but in 1980 he appointed as head of the anti-narcotics campaign Sheikh Khalkhali, who ranged the land publicly shooting and hanging drug-dealers. Today Iran still has 170,000 registered addicts, who are accepted for treatment once only.

A final salutary warning of how rapidly narcotic problems can accelerate is provided by **Australia**, where the country's annual turnover in illicit drugs is now estimated to exceed £1.7 billion. This is despite the fact that the federal police can tap telephones when they suspect drug-dealing is taking place, the only area of crime where they have this power. Australia contains more than 50,000 addicts in a population of only 15 million: a 1984 Royal Commission warned that drug-trafficking is now out of control and 'defies normal policing methods'. Fifty years earlier, in the 1930s, Australia had the distinction of being the heaviest per capita consumer of cocaine and heroin in the English-speaking world,[36] but by 1945 the illegal drug problem was almost extinct because of the rigid wartime controls on importing. The acceleration in the use of first cannabis and then heroin began in the 1970s. Together with LSD and amphetamine trafficking, much of the dealing is based on Sydney's North Shore area, Australia's illicit drug activity being concentrated in the states of New South Wales and Victoria. Dealing is principally entered in the Kings Cross district of Sydney and the St Kilda district of Melbourne, whose trade has been taken over and expanded by organized crime syndicates – a powerful underworld which continues to flourish with the help of corrupt allies in high places. Initially pot and acid's appeal was to dissenting young Australians who sought to expand their consciousness, or to express opposition to government policy over Vietnam and to rebel against their parents and the established order in general. At the same period in the 1970s supplies of heroin from south-east Asia were becoming available, since the withdrawal of the American forces meant that the highly organized traders there were seeking new markets.[37] Australia's large young population was a ripe and wealthy target, geographically accessible to the Golden Triangle and penetrable because of its unpoliceable coastline. Many of the 50,000 Australian servicemen who had been in Vietnam, and the 280,000 US troops who took 'Rest and Recreation' in Australia, brought pathfinding drugs with them. Whereas liberal democracy was complacently unprepared and controls were lax in the extreme, organized crime racketeers like New South Wales's Double Bay Mob – some with links to the American Mafia – seized the opportunity, and Chinese Triad gangs were also attracted by the 10,000 per cent profit they could make by moving heroin from Thailand to Sydney. In 1978 the Sydney football star Paul Haywood was arrested in Bangkok with two other Australians in possession of 8.4 kg. of heroin with a retail value of $2.9 million. In June the same year a former Sydney police officer was jailed for helping to import $70 millions' worth of cannabis; and the convicted smuggler Ronald Tait lost 270,000 cannabis sticks with a street value of $3.1 million, when he was forced to land his plane by a RAAF Hercules that he had been unlucky enough to encounter in a usually deserted part of North Australia. The previous year the politician and anti-drug campaigner Don Mackay had been murdered at Griffith, 600 km. west of Sydney, which is the centre of Australia's own cannabis-growing area, whose Calabrian immigrants make the most of a climate ideal for the crop and control the nationwide market through the Australian branch of the Calabrian honoured society called 'Ndrangheta. Three governmental Royal Commissions on Drugs followed quickly in rapid succession, all of which expressed undisguised alarm. In his interim Royal Commission report, Mr Justice Williams was so critical of the Australian Bureau of Narcotics that it was completely disbanded in 1979; in his final report, the judge catalogued numerous examples of how the police had fabricated and concealed evidence in drug cases, engaged in trafficking themselves, and were susceptible to the 'payment of money to turn a blind eye to criminal activities'. By that time there were estimated to be at least 40,000 heroin addicts in Australia – compared with only 3,000 seven years earlier – plus another six non-addicted heroin users for every heroin addict. Within a single period of two years, fifty-two narcotic-dependent babies were born to addict mothers in four Sydney hospitals. It was a sea change from the 1960s, when an Australian crime syndicate (organized by a former federal Special Branch officer) that was running $22 millions' worth of heroin from Hong Kong to the USA, did not bother to smuggle a single gram of it into Australia because the demand there at that time was virtually non-existent. Meanwhile, some 400,000 Australians were using cannabis at least once a month:[38] a popular Australian joke at the time was 'Grow your own dope – plant a Pom'.

With disquiet becoming ever more rife about the part played in the drug traffic by corrupt lawyers and politicians as well as policemen, Malcolm Fraser set up yet another Royal Commission of Inquiry in 1980 under the highly respected Mr Justice Stewart. Three years later, his report[39] pinpointed the drug operations, more extraordinary than any fiction, of Terrence John Clark (alias Alexander James Sinclair). The Commission, having questioned Clark in England's Parkhurst prison, concluded that he had been responsible for the murder of at least six people, including his lieutenant Martin Johnstone ('Mr Asia' or 'the six-million dollar man'), for diluting heroin and omitting to account for some of the profits. Clark's history is worth describing as an illustration of how far the present-day drug business has altered from the amateur hippy culture of the 1960s. Boasting 'After your first killing, it's downhill all the way,' since 1976 Clark had culled extensive profits by importing bulk heroin into Australia, using female couriers for whom he provided bail and the best legal defence if they were ever caught. The New South Wales police had been warned that he had an agent inside the Australian Narcotics Bureau on an annual retainer of $25,000, plus $4,000 for removing files, but had taken no action about this information. Clark, who was originally from New Zealand, had been arrested in Auckland in 1975 for importing heroin, but jumped bail and transferred his operations to Sydney; his second wife Norma was to die of an overdose of heroin and

75

Mandrax the next year. Twelve months later he lost a small fortune when he failed to recover a large heroin consignment which had been floated overboard from the fishing-boat *Konpira* in a rough sea off the New South Wales coast; but in the next two years he made several million pounds importing heroin and Thai sticks from south-east Asia – via London and New York as well as Singapore and Hong Kong – and then with the proceeds buying investments ranging from silver mines in Indonesia and Sydney restaurants, to a fishing fleet and plantations in Fiji. His speciality was to use a machine from Singapore to compress the heroin into blocks, that were fitted into secret compartments inside suitcases made of fibre-glass (to foil sniffer-dogs) which his female couriers – paid sometimes in cocaine – carried to sell in Britain and Australia. He paid corrupt police officers generously for inside information, including tape-recordings of colleagues' confessions, which frequently enabled him to avoid arrest in Australia. Finally nemesis overtook him in London, where he was charged in 1979 with the murder of Johnstone as well as conspiring to import illegal drugs into Britain. Convicted on all charges after a seven-month trial, he was sentenced to life imprisonment with a minimum of twenty years. Clark claimed to be the richest prisoner in the world, with hidden assets of more than £50 millions; in 1983, however, he died mysteriously in Parkhurst before being able to carry out his threat to name names and reveal how laundered drug money was being used to buy automatic weapons for the IRA.

The killing of Clark's 28-year-old deputy Johnstone was bizarre even by the drug underworld's standards. Accomplices drove Johnstone in a Jaguar to arrange a drugs deal in Scotland, and on Clark's orders shot him at Carnforth, seven miles north of Lancaster, taking care to chop off both hands and disfigure his face and teeth to prevent recognition. Having removed the victim's clothes, ring and watch (but overlooking a Chinese 'long-life' medallion around his neck), they tied weights to the body and slashed the stomach to release the gases which might have caused it to float, before throwing it into a deep and flooded disused quarry at Eccleston Delph. The body, however, caught on a rock ledge a few metres down, where by chance it was found only five days later by two amateur explorers from a sub-aqua club who thought they had found a tailor's dummy. The case was solved after an intensive effort by a team of sixty led by Det. Supt. Rimmer of the Lancashire

Constabulary. Initially Clark's reputation for violence protected him from witnesses (he boasted of breaking every bone in his friend Duncan Robb's arms and hands with a baseball bat as a warning, and of burying two informers in the cement at Sydney International Airport), but he was eventually betrayed by some of the petty criminal addicts and prostitutes he was employing.

Clark's drug syndicate was only one of several operating in Australia, whose power is still increasing. Mr Justice Moffitt, who headed one of the commissions of inquiry, charges that federal and state governments have lacked the courage or will to tackle organized crime, and that political interference with investigations has been 'a disaster'. The Stewart Commission recommended an end to the fragmented approach of law enforcement towards organized crime, and to drug-trafficking in particular; that the surveillance of Australia's northern coastline should be tightened with aircraft and boats using radar; and that 'a system should be introduced and maintained whereby police officers in high-risk corruption areas such as drugs, gambling and vice are frequently interchanged with police working outside those areas, with no more than two or three years' service in any one area.'

Assistant Commissioner Bob Shepherd of the New South Wales police department was reported in 1986 to have said that his force was the most corrupt in the country, if not in the world. One of Clark's leading successors, whom the police believe initially became a cannabis millionaire before going on to market heroin, fled from Australia as a result of a tip-off from a senior New South Wales police officer, but has then continued to control his operations from Europe. He was recently held in Dublin on eighteen Australian extradition warrants alleging murder as well as multiple drug-trafficking, but his release was ordered by the Irish High Court . . . because Australia still possesses no extradition treaty with Eire.

Part Two

The Drugs

4

For Good or Ill:
A Survey of Drugs in General

'Half the vices which the world condemns most loudly have seeds
of good in them and require moderate use rather than total
abstinence.'

Samuel Butler

The history of the world's experience of drugs to date shows they
can be forces for better or for worse, for order or chaos, life or
death. However, no drug ('any substance which has an effect on the
central nervous system') itself can be labelled as 'good' or 'evil'.
Intrinsically there is nothing morally right or wrong about any
substance; this depends on how it is used, by whom and when. As
Dr J. Gaddum said, 'Patients may recover in spite of drugs, or
because of them'; Linnaeus described a medicine as differing from a
poison more in its dose than in its nature. Virtually every drug (legal
or illegal) has a toxic level, and also side effects in addition to those
for which it is used. Certain authorities in societies around the world
define people's use of particular substances as being a 'problem';
though, as we have seen, morphine was once welcomed as a
non-addictive means of weaning opium addicts; heroin in turn was
hailed as a 'wonder drug' to wean morphine dependants; and then

methadone and Diconal were promoted as heroin substitutes – only for the addictive nature of each to become apparent. Nevertheless, many people today would welcome morphine or even the notorious heroin were they painfully ill; while others among the healthy adamantly insist on continuing to take drugs despite warnings of the risks entailed. The largest drug addiction problem – alcohol and tobacco apart – is not caused by the heroin and cocaine on which the media focus, and is hardly ever mentioned. Opiate users in the West are a small minority compared to the army of people dependent on depressant drugs. The Standing Conference on Drug Abuse calculates that in the UK alone 625,000 people have been taking tranquillizers such as Valium regularly for seven years or more, with many of them in consequence unable to live without them. Tobacco and alcohol (discussed in the two following chapters) each kill several hundred times more people than does heroin.

The WHO defines a drug as 'any substance that, when taken into the living organism, may modify one or more of its functions'. Mankind's pharmacological use of roots, grains, fungi or fruits to try to improve his health or mood is as old as agriculture itself. 'Man has an inborn craving for medicine,' comments Sir William Osler, and nature, combined with chemistry, offers him an unlimited choice of potential drugs. The best known natural euphoriants and stimulants – ranging from nicotine to cocaine, caffeine and mescalin – belong to alkaloid chemicals derived from different plants. The physiological action of these on animals can oscillate widely: for in plants alkaloids are not only a defence against predators, but also a lure to attract pollinators. Judging any drug's results is complicated by the fact that the range of effects it can have are as varied as its users themselves: a person in a state of high anxiety may feel euphoric from being calmed down by cannabis or alcohol, while the same drug can have the opposite effect on an inhibited person by giving him more confidence. The user's setting and 'set' (expectations) are also strongly determinant influences: when some non-addicts were given a placebo which they believed was heroin, they reported greater sensations of pleasure from it than a control group who had actually taken the drug.[1]

Methods of taking drugs vary widely. Most stimulants are taken as tablets, though they can also be in the form of liquid, or of powder which can be sniffed, eaten or smoked (sometimes mixed with tobacco). Any drug that enters the body through being swallowed or as a suppository affects the user's brain comparatively slowly; although drugs taken in this way are capable of causing addiction, it is the method least likely to do so. The effect of a wad of coca, tobacco or kat being lodged inside the cheek of a user's mouth is slightly faster. A significantly more rapid method is sniffing or smoking, because of the large surface area of the lungs. Quickest of all to act are drugs taken by injection ('fixing' or 'jacking up') which, carried by the bloodstream directly to the brain, have a much stronger effect than if filtered through the body's natural intake system. (Veins collapse if punctured too frequently, and long-term addicts have been known to inject into their nose-tip, penis or vagina.) Injection carries the highest risk of overdose, as well as of hepatitis, AIDS, gangrene and abscesses from impurities or unsterilized needles. Some medical drugs – including insulin and others based on proteins – cannot be taken orally, since they are liable to become neutralized in the stomach before they reach the bloodstream. Modern administrators of such drugs prefer to deliver them via the nose, where a large network of capillaries – as cocaine snorters know only too well – feeds drugs into patients' blood as fast as by injection. Many diabetics in America are now taking insulin from a nasal-spray rather than a hypodermic needle. The effect of oral drugs can also be spread out by taking them in 'smart pills', in which the drug's molecules are chemically locked with the molecules of a special polymer and sealed with cellulose to control their gradual release inside the body. In medical cases where drugs such as antibiotics cannot be taken by mouth or nose, they can be delivered transdermally through the skin or a flesh wound via impregnated dressings; and bracelets have also been used to release drugs slowly. President Reagan, after his colon operation in 1985, was given morphine from a drip near his spine, in order to reduce pain without making his brain hazier; while a contraceptive implant, now recommended by the WHO, can steadily release progestin in a woman's body for five years. America and Sweden have recently developed Patient-Controlled Analgesia which enables patients to dispense their own pain-killing drug as and when they want it, via an intravenous tube governed by a microprocessor which prevents an overdose: research into this method shows that patients in fact take lower doses when they are able to administer the pain-killer to themselves, besides feeling happier from knowing they can exercise some control over their pain. Of course, such advances also open up the possibility of illegal drugs equally easily being ingested in similar ways.

The main drugs whose use authorities try to control can be grouped as follows:

I   **Stimulants** ('Uppers'): amphetamines such as Benzedrine, cocaine, nicotine, caffeine, kat

II **Depressants** ('Downers') other than opiates: sedatives, tranquillizers, barbiturates, alcohol

III **Hallucinogens and psychedelics**: cannabis, LSD, 'magic' mushrooms, mescalin, PCP ('Angel Dust')

IV **Opiates**: opium, morphine, heroin, codeine, and other synthetic opioids.

V   **Deliriants**: certain glues, solvents and volatile hydrocarbons, etc.

I Stimulants

Amphetamines

Also known as 'speed', 'pep pills', 'hearts', 'lid-poppers', 'copilots', 'truck drivers', 'wake-ups', 'cartwheels', 'footballs', 'splash', or 'crystal' (a list of such slang names may be useful, because many people – including some users – may not know what they are. Nicknames – like euphemisms – have their dangers, since consumers may be lulled into not recognizing what they are really using): Methedrine (methylamphetamine: 'meth'); Benzedrine ('benny'); Dexedrine (dexamphetamine sulphate: 'dexies' or 'yellow bellies'); amphetamine sulphate (known from the colour of its pills as 'blues' or 'bluies'); Durophet (amphetamine and dexamphetamine: 'black bombers'); Drinamyl (amphetamine and barbiturate: 'French blues'; formerly when in triangular pale-blue tablets (known as 'purple hearts'); MDA (methylene-dioxy-amphetamine, derived from nutmeg which is also a potent hallucinogen). Similar to but not amphetamine are: Ritalin (methylphenidate: 'rits'); Preludin (phenmetrazine: 'prellies'); Filon (phenbutrazate); Tenuate or Apisate (diethyl-propion: 'tomb stones', made a controlled drug in 1985); and Ephedrine (hydro-chloride tablets or elixir).

Most stimulants are synthetic amines which perform functions similar to the human body's natural hormone adrenaline. They temporarily arouse a person's central nervous system and blood-sugar level, speed up his breathing and heart rate, widen his pupils, increase his alertness, clarity, and both mental and physical activity, as well as reducing his appetite. The result is that for three to four hours the user gains short-term energy and confidence by postpon-ing fatigue and hunger; but when the debt has to be repaid and the body's reserves drop his feelings can give way to anxious irritation, agitation and insomnia. Stimulants therefore do not create any new energy, but draw on reserves for a limited period of time, from which it can then take a person's body a couple of days fully to recover. However, since the sensation of fatigue, like pain, is in fact a useful safety mechanism for us, to blot out such warning signals can lead to worse consequences. As the body rapidly adapts and becomes tolerant, regular 'speed freaks' come to depend psycho-logically on progressively increased 'hits' in order to obtain the same 'high' or 'rush'. Heavy users graduate to as much as 2,000 mg. a day, moving on from 'dropping' – taking doses orally – to intravenous boosts. By 1943 Adolf Hitler was reported to be having Methedrine injections five times daily. These escalating doses are liable to produce euphoria, disorientation or panic, which is usually succeeded by depression, exhaustion or paranoia when the body, finally rebelling against its lack of food and sleep, 'crashes out' at the end of a 'run'. Hallucinations, suspicions of being constantly watched, or, occasionally, toxic psychosis similar to paranoid schizophrenia can follow. Heavy abuse strains a user's heart and increases his pulse-rate, sometimes leading to death from heart-failure. (Hence the warning among drug-users that 'Speed Kills'.)[2] Over-stimulation can render a person unable to control aggressive or other anti-social behaviour, as a result of his feeling frightened, isolated and persecuted.

For the first time since the 1960s, cheap amphetamine sulphate is now again available on London's streets. Some of it is being home-produced in clandestine laboratories. Stimulants are mainly taken by students, athletes, party-goers, entertainers, pilots, night-watchmen, drivers and other people who want to fend off tiredness and keep awake. Adolescents who lack confidence and self-esteem are especially drawn to rely on them. However, a number of drivers have had crashes as a result of over-estimating their capacity, when their feeling of elation is suddenly overtaken by plunging fatigue. Amphetamines were extensively used on duty by servicemen on each side, including Japan, during the Second World War; US soldiers in the Vietnam War consumed more than 220 million tablets of them. During the 1956 Suez crisis, the Prime Minister, Anthony Eden, described himself as 'living on Benzedrine'.

Although amphetamines were originally synthesized by the German chemist Edeleano in 1887, they were not marketed until 1932 – as Benzedrine inhalers for nasal congestion. Today, because of the likelihood of dependency, amphetamines are less often prescribed than they were in the 1950s as appetite-suppressing slimming-pills or for depression. When taken to counteract the effect of a depressant such as alcohol, users risk becoming simultaneously dependent on both types of drug. Nor is Ritalin any longer given, as it once was, to small children at some American schools 'to raise their learning ability'. The only recognized medical use of stimulants nowadays is for the rare condition of narcolepsy (bouts of irresistible drowsiness, from which the sardonic comedian Lenny Bruce suffered); and also paradoxically – but controversially, with its echoes of the nineteenth-century dosing of infants – for calming disturbedly hyperactive children. In Britain about one in each thousand children is diagnosed as suffering from a hyperkinetic syndrome considered to require treatment from such drugs. But in the USA the proportion is 5 per cent – some half a million children, many of whom are only unusually bright and energetic; the use of drugs on them too often reflects more what their parents and teachers can tolerate rather than indicating any illness. Since amphetamines were restricted by law in Britain in 1964, their illegal production has multiplied, and they now retail from street suppliers for as little as £12 a gram. Seizures in the UK rose from 1.2 kg. in 1978 to 38 kg. in 1984. Amphetamines are comparatively simple to manufacture: one amateur chemist in Edinburgh recently did so with the help of a computer and the Scottish police investigating found three Dutchmen with illicitly produced amphetamine tablets worth over £70 million. Motorcycle gangs specialize in selling speed across the USA and over the border in Canada. In Australian cities such as Melbourne, illegally-made amphetamine rivals heroin as a fashion especially amongst women and the increasing number of multidrug consumers. The interacting effects of any multiple drug combination can be a unique experience for the user – but uniquely catastrophic in the results. Mixing depressant drugs (whether alcohol, tranquillizers, opiates, solvents or sedatives) can be especially dangerous, because a much lower dose will prove fatal than normally is the case.

'Aphrodisiacs'

Amyl nitrite ('poppers', 'reds', 'rush', 'hardware') – an inflammable and volatile liquid, smelling like 'pear drops or old shoes' – produces a heart rush with a deep flush and burst of energy which lasts for less than five minutes. Empty phials of it litter certain disco floors. It is fancied by some older men to assist them sexually (a Piccadilly Circus chemist used to have boxes of its ampoules by the cash register for punters who had picked up younger partners) and also by homosexuals as a muscle relaxant. Other than to relieve heart angina, however, poppers have no legitimate use – and recent medical research now connects them to cancer and strokes. Their cousins butyl and isobutyl nitrite ('snappers') – marketed commercially under sobriquets such as 'Liquid Aroma, to add spice to your sex life' – have lately been banned in New York; but in Britain they are not covered by the Misuse of Drugs or Poisons Acts and few of their users are aware of their danger when swallowed or sniffed excessively.

Despite the authoritative opinion of Professor van Praag that 'There is no known agent (except for dangerous quantities of amphetamines) which has been demonstrated to intensify the libido or enhance potency via a pharmacological route,'[3] alleged aphrodisiacs have had an irresistible appeal to ever-hopeful men and women – sometimes perhaps bringing a placebo benefit by enhancing confidence: another case of 'we are what we think we eat'. Pituitary hormones (such as the serum gonadotrophin which is obtained from pregnant mares) are sought after by the rich in Switzerland, Germany and Australia. Musk, civet, ambergris, borax, valerian, absinthe, henna, mandrake, garlic, juniper, mistletoe, horseradish, ginseng, kava, nutmeg, paprika, shellfish and radish are among the aids that have been optimistically enlisted throughout history by the credulous. Ground rhinoceros horn may be becoming less fashionable – fortunately for the future of that species – but is still prized in the Far East. In China, musk deer glands and powdered deer antlers are also popular, being discreetly named 'Spring Returns'. Currently Stanford University in California is clinically testing, on a record waiting list of volunteers, the claims of the least discredited candidate: the chemical yohimbine, an extract from the shrub *Corynanthe johimbe*, which has been used as a love potion in Africa for centuries; researchers claim that it doubles the sex-drive of rats for up to a week. In 1984 a Frankfurt pharmaceutical company withdrew a drug containing 15 per cent dried testicles and 15 per cent dried brains (whether human it was not specified) which was being marketed as a love potion in Africa. Pheromones – animals' sexual chemicals – are currently added to some cosmetics and bottles of scent (advertised in men's magazines with come-ons such as 'Just a dab and you'll have to scrape the birds off with a trowel'): the fact that they include substances such as sweat of armpits shows how relative attraction is. Other nostrums such as the dried beetle 'Spanish Fly' contain chemicals like cantharidin whose irritation of the urinary tract may be mistaken for sexual desire, but can also cause nausea and death: far from making the heart grow fonder, it can rapidly destroy kidneys. In 1985 the US Food and Drugs Authority declared that most bottles and packets promising sexual joy are not only false but also dangerous to health, and should be banned.

Caffeine

Probably the most widespread stimulant drug in the world is caffeine – like cocaine and strychnine, an analeptic. Caffeine is present in cocoa and cola as well as in coffee and tea. The Aztecs – whose word 'chocolath' we have adopted – prized the cacao bean so highly that they used it for currency; the explorer Carletti (1574–1617) warned that 'the Spanish, and every other nation which goes to the Indies, once they become accustomed to chocolate, its consumption becomes such a vice that they can only with difficulty leave off from drinking it every morning'. Chocolate contains a natural amphetamine chemical called phenylethylamine – which is a traditional antidote for the depression caused by unrequited love since it is believed to be the form of amphetamine released by the brain to give the 'high' feeling when a person falls in love. Today a number of sweet-toothed people are inclined to describe themselves as 'chocoholics': indeed, more money is spent in Britain on buying chocolate than bread. (One such chocoholic was cured by being made to eat ten whenever he wanted one chocolate bar, and by not being allowed to throw the wrappers away.) Mormons, however, frown on the use of caffeine as much as of tobacco and alcohol. Caffeine is a frequent substitute for other constituents in counterfeit drugs; it has recently also been claimed by medical researchers as a cure for cold sore herpes. Caffeine certainly seems to stimulate mental activity (many books like this one might not have been finished without the help of coffee), but it can worsen the perform-ance of any person already affected by anxiety. The syndrome of caffeine withdrawal includes headaches, drowsiness and irritability. Caffeine 'intoxication', characterized by nausea, insomnia and jittery anxiety, can be produced by doses as low as the 250 mg. contained in three cups of brewed coffee or tea. Excessive amounts result in palpitations as well as a dependent habit (rats given massive caffeine doses in laboratory experiments aggressively mutilate themselves as well as each other). Some people come to rely on twenty cups of coffee to get through a day: more than five cups of coffee daily, or nine of tea, invite a degree of risk to your health. The proportion of coffee drinkers who now prefer it decaffeinated has risen to 31 per cent, and in 1985 Castro gave up coffee as well as cigars for health reasons.

Tea contains the mild stimulant theophylline as well as 3 per cent caffeine and 10 per cent tannin. At one period in the nineteenth century it was sold on the mainland of Europe from druggists' shops for indigestion – as was recommended to Madame Bovary. By the 1930s, however, the Egyptian government ordered that tea-shops should be closed because of the dangers of intoxication alleged to result from stewed tea. More recently, Dr Robert Julian has warned: 'It must be remembered that once any stimulant agent is metabolized, there follows a period of behavioural and mental depression. This may be expressed frequently in automobile acci-dents that may occur as a result of people driving for a long time under caffeine stimulation; if people then stop drinking coffee, they may become drowsy and fall asleep while driving.'

Nitrous oxide ('laughing gas'), used medically as an anaesthetic, can also – by stimulating the central nervous system – produce short periods of euphoria followed by disorientation that often seems comical. The leaves of kat ('Arabian tea') contain cathinone, an alkaloid analogous to amphetamine; chewing them can make people dependent, although in the Middle East the habit is considered not to contravene the Koran. Kat is now being imported into Britain, where it is still legal. Other stimulants include ammonia, used in 'smelling salts' such as Sal Volatile, but dangerous in strength; strychnine, incorporated unjustifiably in some 'tonics', since it is in fact capable of causing convulsions and death; ether, which is both a respiratory stimulant and a muscle relaxant, as well as a short-term anaesthetic, but also when taken orally can have an effect similar to alcohol[4] (William James, the brother of Henry, said in his book *Varieties of Religious Experiences* that the ether he used stimulated 'the mystical consciousness to an extraordinary degree'; in Victorian times, ether frolics were the equivalent of pot parties today. At carnivals in Brazil, the traditional intoxicating Lanca spray is a mixture of ether and chloroform);[5] mephentermine, which acts by releasing the noradrenaline stored in our nerve endings, is administered illegally to boost the performance of horses and greyhounds; adrenaline, which can cause dizziness and even cerebral haemorrhage; and the legendary extract of the pineal gland. Two of the most addictive stimulants today, nicotine and cocaine, are described separately in later chapters.

Stimulants and other drugs in sport

In a recent poll of a hundred American athletes, exactly half said they would willingly dope themselves with a drug, despite knowing that it could kill them in a year, if it were capable of making them an Olympic champion. This is nothing new: in the third century BC, Greek athletes ingested several types of powerful mushrooms to try to help their performance. The main banned drugs athletes take today – sometimes in a mixed cocktail – are stimulants (including amphetamines, caffeine or cocaine for cyclists or racing drivers); ephedrine ('Dodo', a synthetic version of adrenaline, which increases the metabolic rate) or strychnine; beta-blocking tranquillizers for snooker players; and in heavyweight sports, anabolic steroids. Anabolic means 'building up' of the body: the anabolic male hormone testosterone, which can be made synthetically in a laboratory, is difficult for sports officials to police as it cannot be distinguished from the natural hormone product of a man's testicles. (The converse anti-androgen drugs given to male sex criminals are cyproterone, oestrogen, or – recently – Depo-Provera.) At the Moscow Olympics urine tests carried out by the International

Olympic Committee indicated that one in five of the athletes, male and female, were using extra testosterone. A dose of an anabolic steroid such as methandienone for therapeutic medical purposes would be 5–25 mg. daily; athletes are known to take – including by injection – more than ten times that quantity. Its side effects can result in liver cancer, heart attacks or strokes as well as stopping sperm production. Drug-dealers are now importing anabolic steroids from France, where they can be bought over the counter, and selling them at a big profit in gymnasiums and health clubs in Britain and America. (Since they are classed as personal chemicals, they escape the restrictions on sale imposed by the Medicines Act.)

Daley Thompson, the world Olympic decathlon champion, has recently alleged that 80 per cent of US athletes, and a third of Britain's track and field internationals, have taken drugs. Paul Dickenson, Chairman of the International Athletes Club, charges, 'Athletes don't get athletics magazines any more; they buy drug magazines meant for doctors and chemists.' Tempted by increasingly rich prizes from sponsorship, athletes use transfusions of drug-free urine to avoid detection. At the 1984 Los Angeles Olympic Games, some marksmen and pentathlon competitors who used beta-blocker depressant drugs to slow their heart-beat and steady their arm for rifle-shooting or archery, escaped disqualification by producing doctors' certificates stating that they needed beta-blockers for health reasons. 'Blood-doping' is the name given to the recent development of transfusing extra blood, which is done in order to improve an athlete's oxygen-carrying red blood cells and stamina: eight of the winning US cyclists confessed to doing this before their races at the 1984 Olympics. The UK Sports Council has now decided to withhold grants from any sporting body that refuses to accept random drug-testing – though it rejected the Amateur Athletics Board's proposal for tests on athletes at their homes on the grounds that it would be an unacceptable infringement of individual liberty. Two new endocrine drugs that some athletes are using and that are so far virtually immune from detection, are somatotrophine (HGH, the 'human growth hormone', used medically to treat patients of stunted stature) and which is obtained from dead people's pituitary glands, and HCG (chorionic gonadotrophin), extracted from pregnant women's urine. The fashion for HGH – which can add 50 lb. of muscle to an athlete – has been blamed for the increasing number of bone fractures amongst American footballers whose body frames cannot stand the strain of the extra weight. Drug-testing is notoriously rare in US athletics. In fact, however, there is little objective evidence that drugs can significantly improve any trained athlete's performance, though stimulants and anabolic steroids may increase his competitive aggressiveness: the calculated 'rage state' of some American football teams is reportedly fomented by heavy doses of amphetamines.[6] Meanwhile many sports stars, who have a key role in giving an example to young people, are happy to continue promoting and being sponsored by those other addictively harmful drugs, nicotine and alcohol.

II Depressants

Sedatives ('sleepers') calm people down, by allaying anxiety and reducing tension for a few hours. In the correct quantity they can also be hypnotic (i.e. induce sleep) or in larger doses anaesthetic. Although some scientists now believe that emotional depression is linked with the brain hormone CRH, the name itself of 'depressant' drugs often misleads non-medical people, because this describes the slowing-down of the users' brain and nervous system; it does not mean causing them to feel depressed – in fact usually exactly the opposite is the case. However, because of the drugs' inhibiting effect on those parts of the brain which are either the pleasure-rewarding (endogenous reinforcement) system, or else receive messages about pain, their result is to mask feelings of hurt and anxiety – though of course the actual causes are not removed. (The effect of alcohol, one depressant, is a good example.) For a person who takes a depressant, the consequences involve risks. Since the drug interferes with the processes of his thought, he is liable to take unwise decisions; and since it slows down the speed and accuracy of the user's reaction to emergencies, it impairs his judgment and ability, for example, to cope with injuries, operate machinery or drive a car.

The most widely taken depressants used to be barbiturates, which inhibit the central nervous system. Employed therapeutically for over eighty years, like most other drugs they are safe when used under medical supervision; but the *Alternative London* guidebook cautions: 'People take sleepers not only to sleep but to make them feel sociable, relaxed and good humoured, yet to others they appear clumsy and unpleasantly drunk.' In their effects they share many features with alcohol: they reduce a person's control of his speech and body, cause chaotic behaviour and leave a hangover after use. Tolerance of them develops easily, leading to a physical dependence so that doses are liable to increase progressively. Barbiturate dependents are estimated to number at least 14,000 in the UK today. Although it is not as easy to become addicted to depressants as injected opiates, the risks can be at least as dangerous: overdoses from barbiturates are the most common form of all drug-related deaths. A lethal dose can be as low as only twice the amount of a prescribed dose – just ten barbiturate pills can be enough; mixed with alcohol, their effect is even stronger. Many doctors regard them as the most damaging of all abused drugs, especially when injected: Jimi Hendrix and Marilyn Monroe are among those who have died from their misuse. Withdrawal from regular high doses of barbiturates can be more severe and life-threatening than withdrawal from heroin: the symptoms include irritability and dizziness, nauseous vomiting, twitching, cramp and delirium tremens, sometimes accompanied by convulsions and hallucinations. However, in a number of countries, barbiturates are still not subject to any control. They are frequently abused in combination with stimulants, heroin or alcohol, and their illegal use in Britain rose sharply when heroin became more tightly controlled.

The most common barbiturates ('barbs', 'blue birds', 'gorilla pills', 'blue devils' or 'idiot pills') include Seconal (quinalbarbitone: 'reds'); Amytal (known in the US as amobarbital or 'amies'); Luminal (phenobarbitone); Soneryl (butobarbitone); Tuinal ('truffic lights'), Nembutal ('yellows', 'yellow jackets' or 'goof balls' are American names for Nembutal capsules, sometimes used by addicts when they cannot get heroin); thiopentone sodium (Pentothal) is used for the induction of anaesthetics – acting in ten to thirty seconds, besides being tried as a 'truth drug'. 'Red chicken' is argot for heroin taken on a barbiturate base. Seconal, Tuinal and Nembutal are the barbiturate sleeping pills most often misused for an intoxicating effect; Tuinal capsules now retail in London at about 50p each.

Some of the better known non-barbiturate sedatives are: methaqualone (Mandrax – 'mandies', also available in the USA and Canada as Quaaludes – 'ludes' or 'pillows' – where they are widely used as a recreational drug despite their addictive potential. At present East Germany is the main source of supply, producing seven tons annually, much of which is illicitly sold in South Africa and Australia); bromide (first used as a sedative in 1857, now largely superseded except for the treatment of epileptics, although still sold in some 'nerve tablets'. This is the legendary additive in army tea to make soldiers feel less sexually active, but bromide intoxication can cause depression and tremors); chloral hydrate ('Mickey Finn' or 'knockout drops': an overdose results in a coma. Though less dangerous than barbiturates, chloral addicts may take enormous amounts: a chloral habit is similar to alcoholic addiction, and withdrawal may lead to delirium); mistletoe; paraldehyde, which is capable of dissolving plastic syringes, and is also addictive; and Thalidomide (Distavel), which used to be prescribed as a sedative before its tragic effects on unborn babies were discovered.

Other tranquillizers ('tranx') range from the major ones like Largactil (chlorpromozine or 'liquid cosh', used for calming violent patients without causing stupor, hence known in mental institutions as the 'chemical straitjacket') and Stelazine (trifluoperazine) to the widely-used benzodiazepines marketed as Valium, Solis, Tensum, Evacalm (all diazepam), Ativan (lorezepam), Mogadon (nitrazepam: 'moggies') and Librium (chloriazepoxide: 'Libs' or 'green and blacks'). The WHO's list of 200 essential drugs contains only one benzodiazepine: diazepam. Because they are safer, benzodiazepines have now replaced barbiturates for most medical purposes, though even they may impair a user's memory as well as produce dependency. In Britain tranquillizers require a prescription, but are not controlled under the Misuse of Drugs Act. The most effective drug for the prevention of travel sickness is hyoscine, though this can cause a greater amount of drowsiness in drivers than most antihistamines. Melatonin, a natural neurohormone which governs the biological clock, is a drug now being tested to counter jet-lag. Alcohol, heroin, morphine, codeine, Distalgesic, Diconal and volatile hydrocarbons, all also depressants, are described later.

Taken briefly in a crisis, a tranquillizer is capable of offering respite. However, the Brain Committee's first report warned that enough barbiturates were then being distributed in Britain to provide twenty tablets a year for each person in the entire population. Today the figure for all sedatives is over 50 per cent higher: 1,834,000,000 tranquillizers are being given in more than 28 million prescriptions annually. Every tenth night's sleep in England is now drug-induced. Apart from the 300 babies per annum which are born addicted in Britain because of their mothers' drug-taking, one in every four babies are being given sedative drugs in their first eighteen months – including some colic drugs recently declared unsuitable for infants. First synthesized in 1864 from apples and urine, benzodiazepine tranquillizers are now the most widely prescribed drugs in the world: in Britain one in five women and one in ten men take them, and the rate is even higher in Japan, the USA, France, Belgium, West Germany and Denmark. If all the regular consumers of benzodiazepines obeyed accepted medical advice and did not drive or operate machinery, the Western world's economy would grind to a halt. In the USA more than 200 million prescriptions for depressants are taken each year, of which 60 million are for diazepam, whose trade name Valium has entered the language as a household word. The consequent profits to drug companies are vast. The Committee for the Review of Medicines, however, found no evidence that depressants continue to be effective after four months' regular use, though more than a third of users go on taking them for longer than this A leading article in the *British Medical Journal* in May 1985 described minor tranquillizers as being no more effective than a placebo; however, because the withdrawal syndrome can resemble the original complaint, both patient and doctor are tempted to continue the pills. In the USA, dependence on prescribed tranquillizers has risen by over 29 per cent since 1962 – exceeding the 23 per cent increase in alcohol dependency. One tranquillizer addict described how hard it is to come off by explaining: 'They cushion the whole world.' Another former user said: 'It took me two years to come off completely. For the last five weeks I had to take leave from the office and go to bed: I had stopped being able to walk. For nearly twenty years, fear was the currency of my life. Today I have to get used to living with no pills of any kind. Very, very slowly things are beginning to come right. I'm alive. I'm a remade person.' Freud commented that, for some people, protection from stimuli is more important than receiving stimuli's signals,[7] but Isbell describes at what cost this may be: 'Chronic barbiturate intoxication always causes marked social and emotional deterioration. Barbiturate addicts neglect their personal appearance and are unable to work or care for themselves adequately . . . They may commit crimes and not remember them.'[8]

Of the significant number of people who have been caught shoplifting when under the influence of depressants, many say this is due to the chemical suppression of the normally deterrent fear of detection. Regular barbiturate users have twice as many car accidents as the average person[9] – indeed a higher accident rate than that of heroin users, which is below the general average – and are also at least five times more likely to have accidents at work. Depressant users' bursts of aggression and disorientation can often cause disruption in hospital casualty departments. (Muggers in Paris and Bangkok, by contrast, have recently taken to slipping a benzo-diazepine sleeping pill into the drink of their victim, believing – incorrectly – that when he awakes he will not remember enough to be able to give the police details. Charles Sobhraj, an international criminal who specializes in drugging tourists, in 1986 made a spectacular escape from Delhi jail by giving his guards food laced with medazapam and chloral hydrate.)

It is disturbing that, according to one recent study, more than half of the patients prescribed drugs (often in bottles merely labelled 'The Tablets') do not understand what they are taking or why they need them.[10] Professor Malcolm Lader of the Institute of Psychiatry believes that as many as one in ten of patients in the UK given benzodiazepines each year develop dependency on them. Just as different personalities can react in diverse ways to alcohol, so individuals' psychology influences other drugs' effects: introverts generally require a much higher dose of sedative to feel the same effect as extroverts. Whereas women form only 30 per cent of the total of drug abusers, they receive three times as many benzodiaze-pine prescriptions as men do. Of equal concern is the extent of the drugging of jailed prisoners – especially female ones – often against their will. During 1983, 295 doses per head of behaviour-modifying drugs were, for instance, administered in the UK's Styal and Cookham Wood women's prisons.[11] One girl who had been in a remand school alleges:

> I used to abscond from school, like everyone else. It was the thing to do. When I got back, if I acted up I would be injected with drugs like Valium or Largactil. I used to object, but I was sometimes handcuffed by the police while the doctor injected me. If you didn't agree to take their tablets you were threatened with the needle. At one stage I was given Largactil

for a year, whether I acted up or not. In the end I got to need it, even though I got hallucinations and it flattened everything out in my mind.

Only comparatively recently has research moved from a 'biochemical solution for every problem' to start instead with the perspective of the consumers; and medical resources in prisons worldwide are often too overstretched to seek to do more than keep inmates quiet. In all, 1.25 million doses of mood-altering drugs were dispensed to the UK prison population of 43,000 in 1981; in Holloway prison every female inmate received an average of more than a dose each day during 1983. This blanket dosing, sometimes without the informed consent of family or patient, has a disturbing echo of the Soma in Huxley's *Brave New World*, which totalitarian governments dispensed to keep the population compliant and easily controlled. Old people in a number of residential homes are also liable to be regularly drugged with tranquillizers and sedatives, sometimes by unqualified staff who want a quiet life. The current widespread employment of major tranquillizers to treat schizophrenics has certainly brought benefits by relieving psychotic and paranoid symptoms, though it has been criticized by Dr Joseph Berke, the Director of the Arbours Association: 'They treat people as symptoms rather than as human beings who can change for the better – mentally, spiritually, emotionally and socially.' Major tranquillizer drugs are used increasingly as an anti-psychotic short-cut because they are simpler and less expensive than the obviously preferable alternative, psychotherapy; however, most people would agree that even a 'chemical straitjacket' is an improvement on its physical forebear. At a surface level, neuroleptic drugs (such as Largactil) have revolutionized the problem of managing behaviour in mental institutions; anti-psychotic phenothiazines have enabled thousands of patients to be released and live out in the community, even though this treatment can cause Tardive Dyskinesia's uncontrollable twitching; and it is certainly true that tranquillizers are valuable anti-convulsants for epilepsy. On the other hand, Professor Bertram Karon of Michigan says, 'I now think that drugs are causing as much mental illness as they cure.' Even before the era of diazepam, in 1956 Thomas Szasz was warning that the use of such drugs might be less for the benefit of the patient himself than for the society having to cope with dissident behaviour, and questioned whether they were not a symptom of what he termed the physician's occupational disease, *furor therapeuticus*.[12] Szasz argues that illegal drugs differ from legal ones such as nicotine and tobacco only through ceremonial reasons of historical chance, and contends that ideas of medication and disease are often a means of social control based on middle-class interests and views of 'normality'. Michel Foucault too has written of the 'strict, militant, dogmatic medicalization of society'. On the other hand, G. L. Klerman warns against succumbing to 'pharmacological Calvinism': the automatic assumption that 'If a drug makes you feel good, it must be bad', based on a suspicion that it violates a Protestant refusal to concede pleasure to one's body.[13]

Voltaire wrote that 'the art of medicine consists of amusing the patient while nature cures the disease'. Nevertheless, on any assessment, why is it that, when there is evidence that tranquillizers and barbiturates are as addictive as opiates, they do not receive a fraction of the attention and warnings the government and media give to heroin? In 1979 the then Head of the US Drug Enforcement Administration, Peter Bensinger, testified to Congress that prescribed drugs present a much greater hazard than any illegal drug, including heroin. Methaqualone Quaaludes, one of the most popular drugs for students in the USA (the former American hit song '7-1-4' refers to the number stamped upon Quaalude tablets), caused death or injury to more than 6,000 people there in 1980. In Britain there are some 2,500,000 people dependent on tranquillizers – compared with an estimated 100,000 on heroin. Part of their routine overuse is because too many doctors resort to prescribing them as a general placebo, especially for women. At least one-third of an average GP's patients, it has been alleged, 'suffer from vague psychiatric and social troubles, inaccessible to his ordinary repertoire of remedies. Simply to stop the weeping and clear his waiting-room, he prescribes barbiturates.'[14] Research shows that doctors are most likely to give prescriptions to patients whose problems they feel are not brought upon themselves. To avoid withdrawal symptoms, however, many users are prone to request a repeat prescription ('Something for my nerves, please'), and some doctors renew such prescriptions by signing bundles of a hundred at a time, without the trouble of re-interviewing the patient. A recent advertisement in *The Times* by the Association of British Pharmaceutical Industry included the significant statement: 'People need medicines for many reasons. The mental comfort provided by a familiar remedy is sometimes as valuable as its more direct medical effects.' But 50,000 hospital admissions a year in Britain for non-suicidal overdoses of prescribed psychotropic drugs is a high price to pay for this clinical largesse. Although such drugs may give some short-term peace of mind to the doctor as well as his patient, they can, far from curing the original problem, make matters worse by masking it. By censoring anxiety, depressant drugs may stop a sufferer tackling its true cause; or by interfering with his emotions and judgment, they may prevent him from coming to terms with reality. The distress patients feel when they try to come off such drugs can in fact be far greater than the original anxiety which first drew them to depressants. Nevertheless, Dr Robert Veatch (the philosopher who has called for the Right to Health to be recognized as a principle of justice) sensibly advocates a balanced attitude overall towards prescriptions:

> We often speak glibly about the overuse of pharmaceuticals without ever having established the true prevalence of the diseases for which the drugs are intended. If by overuse we mean that drugs are being prescribed for the wrong people or for the wrong reasons or that their potential for harm is worrisome, we should say so and then separate these more refined judgments from vague negative generalizations about sheer increases in the volume of prescribing. It is important to remember that better treatment of many diseases and better health care for previously neglected subgroups in the population are quite likely to produce what most people would regard as laudable increase in the overall volume of drug consumption.[15]

Professor Malcolm Lader agrees that there undoubtedly are a few people whose anxiety is such that even a lifelong dependency on tranquillizers is preferable. He believes it is from patients themselves that a healthy mistrust of too easy a use of these (or any) drugs must come, as their powerful propensity to dependency becomes better known. 'Even then,' he says, 'we are left with an enormous number of people who are dependent, who need to withdraw, who must have the right medical help, and for whom at present there is no provision, no money and very little understanding.' In 1980 the American Food and Drug Authority introduced a regulation that all prescriptions for drugs such as Valium should be accompanied by a leaflet with the following information:

> You can become dependent on Valium. Dependence is a craving for the drug or the inability to function normally without it. An overdose of Valium alone or with other drugs can be fatal. You should avoid drinking alcohol while taking Valium. The combination of alcohol and tranquillizers dangerously increases the effect of both. Studies suggest an increased rate of birth defects in children whose mothers took Valium during the first three months of pregnancy. If you have been taking Valium for a month or more your doctor should reassess your condition and your continued use of the drug. The effect of these drugs for the relief of anxiety for periods longer than four months has not been studied.

Should we not focus on what it is about the state of society that causes 28 million prescriptions for tranquillizers annually to be required in Britain? Could not the money spent on the palliatives be better employed to help identify and remove more of the actual causes of anxiety? Might not counselling, psychiatric help, community support, self-help, or even yoga and meditation be preferable alternatives? Jim Reed and Kath Arnold, who run a new self-help group for tranquillizer users in the UK, urge: 'It is time some fundamental questions were tackled. Where are we going wrong when one in seven of the adult population is on tranquillizers? It is not good enough to blame the user for being inadequate. We need to question why so many people feel so bad about themselves that they become the victims of overwhelming feelings of anxiety and depression, and why it is so hard to find the closeness and support of family and friends which could help deal with them.'[16]

III Hallucinogens and psychedelics

Long before the modern development of synthetic alkaloids such as LSD (described in Chapter 9 below), hallucinogenic or psychedelic drugs had been culled from a wide variety of flora. The total number of plants capable of yielding psychoactive drugs is at least 4,000. Psilocin is derived from various psilocybin mushrooms, including the distinctive Liberty Cap; DMT (dimethyltryptamine, whose effect has been described as being 'shot out of a psychedelic cannon') and DET (diethyltryptamine) originate from the bark of the Virola tree and mimosa. Mandrake (*Mandragora officinarum*), mentioned in the Book of Genesis, was used in ancient times and by witches as an aphrodisiac and pain-killer as well as a poison; ZNA – dill mixed with monosodium glutamate – for smoking; Morning Glory seeds ('pearly gates', Convolvulus or Ololiuquil), which contain lysergic acid amide were used by Amerindians for ritual communication with the supernatural. Nutmeg and mace, respectively the seed and pod of the East Indian tree *Myristica fragrans*, are used to produce MDA and MMDA: though nutmeg, used in many kitchens and as a drug by sailors and prisoners, can produce nausea, delirium and fatal poisoning. Henbane, popular in Egypt where it is mixed with tobacco, is difficult to control since it grows wild. Mescalin, from Mexico's peyote cactus, is a derivative of amphetamine long used in North American Indian religious ceremonies, and was also known in nineteenth-century England. The lethal belladonna (deadly nightshade) contains atropine sulphate; and Monkshood contains aconite. Datura (stramonium: also known as Jimson-weed or thorn-apple), whose leaves and flowers are hallucinogenic although nauseous-smelling and bitter-tasting, can also be fatal.[17] Datura-scopolamine (hyoscine) has been used as a 'truth drug', though it has been found less than reliable. Fly agaric mushrooms, red with white spots, are often pictured in children's books. Ginseng, a mildly hallucinogenic stimulant from the root of a northern Chinese plant, is not controlled. Others include Lobelia leaves, which are similarly mild, as also are dried passion flowers (*Passiflora incranata*), valerian, and betel nut which contains the drug arecoline; kava, a mild hallucinogen from a shrub in the South Pacific area; and cannabis, described later separately. Besides those of vegetable origin, hallucinogens are found in certain reptiles and amphibians, such as some species of toads (as used by the witches in *Macbeth*). Synthetic hallucinogens range from THC (tetrahydrocannabinol, one of the active constituents of cannabis) and MDMA (methylenedioxymeth-amphetamine, a.k.a. 'ecstasy' or 'Adam') to the dangerous DOM (dimethoxy-methyl-amphetamine, also called STP – 'serenity, tranquillity and peace') and PCP (phencyclidine, known as 'angel dust', 'rocket fuel', 'killer weed', 'elephant' or 'monkey dust', 'magic mist', 'crystal', 'cyclone', 'goon', 'peace pills', 'hog', or 'scuffle'). PCP, one of the most dangerous, was formerly used as an anaesthetic by vets; in humans a single dose can produce toxic delusions similar to schizophrenia, sometimes provoking violent aggression including self-mutilation. Not to be confused with the Merseyside slang names for heroin ('angel dust' or 'loopy dust'), PCP is a favourite fashion – smoked in marijuana or other cigarettes, but now increasingly taken intravenously – among Los Angeles's many street gangs. Traces of PCP as well as cocaine were found in the body of American soul singer Marvin Gaye who attacked his seventy-year-old father before being shot dead in 1984. PCP's long-term effect can include comas and brain damage, but it is dangerous primarily because the margin between its active and toxic doses is deceptively narrow.

Matthew Huxley, the son of the author who described in *Brave New World* how the fictional hallucinogenic drug Soma was deployed to make everybody 'happy by eliminating unhappiness',[18] in 1984 warned the British Association for the Advancement of Science how a future government might indeed use psychedelic 'drug-pubs' as a means of keeping the unemployed pacified. (Anti-fluoride campaigners allege that a country which allows its government to doctor its water with fluoride invites worse forms of state drugging.) Under the influence of hallucinogenic drugs, a person finds it difficult to distinguish fantasy from reality, or to differentiate himself from his surroundings: rare cases have been highly publicized – amongst a much larger number of apocryphal rumours – of some users having thrown themselves from windows, perhaps believing they could fly, and recently a young Londoner was killed while walking along a railway line after eating 'magic' mushrooms on Hampstead Heath.

In 1983 a young artist was acquitted at a London Crown Court in a test prosecution for cultivating and possessing 'magic' mushrooms (*psilocybe cubensis*), even though these are not indigenous to Britain. (The boundary into illegality is crossed if you extract the hallucinogenic chemical ingredients.[19]) The defendant said that 'psychedelic drugs can be the key to using more of our brain, even if only for a few hours at a time'. Hippie communities have grown up in places in Britain where magic mushrooms can be harvested – in mid-Wales, the New Forest, the Forest of Dean, near Eye in Suffolk and Dorking in Surrey. *Psilocybe semilanceata*, a tiny fungus with an LSD-like effect, is reputed to grow wild in London parks. (One

Pennine-bound bus in Sheffield is known as the Magic Bus to the city's jobless.) But ingesting any hallucinogenic substance is like gambling at Russian roulette. Expertise is also needed to distinguish hallucinogenic mushrooms from other poisonous and deadly ones. Fly agaric mushrooms (so called in medieval times because of their power to stupefy flies: their classical name is *Amanita muscaria*) are found in Siberia and were eaten by Vikings in Scandinavia where they are held to be responsible for the legend of Father Christmas's flying reindeer. They can offer Dionysian visions – but also lead to extinction, because of the effect of the muscimol that similar-seeming arsenic fly agarics contain. A hallucinogenic drug in the latter, bufotenine, is also found in certain toads; the natterjack toad has glands on its back which release a lysergide resembling LSD.

Hallucinations (sensory perceptions without sensory stimulation – in contrast to delusions, which are the faulty interpretation of sensory signals) are also experienced by people who fast and by solitary travellers or prisoners. A number of individuals undergoing sensory deprivation claim they have seen visions – including the most famous mystics and religious leaders: the Buddha, Muhammad, Moses and Jesus each experienced revelations when alone in a wilderness.[20] Artists and writers as well have experimented with hallucinogens for their work – not always with great individuality: at one London art college a group of students who took LSD all painted a similar composition incorporating a rainbow-coloured ladder.

IV Opiates

People can take opiates either in an attempt to regain 'normality' as an antidote to pain, or conversely to try to escape from their normal life through intoxication. Opiates are often confused with narcotics, a term – from the Greek *narkosis*, meaning benumbed – which more accurately describes drugs used to induce stupor or sleep. Opium (known as 'mud' or 'brown stuff' to distinguish it from the 'white stuff', heroin), the coagulated milky juice from poppies' unripe capsules, has been used both medically and recreationally in temperate and tropical climates for several thousand years. Shakespeare wrote in *Othello*:

> Not poppy, nor mandragora,
> Nor all the drowsy syrups of the world
> Shall ever medicine thee to that sweet sleep
> Which thou owd'st yesterday.[21]

For pleasure, opium was originally eaten or taken in a drink. Smoking it is a comparatively recent refinement, following the introduction of pipe-smoking from the New World. Today it is legal to grow poppies (unlike cannabis) in Britain and elsewhere, but in most countries it is illegal to milk them. Whether smoked or eaten, the effect of opium can be to conjure a floating trance during which worries vanish and fantasies are woven. In 1700 John Jones, a London physician, wrote: 'It has been compared (not without good cause) to a permanent gentle Degree of that Pleasure, which Modesty forbids the naming of.' Opium's main alkaloid constituents, morphine and codeine, inherit its medicinal qualities but also its dependence-producing character; although the 'tourist's friend' paregoric – a weak solution of camphorated opium in alcohol – can still be bought without prescription in some US states. Opium, which contains 10 per cent morphine and 0.5 per cent codeine, continues today to have an important role for the licit production of these two medical drugs. Most morphine ('M' or 'morph') is now extracted from poppy straw – the dried capsules and upper stems of cut poppies – and is still used as the classic analgesic for the mitigation of severe pain such as burns, although it can cause nausea and vomiting as well as euphoria. Research suggests that opiates take effect by acting (like acupuncture) as 'keys' which unlock natural pain-killing receptors. Whether an opiate makes a person feel good or ill can depend on whether its effects are felt (positively) on receptors in the brain or (unpleasantly) on nerves in his gut. Opiates cause constipation and reduce sexual drive and performance, but they are not toxic unless taken in bulk or an impure form. Unlike barbiturates, they cause little interference with a user's intellect, motor skill or sensations. With higher doses, sedation occurs; an overdose results in a coma or death from respiratory failure. Heroin (diacetylmorphine: described in detail in Chapter 7) is over twice as potent as morphine, from which it is obtained by a simple chemical process of acetylation. When the UK government attempted to ban it in 1955, the British Medical Association rallied to its defence, describing it as 'a most excellent sedative'; and it is used in a number of countries for terminal cases, such as of cancer, where the possibility of dependency is not the paramount concern. Recently a battery-operated syringe has been developed to deliver subcutaneous diamorphine steadily at a pre-determined strength, as well as a new tablet for the control of pain which releases morphine slowly over a twelve-hour period and thereby ensures a night's sleep.[22] Nevertheless many doctors – except in the growing number of hospices – will not prescribe morphine or heroin even to ease the anxieties of the terminally ill. Dame Cicely Saunders, the pioneer of hospices, believes that many cancer patients die in unnecessary fear and agony because doctors deny them the pain-killing drugs they need: she told the British Association in 1984 that some terminal patients were being reduced to the state of demented animals because of prejudices about opiates. The writer Colin MacInnes, who himself died of cancer without adequate pain-killing drugs, called this 'a cruel and callous disgrace. This is the non-chalant attitude of the medical profession towards quite unnecessary suffering.'[23] Dr H. G. Miller, the Vice-Chancellor of Newcastle University, denounces 'an unholy combination of neurotic fear of addiction with the traditional Christian glorification of suffering' as the reason why 'a minority of physicians practise unjustifiable parsimony in the dispensation of pain-relieving drugs'.

Codeine (methylmorphine) is used extensively as a cough-suppressant, and is a mild analgesic drug, comparatively less addictive than morphine or heroin. More than 90 per cent of the current licit production of morphine in the world is now converted into codeine. However, it too can result in dependency: Goering at the end of his career was taking forty codeine tablets a day, and when he was arrested had 20,000 tablets with him. Other, less notorious people have become dependent on well-known cough mixtures which contain codeine linctus and chloroform, some of which are still obtainable without prescription. Addiction to opiate drugs can comprise both physical dependence (causing withdrawal symptoms after discontinuance) and psychological compulsion, coupled with the development of tolerance – desensitization that requires an increasing dose to maintain the original effect. Dependence may be acquired comparatively rapidly – though not (see Chapter 7 on heroin below) from the first dose, or inevitably. The all-important search continues for an effective synthetic opiate pain-killer that will be non-addictive. Some thirty years ago German chemists marketed pethidine with this claim, but experience has proved otherwise, although addiction to it is slower to develop than with morphine, and it is the drug of choice for relief of pain in childbirth.

Modern synthetic opiates include Palfium (dextromoramide), DF118 (dihydro-codeine tartrate), Fortral (pentazocine), Distalgesic (dextroprop-oxyphene); and Diconal ('dikes': dipipanone hydrochloride; in America, Wellconal) and methadone (Physeptone) which are used as substitutes for heroin. Palfium, a strong pain-killer taken orally by terminal cases, is used by addicts and its overdose can be fatal. A number of patients who were prescribed Diconal for the relief of post-operative or common back pain became addicted to it: preferred even to heroin by some addicts and a Class A controlled drug, most consultants will now no longer prescribe it for non-malignant conditions. Sold illegally by street-dealers in Britain for £5 a tablet, recently Diconal is being ground down to powder, mixed with water and then injected to give a heroin-type 'buzz'; but because the tablet is silicon-based and contains chalk, this clogs up and collapses the user's veins (sometimes resulting in limbs having to be amputated). Methadone, developed by I. G. Farben as a morphine substitute during the Second World War and originally named Dolophine after Adolf Hitler, is given orally as a replacement for heroin, especially in the USA. It has the advantage of being long-lasting, one dose of it substituting for a heroin addict's five injections a day; and this at least helps users to keep a job. However, it is only a substitute for heroin rather than a cure, especially since it too is highly addictive (with now over 5,000 addicts in the UK); withdrawal from methadone can be even harder and more painful than from heroin. An illicit market for it has spread in US cities: Washington DC now has more people addicted to methadone than to heroin.

'Designer' drugs

MPTP is one of the recent synthetic by-products of MPPP, the analogue which Californians call 'new heroin'. Those who inject themselves with it are in danger of developing the symptoms of Parkinson's disease, becoming crippled and suffering brain damage. One scientist synthesizing MPTP as part of his work with benzomorphine analogues is reported to have developed irreversible Parkinsonism; and since he was not ingesting the drug, he must have absorbed it either through his skin or by inadvertent inhalation.[24] This case illustrates the potency of the new synthetic mimic or 'designer' drugs (more of which will inevitably be developed in the future) as well as the risk they present to those who research – let alone abuse – them. In the last four years there have been at least eighty-seven deaths confirmed from synthetic opioids in California alone. Such analogues of heroin and cocaine are disturbing in the extreme for any government because most are not illegal to possess or manufacture, since the variants' chemical formulae continually differ slightly from legal definitions of the molecular structure of banned drugs. Some, but not all, of the new generation of designer drugs are as addictive as natural narcotics; others can be up to 3,000 times more potent: a single chemist working an eight-hour day would be capable of supplying a nation's daily heroin demand. The production of some designer drugs requires only basic equipment in a garage or kitchen and a degree in chemistry, to reap enormous profits for a very modest outlay. According to Dr Roberton, the Head of California's Drugs Division, at least a fifth of the heroin used in the state is now some kind of synthetic variant. Concern centres on analogues of fentanyl, a common anaesthetic. Addicts opt for such opioids in the belief that they are less adulterated and last several times longer than ordinary heroin, but are often liable to overdose because they do not realize the vastly higher potency of, for example, alpha methyl fentanyl ('China White'). Even stronger variants, such as 3-menthal fentanyl – 3,000 times stronger than morphine – and su-fentanyl, have recently emerged on the West Coast. The variations of possible analogues are, worryingly for the future, potentially as limitless as the profits ($2,000's worth of materials can produce a kilogram of 3-menthal fentanyl – enough for several million doses), even though under a proposed new Bill the US Federal Drug Enforcement Administration will be able to outlaw a new drug variant in thirty days, compared with more than a year hitherto. Designer drugs are beginning to spread from California to New York and, since control of them is virtually impossible, are bound to reach Europe in the near future.

Nevertheless, continuing research into drugs – including narcotics – is not only inevitable, but vital. As many as one in three of the population is reckoned to suffer some form of consistent or recurring pain (which Sir Charles Sherington defined as being 'the psychic adjunct of an imperative protective reflex'). Yet strikingly little is known about how people feel pain, or how to treat it. A great number of analgesic (pain-killing) drugs can be harmful or fatal in overdose – including several which are available without prescription. Propoxyphene drugs are the most commonly prescribed in the USA, but their non-medical consumption also is now rising at a disturbing rate. Their potential for abuse and addiction is not generally realized: a single high dose can result in pulmonary oedema and death. Besides opiates, the principal pain-killers at present available are aspirin (supposedly first identified by Hippocrates in 400 BC from the bark of willow trees), which can cause stomach bleeding and kidney damage, and whose use by children under twelve in the UK received official discouragement in 1986; and paracetamol, milder, but capable with heavy use of causing liver damage. The USA consumes more than 9,000 tons of aspirin each year – some 45 million tablets a day. However, although aspirin has been in very widespread use for over eighty years, its precise action on the body still remains uncertain – and the same is admitted to be true of a great number of other drugs.

Research for the elusive key to separate analgesia from addiction is now concentrating on the natural peptide chemical neurotransmitters which serve to police pain in the human body. Upjohn recently discovered by accident a synthetic chemical equivalent for the natural pain-killer dynorphin. Other researchers at Kyoto University are trying as an alternative to develop drugs that could trigger or promote the release of the natural pain-killers already contained in our bodies, while Tokyo and Singapore scientists believe that lasers might achieve this by being focused on certain points of the body in the same way as in acupuncture.

V Deliriants

The various organic solvents and volatile hydrocarbons which are sometimes inhaled for intoxication include – besides glues that contain ketones, toluene, acetone or naphtha – chloroform; paints and paint thinners; nail-varnish removers that contain acetone and amylacetate; lighter fuel that contains butane; propellants in aerosols such as anti-insect sprays, some hair lacquers and fire-extinguishers; typewriter correction fluid; anti-freeze; bicycle-tyre rubber solutions which contain benzene; dry-cleaning fluid that contains carbon tetrachloride; oven-cleaning chemicals; and petrol. The Canadian Le Dain Committee found no less than thirty-eight different household products in this category that were legally obtainable on the shelves of a typical service station store in Ottawa. Inhaling them can cause a light-headed feeling of relaxation, and occasionally hallucinations with blurred vision or memory. Although most concern has been concentrated on glue sniffing (described in more detail in Chapter 10), that practice is in fact less dangerous than any involving vapours containing the metallic, chlorine or fluorine components of some other solvents. Lead and other additives in petrol, or the tin, copper or zinc particles in paints, for example, can be toxic and damage an inhaler's liver and kidneys. Pilots are warned against inadvertently inhaling the fumes of aviation fuel, which could cause a crash through disorientation. The fluorinated hydrocarbon propellant gas in aerosols may, when inhaled, damage lung tissues or cause a spasm in the larynx that results in asphyxiation by cutting off air to the lungs. In Virginia in 1984 a girl died after inhaling fumes from ordinary typewriter correction fluid, because the drying agent in the fluid interrupted the flow of her blood. Children, forbidden glue, have been known to switch to butane gas, which is much more dangerous: deaths in England and Wales from deliberately inhaling this increased from four in 1979 to fourteen in 1983. Students at more than one exclusive school are reported to rely on illegal sniffs of glue for a boosting 'buzz' or 'trip' as an alternative to pep pills before taking examinations. In a very different case, a young motor mechanic who accidentally swallowed some petrol when siphoning a tank developed the habit of drinking or inhaling a litre of petrol each week for almost three years: admitted to hospital with peripheral neuritis with his nerves so affected that he could hardly move his feet, he was fortunate to recover after eight months' treatment.[25] Solvent abuse is a habit mainly practised – and then grown out of – by adolescents. Generations of younger children have enjoyed the sensation of dizziness from spinning themselves round, or hyperventilating by breathing into paper bags; adult 'whirling dervish' fraternities in Islam ritually enter a form of cataleptic trance through gyrations during their devotions.

In a 1979 survey of US high school senior students which revealed that 65 per cent of them had taken some form of illicit drug, 18.7 per cent said they had tried an illegal inhalant. By comparison:

    60.4 per cent had taken marijuana or cannabis (10.3 per
      cent daily);

    24.2 per cent illegal stimulant drugs;

    18.6 per cent hallucinogens;

    16.3 per cent illegal tranquillizers;

    15.4 per cent cocaine (an increase of 200 per cent in four
      years; 46 per cent of the students said that supplies of
      cocaine were readily available to them);

    14.6 per cent illegal sedatives;

    12.8 per cent PCP;

    11.1 per cent amyl or butyl nitrite;

    10.1 per cent other illegal opiates; and

    1.1 per cent heroin.[26]

Such findings once again underline the illogicality of current concern and education about drug abuse focusing so exclusively on
heroin.

Other varieties of addiction and drugs

The context in which a drug is used may crucially affect its results:
social usage – in contrast to 'solitary vice' – can provide control
against abuse. The circumstances and traditions in which they are
consumed can help to determine whether alcohol, cannabis, or
opium make users feel euphoric, serene, elated or depressive.
Cannabis has been used in one culture to assist religious meditation;
in another to stimulate jazz-playing or sex; in yet another to give
soldiers aggression. The anthropologist Francis Huxley points out
that shamans in south-east Asia are made alert, not more sleepy, by
opium; and also that tobacco smoking in some Brazilian tribes is
solely a communal activity, with a cigar being passed round like a
joint.[27] In addition to context and mood, auto-suggestion – the
result the user believes and expects he will feel – plays a significant
part in the effects a drug will have. People who in experiments have
been given a harmless inactive placebo that they believed to be
heroin or cannabis have exhibited the symptoms, including intoxication, customarily produced by those drugs. (When drug-users
unknowingly take placebos because they are unaware that they
have been sold counterfeit 'look-alike' drugs, they run the risk of
overdosing as soon as they revert to the unexpected potency of a

non-counterfeit drug.) Other heroin dependants have been known to transfer their addiction to the hypodermic needle they have been using, and begin to inject themselves regularly with other substances such as milk, mayonnaise or water. The psychological nature of addiction is demonstrated by the fact that there have been cases in which people have in fact become dependent on a placebo, and that this has continued even despite their being told it was a placebo.[28] In one spectacular case in 1984, I. Khint, an Estonian biochemist in Tallin, successfully marketed a universal 'Health Elixir' drug brewed in a bathtub out of ingredients recalling the witches' cauldron in *Macbeth*, ranging from blood, nettles and animal entrails to dandelions, pigs' feet and mushrooms. This concoction, having been widely recommended at lectures and conferences as a panacea for virtually every complaint including cancer, soon acquired a devoted following, and it was claimed that productivity had risen by 30 per cent when the elixir was introduced into livestock's drinking water, although analysis eventually determined it to be not only devoid of medical value but also toxic and addictive.[29]

Not all drugs come in tablets or bottles – nor are we always aware of being under their influence. Recent research suggests that kissing is a mechanism people exchange in order to imbibe and test semiochemical reactions. (Semiochemicals are chemical substances that communicate biological signals between animals; unlike pheromones – which are scent-like chemicals that attract the opposite sex and are produced by secretory glands – they remain on the skin and are not discharged in the air.) Contentedly kissing lovers, according to Dr Bubba Nicholson, are in thrall to such substances secreted in the love-object's sebaceous glands; falling in love may in unromantic scientific reality only be addiction to a particular bonding semiochemical – perhaps the only true aphrodisiac. Nor is it only chemical drugs from which people get their kicks and to which they become addicted. The scientist J. B. S. Haldane recorded: 'I have tried morphine, heroin and hemp. The alteration of my consciousness due to these drugs was trivial compared with those produced in the course of my work.' An MP said of a cabinet colleague whom he described as 'a messianic, driven figure': 'One can become hooked on adrenaline like a junkie. What would probably make him crack up now is a week sitting down doing nothing. Adrenaline becomes a narcotic, you live off it.' As another illustration of 'workaholism', Dr Toru Sekiya, the head of a psychiatric clinic in Tokyo, says that the introduction of a five-day working-week in Japan has resulted in many cases of neurosis in middle-aged men, including severe withdrawal symptoms of stomach pains and insomnia.

Compulsive gambling

Dr Mark Dickerson has found that compulsive gamblers, too, can suffer physical withdrawal symptoms when weaned from their habit. The addiction of many pathological gamblers – like that of some sexual seducers – seems to be centred on the hypnotic ritual more than on the lure of success. Gordon Moody, the founder of Gamblers Anonymous, says:

> Real gambling is continuous and circular in its action: staking, tension, release and staking again. For compulsive gamblers this becomes a squirrel's cage. Win or lose, they cannot escape – this distinguishes them from heavy and professional gamblers. As time goes on they develop a need for 'the action'. Because it contains the elements of tension and release some observers have made a comparison with orgasm, and decided that gambling is a sex substitute. But those who have experienced all three say that, as an experience, gambling has more in common with breaking and entering than with sexual intercourse. If you must have the action and, win or lose, cannot leave it, then because the odds are against you, you must lose till it hurts. There can be no ultimate win for those who must continue to gamble. When in Sydney, Australia, I heard of a man who 'cleaned up' in a two-up school, and was so frustrated that the action had ceased, that he divided the money among his fellow gamblers to make a fresh start.[30]

Although the actual form gambling takes varies according to opportunity as well as socio-economic class, the overwhelming preponderance of all gamblers are male. The effects of compulsive gambling are of course shared by families too, but recently it has also spread to a striking number of children – some as young as ten. One teenager recently said: 'Since 9 o'clock this morning I've burnt my way through £60, most of it on fruit machines. I can't afford it, but it's an addiction, I can't help it. It caught up with me before I realized what was happening . . .' The nineteen-year-old secretary of Young Gamblers Anonymous in the UK recalls: 'Crossing the line from "normal" to "uncontrolled" gambling was a gradual process. Compulsive gambling is a symptom of my illness. If I hadn't gone for gambling, it could equally have been alcoholism, drugs or a mental breakdown.' Regular users of one-armed bandits recount that they 'get a buzz', with a raised heart-beat similar to when they take a pep pill. Gamblers Anonymous now has among its members 1,500 slot-machine addicts; but this is not just a teenage craze: a 48-year-old policeman was recently ruined and jailed in England because of this addiction.

Probably the most benign drug of all is music. Other people are hooked on status, money-making, publicity, religion, consumer goods, erotica, horror films or competitiveness. To be 'addicted' under Roman law meant to be formerly delivered over to an owner. By Elizabethan times this came to be used as a habit: Shakespeare in *Twelfth Night* speaks of addiction to a melancholy; Greene of addiction to virginity. Today, besides those hypnotized by television, many young people get a buzz from the beat of rock music, strobe lighting, or associations with excitement and danger. Is the risk of dicing with death a drug for some soldiers, racing drivers, motor-cyclists, mountain climbers? For others sex or power may be the narcotic they crave. (Sexual activity causes the body to release some of its natural opiates, and thus can soothe anxiety and induce euphoria or addiction in the same way as a morphine-type drug.) There is also the infatuated love of couples who become fixatedly dependent on everything about each other: does a great obsession exert so unbalancing a power that it can excuse, as some courts allow for crimes of passion, major offences? *Amour fou* – what D. H. Lawrence called *egoisme à deux* – may, like drugs, be a panacea for insecurity, and can be equally destructive of the dependent person as it is of the loved one on whom he is fixated. It can be another example of the truth that it is not drugs which addict people, but people who addict themselves. Sartre said lovers eat each other; yet society (at least since the time of the troubadours) admires and envies romance as much as it condemns and fears drug-taking.

Alternatively, violence may be the pull. Professor Ivor Mills of Cambridge writes:

Since the demonstration of the production of morphine-like substances in human beings (endorphins and enkephalins), it has become apparent that the release of these substances under stress can be sufficient to prevent pain being sensed in the normal way. We have studied patients who produce violence to themselves and deny that they feel pain at the time. In one case all such activity ceased when an antagonist to morphine was continuously given it intravenously. Seeing violence on the screen is known to produce stress responses in the viewers and such stress responses are known to include release of enkephalins with the adrenaline (which is the so-called fight or flight hormone). A state resembling addiction occurs in people who constantly inflict violence and it is extremely difficult to cure them of this state. Watching violence on videos must surely stimulate similar responses in the viewers and the release of morphine-like substances can be high enough to produce a state of addiction.[31]

These endorphins or natural opiates in our bodies can act as even stronger pain-killers than the purest codeine, morphine or heroin. Recent medical treatment of heroin addicts has thrown light on the workings both of endorphins and of acupuncture. When an addict is given naloxone to bring him down from his 'high', this drug blocks the heroin receptor sites in his body – and equally has the effect of blocking the anaesthetic effect of acupuncture. The endorphin opiates that injured soldiers or sportsmen produce are the reason why they often do not feel pain from a wound during the immediate excitement. Physical exertion such as jogging or walking, like sex, leads to the release of endorphins in our bodies which acts to counter depression – so that athletes have been known to complain of feeling depressed if they do not have their daily 'fix'.

The 'addictive personality'
Is there an 'addictive personality'? Most informed opinion today regards addiction as learned behaviour rather than as a disease (see Chapter 12). 'Whilst personality make-up is obviously important – factors such as depression, anxiety or an impaired ability to make or sustain personal relationships can be crucial in particular cases – the notion that there is an "addictive personality", i.e. a distinct personality type which distinguishes addicts from non-addicts, must be regarded as far too simplistic,' says Sir Bernard Braine, MP.[32] There may be support for this from the fact that some people – such as 'weekend binge' alcoholics – are only part-time addicts. Other

people who start slimming or jogging from a healthy motive may go on to find starvation a cerebral excitement through anorexia nervosa, or else channel their depression and self-anger into bulimia – compulsive eating.[33] Fasting, like other sensory deprivation, changes the body's biochemistry and can produce light-headed euphoria and fantasies.

Even a summary catalogue of drugs (and addictions) can never be complete, because new ones will continually be developed. This is impossible to prevent – even were it desirable to do so. It would be wrong if society lost the positive value of drugs because of ill-informed panic, or through making them the scapegoats for a minority's misuse or overuse. Indeed, because of the negative emotions generated by the word 'drug', it is deviant drug-users – in the view of Szasz or of Du Quesne and Reeves – who are in danger of persecution as scapegoats for other ills in our society.[34] It is important to understand as much as possible about drug use and abuse, if only because attitudes and policies based on ignorance lead to witch-hunts capable of harming society as much as the victims.

Medical drug use – and abuse

In contemporary society many of us consume ever-increasing amounts of drugs to escape – or at least postpone – evidence of our mortality. Medicine has replaced morality; what our ancestors called gluttony or lechery today is diagnosed as 'having an obesity or libido problem'. We prefer the illusion that our physical ailments are in some way separate from ourselves: that our portrait can be changed or repainted by external medical agents. However, virtually every drug, whatever its benefit, also carries dangers.[35] Dr Arabella Melville and Colin Johnson, amongst others, warn that the spread of chemotherapy has diverted Western medicine away from the positive promotion and protection of health. They estimate that the unintended side effects of over-prescribed – and inadequately tested – drugs in the USA and Britain cause at least as many deaths and injuries as do road accidents.[36] Casualties are inevitable in a culture whose faith-healing belief today is that health can be bought in a packet over the chemist's counter, and that happiness can be acquired out of a syringe or plastic bag. Placebo research demonstrates people's credulousness about magic bullets and our blind reliance on the totem of medicine and miracle drugs instead of managing our nature and bodies ourselves.

Most of the public appear unaware of drugs' risks, despite the publicity for cases such as Thalidomide and Opren. More and more patients demand magical nostrums; doctors and chemists today have assumed the role of shamans and priests. The modern tendency is for various age-old human conditions (such as anxiety or depression) to be categorized as new illnesses; but instead of attempts to cure them by tackling their causes, a plethora of new drugs are promoted to mask our bodies' signals. Depression, for example, can be a perfectly rational response to adverse circumstances; but a patient diagnosed and stigmatized as mentally depressive is liable to feel anxious if not guilty and consume yet more pills. An estimated 28 per cent of women and 18 per cent of men in Britain now constantly take some form of medication prescribed by doctors. The prescription of drugs per head in Britain has risen by 40 per cent since the National Health Service began, though West German and Italian doctors give even more: almost twice as many prescriptions per patient as in Britain. Some drug companies are among the most profitable corporations in the world, spending massively on pushing their products in a market now worth in excess of £60 billion a year. Developing countries may squander their limited resources on importing these products, instead of concentrating on providing basic health essentials such as a clean water supply. Melville and Johnson believe that most prescribing in Britain could beneficially be rationalized at around 20 per cent of its present level – thus saving over £800 million for other health services, including the provision of more counselling and positive health promotion. Furthermore, they argue, the research and development of drugs should best be done by independent academic bodies whose primary motive would not be to maximize profits at any cost, since Dr John Griffin's expert analysis of new medicines in the UK caused him to conclude that innovation in the drug industry was 'directed towards commercial returns, rather than therapeutic need'.[37]

Despite doing their best, few busy doctors today have the training, time or experience to assess drugs by analysing the proliferating details of their tests and trials. Meanwhile they are under increasing pressure to prescribe from both patients and drug companies. How many doctors or patients know, for example, that the authoritative *British National Formulary* guide says of the numerous cough expectorant medicines prescribed that there is no evidence that they work, and 'There is thus no scientific basis for prescribing these drugs, although a harmless expectorant mixture may have a useful role as a placebo'? Or of many so-called tonics that 'All depend on suggestion, and there is no advantage in prescribing the many exotically-coloured and flavoured products which are available'? Or that the use of vitamin pills as general pick-me-ups is 'of unproven value . . . and may actually be harmful'? Fraudulent cures for AIDS have provided a huge new market for the unscrupulous. Many members of the public prefer to buy ranges of pills in an uninformed attempt at self-help so as 'not to bother the doctor' – which often really means because they are afraid of him or what he might diagnose. The current campaign by pharmacists that people should bring minor ailments to them rather than to a doctor makes it likely that even more drugs will be dispensed, because chemists receive no payment for giving advice alone. Particularly when they are not feeling well, patients easily forget the all too frequently illegibly written instructions for taking drugs, before hoarding and forgetting them. Controls vary from country to country: antibiotics available only through doctors in the West are sold from vans touring the countryside in much of Africa; drugs which can only be dispensed through pharmacists in Europe may be sold by any retail outlet such as a petrol station in the USA. There are 17,000 drug products licensed in the UK, and over 24,500 different drugs available in Brazil – but a total of less than 2,000 in Norway, which enjoys much better health than Brazil, and where new drugs are licensed only if they are safe and have clear advantages over what is already available.

If each country had a national agency to acquire the drugs it needs on the world market, this would cut costs as well as being more efficient. Research by Charles Medawar of Social Audit shows that the price of brand-name drugs is many times the cost of the same ingredients obtainable under their generic (chemical) names.[38] Drug companies often price differently in each country according to what they think the market will bear. Several British chemists regularly go to buy on the continent, where the same drugs are one-third cheaper than in the UK. The drug industry argues that to develop a successful new drug may cost as much as £50 million and can take up to ten years. Discoveries of new drugs have indeed been of inestimable benefit – including, for example, the sulpha drugs, penicillin, the heart-protecting beta-blockers, and the anti-ulcer drug Tagamet (currently the most profitable drug in the world with sales of $1 billion annually). On the other hand, it is pressure from pharmaceutical companies that causes unnecessary drugging, with misleading advertising, deceptive competition, and often an identical drug being marketed under different names by the same maker. Salesmanship is backed up by extravagant 'hospitality', together with hyping from bogus and inaccurate tests; sales representatives regularly visit surgeries and health centres with gifts such as wine, and one UK doctor reports that he was offered £10 a time to prescribe a particular drug. Other doctors try out new drugs on patients without their consent or knowledge, at times because a drug company is paying them to do so. It has been known for drug companies to withdraw their advertising from those medical journals which dare to criticize their products. In the UK, the Department of Health allocates a derisory £7,000 a year to monitor drug advertisements. Against this, there is now one drug company sales representative active in Britain for every seven GPs; and many companies spend more on promotion than they do on research – the equivalent of some £5,000 a year for each GP. Even lower standards are practised by door-step pill peddlars who currently operate without any qualifications on pyramid-sale commissions, and have been known to market drugs employing bogus questionnaires to worry customers with questions such as 'Is your fifth finger particularly short?'[39]

One reaction against burgeoning drugging has been the rise in popularity of holistic (complementary or alternative) medicine, with its assertion that physical symptoms are merely a sign of spiritual dysfunction, and its preference for treatment such as homeopathy in place of drugs. One of the reasons for the attraction of holistic medicine is the amount of time its practitioners spend listening to their patients – something orthodox doctors should also do: a recent study in the UK found that on average an alternative therapist spends ten times longer over a consultation than one average GP. Farmers in Europe and North America are now starting to market crops of Evening Primrose plants, whose oil produces prostaglandin, for use as herbal medicine. Traditional tribal healers led the way to the discovery of quinine (still the most effective drug for treating malaria), derived from the bark of the Cinchona tree. However, the value of many other homeopathic remedies is unproven: 'laetrile' made from apricot stones is still used as an alternative treatment for cancer, despite research having suggested it is not only valueless but possibly toxic from cyanide. Most homeopathic remedies, including some that contain arsenic, toxic mistletoe, mercury and antimony, have not been clinically tested for either safety or results. Overall, Charles Medawar and the UK Consumers' Association conclude: 'There is a clear need for better education for doctors and patients about what drugs can and cannot do. Doctors do not get enough training in drug prescribing, either before or after they qualify. Patients would benefit if they learned from their doctor – or even at school – what to expect, and what to ask in a consultation.' And, wisely, they advise members of the public: 'Don't automatically expect to be given a prescription, and don't feel you're wasting the doctor's time with an unnecessary visit if you don't get one. If you are prescribed drugs, find out all you can about what you're taking.'

The Third World's problems

The problems in rich countries are compounded many times over in the developing world, where most countries have no choice but to buy their drugs from the dominant Western companies. Africa, Asia and Australia now form a larger share of the £72 billion market in the non-communist world than either Europe or North America. Developing nations spend about £12 billion a year – almost half their health budget – on medical drugs, but less than 3 per cent of the funding for biological research world-wide has been devoted specifically to Third World health problems. (Illnesses in the poor world are markedly different from those in the rich world: caused principally by malnutrition and dirty water, the most frequent diseases of the poor majority are bacterial, parasitic or viral infections, such as malaria and diarrhoea; degenerative illnesses of the rich world like heart disease or cancer are relatively rare.) Some countries – including India, Mexico and Bangladesh – have tried to meet this problem by creating a domestic drug industry to meet their needs. Nevertheless, although the Indian market is flooded with 15,000 different brands of drugs, spending per head of population on drugs there is only $1 a year (compared to $103 in West Germany), and since 90 per cent of drug sales are for private health care, drug consumption in rural areas averages a mere $0.4 a head annually. The public health services of the sixty-seven poorest developing countries (excluding China) have a total budget of less than the rich countries spend on tranquillizers alone.[40] Pricing anomalies abound: in Africa, the antibiotic streptomycin, for example, recently cost twelve times as much in Guinea as it did in Egypt. Allegations of cartels and monopolies are common. In 1982 the Bangladesh government announced its New Drugs Policy, which aims to: (i) eliminate harmful and useless medicine; (ii) increase domestic research and production of essential drugs, which would be publicly distributed; (iii) import pharmaceutical raw materials in bulk, to reduce costs; and (iv) use generic drugs rather than more expensive brand names. A Bangladeshi official suggested, 'It is a policy which should be adopted by many other countries, including Britain, where there are a lot of unnecessary medicines.' The multinational companies are indeed worried that Bangladesh's example might be followed.[41] They successfully lobbied against attempts by Sri Lanka and Pakistan to get rid of brand names, and in 1982 a Delhi court also quashed an Indian government order which sought to abolish brand names for a number of basic drugs.

Drugs are pushed overseas uncontrolledly and often irresponsibly. Oxfam's medical experts were alarmed to find that one Dutch multinational's powerful anabolic steroids (produced for the treatment of rare bone diseases) were being sold as an appetite stimulant for children in Peru.[42] Malnourished children in Africa, at risk from famine and kwashiorkor, are being sold appetite-stimulant drugs by European multinationals – despite the side effects for which these drugs are known in Europe; and as a result of international criticism, another Swiss company recently phased out its anti-diarrhoea drug that produces neurological side effects. To get overseas doctors to prescribe certain drugs, they are offered every inducement ranging from free trips to Venice to promises of 'a visitor for the night'. Much consumer drug advertising is targeted at the ready market caused by male insecurity: Pasuma Strong, produced in West Germany from testosterone, yohimbine and strychnine, is widely promoted in Africa as 'the successful answer to impotence'. The use as a tonic of an anabolic steroid – promoted in India as a life-enhancer and in the Philippines as being safe even for children – is criticized in the *British National Formulary* as 'quite unjustified': Social Audit has documented how contradictory tailored advice is given by some drug manufacturers in different areas of the world. Drugs, withdrawn on safety grounds in the UK and US, continue to be marketed – and sometimes dumped in bulk – in the developing world. Another disturbing hazard is caused by the increasing manufacture of dangerous counterfeit drugs, especially in Thailand, Nigeria and the Lebanon. At least one Bangkok factory has recently been producing counterfeits, adulterated with tapioca and starch, of reputable drugs, and some of its potentially lethal but cleverly simulated fakes were exported to Europe via Singapore. In Nigeria, Pfizer's Terramycin suffers from fifteen different illegal imitations; and recently pseudo birth-control pills are increasingly being marketed from the Far East.

Monitoring

Even established drugs should have their complete effects regularly re-appraised and carefully monitored. An unprecedented number of drug products have been withdrawn from the market in recent years – but not before some of them had caused serious injuries or deaths. Clearly a balanced perspective is necessary, because not only is the world crying out for antidotes to scourges such as cancer or AIDS, but also because it is true that for every person damaged by most new drugs, thousands are likely to be helped. Every drug generates some side effects; the decision to prescribe any drug in an individual case is always a matter of weighing likely benefits against possible adverse reactions. Psychotropic and tranquillizer drugs have helped to lower the number of in-patients in UK mental hospitals by more than 40 per cent. Nobody wants that kind of progress halted. On the other hand, it is inequitable that there is as yet no formal arrangement for compensating patients who suffer adverse effects from drugs: a 'no-fault' restitution scheme for such damage is long overdue. Nor is there yet any statutory protection for people being used in trials for new drugs: old-age pensioners are being paid to act as such guinea pigs in Britain, and 'double blind' tests continue which are based on patients not being able to give informed consent. It is also wrong that local authorities lack – as they do – powers to protect the public from retailers offering deteriorated or worthless drugs.[43] The anti-arthritis drug Opren was withdrawn in late 1982, but not before a number of disturbing cases, despite advertisements for the drug in the *British Medical Journal* informing doctors, 'The side-effects story as a whole is very impressive indeed, as they are generally mild and transient.' The pain-killer Zomax was withdrawn by its American makers in 1983 following five deaths – though not until after it had been used by a million people in Britain; in the same year a US federal jury awarded over $4 million to a man who claimed that his mother had died from taking another drug, and that its makers had failed to report other deaths linked to its use in Europe before the drug was approved for sale in the USA.

Professor John Kaplan points out that, just as a weed is any plant growing where it is not wanted, so a side effect is a consequence of a drug use not wanted by its user. (For some people, excess salt has caused delirium and death.) Sir Derrick Dunlop said, 'Show me a drug with no side effect, and I'll show you a drug with no action.' It is scarcely feasible to calculate scientifically every drug's full effects upon every user, because no two people – or their perception of pain – respond equally to any particular drug (licit or illicit). However, in the past, as many as five years have elapsed between the first reports by doctors of significant adverse reactions to some drugs and the issuing of cautionary notices to prescribers by the UK Committee on the Safety of Medicines. Michael Meacher, MP, in February 1984 cited a case in Parliament where four drugs linked with twenty-nine deaths were still being prescribed and dispensed about 250 times a week, several months after they had been withdrawn. Dr Dannie Abse also criticizes some drug manufacturers whose warnings about the possibility of serious adverse reactions are printed 'in the smallest of type, legible only with a magnifying glass'.[44] Indirectly ingested substances also can have their dangers. Cattle are being injected with fattening drugs which are risky for human consumption; and at least one-third of all the beef cattle in Britain continue to be given hormone implants, despite the fact that the EEC's Scientific Committee on Food says there is not yet sufficient evidence to prove that the use of artificial hormones is safe. The WHO estimates that there have been some half a million cases annually – involving 9,200 deaths – of people being accidentally poisoned by pesticides: in Sri Lanka, the number of deaths in 1979 from pesticide poisoning – 938 – significantly exceeded the total of those from malaria, tetanus, polio, whooping cough and diphtheria combined.[45]

What can be done to reduce harm from drugs whilst at the same time not forgoing their benefits? For society seems hyper-sensitive to any damage which drugs may cause: one in 10,000 is considered an unacceptable risk in using drugs – yet people largely ignore that major surgery carries at least a one in 100 chance of something going seriously wrong, or that the use of any general anaesthetic can be potentially dangerous.[46] Several patients have stated that they wish to be allowed to continue taking Opren and Zomax, despite the risk, because of the relief these drugs give them. If it is the price of release from constant pain, you may be willing to consent to run a risk of danger from a drug – but that essentially requires your first being told completely frankly all the known facts about such risks. Only recently has the principle of drug data for consumers been grudgingly conceded. Information should be provided – for doctors, chemists, and patients – with any advertising and distribution of each drug, stating in simple and clear language how it works, what possible side effects to look for and what to do if these occur. It should also warn which drugs contain any potentially harmful additives (such as the yellow dye tartrazine, which can cause bronchial asthma and skin rashes): at present – inexplicably – while food manufacturers have to provide such details, drug firms do not.[47] All such data should be constantly updated; and licences should be withdrawn internationally for those drugs which have been superseded by more effective and safer products.

In an ideal world, research into drugs should be wholly separated from their marketing. (Possibly the advance of bio-technology may hasten this happening.) Meanwhile, developing countries in particular require international help to deal with pharmaceutical problems. The WHO has done its best to meet this need. In 1984 one hundred governments voted for it to develop a marketing and advertising code for drugs – a mandate it has in fact had since 1978 – despite sustained lobbying against this move by the USA and drug companies. (Britain voted for the proposal; West Germany and Japan abstained; the USA was the only country to vote against.) It is reported that the US, which provides a quarter of WHO's funds, has privately threatened to leave the world body should a mandatory drug marketing code ever be adopted. However, drugs are too powerful for society to leave their regulation to commercial interests. The poet may counsel us not to let daylight in on magic; but only when an individual has first been given the complete objective information on which to base a decision, will he be in a position to decide whether to consent to allow a drug to enter his body. The ethics of the international medical-scientific community should insist on nothing less.[48]

5

'Some More Poison?' – 'I Don't Mind If I Do':
Alcohol

'Ah, my Beloved, fill the Cup that clears
Today of past Regrets and future Fears:
Tomorrow! – Why, Tomorrow I may be
Myself with Yesterday's Seven thousand Years.'
The Rubáiyát of Omar Khayyám,
translated by Edward Fitzgerald

'Why do you drink?'
'It gives me the impression I'm alive.'
Chekhov, *Uncle Vanya*

'He who makes a beast of himself gets rid of the pain of being a man.'

Dr Johnson

Which is the world's most widely used psychotropic drug? Which has more than three-quarters of a million dependants in Britain and 10 million in the USA, causes more deaths in both America and Europe than murder does, and plays a part in over 50 per cent of violent crimes?

The total number of people dependent on alcohol is far larger than those on all other drugs (except for nicotine) put together. Alcoholic consumption in Britain, for example, has risen inexorably since the Second World War: per capita, the British now imbibe over twice as much as the Norwegians. Alcohol abuse is now estimated to be responsible for between 6,500 and 25,000 premature deaths a year in the UK. One in three UK drivers plus a quarter of all pedestrians who are killed in road accidents had an alcohol

124

level over the legal limit; and the annual total of people entering mental hospitals with alcoholism or related problems more than doubled in the decade up to 1975. So ubiquitously popular is alcohol in Western culture that it has made a take-over bid for the verb 'to drink'. Participants at conferences on drug abuse see no irony in propping up the bar late into the night.

The active ingredient in all alcoholic drinks – the one that changes mood and behaviour – is ethyl alcohol (ethanol); although fortunes are spent in advertised hype to try to pretend otherwise, all such drinks are merely ethyl alcohol flavoured for taste. It is a clear, colourless and almost odourless liquid that is less toxic than the wood or methyl alcohol contained in anti-freeze, paint-strippers and methylated spirit, or the isopropyl alcohol found in eau de Cologne or after-shave lotions which some people also tipple.[1] In 1986 it was methyl alcohol added to some Italian wines which caused injuries and death; in Austria the previous year some wine was adulterated with diethyleneglycol. Industrial alcohol can cause its drinkers irreversible blindness and death; only ethyl alcohol is comparatively safe to imbibe in moderation. Any alcohol we drink is absorbed from the stomach into the bloodstream and thence to the brain, since the liver can only process a limited amount at a time; the quickest way to get drunk would be to inject it.

Contrary to many people's delusion, alcohol is neither thirst-quenching nor a stimulant. All alcohol in fact has the opposite effect: its depression of the brain's functions induces a feeling of relaxation by making worries hazier; but it also blurs judgment, inhibition and self-control – as well as weakening an intention to drink less. The expert Malcolm Lowry described in his brilliant *Under the Volcano* how alcohol can have a habit of releasing a person's second self, normally kept hidden. It also speeds up drinkers' heart rate, enlarging the blood vessels on their skin surfaces and causing reddening of their face and shoulders. Dr John Havard, the Secretary of the British Medical Association, says, 'Alcohol is the most powerful depressant of the central nervous system available without a doctor's prescription. If it were being introduced now, it would be a prescribed drug.'

The European Economic Community has proposed that all alcoholic drinks should at least be labelled with the percentage of their alcohol content (the determinate factor), but any such idea is being resisted by the drink industry. Most beers and lagers in fact contain between 3 and 8 per cent ethyl alcohol by volume; cider 4–13 per cent; wines 9–15 per cent; fortified wines such as sherry, vermouth or port 15–22 per cent; liqueurs 25–50 per cent; and spirits 35–55 per cent. People, however, can develop into alcoholics on beer alone. Liqueurs, distilled with herbs, were originally used as medicines in medieval times; brandy too was regarded mainly as a medical aid and few spirits were drunk recreationally in England before the end of the seventeenth century, when 'Geneva' (as gin was first called) was popularized by William of Orange, whose soldiers drank it for 'Dutch courage'.[2] It was soon recognized as a cheaper and quicker way of getting drunk than beer ('drunk for a penny, dead drunk for two-pence'); consumption rose twentyfold, and by the mid-eighteenth century a quarter of Londoners were reputed to be drinking a pint of gin daily. One brand of gin was known as Strip Me Naked, because addicts used to pawn their clothes for the price of a glass. The social consequences were recorded by Fielding and Hogarth, but – as today – its spread was not discouraged by governments which benefited so richly from the duty on it. There were protests and rioting against any idea of controlling it; Lord Chesterfield's argument against attempting to control drinking through taxation was 'Would you lay a tax upon a breach of the Ten Commandments?', and Lord Harvey compared this to 'mortgaging the prostitution of one's wife or daughter'. As late as 1889, morphine was recommended in medical journals for the treatment of alcoholics since it 'calms in place of exciting the base of the passions, and hence is less productive of acts of violence and crime'. Today there are in Britain over 150,000 officially sanctioned centres which encourage alcoholic drug use and abuse – known as 'licensed premises', where new experimenters can consort with old addicts.

The average American devotes more than 5 per cent of his weekly budget to various kinds of alcohol. Nine out of ten people in Britain drink it in some degree: more than one in ten do so each day. The majority of people drink sensibly and with moderation, and derive sociable pleasure from doing so: small amounts, say, of up to a pint of beer or two glasses of wine a day cause no known harm and may help some people by relaxing tension. Social drinking usually has the benefit of some mutual control being exercised – unlike solitary drinking. Alcohol, however, is also a powerful drug: it acts on the nervous system like an anaesthetic and in large amounts is a poison that can kill. To a greater extent than several illegal drugs, alcohol causes physical deterioration. A drinker's liver is particularly vulnerable, since that is the part of his body which breaks down and oxidizes the alcohol he consumes: regular heavy drinking damages liver cells – their irreversible substitution by fibrous tissue being known as cirrhosis – as well as foetuses in pregnant mothers. The US Surgeon General has recommended that pregnant mothers should not drink any alcohol at all. Alcohol can also cause obesity (because it contains calories but few vitamins or minerals), heart disease, and high blood pressure; lead to sexual impotence in males ('brewers' droop'); damage the brain and nervous system, impairing – often irreversibly – intelligence, memory, co-ordination, sensation, muscle power, even when the drinker is sober; and also increase the likelihood of stomach ulcers and cancer of the mouth and throat. People have died from overdoses of acute alcoholic poisoning. In Britain, alcohol is the fourth largest cause of all premature deaths; in the USA it is the third biggest cause of illness, exceeded only by cancer and heart disease.

How alcoholic consumption and intoxication is inwardly experienced or outwardly expressed depends – as it does for other drugs – on the psychology and physique of the drinker as well as the context in which he drinks. The same quantity of alcohol is likely to have a different effect on a man or woman drinking alone from what it would at a party. Cultural expectations or who a person drinks with can be determinant; another influence is a person's beliefs about what booze does to him or her. *In vino veritas*: the symptoms of a drinker's disinhibition may vary from tears, loquacity, belligerence or sleepiness, to over-familiarity, guilt, song or maudlin despair.[3] Contrary to what almost every drinker believes, alcohol makes his thinking slower and more superficial. Heavy drinking in some societies is admired; in some it is regarded as comedy; in others a cause of shame. The Book of Proverbs (23:30–2), however, warns: 'They that tarry long at the wine; they that go to seek mixed wine . . . at the last it biteth like a serpent and stingeth like an adder.' Vomit and hangovers are only the short-term retribution. 'Drinking that results in regular loss of control means you're a lush,' a former drinker said.[4] If, to cope with his hangover, a dipsomaniac persists in further 'morning after' alcohol, he is showing a classic symptom of alcoholic dependency: Dylan Thomas, for instance, had a habit of drinking lines of light ales as soon as a pub opened to get over his hangovers. The 'hair of the dog' may – as for those who use heroin and other addictive drugs – postpone immediate physical and mental distress, but only does this at the price of greater addiction. As an old Chinese proverb puts it, 'First the man takes a drink; then the drink takes a drink; then the drink takes the man.' Individuals' experience varies: cirrhosis is not inevitable for all drinkers; on the other hand a person can be chronically dependent on alcohol without showing any of the usual signs of drunkenness.[5] Dependence can be psychological, with alcohol becoming increasingly important until it takes over entirely; or physical, when heightened tolerance causes withdrawal symptoms of shakiness, sweating, anxiety, insomnia, convulsions or delirium. As with barbiturates, such symptoms can take a matter of days or only hours to occur. The hallucinatory suffering of an alcoholic's delirium tremens (DTs) is one of the severest experiences of withdrawal from any psychotropic drug, being far more painful and dangerous than heroin withdrawal: it can resemble a nightmarish LSD trip, but one that lasts for two or three days. Drying-out recovery usually takes seven to ten days; though occasionally, unless treated, people may die from respiratory failure while withdrawing from alcohol.

Alcoholics, besides showing resentment towards abstainers or those people who drink less than themselves, can show obsessive persistence and cunning. One housewife recounted: 'I used to keep vodka in an Ajax bottle. We had a cooker that stood on a work surface and beneath it was a space that took a half-bottle of vodka lying on its side. The man I lived with then would take the dog out last thing at night for ten minutes and that's when I would drink.' Another toper hid bottles of what she disguised as her 'sauce' in the washing machine, with dramatic consequence when she forgot this before switching on. Although several narcotic addicts who survive their twenties mature out of their habit, alcoholism has no age cut-off. 'Most alcoholics', said Professor Sedon Bacon, 'hate liquor, hate drinking, hate the taste, hate the results, hate themselves for succumbing, but cannot stop.'

Dr Dannie Abse suggests that many alcoholics are people still fixated at an oral stage, and may have unconscious doubts regarding their sexual identity – which could explain the association of drinking with masculinity in Scottish and French culture.[6] Other studies have found no single explanation, although several describe a large incidence of drinkers with inferiority feelings and high anxiety.[7] Karl Menninger has perceptively portrayed alcoholic addiction as 'a form of self-destruction used to avert a greater self-destruction, deriving from elements of aggressiveness excited by thwarting, ungratified eroticism, and the feeling of a need for punishment from a sense of guilt relative to the aggressiveness'. The cause of death at Dylan Thomas's autopsy was described simply as 'insult to the brain'.

Each person who has a serious drinking problem is liable to affect and threaten – besides himself – the health, happiness and safety of family, friends, or workmates. The popular picture of the typical alcoholic as being a solitary tramp or wino is out of date: only 5 per cent of those with chronic alcoholic dependency are social derelicts, and even allowing for the smaller proportion of poor people who seek help for such problems, the majority of alcoholics are married people with homes and jobs. Significant factors which can induce alcoholism include: firstly, the ready availability of alcohol – publicans are fifteen times as likely as the average man to die from cirrhosis of the liver; secondly, boredom, loneliness, and separation from normal social and sexual relationships – among, for example, sailors, commercial travellers, journalists, some divorced or shy people; and thirdly, social pressure to drink (a doctor who works at a university describes that she sees 'students and teenagers, who originally didn't like beer or spirits, gradually programmed to drink more and more so they could regularly go drinking in pubs with their friends, because it's the thing to do').

One survey found that by the age of fourteen 92 per cent of boys and 85 per cent of girls in Britain have tasted alcohol: often introduced to it as exciting bravado by other teenagers.[8] A schoolgirl described the attraction of 'being taken for eighteen and getting away with it time and again'. Most young people copy the way they see their parents or peer group handling alcohol. In many schools today, it is spreading faster than other drug use. Adolescent slang words for alcoholic states are on the increase and there are now some 2,000 connected euphemisms: the word 'booze' dates from at least the fourteenth century; 'slugs' and 'shots' of whisky point to the macho connection. It has been suggested that among the reasons why the ratio of doctors and surgeons with alcoholism or liver cirrhosis is three times the national average is the formative tradition of heavy drinking amongst medical students. (One doctor with a drink problem piled all the drugs in his surgery into a bucket, which he left in his waiting-room with a note telling patients to help themselves and not to bother him, saying this was no more random a method of prescribing drugs than that used by most other doctors.) It is far from generally realized how rapidly tolerance to alcohol can develop – often after only a week of heavy use – and that once tolerance has been acquired, it quickly recurs if drinking is resumed after a period of abstinence.[9] Some doctors believe that human livers today can absorb alcohol less easily because of the amount of agri-chemicals contemporary people ingest.

Counsellors often advise client cases to minimize temptation and avoid off-licences; and to try to be happier rather than wallow in self-pity: 'If you're feeling very lonely, meet, or at least telephone, someone.' Although Whistler said, 'I drink to make my friends seem witty,' it is rare that alcohol makes a drinker (contrary to what he thinks) more amusing or good company; Dr Anthony Clare points out that, as regards creativity also, it is a great leveller – downwards: 'It drags the man of genius down while bemusing the second-rate into believing that he or she is up there with the gods' – or at least on the same cloud, sharing a lost weekend, with Scott Fitzgerald, Jack London, Dylan Thomas, Hemingway, Lowry, Brendan Behan or Eugene O'Neill. One writer who preferred the reality of sobriety to periodic oblivion was Dr Johnson, because, he explained to Boswell: 'It is so much better for a man never to lose the power over himself'; he conceded that abstinence might be a diminution of pleasure, ' . . . but I do not say a diminution of happiness. There is more happiness in being rational.' By contrast, an eloquent account of the changes alcohol can create or uncover in the human psychology has been given by the admittedly unusual Dennis Nilsen, prior to his recent conviction for several London murders. Mr Nilsen, a 37-year-old civil servant and former probationary policeman, described himself as a chronic alcoholic, and said that when he drank:

> I see myself drawn along and moved out of my isolated prison . . . I guess that I may be a creature – a creative psychopath – who, when in a loss of rationality situation, lapses temporarily into a destructive psychopath, a condition induced by rapid and heavy ingestion of alcohol. At the

subconscious root lies a sense of total social isolation and a
desperate search for a sexual identity . . . I am not in sympathy
generally with the state of women who are the worse for wear
for drink . . . In the normal course of my life I feel I have
normal powers of mental rationality and morality. When under
pressure of work and extreme pain of social loneliness and utter
misery I am drawn, compulsively, to means of temporary
escape from reality. This is achieved by taking increasing
draughts of alcohol and plugging into stereo music which
mentally removes me to a high plane of ecstasy, joy and tears.
This is a totally emotional experience. This glorious experience
and feeling is conjured up in this manner. I relive experiences
from childhood to the present – taking out the bad bits.

Public attitudes towards heavy drinking, and hence any social
control of it, vary within regional as well as national cultures. The
rate of mortality from liver cirrhosis in Scotland is almost twice that
of England and Wales, and a Scots Chief Inspector of Police said
there is no doubt that alcohol is the country's greatest drug problem.
Among the reasons advanced for this are: 'In the past five years
there's been five or six new pubs opened and very little else – no
swimming pools or sports grounds; I think this is one of the main
causes of under-age drinking. . . . Our pubs, of course, are places
that predominantly sell alcohol. We don't have any of the café pubs
of some other parts of the world where you can have been if you like,
but equally and without social pressure to do otherwise, you can
drink a cup of coffee or a glass of orange juice . . . You see
emphasized in so many advertisements that being a real man is
taking strong drink, and you want to display your membership of
the club . . . Advertising about lifestyles subtly associates alcohol
with a desirable way of life and implies it's sophisticated, exclusive
or luxurious to drink regularly.' One headmaster traced the cause to
teenage loneliness: 'not being one of the gang: drink is the easy way
out'. To adolescents, adult society's signals about alcohol are
ambiguous and confusing in the extreme. Drinking and intoxication
are publicly simultaneously cheered and disapproved. Sports clubs
– sometimes with violent drunks as supporters – accept sponsorship
from drink manufacturers, who are delighted that star-heroes
promote their products to young fans: the image of this drug-ring
was only temporarily dented by the Brussels football tragedy of

1985, when mainly drunken fans killed thirty-eight people. Alcohol remains a strong social symbol as well as a powerful drug. The giving and receiving of alcohol symbolizes a wish for friendship: it is a traditional means to instigate or promote a relationship, which it can equally be a way of cementing or dissolving. Hence the disdain often held for a man who refuses a drink, and also the ritual and rules which determine who buys a round.[10]

Both the number and proportion of women drinkers have recently risen, helped by the prettying-up of pubs, drink advertising campaigns targeted specifically at women, and the spread of wine bars and supermarkets where women can buy supplies of drink without feeling conspicuous. The number of females admitted to hospital for alcoholism has more than doubled in recent years: Women are likely to be more physically vulnerable than men to the same amount of alcohol, because they tend to have lower body weight and smaller livers; due to the effect of female hormones on the metabolism of drugs, their response to alcohol can also vary according to their menstrual cycle, and whether they take oral contraceptives. Nothing reveals more clearly society's ambivalence towards alcohol than the double standards it shows (as with promiscuity) towards male and female drinkers. Whereas getting drunk is often thought proof of a 'real' man, and boys get hog-whimperingly legless as part of their initiation into manhood, women who drink much are made to feel ashamed. One in every ten wives who are married to alcoholic husbands leave them, whereas the proportion of husbands who leave alcoholic wives is nine out of ten. 'Drunken women are totally unacceptable to society,' says Rosie Boycott. 'It's worse for a woman to be alcoholic than mad; this has to do with the myth of motherhood: women are meant to be perfect. My friend would be visited by her family when she was ill in hospital, but never at the clinic.' Although female drinkers are more reluctant to seek help for fear of being judged and condemned, today one-third of Alcoholics Anonymous's members are women (whereas twenty years ago the proportion was only a fifth), although many women with problems prefer to seek help from women-only groups.

At the same time, drinking is rising overall, amongst all ages of both sexes. Britons consume 50 per cent more alcohol a head than they did a generation ago. In England and Wales, convictions for drunkenness offences climbed from 47,717 in 1950 to 161,803 in 1977, while in Scotland such offences known to the police rose in the same period from 9,013 to 79,501 – an increase of 782 per cent. Apart from the boost due to the fact that alcohol is today comparatively cheaper, expenditure on it has also increased as a proportion of consumers' budgets in Britain, as Table 3 shows.

Table 3: **Comparative percentage increase in items of UK consumers' expenditure between 1963 and 1973**

Food	6.3		
Clothing	34.8		
Beer	49.1		
Spirits	102.6	Total alcohol	76.0
Wine	150.0		

In 1984 Britain's imports of champagne – 'the cocaine of alcohol' – rose by 58 per cent, making it the world's biggest importer of the recreational drug. Overall, alcohol consumption and abuse in Britain has at least doubled over the last two decades. It is today responsible for killing far more people than all other drugs (except nicotine) combined. The suicide rate of alcoholics is fifty-eight times that of non-alcoholics, and drinkers' overall life expectancy is twelve years shorter. 'Alcohol intoxication is involved in the deaths of over 500 young people each year,' Professor John Strong[11] points out. 'Alcohol abuse is also responsible in Britain for 80 per cent of deaths from fire, 65 per cent of head injuries and 35 per cent of fatal accidents – besides the loss of at least 8 million working days a year.' The annual economic cost of alcoholic damage in Britain is now estimated to exceed £1,600 million, and in the USA $100,000 million, but the real cost in human terms is beyond price. 'No matter how large the heroin problem,' says Dr Anthony Clare, 'at the moment it really pales into insignificance beside the enormous impact of alcohol abuse.'[12]

The pattern is similar elsewhere: alcohol consumption has risen dramatically in almost every country in the world outside Islam. Consumption in both Hong Kong and North Korea has increased by a factor of eight in the last twenty years; in Gabon it is up by more than eleven times. Japan drinks over 200 million cases of sake annually; Brazil each year consumes 88 million cases of the local distilled spirit cachaca; Western non-communist countries now swallow 60 million cases of vodka a year – more than they do of gin or rum. The nations with the highest consumption of alcoholic spirit are Hungary, East Germany and Poland, which drink some fifteen bottles of spirits a head annually: nearly half as much again as either the USSR or the USA, which themselves both consume twice as much per head as the UK. East Germany's consumption per capita is very nearly twice that of the average West German. Almost half the hospital patients in the Soviet Union are reported to have illnesses connected with alcoholism; in Czechoslovakia, some 2 per cent of the population are considered to be alcoholics. Child alcoholism is a widespread problem in Portugal, especially in northern areas where it is customary for mothers to add wine to babies' bottles, as well as to give children brandy 'so as to make them strong'. In 1984 Professor David Hawks warned that in Australia alcohol abuse was reaching the proportions of an epidemic, with the number of alcoholics amounting to 250,000 out of a population of only 15 million. The Antipodean tradition of associating heavy drinking with masculine prowess is a legacy of the early settlers, as it is in parts of mid-Western USA; one-fifth of Australian hospital beds are taken up with alcoholic cases, and the cost of alcohol to Australian industry has been estimated at A$1 billion a year.

Europe, with only one-ninth of the world's population, still accounts for almost half the total consumption of commercial alcohol, but alcohol manufacturers – several of which have recently been taken over by tobacco companies – now concentrate on aggressive marketing in the Third World. The WHO reports that beer consumption in the developing countries has increased by a factor of at least four in the last two decades, boosted by vigorous advertising especially aimed to convert non-drinkers: in Paraguay it has risen by a factor of eight, and in the Congo by more than ten. Greenland's alcoholism has overtaken tuberculosis as its biggest social problem. In an attempt to stem the increase of drunken violence there, a coupon system was tried in 1979: seventy-two coupons a month were issued to each drinker, with one coupon allowing the purchase of a beer, six for a bottle of wine, and eighteen for one of whisky, gin or brandy. The system, however, was not popular and was undermined by a black market. By contrast, the South African government is vigorously promoting the sale of beer to its black population, since this provides the chief source of revenue for the Pretoria-appointed 'administration boards' who own beerhalls in the black areas. The Port Natal Administration Board in Durban, for example, derives an annual estimated profit of $7 million from the sale of its Zulu beer, so that recently the authorities there called on employers selflessly to encourage their African workers to consume two litres before starting work.

> Dred delitable drynk & thou shalt do the betere.
> Mesure is medicine theiy thou muche yerne.
> Al is not good to the gost that the gut [ask]ith,
> Ne liflode to the lycam that lef is to the soule.[13]

Ever since man's Neolithic forebears accidentally discovered the intoxicating effect of fermented grain, he has been undecided what to do about it. For years it was the only available anaesthetic. Jesus is recorded as enjoying wine, but Muhammad eventually came to forbid it. The Prophet's first Revelation did not condemn alcohol: 'And of the fruits of the date, palm and grapes, whence you derive strong drink and good nourishment. Lo! there is indeed a portent for people who have sense.' His second Revelation, however, revealed greater caution: 'In both strong drink and games of chance is great sin, and utility for men: but the sin of them is greater than their usefulness.' By the time of his fourth Revelation the Prophet had no doubt that drink was 'an infamy of Satan's handiwork'. This progressive prohibition may also have had a religious motive, since wine played an important part in Christian as well as some pagan rituals.[14]

A similar view was supported by a minority of infidels such as La Bruyère, who exclaimed: 'If we heard it said of orientals that they habitually drink a liquor which went to their heads, deprived them of reason and made them vomit, we should say "How very barbarous!"'[15] The first Methodist campaigns against alcohol abuse in England during the eighteenth and early nineteenth century concentrated on the harm caused by spirits and especially gin and rum, rather than all alcoholic drinks: John Wesley himself described wine as 'one of the noblest cordials'. In 1835 a national society of teetotallers was founded, and several thousand people signed a pledge of voluntary abstinence in Ireland as well as England. Across the Atlantic, the state of Maine passed the first Prohibition Act as early as 1851: cider was excepted, but otherwise alcoholic liquor could only be taken by medical prescription. Two years later in Britain, an Alliance movement was formed 'to procure the total and immediate legislative suppression of the traffic in all intoxicating

135

liquors' – though this idea was attacked by J. S. Mill as a threat to individual freedom. In Sweden, the city of Gothenburg tried taking the supply of liquor out of the hands of commercial enterprise and placing it under the control of a disinterested board. The aim of the experiment was to reduce excess alcohol and encourage beer in place of hard liquor; its success was copied throughout Sweden and Norway, and a similar plan was advocated in vain by Joseph Chamberlain and forty-nine other MPs in Britain in 1876.[16] Denmark is today about to adopt the same policy.

Twelve other American states followed Maine's example and became 'dry'. By 1890 the National Prohibition Party – aiming to hold the balance of power between Democrats and Republicans – won its first seat in Congress. At social functions at the White House disgruntled visitors reported that 'iced water flowed like champagne'. In saloon bars, however, people were beginning to treat each other with rounds of drinks, like party-goers proselytizing cocaine today. In response, prohibitionists in 1893 founded the Anti-Saloon League which endorsed candidates from either of the major parties provided they backed Prohibition. The First World War assisted the abstentionist cause: several of the brewers opposing Prohibition were attacked for their German origins, while industrialists lent their support to temperance because they thought it would ensure more reliable labour. During the war the Anti-Saloon League campaigned with the slogan that alcohol was 'unAmerican, pro-German, youth-corrupting and treasonable'. In Britain, the court of King George V renounced drink for the duration of the war; Lloyd George introduced licensing hours for public houses, and in 1916 declared that, while Britain was fighting Germany, Austria and drink, 'the greatest of these three deadly foes is drink'. During the hostilities, consumption of spirits fell by half, and the total of convictions for being drunk and disorderly dropped from almost 200,000 to less than 30,000 a year. The D'Abernon Committee, which was set up to consider alcohol as a drug in 1917, none the less found that Britain was still spending more than twice as much on alcohol as it did on bread, and that toal expenditure on alcohol was as great as the whole peace-time revenue of HM government.

Prohibition nationwide began in the USA with the passing of the Volstead Act together with the 18th Amendment in 1920. Leaks and loopholes sprang up immediately. The American government was forced to exempt communion wine, bottles of which soon found their way to numerous other supper tables. Doctors and chemists dispensed spirits for a surprisingly heavy number of 'medical' cases. The demand for industrial alcohol expanded as people learnt how to redistil it as a drink. With the help of the Mafia, moonshine and bootleg smuggling flourished: Canadian and British boats ran consignments of rum and whisky – making as large a profit as earlier from opium in China – despite the indignant anger of William Jennings Bryan: ocean-going rum-runners would anchor just outside the USA's twelve-mile limit, while mobsters ran the liquor ashore in motor-boats. Deaths increased from lethal forms of adulterated moonshine, as corruption percolated throughout the law enforcement system, helped by the tacit support of much of American public opinion. Gangsters were able to pose as public servants and benefactors; Al Capone smugly philosophized: 'I make my money by supplying a public demand. If I break the law my customers, who number hundreds of the best people in Chicago, are as guilty as I am. The only difference is that I sell and they buy . . . I call myself a businessman.' President Hoover began to grow disillusioned with what he called 'this noble experiment'; by 1930, more than half a million Americans had been arrested for drink offences, and another 35,000 had perished from drinking illegal hootch. F. D. Roosevelt, faced with the Depression, realized from the continuing demand for liquor that a duty imposed upon it would raise revenue as great as income tax. He put the issue to the individual states to decide, which resulted in the repeal of Prohibition in 1932.[17]

Illegal distilleries still flourish on a small scale in several places, particularly on both sides of the Irish border. In 1984 the police in Counties Tyrone and Antrim seized seven big stills which had been selling 100 per cent proof poteen for IR£4 a bottle, in competition with whisky's price of over IR£8. In Ireland private enterprise has for generations distilled moonshine spirits out of sugar, yeast and treacle, which are left to ferment for ten days before being boiled. Older people also use the raw spirit for rubbing on rheumatic aches and pains; it tastes smoothly fiery, not unlike tequila – though a local police officer commented: 'With some of the bad stuff, you'd be better off drinking paraquat,' and some cases of resulting blindness have been reported. The maximum penalty for those caught making poteen is a scarcely swingeing fine of IR£1,000 and/or six months' imprisonment. Recently the illegal Irish trade has been near modernized by the introduction of mobile stills hidden in vans, and a modest export trade has started to England and the USA. In the USSR the authorities have had to introduce a cheaper brand of state vodka in order to compete with the flood of home-produced 'samogen' spirits (known by a variety of names ranging from 'white lightning' in Georgia to 'bimber' in Poland), which are estimated to total 1,500 million litres annually, and are 80 per cent proof.

Since abstinence is unlikely in either Western or Eastern-bloc countries unenthusiastic to accept the severe Muslim penalties against alcohol, what else can be done to limit the damage from its abuse? Several of the lessons of Prohibition are relevant when considering drugs policies generally. One option, which would permit the moderate enjoyment of alcohol while attempting to curb its excesses, would be some system of rationing. Between 1917 and 1955, Swedes could buy alcohol only with a ration book – which was not issued to people under the age of twenty-five, to married women or to known alcoholics. At one stage, the permitted allowance rose to four litres of spirits a month, but the system collapsed because virtually everybody felt compelled to acquire their full ration and sell any surplus. Recently 150 Swedish professors of medicine have urged that an alcohol ration with a maximum of 1.5 litres a month should be reintroduced to mitigate the medical and social problems caused by alcoholism; although alcoholic consumption has not grown in Sweden as much as it has elsewhere, doctors there point out that it is killing more than 7,000 people a year.[18]

For governments reluctant to limit by rationing, the alternative control mechanism is to influence the price through taxation. In Britain, alcohol's price in recent years has become progressively cheaper compared with other items on the retail index: it now requires less than an average of two hours' work to earn the price of a bottle of whisky, compared with six and a half hours a generation ago – whereas it takes longer to earn the price of a loaf of bread today than previously. In both the 1985 and 1986 budgets the UK Chancellor of the Exchequer raised duty on spirits by less than the rate of inflation, because he wanted to help the whisky industry. Professor Robert Kendall, pointing out that the amount of alcohol consumed is largely determined by government policy on its price plus controls on its availability through opening hours and outlets, says: 'The most important single act would be for the government to increase the price of alcohol slowly year by year for a decade.' Leaving aside argument about the morality of a policy whereby eventually only the rich could afford to harm themselves, the reality is – as Sir George Young, MP, admits – that the prevention of alcoholism is 'not a medical but a political problem'. Some 90 per cent of the voters in Christian democracies drink some form of alcohol. In Britain 700,000 people are also directly employed in its manufacture, distribution and sale, including the export trade. The British government is in fact planning to extend licensing hours, allegedly to encourage tourism. Significantly, however, ministers pusillanimously refuse even to publish the key 1979 Study on Alcohol Policy carried out by the UK government Think Tank – despite the fact that it has been published in Sweden.

The Study says that, in the absence of a firm government initiative, misuse of alcohol will inevitably continue to increase. 'We suggest that the initial goal of seeking to prevent per capita alcohol consumption from rising above present levels is both feasible and necessary, and that it should be coupled with measures to prevent levels of alcohol-related disability from rising.' It goes on to urge the UK government to adopt a co-ordinated policy (equally necessary in other countries), including: public education programmes; tougher drinking-and-driving laws; a commitment to hold consumption level at no higher than its present rate, by at least maintaining the real level of duty and tax on alcohol; better treatment facilities; and establishing an Advisory Council of Alcohol Policy.

The Study roundly castigates government departments for turning their backs on the problem. Alcohol constitutes the commonest cause of recurrent absenteeism from work. Here, the Study suggests, is the key place to identify and tackle abuse: cases are often easier to recognize because of decreased performance; a job is a significant incentive to reform; and everybody – whether capitalist or socialist – has an interest in achieving a healthier and happier work-force. Both Canada and France have recently introduced new ideas to help employees cure alcoholism; and there are over 25,000 programmes for treatment, rehabilitation and prevention in companies in the USA, which is recently taking much firmer steps than Britain to reduce damage from alcohol abuse. In twenty US states people cannot buy an alcoholic drink until they are aged twenty-one, and in nine other states together with the District of Columbia they cannot purchase spirits before that age. President Reagan has recently signed a Bill to encourage this age-limit throughout the nation, by cutting federal highway funds for any state which refuses to accept the minimum within two years – even though at the President's 1985 inauguration a star singer sang 'One More for the Road', holding a glass in his hand. Research indicates that at least 1,250 American lives would be saved each year if every state raised the drinking age to twenty-one. As a further deterrent, resulting from a recent decision by the Supreme Court in New Jersey, party hosts as well as saloon and restaurant owners are now held legally liable for accidents caused by their drunk guests. Several states lowered their drinking age during the Vietnam War, arguing that if a teenager could die fighting, he should be allowed to die drinking; this led to a sharp rise in alcohol-related accidents, and during the late 1960s, more people were killed on the roads of America by alcohol than were slain in the War. Nevertheless, drinking while driving is permitted at present by no less than twenty-six of the fifty US states: A motorist can drive on roads across the country from Florida to Canada, drinking non-stop with legal impunity for the entire 3,700 miles.

Oslo's threat of a year's jail sentence for drivers who fail a breathalyser test has resulted in most people going home from parties by public transport. It is difficult to argue why in Britain motorists should not be stopped for random tests, as a deterrent against drunken driving, especially since the police are legally permitted to stop pedestrians. Anthony Clare points out:

> Whenever anyone so much as breathes opposition to the current lily-livered approach to drunken driving and suggests that we take serious action, every hack in the land emerges from taverns and winebars, pubs and lounges, to shriek that the Gestapo are around the corner. The racket kicked up by the so-called 'libertarian lobby' conveniently drowns the moans of the maimed flooding into hard-pressed casualty departments up and down the land. Everyone conveniently forgets – or perhaps some just don't know – that the police already have 'unfettered discretionary powers' to take someone to a place of safety, such as a hospital or police station, if they so much as suspect him of suffering from mental disorder.[19]

In addition, the system of duty-free alcohol on planes takes up weight and space, besides being a fire hazard, and gives a tax benefit only to those already well-off enough to fly abroad.

What help or treatment is available for alcoholics? Since the average family doctor has 250 patients with an alcohol problem, he rarely has time to give them all sufficient diagnosis, counselling or support. Until E. M. Jellinek argued in 1960 that alcoholism was a disease,[20] it was seldom accepted to be a medical problem: most people arrested for drunkenness were left to dry out overnight in jail. The new medical concept of the problem at least reduces the social stigma of alcoholism and encourages more of such dependents to seek help. On the other hand, many people believe it would be unfortunate if the 'disease' approach led to the condonation of alcoholic cases who absolve themselves from any responsibility or feel that their problem is inevitable. Contemporary research has questioned the validity of two previously held views: first, that all alcoholics suffer from the same disease, and second, that they all should aim for total abstinence. The contemporary approach believes that each case requires individual diagnosis, backed by a programme of counselling, support and a target, which essentially should aim to reduce the life problems associated with a dangerous level of drinking.[21] Unfortunately, in the public health service facilities for alcoholics are very overstretched, and many people cannot afford £7,000 for in-patient treatment at a private clinic.

One treatment technique is to use aversion drugs, such as Antabuse (containing disulfiram as its key component), which, when taken regularly, remain in the bloodstream and block the alcohol's breakdown in the body, causing unpleasantly strong reactions if any alcohol is drunk for some days afterwards.[22] (Anyone who uses such drugs should remember that vinegar, and some types of medicines or cough sweets contain alcohol and glycerol.) As a recent development of this approach, an anti-alcohol implant in the wall of a drinker's abdomen can be used which will continue the results of such aversion drugs for six to nine months. In order to be effective, such a treatment requires the full co-operation of an alcoholic patient; a number of people convicted of alcoholic-related offences have consented to it under the threat of being given a prison sentence as the alternative. Aversion treatment nevertheless has its critics: 'Alcoholism comes in people rather than in bottles,' says one, 'booze isn't the illness, but merely a symptom of an illness that can only be treated when booze is removed. And booze can only be removed when the alcoholic wants it removed, when he or she reaches their own, personal gutter. Fear never kept anyone sober.'

Reformed alcoholics often flow with evangelical fervour strongly laced with confessions: 'This is because drunks are constantly asking for help,' one of them said, 'and it's wonderful to be able to help other people.' Alcoholics Anonymous (AA) is the principal mutual-help fellowship organization that offers group treatment and is flourishing throughout many (mainly Western) countries. It is the model which has influenced other organizations such as Narcotics Anonymous, described in Chapter 12 below.[23] AA was started at Akron, Ohio, in 1935 by a surgeon and a New York stockbroker, both of whom admitted to being 'hopeless drunks' but were impressed by the religious Oxford Group movement's precepts of 'confession, honesty, talking out of emotional problems, unselfishness, making reparations and praying to God as personally conceived'.[24] The start was slow: it took four years to gather the first hundred members into three groups. During that time, however, AA formulated its distinctive Twelve Steps to Recovery, based on its core idea that members admit they are 'powerless' over alcohol which has made their lives 'unmanageable', and that they must recognize 'you can't overcome it alone, but you alone can overcome it'. Growth since has been impressive: in Mexico 4,000 groups have been formed in the last fifteen years. The first UK group was started in London in 1948: today there are 2,000 groups in Britain, and throughout the world more than 40,000 groups containing well over 1 million members in a hundred different countries.[25] Such expansion certainly shows that AA is meeting a previously unfulfilled need, particularly for those whose drinking problems stem from some form of loneliness. AA's contention is that alcoholism is a progressive illness, and it asks from its members a lifelong commitment ('a day at a time') to total abstinence, believing (without any real scientific proof) that alcoholics possess a constitutional abnormality which prevents them from drinking normally. A survey of AA showed that a quarter of its members attending meetings had not had a drink for over five years, and that some 90 per cent of each annual intake keep off drink and say they intend to remain active members.[26]

The Economist recently estimated that alcoholism overall is costing businesses and governments across the world more than $100 billion a year.[27] It is obvious that to change attitudes to alcohol abuse will require much greater courage from ministers, together with a real commitment to proper education about the damage it causes. The role of the rest of society in not pressing alcohol on drinkers can be, literally, vital. Members of the American Medical Association have proposed that bottles of alcohol should carry health warnings similar to those on cigarette packets. Each person has a right to better information about the potential risks of inappropriate drinking – which should be presented at least as fully as the glamorous image peddled by drink-pushers. The recent gradual waking up by most members of the public to the risks of smoking hardly seems to have started in the case of alcohol. (So far, Yugoslavia is almost the only non-Muslim country to have banned alcohol advertising.) The real treatment to help this problem is inseparable from better education; but in the UK, government expenditure on health education about alcohol is less than 5 per cent of the £109 million budget the alcohol industry annually spends on counter-persuasion.[28] Is it coincidence that most of the media which welcome drink advertisements seem to give far less coverage to the problems of alcohol addicts than they do to dependants on other drugs?

6

The Fatal Habit: Tobacco

'Pernicious weed! whose scent the fair annoys,
Unfriendly to society's chief joys.'

William Cowper

Which drug – obtained from the most widely cultivated non-food
plant in the world – has killed more people in this century than has
war, yet whose pushers, far from being arrested, are rewarded with
public honours and a royal warrant in addition to financial fortunes?

Pharmacological research shows that smoking is an exceptionally
fast and efficient way of getting a drug to act on one's body. Shortly
after the European discovery of America, Gololamo Benzoni reported his amazement that the Indians appeared to be intoxicating
themselves by drinking tobacco smoke. When Bartolomé de las
Casas criticized the Spanish colonists on Hispaniola for copying
such a 'disgusting habit', he recorded: 'they found it impossible to
give it up. I cannot understand what enjoyment or advantage they
derive from it.' Sailors carried the fatal habit to Europe, where
tobacco initially became popular as a prophylactic panacea for
everything from headaches and syphilis to cancer and worms. Even

children were encouraged to use it. Nearly a century later in 1586, Sir Walter Ralcigh introduced tobacco from Virginia to the English court, and made pipe-smoking for pleasure fashionable; in *The Faerie Queene* Spenser described tobacco as 'divine'. Partly motivated by his dislike of Raleigh, however, King James I of England and VI of Scotland published – initially anonymously – in 1604 his polemical *Counterblaste to Tobacco*: its 'manifold abuses of this vile custome', he said, were 'loathsome to the eye, hateful to the nose, harmful to the braine, dangerous to the lungs, and in the black stinking fume thereof nearest resembling the horrible Stigian smoke of the pit that is bottomless'. He increased by a factor of forty the customs duty of twopence a pound that Queen Elizabeth had placed on the import of tobacco: the first experiment to control drug use by imposing a heavy tax. When the inevitable smuggling resulted, James farmed out the collection of the duty. In France, by contrast, Louis XIII forbade the use of tobacco unless this was ordered by a physician; but Richelieu made a profitable state monopoly of it, which continues to this day. Both governments became dependent on the drug's revenue, as they were later to do in the case of alcohol.

The economy of the colony of Virginia came to be so identified with growing tobacco that Virginians used it as money. Pepys meanwhile employed tobacco in an attempt to ward off the Great Plague of 1665. However, among the grumbles against it was that it caused male impotence and sterility:

> Tobacco, that outlandish weed
> It spends the brain and spoils the seed,
> It dulls the sprite, it dims the sight;
> It robs the woman of her right.

Other countries were less permissive: the Swiss placed the prohibition of tobacco amongst the Ten Commandments: Turkey mutilated, and the Pope excommunicated, smokers; in both China and Russia they were executed; in Iran they were killed by having molten lead poured down their throats, while German smokers faced the death penalty until the end of the seventeenth century. Not one of these deterrents succeeded. In America, Massachusetts tried to forbid smoking in other people's company. Dr Benjamin Rush – one of the signatories of the American Declaration of Independence – called for a ban on it in 1798 on the grounds that it was not only unhealthy and anti-social, but it increased a person's thirst for strong liquor, so that in time the Evangelical and Non-conformist anti-smoking alliance joined forces with the temperance campaigners. The British, meanwhile, acquired the habit of smoking cigarettes from Turks during the Crimean War; cigarette-making machinery lowered smokers' costs and widened the weed's popularity. In the nineteenth century tobacco was still being medicinally advocated by some doctors – to be taken either as snuff, by injection, as an infusion, or conversely by its smoke being blown into the rectum.[1] Its powerful principal constituent, nicotine, was isolated in 1828, but as late as 1901 the pharmacological authority W. Hale-White was still recommending it as a valuable drug for treating – of all things – respiratory disorders.[2] Long before in 1761, however, others had noticed the relationship between nasal cancer and tobacco dust among workers who were manufacturing snuff. Twenty years later Sir Percival Potts announced his discovery that scrotal cancer in chimney sweeps was caused by the tars contained in soot. By the 1860s the *Dictionary of Daily Wants* was warning the public about the habit-forming nature of tobacco smoking, saying that 'The occurrence of cancer in those who habitually smoke from a short pipe . . . are notorious: further there is a tendency to disease of the throat and air passages when this indulgence is followed to any great extent.'

Why smokers and governments have for so long contrived to ignore the evidence concerning damage caused by smoking is a recurrent mystery. It is now over twenty-four years since the British Royal College of Physicians warned that '. . . cigarette smoking is the most likely cause of the recent world-wide increase of deaths from lung cancer, the death rate from which is at present higher in Britain than in any other country in the world.'[3] Two years later the US Surgeon-General reported that 'Cigarette smoking is causally related to lung cancer in men . . . [it] is the most important of the causes of chronic bronchitis . . . [it] increases the risk of dying from chronic bronchitis and emphysema.'[4] Not many women smoked before the Second World War, but by the date of this warning 42 per cent had taken up the habit. In 1971 the Royal College of Physicians was warning in even stronger terms 'cigarette smoking is now as important a cause of death as were the great epidemic diseases such as typhoid, cholera and tuberculosis . . .'[5] Six years later its next report highlighted a further danger: the link between smoking and the cause of most deaths, coronary heart disease; but also warned:

'Patients who ultimately die from chronic bronchitis or emphysema usually endure about ten years of distressing breathlessness before they die . . . Between 2.5 and 4 out of every 10 cigarette smokers will die because of their smoking.'[6] Only two years later the US Surgeon-General presented an even more devastating bill of indictment:

Cigarette smoking is causally related to lung cancer in both men and women . . . is a significant causative factor in cancer of the larynx . . . the development of oral cancer . . . cancer of the oesophagus . . . is related to cancer of the pancreas . . . is one of the three major independent risk factors for heart attack . . . and sudden cardiac death . . . a major risk factor in arteriosclerotic peripheral vascular disease . . . a cause of chronic obstructive lung disease . . . increases the risk of foetal death . . . [7]

His successor in 1982 concluded unequivocally that 'cigarette smoking . . . is the chief, single, avoidable cause of death in our society, and the most important public health issue of our time.'[8] In Eire, the health warning on packets of cigarettes now minces no words: 'Smoking kills'. Dr Richard Pollin, the Director of the US National Institute of Drug Abuse, describes cigarette smoking as being worse than heroin and now the most serious and widespread form of addiction in the world.

How has it come about that this seemingly mild habit has caused tens of millions of people to 'die for a smoke'; and currently continues to cause the premature deaths each year of 355,000 people in the USA, 140,000 in West Germany, 100,000 in Britain and at least another 250,000 elsewhere in Europe?[9] Four out of five smokers say they want to give up the habit but cannot face nicotine withdrawal. They include even chest surgeons who are in close contact with tobacco's horrific results in their daily work. Hospital patients have been known to resume smoking as soon as they emerge from an operation for lung cancer. 'Cigarette smoking', Dr Michael Gossop points out, 'is one of the most addictive of all drug habits. It is more likely to produce dependence than using either barbiturates or alcohol: the nearest drug habit, in terms of the risk of becoming dependent, is injecting heroin.'[10] Although almost everybody's first experience of tobacco is nauseating, research shows that out of every hundred young people who smoke more than one cigarette, eighty-five will continue the habit. This happens despite the fact that, so far from filling any cultural, spiritual or nutritional need, smoking is ostensibly disliked and condemned by many of those who practise it. Smokers have variously claimed tobacco to be either a minor stimulant or a minor sedative: depending on whether a cigarette is smoked in short puffs or deep drags, a smoker can be briefly aroused or calmed. Most smokers inhale, as a way to self-administer nicotine: the time taken for the active constituents of tobacco to travel from the lungs to the brain is about seven seconds – roughly the same as when a drug is injected into a major vein.

Not every smoker may be aware that raw nicotine is among the most potent poisons known: one drop of pure nicotine, extracted from tobacco, is capable of killing a man within a matter of minutes. New research shows that it affects the release and synthesis of brain chemicals, neuropeptides, and probably the body's own endorphines. It can also increase the tolerance of pain, and makes people eat less sweet food. Many people think only heavy smokers are at risk: in fact a third of smoking-related deaths occur to smokers of fewer than twenty cigarettes a day. There is no such thing as a safe number of cigarettes (or of pinches of snuff, each of which provides as much nicotine as smoking a cigarette): each single cigarette smoked reduces a smoker's lifespan by five minutes. Nicotine harms smokers' cardio-vascular systems, but the really lethal damage in smoking is due to tar, which causes cancers, plus the carbon monoxide and other gases which are responsible for heart disease and broncho-pulmonary trouble. Besides the immediate results of coughing and bronchitis, other long-term damage appears later: smokers are markedly more likely than non-smokers to develop stomach ulcers, coronaries, diseases of the digestive tract, and weakening of the heart muscles.[11] As a final blow to the macho image of smokers that tobacco advertising tries so hard to promote, recent research by French doctors – corroborating a seventeenth-century accusation – suggests that smoking can cause the restricted blood circulation which is a principal reason for male impotence. Both women and men who wish to conceive a child are now advised to give up smoking; and pregnant women who smoke risk a miscarriage as well as causing harm to their unborn offspring: such children run double the risk of developing leukaemia, as well as kidney cancer and lymphoma – although British surveys show that more than one-third of mothers continue to smoke during pregnancy. Lung cancer has now overtaken breast cancer as the commonest of all causes of death in women. A recent report from Harvard notes that former smokers are as likely as former heroin users to revert to their habit; and that people who smoke may increase their likelihood of getting Alzheimer's disease by a factor of four. Although the act of smoking itself wreaks the most destruction, it is nicotine which hooks the addicts: the American National Cancer Institute is consequently considering whether it might be better for people who are addicted to nicotine to bypass smoking by taking the drug through chewing-gum or an inhaler, and other research is concentrating on steroid injections of drugs such as corticotrophin, which has helped some smokers to stop for periods of several months.

What type of people continue the fatal habit in the face of such a conclusive battery of warnings about its dangers? Research indicates that people who smoke change jobs more often, divorce more frequently, and have more traffic accidents than non-smokers; that they consume greater quantities of alcohol and caffeine; and are more prone to exhibit anxiety, neuroticism and hysteria.[12] Psychoanalysts point to smokers' oral need for a breast or phallic substitute, or to their unconscious desire to set something alight.[13] Several smokers use the fear of putting on weight as an excuse for their reluctance to stop. Most agree, however, that the key influence is the social example of other smokers: friends, film-stars or fellow-workers who smoke are insidiously infectious. For a large number of people, smoking is a social prop: many smokers have never unlearnt a teenage habit they adopted as a defence against their gaucheness or swings of mood. For a high proportion of them, it is the ritual – including offering and cadging cigarettes, searching for and striking matches, restating yet again how they despise themselves and intend soon to give up smoking – which obviously fills a deeply significant need. Perhaps these people, who depend on the paraphernalia and fidgety theatrical performance of smoking to relieve their nervousness, could be diverted to some other less lethal ritual. On the other hand, cigarette smokers who believe they have escaped their habit by switching to cigars, or sniffing, sucking or chewing tobacco are unwise. Besides the fact that cigar smoke contains more of the dangerous tars than that of filtered cigarettes, former cigarette smokers nearly always inhale when they smoke cigars or pipes, and are hence just as liable to lung cancer, heart disease, bronchitis, oral and throat cancer. Sir Richard Doll, formerly the Regius Professor of Medicine at Oxford and perhaps the world's leading expert on cancer epidemiology, points out that alcohol reduces resistance to oral cancer, so that people who both smoke and drink are particularly vulnerable. And those who use snuff (the tins and packaging of which carry no health warning) or chew tobacco – 22 million in the USA alone – equally are inviting oral cancer. The use of 'smokeless tobacco' has increased by 11 per cent a year since 1974: recently it has become popular, especially in the USA, for a person to take nicotine by sucking a bag of tobacco between the lip and gum of his mouth. An American tobacco company is paying students £30 a month to promote this habit (particularly worrying since schoolchildren may think it similar to sucking sweets) in Britain, which Richard Peto, Reader in Cancer Studies at Oxford, warns could cause the deaths of many people from mouth and throat cancer; it is banned altogether in Eire. Snuff, which is used by many miners because matches are not allowed underground, unlike cigarettes carries no excise duty.

The Royal College of Physicians sums up smoking as creating an avoidable 'hidden holocaust'. It is by far the single most important contemporary cause of preventable ill-healh and death. The human body is not designed to cope with absorbing such dangerous chemicals through its respiratory system, even though some of the harm may only manifest itself several years later. Smokers are overall twice as likely as non-smokers to die before the age of sixty-five; a twenty-cigarettes-a-day person will cut five years from his life.[14] Smoking is in a uniquely dangerous category because – unlike alcohol and other risks whose harm derives from their abuse – it is the 'normal' use of tobacco which causes both addiction and a sharply increased vulnerability to killer diseases. The research provides a conclusion which is devastating: out of every 1,000 young people who smoke a packet of cigarettes a day, one of them is statistically likely to die from being murdered, six will be slain in road accidents, but no less than 250 will be prematurely killed by tobacco. In Britain, tobacco now destroys four times as many people as the combined total killed by other drugs, murder, suicide, road, rail or air accidents, fires, drowning, poisoning, falls and every other known cause of accidental death. From these figures it would be logical for any responsible government to concentrate on doing everything possible to prevent smoking.

Among students themselves, 70 per cent have tried to give the habit up at least once. 'I really hate myself for smoking,' one teenager said. However, the power of the addiction is bleakly evident from the fact that even 48 per cent of those patients who have undergone major cancer surgery start smoking again. Virtually every smoker, certainly in the Western world, cannot now fail to be aware of the known risks. It may be argued that it is only his own concern if he chooses to undergo the dangers – apart from the cost caused to the public health services (including more than 4,000 hospital beds each day in Britain), the effects on his family and friends if he falls victim, and aside also from other consequences such as the several million pounds of damage caused annually by fires from lighted cigarettes. In their defence, smokers argue that they do not lose control of themselves as alcoholics do, nor do they steal to get money for their drug. Unfortunately, however, non-smokers are put at risk in a more direct way by other people's smoking. This is not just from annoyance, though Suzanne Lowry says she is always puzzled by 'the smoker's indifference to, or oblivion of, how he or she smells. I cannot understand how people otherwise very careful to make themselves attractive should not mind stinking of stale tobacco. Yellowing teeth and fingers can be dealt with; the smell is beyond redemption.'

John Mortimer warns against persecuting smokers so that they appear to be taking an exciting risk, and suggests that opponents instead should emphasize that the habit is messy, unsexy and boring.

More crucially, recent Japanese research has confirmed that non-smokers suffer significant health risks from breathing cigarette smoke: exposure to a person who smokes two packets a day causes a danger for a non-smoker equivalent to himself smoking three cigarettes daily. Dr Shigum Matsukura and his colleagues at Kyoto University School of Medicine conclude from analysing the amount of cotinine (a constituent of nicotine) in bodies: 'the deleterious effects of passive smoking may occur in proportion to the exposure of non-smokers to smokers in the home, the work-place, and the community'.[15] Smoke inhaled through tobacco by a smoker is known as mainstream smoke, whereas smoke which curls from smouldering tobacco into the surrounding air – whence it may be inhaled by smokers and non-smokers alike – is called sidestream smoke. Nicotine, benzpyrene, carcinogens, ammonia and carbon monoxide are all in fact found in stronger concentrations in sidestream than in mainstream smoke. Toluene in sidestream smoke has been found at six times the mainstream level, and the carcinogenic dimethylnitrosamine at fifty times. At least half of non-smokers (involuntary or 'passive' smokers) who live in cities have significant amounts of nicotine in their blood; Dr Takeshi Hirayama of the National Cancer Centre Research Institute in Tokyo, in a study of lung cancer mortality in over 142,800 women, found that non-smoking women with smoker husbands developed lung cancer at a rate nearly double that of women whose husbands did not smoke. The conclusion must be that several thousand non-smokers are killed each year by others smoking. A report from the US Center for Philosophy and Public Policy[16] questions the double standard permitted to tobacco smokers, which allows the pollution they cause to be regarded differently from traffic or industrial pollution: 'If ambient tobacco smoke were emitted from a polluting industry into the outdoor air, it would be judged to be both a toxic and a carcinogenic pollutant, subject to national hazardous air pollutant emission controls.' The report points out that Section 112 of the US Clean Air Act regulates any airborne pollutant that may reasonably be anticipated to result in 'an increase in mortality or an increase in serious irreversible, or incapacitating reversible, illness' and goes on to argue:

> The smoke pollution inhaled directly from cigarettes, pipes, and cigars indoors is not only chemically related to the smoke from factory chimneys, but routinely occurs at far higher levels indoors than does factory smoke or automobile exhaust outdoors. Daily exposure to tobacco smoke can amount to the single most important source of exposure of the population to this harmful kind of air pollution . . . In public areas such as restaurants, measurements indicate that simply providing separate sections for smokers and non-smokers can halve the risk to non-smokers at very small social expense . . . The time has come to treat ambient tobacco smoke as the air pollutant it is and to subject the tobacco industry to the same sort of controls that all other polluting industry must bear.

Sir Richard Doll puts it even more forcefully:

> The case for reducing air pollution by tobacco smoke is thus comparable to that for reducing pollution with lead, automobile fumes, ioning radiations and asbestos. Indeed, it is a good deal stronger than the case for reducing the two last, as the calculated (and observed) excess of cancer produced by passive smoking is some fifty times greater than that estimated to be the effect of forty hours' a week exposure to asbestos in asbestos-containing buildings and two orders of magnitude greater than the estimated risk to the general population of all cancers from the operation of the nuclear industry.

Today the British cabinet has only one member who is a smoker, an exact reversal of the situation in 1964. Smoking is now the habit of a shrinking minority, whereas it used to be practised by 65 per cent of adult males in the UK.[17] Of those who smoked ten years ago one person in five no longer does so today. The slow turn of the tide of public opinion against smoking is one of the few positive developments to have taken place in the whole field of drug addiction in recent years. It has been slow partly because it is an issue on which sections of the public have had to lead governments rather than vice versa. 'I can guarantee', Ronald Reagan assured North Carolina tobacco farmers when he was running for President, 'that my own cabinet members will be far too busy with substantive matters to waste their time proselytizing against the dangers of cigarette smoking.' The farming of tobacco is now on the increase in Britain. Governments of several countries avert their eyes from the medical data because they have come to enjoy the revenue from cigarette sales or the growing of tobacco. Tobacco is Zimbabwe's largest cash crop; in Britain the government draws £5,000 million a year in tax from smokers. The British government was first alerted to the causal link between smoking and lung cancer in a report from the government actuary as long ago as 1954, but decided to take no action on the warning because of the tax revenues (a decision possibly facilitated by a £250,000 grant to the Medical Research Council from the tobacco industry).[18] A recent British government study cynically concluded that to save lives by reducing smoking would mean a net loss to the Department of Health and Social Security because of the consequent increase in elderly and retired people.[19] When smoking was banned from London Underground stations in 1985, it was announced that this was because of fire-risk and not health-risk. Dr Charles Fletcher, Emeritus Professor at London University, comments, 'Politicians are not in the least interested in health, except their own. Banning cigarettes is not going to win them an election, but it will hurt their relations with manufacturers who give them a lot of funds.'

Understandably many GPs were among the first to give up smoking; the number of doctors who die from lung cancer in Britain is now half what it was fifty years ago. The Royal College of Physicians points out that the £100 million the tobacco industry spends each year on advertising is more than ten times the amount of the UK Health Education Council's total budget. Today the cost to the British health service of treating smoking-related diseases is at least £175 million. The 1977 Royal College report highlighted the urgent necessity for education programmes to discourage children from smoking; the restriction of smoking in public places; the phasing out of tobacco sales promotion; the withdrawal of high tar/nicotine cigarettes; and a large increase in research. Nine years later, hardly any of these steps have been taken – although, significantly, many smokers themselves say they would welcome and support more restrictions on smoking in public. In 1984 a medical tribunal ruled, against the wishes of the government, that the UK health service should pay for Nicorette, an effective anti-smoking chewing-gum, when it is prescribed by doctors. However, as soon as Sir George Young showed himself to be a responsibly anti-smoking junior Minister of Health, he was quickly transferred elsewhere following protests by the tobacco industry (which happens to be a substantial contributor to Conservative Party funds). One of the most damning of recent research findings is that nearly half of smokers say that smoking 'can't really be dangerous or the government wouldn't allow it to be advertised'. In the House of Lords in 1984, Lord Ennals asked for a complete ban on the promotion of tobacco, more prominent health warnings on cigarette packets with an increased amount of information about smoking (especially for young people), leadership from the government to encourage non-smoking as the norm in public places (with smoking areas set aside rather than vice versa), plus a substantial increase in the tax on tobacco. The Duke of Gloucester in the same debate pointed out that Norway's ban on cigarette promotion has resulted in a dramatic fall in the number of children who smoke, and asked for Britain to phase out tobacco advertising and sponsorship (which together form less than 3 per cent of the national total of advertising expenditure). The British Medical Association recently described the government's voluntary agreements on tobacco advertising and sponsorship as a 'farce' and a 'sick joke', and warned that 'every day we delay in banning the promotional activities of this industry, on average another 274 premature deaths occur' in Britain. None the less, the tobacco industry is a formidable adversary. When in 1976 Peter Taylor made a TV documentary called *Death in the West* which showed cowboys dying of lung cancer, an American tobacco company took weighty legal steps to prevent the film from being seen anywhere in the world.

Tobacco companies' advertising is frequently targeted at younger people in a calculated strategy to hook them as clients by making them acquire nicotine dependency at as early an age as possible. (Since the companies kill off thousands of their customers every week, they understandably have a continual need for new recruits.) Cigarettes' addictiveness is well understood by the manufacturers who give free packets of them away to students. The majority of all smokers establish their addiction before the age of eighteen. Against the overall trend, it is disturbing that 42 per cent of Britons between the ages of eighteen and twenty-four are now smoking, a figure which has risen from 37 per cent three years ago. Despite the fact that the law forbidding the sale of tobacco to those aged under sixteen dates from as long ago as 1908, several thirteen- and fourteen-year-olds today smoke more than their parents. (Even though children cannot legally be sold tobacco, the law allows them to possess and smoke it.) Professor Griffith Edwards points out that most youths smoking in a street are unlikely to have read the Royal College of Physicians' report, though they may well have seen on TV last night's snooker or car rally – both promoted by cigarette companies. The companies' expert researchers have advised them that the problem they need to surmount is that many smokers consider their habit irrational and stupid; so the images they spend massively to promote are to associate smoking with style, rugged individualism, success and sexual attractiveness. Skilful advertising campaigns straight-facedly seek implicitly to link cigarettes with outdoor health and sophistication. Sponsorship of sport and the arts endeavours to delude the public into believing tobacco is life-enhancing. (One mother at a Hertfordshire school meeting about drugs said that her small daughter had asked why she should take any notice of warnings against cigarettes since they are advertised as 'By Appointment to Her Majesty the Queen'.) Amongst teenagers and young women the incidence of smoking is today actually rising. In France, where smoking among adolescents is increasing and the total of cigarettes sold has risen by 12,500 million in the last ten years, cigarette promoters have evaded Madame Veil's restrictions on advertising by advertising their matches and lighters. When San Francisco voted in 1983 to give non-smoking employees the right to work in a smoke-free environment, the tobacco industry spent $1 million in efforts to defeat the law. Research, however, has shown that a smoker costs his employer $4,600 a year more than a non-smoker; Pacific Northwest Bell has decided it is better to invest in helping its employees to stop smoking rather than to pay for smoking areas.[20] While 34 per cent of all West German smokers themselves say they wish smoking were banned at work, in Britain, Clarks the shoemakers have for many years banned smoking completely, and Birmingham City Council is now offering its employees time off with pay to attend courses on how to rid themselves of the habit.

A 1985 congressional study calculated that smoking is costing the USA a total of at least $65 billion each year in medical bills, premature deaths and time lost from work – or more than $2.16 for each packet of cigarettes consumed. Although 33 million Americans have given up smoking, 53 million still smoke, and these now do so more heavily, increasing the number of cigarettes being sold by about 1 per cent a year. Although it goes to great lengths to keep the figures secret, the multinational tobacco industry is estimated to spend at least $2 billion each year on advertising and promotion. In a law-suit currently being heard in California, a tobacco company faces a charge of being directly to blame for a death from cancer; if the claim is upheld, this could be a watershed. Some US tobacco companies are reported to have sought to take out patents on marijuana, as an insurance against a possible future where pot has been legalized and tobacco banned. Most are desperately diversifying – including one which has invested by buying crematoriums. The strongest push by tobacco companies for sales and new addicts is being concentrated on the Third World, where Western enterprises now promote the drug with the same energy – and profitability – with which Britain used to trade opium in the

Far East. The Indonesian market is expanding by 7 per cent a year; in Uruguay 46 per cent of teenage boys smoke today, compared with 16 per cent in the US. In Japan, sales have risen by 135 per cent since 1960, and one in three adults now smoke, although smoking under the age of twenty is prohibited by law. Over the last twenty-five years the USA has even cynically exported $1,000,000,000 worth of cigarettes under its 'Food for Peace' programme. The EEC is spending £500 million a year maintaining a tobacco mountain, composed of low-quality leaf grown in Greece and Italy. There is also a flourishing international black market in cigarettes, estimated to account for some 30 per cent of sales, under the control of five of the biggest Mafia families. The total of cigarettes produced in the world has risen to 4,569,597 million annually, with a market now worth some $100 billion a year. In industrialized countries, despite the increasing unpopularity of smoking, an average of no less than some 2,500 cigarettes are still consumed per person each year. In the developing countries the figure is at present lower than 300. To the WHO this means that an epidemic is still preventable. To the tobacco industry, the figure indicates a tempting target for vastly increased sales and profits. Few developing countries – other than Singapore, where Lee Kuan Yew detests the habit – have started to take seriously the medical truth about smoking, the uncontrolled promotion of which carries no health warning. The tobacco sold is commonly the high-tar variety that is now unsaleable in the West. During the famine in Africa, Britain and America continued to export several million cigarettes to the impoverished countries, which had to be paid for in hard currency (thus reducing the Africans' ability to buy agricultural essentials and infrastructural development). Two brands of cigarettes popular in Africa are ironically named 'Life' and 'New Life'; another is somewhat more truthfully named 'New Paradise'. In China, which is the world's biggest producer of cigarettes, production has risen by 50 per cent in the last few years. The tobacco companies, however, received their first major setback in the developing world when Sudan recently banned all cigarette advertising; none the less precious, fertile land which could be producing badly-needed food is meanwhile being diverted to growing this inedible and anti-social crop which has no long-term future, and, in addition, more than 1.2 million hectares of trees are consumed every year by being burnt for tobacco curing.[21]

Education, as in all drug matters, is the key to any solution.

'Many young people now see smoking as sick and neurotic, not heroic as they used to,' a London teacher said. 'Though secret smoking in toilets in some schools makes them disgusting. One sixteen-year-old girl I used to teach works solely to pay for her smoking, which costs her over £500 a year.' Children in Britain are estimated in all to buy £80 millions' worth of cigarettes a year – an average of five a week for every child at secondary school. An official survey of schoolchildren shows that 1 per cent had tried a cigarette by the time they were four, and 20 per cent by the age of nine; 30 per cent of fifteen-year-olds and 45 per cent of girls aged sixteen say they smoke regularly.[22] Proportionally, a greater number of schoolchildren in several countries smoke more than adults. One fifteen-year-old boy admitted to smoking eighty-five cigarettes a week, which were given to him by his mother; and even primary schoolchildren are encouraged to start smoking by some tobacconists who offer them loose cigarettes. A few schools, such as the Abraham Moss Comprehensive in Manchester, have countered by successfully offering counselling through anti-smoking clinics. Others are showing films, some of which are educational and others frightening, like the powerful video film *Suckers?*, which shows a man who has had to have his legs amputated and has lost one eye as well as part of his stomach, all through smoking-induced disease, but who nevertheless continues to smoke cigarettes.[23]

Should smokers be left to self-destruct? If this is allowed to be a matter for personal choice, two further questions arise: should some people be permitted to make profits out of encouraging other people to kill themselves? And, if smokers are shown to endanger non-smokers (in a way that the users of no other drug do), does that affect the freedom we should allow consenting adults? 'Smokers will give up the habit', one Welsh doctor says, 'when they are intelligent enough to realize that it isn't the cigarette in their mouth which gives them confidence.' Meanwhile, however, tobacco dependence remains the most damaging type of drug addiction, and it is also the biggest single preventable cause of premature death in the Western world. The number of its victims dwarfs killings from road accidents, alcohol, heroin, murder, and a host of other highly publicized culprits. A 1980 Australian survey concluded that drugs were responsible for 19 per cent of all the deaths in that country; of these deaths no less than 79 per cent were caused by tobacco and 18 per cent by alcohol, while 3 per cent were due to all other drugs. Solvent abuse, which has claimed 200 lives over a decade in Britain, seems to agitate public opinion more than the million deaths caused by smoking in the same period. Michael Daube, a senior lecturer at Edinburgh University, comments: 'Eventually it will be impossible for future generations to comprehend that millions of us smoked, knowing that we risked and suffered fatal disease in vast numbers as a result.' A determined policy of attack by governments is long overdue; as a recent leader in *The Times* concluded, 'It is the industry that should be dying more quickly, not its customers.'[24] The fairest way might be to make tobacco companies legally liable for the costs of all the damage caused by smoking.

7

The Faustian Pact:
Heroin

'The undiscover'd country from whose bourn no traveller
returns, puzzles the will . . . '

Shakespeare

'In themselves narcotic drugs are neither dangerous nor harmful.
Indispensable to modern medicine, they are used the world over
to alleviate pain . . . Thus they bring a very great benefit to
mankind. But abused they can cause havoc and misery . . . the
dual nature of narcotic drugs has made it necessary to submit
them to the most stringent international control.'

Trygve Lie, *Bulletin on Narcotics*, vol. I

In his *Devil's Dictionary* Ambrose Bierce defines 'opiate' as 'an
unlocked door in the prison of identity. It leads into the jail yard.'[1]
One of the most addictive of all drugs – and perhaps for that reason
the one whose reputation arouses the most emotion – is the opiate
heroin ($C_{21}H_{23}NO_5$), whose medical name is diamorphine hydrochloride. To its illegal users it is known as smack, H, stuff, junk, horse,
skag, shoot, heavy, Henry, thing, dope, white stuff, boy, happy or
loopy dust, or tragic-magic. Heroin is made from morphine, which
in turn is derived from the gum of the pods of the white and blue
opium poppies that are legally grown widely in Asia (and also in
Europe for their seeds which are sprinkled on bread). Whereas
morphine is ten times stronger than opium resin, heroin is twenty-
five times more potent.

Myths about heroin are as resilient as dependence on the drug
itself. Hailed in the nineteenth century as a miraculous medicine,[2]

subsequently heroin has been equally vehemently demonized and in many countries ostracized even for medical use. It does not appear in the US Pharmacopea at all, the US authorities having decided that it is too addictive to be used by doctors. By contrast, the UK is one of only four countries where heroin can still be medically employed in the control of severe pain, although the number of doctors licensed by the Home Office to supply it is now less than 200. Heroin, like morphine, enables seriously ill patients to distance themselves from their agony and so end their lives with a degree of dignity and composure. (Any powerful opiate has the benign effect that, while a patient may still be conscious of pain, she or he no longer feels so terrified at being in its power.) In 1984, however, Congress again overwhelmingly defeated a Bill that would have allowed US hospitals to conduct a trial of heroin to treat cancer pain. Professor Arnold Trebach as well as many medical authorities argue that to cut American patients off from such relief is an irrational and misguided deprivation.[3]

The dramatic shock-horror role in which heroin has been popularly cast inflates its danger by lending false glamour to its image. Chris Brazier, one of several experts who deplore such hysteria, points out: 'Heroin is a dangerous drug, but it is less addictive than nicotine; people can use it regularly without becoming addicts; those who do become addicted can stop using it more easily than can alcoholics; and it causes no long-term physical damage.' Stripped of exaggerated hyperbole and its mystique, the reality is that heroin has – like almost every chemical substance – both positive potential and serious hazards. Contrary to popular belief, it is not the most dangerous drug; whereas people under the influence of, for example, alcohol cannot function normally and often act violently, heroin has the opposite effect and makes behaviour more peaceful.[4] One police officer pointed out to me that heroin does not dangerously affect driving a car in the way that cannabis and alcohol do. A widely held misapprehension about heroin arises through failure to recognize that it is not organically harmful when taken in pure form under controlled conditions – except in overdose, like many other substances.[5] Dr Sathananthan, a London practitioner, states, 'It's less dangerous than barbiturates and amphetamines, or killers like nicotine and alcohol which we accept. If you take heroin you are not poisoning me, but if someone smokes in this room I am poisoned.'

Unlike alcohol or nicotine, heroin does not itself have the effect of destroying human organs. Almost all deaths and injury from its use result either from its being adulterated or 'cut' with washing, baking or talcum powder, caffeine, cement, brick dust, bleach, flour or chalk; because of the physical neglect its spell can cause; or as a result of hepatitis or blood poisoning due to injection with dirty equipment. Sharing infected needles has caused drug-addicts to be second only to homosexuals in the degree of risk from catching AIDS: more than 2,000 British addicts have been infected in this way.[6] (Proposals by doctors in Edinburgh and elsewhere to provide clean needles – as in Amsterdam where hospitals will issue addicts with new needles in exchange for used ones – have been opposed by the British government officials on the grounds that this might encourage drug-taking.)

When pharmaceutically pure, heroin is a white powder, indistinguishable to the non-expert eye from cocaine or barbiturates. It is made from boiling morphine with acetic anhydride, a thick colourless liquid used in manufacturing celluloid. Poorer quality heroin from Turkey or Iran can be brown or pink, whereas black tar, a dangerously potent cheap heroin from Mexico, is now increasingly dominating the US market. Since dilution and adulteration is the easiest way for traffickers to boost their profit, illegal supplies – especially in North America – may be less than 5 per cent pure. The dangers from this are obvious: the brown heroin cut with crushed brown yeast tablets, at present freely sold on South London streets, causes bodies to swell up dangerously when it reaches the bloodstream; other adulterants with a plastic base stop up veins and result in ulcers and coronaries. The street price of heroin has currently fallen to around £60 a gram in London – where illegal supplies have a purity of 40 to 90 per cent – and to as low as £40 a gram in Liverpool. Heroin is sometimes eaten despite its bitter taste, but more often it is smoked or sniffed: 'skag' is heroin mixed with powder such as glucose, the fumes of which are then inhaled; 'chasing the dragon' is inhaling through a straw or paper tube the smoke of heroin which has been heated on silver paper. It may also be dissolved and injected ('fixing', 'shooting', 'jacking up', 'banging' or 'popping'); such injections can be subcutaneous – just under the skin ('skin-popping' or 'joy-popping'), intramuscular, or intravenous ('mainlining': a recidivist mainlining addict will puncture veins all over his body, from his foot and groin to his neck). Users describe the effect of this as being 'like a hammer' compared with the slower results of sniffing.

A person who takes heroin or morphine for the first time often experiences nausea and may vomit. The physical symptoms produced by heroin are dilation of the pupils, chronic constipation and sexual impotence; but internally there is an almost instantaneous sensuous kick ('buzz', 'rush', or 'flash'), which has been compared to orgasm and lasts only one to four minutes, followed by a calmer 'high' of drowsy and detached well-being that may continue for up to four hours. Research suggests that opiates give pleasure by affecting the central discharge of transmitters from those parts of the brain which are sensitive to anxiety and painful stimuli, through mimicking the action of the body's own endogenous morphine chemical B-endorphin, which regulates the sensitivity of the nervous system. Release, the drug information organization, points out: 'The problem with opiates is linked to their greatest advantage: that they kill both mental and physical pain, not so much by numbing and blocking it, as by producing a euphoric detachment which makes pain irrelevant and bearable. They give people the feeling that nothing matters.' One recently addicted Glasgow man warns, 'Heroin is very seductive: it can destroy one's better judgment – especially in relation to itself. It seems to supply all one's needs. Above all, it's a totally selfish drug; nobody and nothing else becomes any longer important.' Users' problems escalate because, since heroin's effect diminishes as the body grows accustomed to it, they therefore seek ever-increasing amounts. Eventually the addict requires continual supplies to ward off the symptoms of withdrawal. The main problem for many opiate users is the extent to which their life becomes centred round the drug they are using: so totally absorbed are some addicts that they forgo even eating or looking after themselves. Because they are dependent upon an illegal activity, they become increasingly cut off from the ordinary world, with their lives crabbed in the confines of a small drug-orientated milieu. In time, many have no friends left who are not also involved with addictive drugs, and retain no interest outside the pursuit of scoring to maintain their way of life. This situation compounds the difficulty of staying off if an addict tries to withdraw: it is the aura attached to heroin, as much as its euphoric effect, that makes escape from the habit so hard. Dr Charlotte Feinmann, a consultant at a London drug dependency unit who opposes easier maintenance, recounts: 'When you are prescribing, the only conversation you have with the drug-user is over the size of the prescription. You cannot get them to change any aspect of their life.'

A baby which is born to an opiate-addicted mother can be itself addicted – although, if breast-fed by a mother still using drugs, withdrawal symptoms may not show until it is weaned. Such a baby may die unless it is carefully withdrawn under medical supervision, though if properly treated no long-term effect will result. (The very young and old are particularly sensitive to opiates: in 1983 a Birmingham man unintentionally killed his fifteen-month-old child by giving her heroin to lick off his finger to stop her crying.) Dr Martin Mitcheson, recently the senior consultant in charge of the University College Hospital drug clinic in London, explains how a dependent body comes to resent withdrawal:

> There are in the human body naturally occurring substances called endogenous morphines – or endomorphines for short. They perform certain functions in transmitting impulses between nerve cells, particularly in the brain but also in other areas such as the gut. Normally they are produced in minimal quantities, controlling how we feel – our appetites for food or sex, our feelings of anxiety, depression or pleasure. In essence heroin and other exogenous (externally administered) morphines replace the function of the endomorphines, but in a rather crude fashion. By taking large amounts, whether by injecting, smoking or sniffing, the addict swamps the body's delicately-balanced morphine mechanism. Moreover, the body stops producing its own endomorphines. This means that when a regular user stops taking heroin, he experiences withdrawal symptoms that can last for several weeks. These include anxiety, emotional instability, feelings of insecurity, as well as physical symptoms such as violent fluctuations in body temperature, an overactive gut, an exaggerated sense of pain.

Withdrawal symptoms peak some thirty-six to seventy-two hours after the last dose, and disappear altogether within seven to fourteen days. 'Cold turkey' is so called because of the goose-pimples frequently experienced during withdrawal; 'kicking' the habit derives from another symptom, twitching of the legs. The discomfort involved – a feverish ache, sweating and insomnia – is unpleasant but manageable. 'No worse than flu' is the most common verdict, though users tend to feel stronger effects if that is what they are expecting to experience. 'One of our main bugbears,' said one doctor, 'is the hyped melodrama of scenes in novels and films like *French Connection II* which deter a good many people from trying to come off and detoxify.'

The reasons for vulnerability to drug dependency are discussed in Chapter 12. Where the borderline lies between physical and psychological dependency is never easy to determine: mental distress can often evince itself in physical symptoms, and vice versa. In acquiring or retaining dependency, the processes and associations of a drug can be as significant as its chemical content. Even after detoxification is completed, reconstructing and keeping to a new way of life can be the hardest part. One expert declared: 'Being "untogether" can be as much the cause of drug abuse as its result, and such a person is likely to be even more disorganized after a period of fixing. The real problem is not just the coming off, but to make life meaningful and satisfying without drugs.' Many users take heavily to alcohol after giving up opiates.

The most common myth about heroin is that all its users are addicts and destined for an early grave. In fact, addiction is neither instant nor inevitable. The rapid increase in tolerance that a heroin addict can develop is demonstrated by the fact that whereas 10 mg. of heroin might be fatal for a non-user, a high-rolling addict's body is able to cope with 1,600 mg. daily. A minority of heroin users, however, succeed in controlling their intake so firmly that they continue to lead a stable existence and carry out professional and other jobs – in the case of one London man, for over thirty years. The total number of these stable or occasional users is unrecorded but is estimated to run to several thousand. Whether, and how easily a user becomes dependent is very much determined by his or her personality: addiction, it must be emphasized, is the result, not (as is popularly believed) of a one-off chance, but of continuing to repeat a conscious action often in the face of initial discouragement. Most healthy people given a heroin injection would certainly not want another; in fact only 2 per cent are willing to accept a further dose, unless they are suffering great pain. In the setting of a clinical experiment, it has taken at least two weeks of thrice-daily use before dependency is evidenced by withdrawal symptoms on cessation.[7] However, this carries a paradoxical danger: new users, deceived by the absence of the immediate dependency reputed by popular mythology, make the mistake of underestimating heroin's real potency. Any user in fact gambles with his life every time he takes a shot, because he can never be sure of the strength or purity of what he buys illegally. Another major current problem is that users who experiment with heroin by snorting or smoking it wrongly believe that they are avoiding the risk of addiction. A number of them overdose, usually as a result of mixing opiates with other drugs such as alcohol or barbiturates, or else from resuming the same level of dosage after a period of abstinence during which their body has shed its capacity to tolerate opiates. (The symptoms to look for in overdosing are pinpoint eye-pupils and a cold clammy skin; the user falls into a sleepy stupor, followed by a coma that can last four to six hours, during which there is a danger that breathing may stop.[8]) Overall, heroin abuse is a problem which is closer to alcoholism than to suicide; none the less, as a social worker in a Liverpool clinic said, 'We have developed in society some traditions – I agree not effective enough – of teaching people to use alcohol, but we've never done this for heroin. The result is whereas one in ten alcohol users have a serious problem from it, the proportion of addicted heroin users is as high as one in two.'

In the face of so much adverse publicity, why do increasing amounts of people still try heroin? In the USA the total number who take it at some time or another, despite the threat of severe penalties, is believed to be 4 million, of whom 500,000 are addicts. Roger Lewis, when he was at the Drug Indicators Project, estimated that 750 kg. a year were currently being consumed in the UK. Until recently in America and Britain its use was mainly concentrated in downtown urban areas – 'as a counter to either puritanism or despair,' according to one New York authority. Today, supplies are available not just in cities but in rural farmland areas: cheaper than cocaine, and, at £5 for an evening's high, heroin is no more expensive than alcohol. As cheap – if not yet as easily obtainable – as cannabis, heroin use now spans every social and economic group, with the consequence that the taboos surrounding it appear to be breaking down. Due to expansion of supplies and marketing, in 1982 its street price, set against inflation, was only half what it had been five years earlier; by 1986 it was half as cheap again – and purer in quality. When a gram of heroin began to cost no more than an ounce of quality cannabis, drug samplers who would never have touched opiates previously started to experiment with heroin for recreational use. People who snorted cocaine lost their fear of heroin when chasing the dragon became fashionable: its 'social acceptability has widened since smoking it replaced the dreaded needle', according to Bernard Simon, an experienced solicitor who handles many drug cases. A trip became a trendy way for some young people to get stoned at the weekend; in America, heroin has become the drug of preference for a number of wealthy and professional users who no longer get a kick from cocaine, and want to try a new sensation. One young British academic who has tried a variety of drugs suggests why heroin has become fashionable in place of LSD:

> It was a reaction to the 1960s drug culture. It didn't really give you any transcendental feelings. (And also it did you damage, which is very much part of it. A lot of the experience connected with it is at least in an ordinary sense quite unpleasant. Under the drug you can even come to like that.) But it has some effects analagous to the psychedelic drugs. It does make you feel at one with your surroundings, but while allowing your surroundings to remain intact. They are not distorted, as with cannabis or LSD. Nor does heroin make you gregarious, like cocaine does. What it does is to make you very happy to be married to the moment. Under its influence banality becomes understandable, acceptable. Certainly it can reconcile people to the experience of being surrounded by urban squalor and decay. Things are not made more beautiful. You can simply be – as it were – magically reconciled to how they are now.

The writer Malise Ruthven reinforces this view:

> Unlike the psychedelic drugs of the 1960s, which encouraged people to drop out of ordinary society, heroin does not distort people's perceptions so seriously as to make them incapable of performing ordinary functions or holding jobs. This could be a factor adding to its popularity and acceptability among working-class teenagers who have not been influenced by the 1960s 'drug-culture'. Its analgesic effects – killing pain, relieving anxiety and generally making life seem more bearable for young people who live in deprived or squalid urban areas and whose employment prospects are poor – all this has made it the drug of the 1980s par excellence.

The feeling of relaxed introversion which is characteristic of opiates runs directly counter to the traditional emphasis in Western societies on aggressive achievement, competitive anxiety and collective extravert values – which may explain their attraction for many users today. Dr Timothy Leary, the apostle of LSD, declares: 'I have always criticized heroin as a drug to be avoided by intelligent, life-loving people.'[9] As Lyn Perry of Release says, 'The truth, and trouble, is that heroin is a very effective drug for those who want to escape.' One woman user explained that she needed it in order to provide her with a second skin as a shield against a hostile world, in much the same way as almost half the enlisted American soldiers in Vietnam turned to opiate drugs as an internal defence against the trauma of the war. 'The dominant emotional characteristic of the addict', Jean Liedloff suggests, 'is said to be his enormous compulsion to abdicate responsibility for his own life.'

This abdication is, however, not necessarily pleasant – quite apart from the initial nausea and loss of appetite and sex-drive. A British medical investigator, who took heroin regularly for research purposes, recorded in his diary:

My personal view at present is just one made grey and utterly grim by heroin. The extraordinary thing is that it brings no joy, no pleasure. Weariness, above all. At most, some hours of disinterest – the world passing by while you just feel untouched. Even after the injection there is no sort of a thrill, no mind-expansion nonsense, no orgiastic heights, no Kubla Khan. A feeling of oppressed breathing, a slight flush, a sense of strange unease.[10]

Others explain the fascination of heroin in terms which recall De Quincey's explanation of opium's attraction:

Whereas wine disorders the mental faculties, opium on the contrary (if taken in the proper manner) introduces amongst them the most exquisite order, legitimation and harmony. Wine robs a man of his self-possession . . . opium on the contrary communicates serenity and equipoise to all the faculties, active or passive: and with respect to the temper and moral feelings in general, it gives simply that sort of vital warmth . . . the opium-eater feels that the diviner part of his nature is paramount . . . he naturally seeks solitude and silence, as the

indispensable condition of these trances or profoundest re-
veries . . . but his intellectual apprehension of what is possible
infinitely outruns his power, not of execution only, but even of
power to attempt . . . the sense of space and in the end the
sense of time were both powerfully affected . . . opium had
long ceased to found its empire on spells of pleasure; it was
solely by the tortures connected with the attempt to abjure it,
that it kept its hold . . . But my case is at least a proof that
opium, after seventeen years' use and eight years' abuse of its
powers, may still be renounced.[11]

Today, several users with the self-control to regulate their habit
have, like De Quincey, taken opiates for many years without
deteriorating physically or intellectually; others who claim that it is
doing them no harm belie this assertion by their tremulous and
preoccupied manner. Giampi Alhadeff, the Director of the London
City Road Crisis Intervention Centre, indicates the problem caused
by the fact that people are using heroin occasionally – 'even small
amounts twice a week for a year' without being hooked; the
Community Drug Project in South London, one of whose main
concerns is to educate and warn young people about drugs, points
out: 'You can't say "Don't use it, it kills", because children will see
their mates using it but being unharmed, and they won't listen to
you again. You've got to tell them the truth – these are sixteen-to
eighteen-year-olds, bored, lacking any proper facilities or hope of a
job, who want to escape for an hour or two – but warn them of the
dangers.' The apparent innocence and immunity can indeed be
deceptively seductive. William Burroughs testifies to this: 'The
addict himself has a special blind spot as far as the progress of his
habit is concerned.' New users, who start by being able to afford to
blot out the dreary despair of unemployment with £5 for a 'ching
bag', find that as their tolerance increases, so does the cost of the
dose they need to obliterate anxiety. A not untypical case is that of
a graduate who recounted, 'I'd had an abortion and was very
depressed, and heroin closed off those feelings. I shoplifted to pay
for it, but I needed more and more money. So I went on the game.'
Many of these new users are not the junkie stereotype derelict
drop-outs, but normal and sometimes highly intelligent young
people. Heroin use is now rife not just in London, Amsterdam and
Berlin, but among farm-workers and in the sober housing estates of

places such as Edinburgh, where social workers estimate that as many as one in twelve young people have taken it. Jimmy Boyle, who, after his own son had become hooked whilst he himself was in Barlinnie Prison, is working with anti-drug community groups on Edinburgh housing estates such as Pilton and Muirhouse, says: 'In the last two years we've found heroin coming in at a frightening level. Children of ordinary working-class people, the salt of the earth, who have never heard of heroin before, have habits needing £50–£200 a week.'

Why is the habit spreading? One reason is that many addicts are driven to deal in the drug in order to be able to afford their increasing needs. Wider availability leads to more experimentation: though most initiation is a result not of pushers, but of the example and pressure of peer groups. Some cannabis dealers have switched to heroin, because of the constancy of the profits to be made out of opiate customers' dependency. One former addict in Glasgow described how some dealers start off by giving away free heroin a number of times to teenagers 'to make them feel good' and 'then when they've been using it for a while, they start charging them, and by that time they really need it'. Carol Woolley, a Merseyside drug counsellor, said that young children in that area at first may not realize that it is heroin they are using, and are deceived into starting by pushers describing it as happy powder or rainbow dust who offer this to schoolchildren on easy credit. (Other Liverpool addicts are selling bottles of their urine to traders who take this to clinics and are then prescribed methadone which they can sell for £40.) In Bermondsey a teenager said that schoolkids were 'so ignorant about heroin they couldn't tell skag from pot'. The supply network spreads like a pattern of capillaries as hooked youths become mini-dealers themselves, if they do not turn to crime and prosti-tution. An eleven-year-old in Liverpool who admired a group of older 'skagheads' taking heroin, copied their habit in order to become an accepted member of the circle; by the time he was thirteen he was spending up to £20 a day on heroin, to pay for which he developed successive skills at shoplifting, mugging and burglary. Other children sell their food or the clothes they are wearing to buy the drug. A fourteen-year-old 'skaggie' in Southwark recently 'borrowed' a furniture van, and proceeded to ransack his parents' flat, removing every portable item which he then sold.

Carol Woolley says of Merseyside, parts of which are known as 'Smack City' since Liverpool is a major entry port for drugs:

> There are not hundreds, but thousands of kids out there who are not receiving any help at all. They must be going through a living hell. This has to be stopped, now, before a catastrophe happens. What is needed is positive education at all levels. In my view that means teaching children as early as seven or eight to be aware of the dangers of drugs. The education should be progressive: as a child grows older he or she should be given more information about the devastating effects drugs can have. And parents and teachers have to be taught to look for drug abuse symptoms at a very early stage: it's often very difficult to detect because children of twelve or thirteen are at a difficult age anyway, coming to terms with growing up.

Of the thirty-seven children under the age of sixteen who sought help from the Merseyside Drugs Council in 1983, every single one was on heroin; one of the children was only ten years old; out of eighty clients in the sixteen to eighteen age group, seventy were on heroin and ten were on solvents. However, a sixteen-year-old London girl recalled: 'When I was trying to get off it, I went round to a doctor for help. But he said, "I don't deal with heroin addicts."' The mother of a 22-year-old man who went for help to her GP stated: 'He just said that if my son couldn't help himself, he certainly couldn't.' Another mother living on the grey concrete Avondale estate in south-east London recounts: 'The pushers come on Tuesdays and Thursdays. They roll up in Jags and Porsches, all sorts. The kids wait for them in the launderette – they pip their carhorns, and out go the kids as though the ice-cream van's arrived.'

Users describe the change which overwhelms their lives: 'Sex just goes out the window.' 'All you seem to need to get you through the day is your heroin. First thing you think of in the morning is your heroin and the last thing you think of at night is your heroin. There are also changes in your personality. I mean, I'd do things for money for heroin that once I would never have dreamt of doing – stealing, shoplifting, burglary, anything, it doesn't matter what it is. You'll even rob your mother and father. Personally, I haven't stooped that low, but most of my friends have. Then there's the lying. Your whole life's a lie. From the time you wake up in the morning until you go to bed you are just telling one lie after another to con people, to get money. Heroin completely changes a person to a totally different person, a bad person.'[12] 'The ritual of chasing the dragon ("Puff, the magic dragon" in the children's song) virtually becomes a religious experience. People sit around afterwards going over each stage of the operation, analysing how pure the heroin was.' 'I was very shy when I was a teenager . . . only when I was actually taking drugs did I feel the way I wanted to feel: kind, considerate, honest.' 'When I was fifteen someone gave me heroin . . . I found that was the cheapest, fastest way of getting a buzz. What was insidious was the way in which my drug-taking changed . . . I started relying on being high as a way of coping with any difficult situation. And since getting high made me feel guilt and disgust with myself, I had to take more drugs to feel all right . . . I have used drugs and drink for fifteen years as an escape from growing up, and from the real world. In that respect I am still today a fifteen-year-old schoolboy.' 'We think we're in a blissful state, but there is a lot of introverted aggression.' 'When you score from a dealer, the dealer is God. He controls your entire existence, rules your life.' As the novelist James Buchan says, 'Heroin reduces all problems to a single problem.'

Alexander Trocchi, the writer from Glasgow who was a friend of William Burroughs, had a heavy heroin habit which ironically he originally adopted because he had a very weak head for alcohol. He could control his heroin intake, but unfortunately assumed others were equally able to do so, and a circle of young admirers in the Brighton area have become addicts through his proselytizing example. In his bleakly frank autobiographical novel *Cain's Book*[13] Trocchi describes how the illegality of heroin impels users to membership of a secret exclusive club. William Burroughs's testimony, however, is, 'Junk takes everything and gives nothing but insurance against junk sickness.'[14] He warned users in the *British Journal of Addiction*[15] that the habit of smoking opiates 'is as difficult to break as an intravenous injection habit'. For over twelve years Burroughs used opium, heroin and morphine, but concluded:

> Opium is profane . . . I had not taken a bath in a year nor changed my clothes or removed them except to stick a needle every hour in the fibrous gray wooden flesh of terminal addiction. I never cleaned or dusted the room. Empty ampule boxes and garbage piled up to the ceiling. I did absolutely nothing. I could look at the end of my shoe for eight hours. I was only

roused to action when the hourglass of junk ran out . . . I
Don't Want To Hear Any More Tired Talk And Junk Con – the
same things said a million times and more and there is no
point in saying anything because NOTHING Ever Happens in
the junk world.[16]

How much crime is heroin responsible for? No drug itself 'causes'
crime; but in New York, almost half of all street crime is attributed
by the police to heroin users.[17] An unquantifiable proportion of
these offences is committed by people who would be likely to
commit crimes in any event; professional criminals in Europe and
North America increasingly are taking control of the wholesale drug
trade, finding they can make considerably greater profits – with a
higher chance of impunity – than they could from bank robberies,
and the violence of their methods is permeating down to retail drug
distributors. Protection rackets are now reported by small dealers in
Liverpool. In June 1984 a Hollywood antiques dealer was jailed for
fifteen years for robbing sixty-four banks in order to support his
$800-a-day heroin habit; three months earlier two nineteen-year-
old heroin addicts had killed a hotel receptionist in Torremolinos
when stealing 3,000 pesetas (under £15). The murder for drugs of a
film producer in the Fulham area of London in 1985 aroused
apprehension that it heralded the arrival of the violence of the
American drug scene in Europe. Although policemen as a whole
are more optimistic about heroin than they are about cannabis –
'With heroin we can zero in on a group that has little public
sympathy or co-operation, unlike the position with cannabis' –
prison does not necessarily deter the trade; a highly organized
heroin gang continued to operate successfully throughout the time
they were jailed in Tijuana Prison.

Pharmacologically, opiates do not induce criminal behaviour; it is
the restriction on their supply which forges this connection. While
the cost to society, the police and the criminal law as a result of the
prohibition shows every sign of growing, all too little is being spent
on breaking the cycle by education or the treatment of addicts.
Stimson and Oppenheimer's research[18] found that out of 128 heroin
addicts (a one in three sample) attending London clinics, after ten
years 38 per cent were off drugs, while a similar proportion were still
attending the clinics and receiving prescriptions. The fact remains
that only a small minority of addicts are temperamentally willing

to contact clinics or doctors, and today less than one-tenth of Britain's addicts are attending any of the country's forty drug dependency units. One of the most expensive private clinics in England has a long-term success rate of only 7 per cent with heroin patients who are well orientated and drawn mainly from privileged and stable backgrounds. Many clinic workers seem uncertain whether their function is maintenance of drug-users – to keep them out of criminal subcultures – or to attempt to cure them. Almost all clinics now have waiting lists of at least six to eight weeks: addicts who decide to come off are not likely to have the long-term restraint to wait this long. One young mother who begged for treatment was turned away and told, 'If we saw everyone without an appointment this place would be overrun.'

Which people are most at risk? Research recently carried out for the UK government by Andrew Irving Associates found that the people most likely to reject heroin are either those who have tried and rejected soft drugs or who are described as 'discerning cannabis users' – to whom presumably should be added those who decline to take any drug at all. At most risk are those people who will try anything or who have friends heavily into drug misuse; those who are emotionally or socially vulnerable; and people living in areas where heroin misuse is common. The hardest group of users to treat are those who use a range of drugs and do not see heroin misuse as a problem. Professor Kaplan believes that heroin users share several analogies with alcoholics: 'Some drinkers use alcohol moderately while others become problem drinkers and alcoholics; some use moderately for quite a while and then gradually seem to lose control over their intake; some, who are clearly problem drinkers or alcoholics, stop drinking completely but relapse again and again; while others give up alcohol permanently with or without social support.'[19]

However, the situation, although serious, is not without hope. We could learn from the history of the large number of US soldiers who started to take heroin in Vietnam: on their return home after the war, only 7 per cent used any opiate drug, and less than 1 per cent continued to be addicted. This may provide some clues for us. It shows that addiction is not, as some allege, irremediable; and also the powerful effect of social circumstances on drug use: whereas in Vietnam many of the usual social and moral restraints inhibiting drug abuse were absent – the soldiers felt their war duty was a period away from 'real life', and saw other people using freely available drugs – the psychological sets changed after demobilization. In a modern society like ours, which is full of tension and which places a premium on self-reliance, the attraction opiates offer is the insulation of a womb-like retreat. An addict's needs for achievement are reduced to only one: maintaining the cocoon that shelters him from worry. Perhaps the key to escape from this destructive chimera is to offer him the self-respect of a life more worthwhile than drugs.[20]

8

The Land of Cocaine

'Does any man doubt, that if there were taken out of men's minds, vain opinions, flattering hopes, false valuations, imaginations as one would, and the like; but it would leave the minds of a number of men poor shrunken things, full of melancholy, and indisposition, and unpleasing to themselves?'

Francis Bacon, *Of Truth*

A writer who takes cocaine says: 'Coke makes you feel on a wave-crest: the cleverest, most amusing person in the world – for a few minutes. Then you need some more to go on feeling this, and then some more, and you suddenly find you're tied to a treadmill.'

Cocaine – $C_{17}H_{21}NO_4$, also known as coke, happy dust, C, charge, Charlie, cubes, her, lady or girl, snow, blow, leaf, flake, freeze, cake, toot, Bernice, nose candy, snort, Mother of Pearl, crack, rock, champagne, Cecil, gold or star dust, sea snow, Bolivian marching-powder, bouncing powder, *la nieve* in Bolivia, *la tía blanca* in Peru, and *la perica* in Colombia – used to be described as the champagne of drugs. Cocaine is still a tonic of the trendy and a status symbol at jet-set parties; however, as it has become increasingly cheaper and more widely available, its popularity has spread democratically, with the fashion for it today expanding faster even than that for heroin. Its regular users now include, besides those 'born with a silver spoon in their nose', a number of athletes and executives who began to take it for energy, only to discover they cannot do without it. 'People who stay up all night in a disco or club and then have to be at their office in the morning think a line of coke is the solution,' declared a company director in Madrid, 'but now they snort first thing in the morning, and feel they can't make decisions without it.'

In America cocaine is wrongly called a narcotic because it was banned together with heroin and opium by the 1914 Narcotics Act; in fact it has the opposite effect and – although also an effective local anaesthetic since it blocks the painful effects of the brain chemical, serotomin – is an intense stimulant of the central nervous system. One fancier described its 'hit' as like 'taking off in a space rocket'. Research by Swiss chemists shows that monkeys self-administer cocaine in preference to any other drug – and even to food or sex. Steve Abrams's view, however, is that 'One stimulant is much like another. Cocaine is not very different from benzedrine; there's a lot of snobbery attached to it.'[1] The white powder of cocaine hydrochloride is derived from an alkaloid of the leaves of the bush *Erythroxylon coca*, a stocky evergreen shrub cultivated throughout the moist northern uplands of South America and Java. Some 11 million Andean Amerindians today still chew its leaves to counter feelings of hunger and fatigue; but slowly to absorb tiny amounts of cocaine from coca leaves in this way is, for the body, as different from snorting a powerful refined drug as sipping a glass of wine is from gulping raw spirits.

Besides 'tooting' cocaine through the nasal membranes via a straw or rolled-up bank-note, abusers also inject it into their veins; 'freebase' by smoking its salt or paste; or 'speedball' by mixing it with heroin or morphine. One consumer explained, 'Freebasing is more of a high for your whole being. When you toot, the whole rush tends to go right to your head, whereas freebasing gives within ten seconds a tingling that goes right down your body.' The strong stimulus produced by cocaine is probably the result of its activating neurotransmitters which release the brain chemical dopamine. The resulting euphoria is stronger than that gained from heroin, but it does not last so long: cocaine boosts the user's ego and enhances his confidence and feeling of mental vigour, giving him indifference to hunger and fatigue together with an illusion of physical strength – but only for a period of ten to forty minutes. After that, anticlimactic tedium sets in, to counter which users often seek further cocaine. In the UK illicit 30–70 per cent pure cocaine currently costs £40–£60 a gram, compared with $50 for a less pure gram (or $10 for a slug of crack) in New York. Occasional users sniff ¼ gram or so; habitual users consume 1–2 grams a day. Unlike heroin, cocaine does not produce physical withdrawal symptoms when use is discontinued; although its abuse, in common with that of all stimulants, brings on fatigue and ageing by prematurely exhausting finite reserves. The habit for cocaine is psychologically addictive, except for extremely strong-willed users who are able to keep to small, non-increasing doses. So great is its spell that overuse has been known to result in those in thrall becoming recluses, interested in nothing except the drug; one doctor warned me, 'Like heroin, it's so good, don't try it even once.' Large or repeated doses lead to agitated anxiety and paranoia, since the user who feels omnipotent comes to attribute his actual ineffectiveness to a conspiracy. Diana Willis, convicted of drug-dealing in Kensington in 1985, said, 'Cocaine makes you completely crazy. Everything becomes distorted and you think everybody's against you.' William Burroughs cautions that although cocaine is the most exhilarating drug he has ever used and the desire for it can be intense, its continued use 'leads to nervousness, depression, sometimes drug psychosis with paranoid hallucinations. The nervousness and depression are not alleviated by more cocaine.'[2] Such hallucinations commonly take the form of phantom insects crawling on or under the skin, and abusers claw and lacerate themselves in attempts to free their bodies from this imaginary infestation. Some heroin injectors hazardously speedball or 'boy-girl' by adding cocaine to prolong heroin's euphoria; conversely a number of cocaine users mix the drug with heroin or Quaaludes to calm down or to counter the irritability caused by prolonged cocaine use. Overdose may in rare cases result in cardiac or respiratory failure: although the danger level is often quoted as 1,200 mg., as little as 20 mg. has proved fatal. Besides deaths amongst 'mule' smugglers (see below), cocaine-related fatalities in the USA rose to 617 in 1984; in the previous year, deaths from cocaine overdose in San Francisco for the first time overtook those from heroin. It is important, however, not to exaggerate cocaine's toxicity: in Britain before the boom started in 1983 there was only one death from dependence on cocaine besides four from overdoses.

Until very recently cocaine was not considered physically addictive, though there has never been any doubt that it is highly seductive; freebasing (smoking coca paste) is particularly liable to cause psychic dependence.[3] Lately, however, the dichotomy between physical and psychological dependence has begun to be questioned, but experts have suggested that in any event there may be a physiological basis for the depression and insomnia many cocaine users experience when they cease their habit.[4] In the USA, some quarter of a million users are now thought to be dependent on it to a significant degree. The minority of compulsive users mainly take it intravenously or freebase, although cure is readily possible after detoxification. Freebasing, however, is liable to damage smokers' lungs, causing injury similar to pulmonary emphysema; the powder used for this is produced by dissolving cocaine in ether and then evaporating it over a flame, preparatory to smoking it, usually in a pipe. (It was volatile ether that exploded in 1980 at the home of the actor Richard Pryor, badly burning his body; and investigators believe that it was a freebasing fire which on 31 December 1985 caused the plane crash which killed the cocaine addict rock star Rick Nelson together with six others.) Since 1985, 'crack' (also known as 'jumbo' or 'rock') – a new pure form of cocaine base that is ready for smoking – has become cheaply available in New York. Within a mere eight months, its use spread like an epidemic: street sellers signal they can supply it by making a sign like cracking a whip. Smoking crack (which can be illegally made in an ordinary kitchen with baking soda) creates almost immediate compulsive addiction, whereas people can snort ordinary cocaine for several weeks before they acquire dependence. More common but less serious physical damage is caused by the hydrochloric acid with which cocaine is produced eating away the septum separating the nostrils of those who snort it: the coke boom has led to lucrative spin-offs in plastic surgery to repair these among the rich.[5] Cocaine's former use as a local anaesthetic – especially in dental and optical work – has now largely been replaced by less toxic alternatives such as lignocaine and, in the USA, Novocain. Illicit supplies are often cut with Mannite, an Italian laxative which looks and smells very similar; other users, because of their expectations, do not notice when they are supplied with amphetamine or Novocain instead. Due to a shortage of ether, illegal cocaine is now increasingly being made from the more dangerous benzene.

High rollers, because of the grandiose feeling of enhanced strength and mental clarity that cocaine engenders, are liable to overestimate their capabilities. Businessmen feel supreme self-confidence and personal rightness, in the face of any amount of evidence to the contrary. Some users display aggressiveness from an arrogant assumption of superiority; it is possible that the use of cocaine and amphetamines was one of the factors contributing to the Nazi leaders' delusions of invincibility.[6] (Goering was addicted to both cocaine and morphia.) It is not only criminals who borrow energy and confidence from coke prior to embarking on assignments; ballet dancers as well as a range of sportsmen admit that they rely on it. Kirk Stevens, the former snooker champion, has stated, 'At first I was hooked just mentally, but now it has a total physical hold over me.' In 1986 the deaths of two exceptionally talented US sports stars, the footballer Don Rogers and the country's most promising football player, Len Bias, were attributed to cocaine. It is estimated that a total of at least 40 tons of cocaine is being illicitly imported into the USA annually; each ton can produce 100 million doses. (The police in Miami report that since every banknote in the city now has an average of 35 micrograms of cocaine adhering to it, their sniffer dogs are bewildered.) In a growing number of circles in Western Europe as well as throughout North America, not just among the jet-set and in show-business, cocaine now enjoys a symbolic status: it has become a cult among upwardly-thrustful Yuppies, who consider snorting like buffaloes and the conspicuous consumption of coke to be a signal of success. Its main popularity lies in business, media and entertainment circles, where people rely on it for stamina during long meetings or cyclical periods of intense work as an expensive alternative to jugs of coffee. Certain lavatories in the London and New York Stock Exchanges are now known as the 'Powder Rooms'; in a number of advertising firms cocaine is given to clinch deals or to reward favours. Wealthy people present cocaine to lovers or friends where they once gave alcohol or chocolates. Buñuel signalled the trend as long ago as 1973 in his film *The Discreet Charm of the Bourgeoisie*. A man working in a large computer company stated that among his office of twelve people, eight frequently take breaks to smoke crack. A couple who moved to Fort Lauderdale said they felt ostracized because they did not want to join the coke circles of the Florida doctors and lawyers who tote the drug at evening and weekend parties. In some areas, coke is now a recognized currency, accepted as fees by accountants or doctors; a little pile of the powder is sometimes left on tables in Aspen, Colorado ('Toot City') as a tip for the waiter or maid. Today the USA's cocaine business is estimated to have expanded to be worth three times as much as the nation's film and recording industries put together. Fortified 'rock-', 'base-' or 'crack-houses' in Los Angeles and New York dispense cocaine, both wholesale and retail; a Hollywood agent lamented to me of her difficulty in working with people who 'disappear every twenty minutes to take coke, and when they come back think every word they say is a pearl of wisdom when in fact they're just repeating themselves'. One French film director recounted, 'Using coke I once turned out a script in three days. It was terrible. Of course coke is a stimulant but it doesn't make you intelligent.' Its effects are visible in the disjunction of several recent films made in Hollywood: 'When the director or stars are on cocaine, they seem to have tunnel vision,' a producer said. 'On screen there's a party going on, but the audience isn't invited; you can't enter into the logic of the film.' The actress Julia Phillips, who produced *Close Encounters of the Third Kind*, says she spent 1 million dollars on cocaine in ten years, and the habit is costing some other individuals in California $750,000 annually. The president of a large American medical corporation spent $2.5 million on his habit; one major Paris couturier was driven to bankruptcy within two years because of his consuming passion for the drug. Before he became a star, John Belushi's large appetite for cocaine had been restrained by a limited income; fame and wealth helped him to become a 'man with a golden nose'. His sordid death from speedball injections off Sunset Boulevard in 1982 – followed by other tragedies such as those of David Kennedy at Palm Beach and Pascale Ogier in France – cast a temporary cloud over coke's high-octane acolytes, who prefer to associate it with glitzy charisma rather than the post-mortem on the American dream represented by a corpse in a hotel room.

What are the reasons which underlie the pull of cocaine? For some, the glamour of its expense represents the draw, since their noses twitch with equal satisfaction over chalk powder: they believe 'because it costs £100, it must be cocaine' – and react accordingly. A growing number of young professional people are now succeeding in adding thousands of dollars to their income, tax-free, by cutting and dealing in coke. Undoubtedly the ritual and ancillary hardware also perform a role that is highly significant, as they do in the consumption of several other illicit drugs. Crystals are carefully crushed, prior to the powder being laid out in straight lines on a smooth glass surface or mirror; the rolled banknotes used for snorting must be of as high a denomination as possible. (Woody Allen immortalized the true experience of one neophyte who, nervous at trying his first sniff, sneezed $25,000's worth of coke over the carpet.) The totemistic paraphernalia deployed in the devout rites – exclusive straws, expensive spoons, impressive sieves, folding scales, caskets, grinders and razors in silver, jade, gold or platinum – are sold legally by mail-order and in several smart Paris and Beverly Hill stores. California boutiques offer 'Hot Boxes' to test the quality of purchases; and 'head shops', such as Lady Snow's in Hollywood, do a flourishing business. Unless customers are incited to commit an offence, trading in associated merchandise is not unlawful; cocaine-snorting kits were openly on sale in London shops in 1986.

The absence of withdrawal symptoms deludes fanciers into thinking that cocaine does not produce addiction. 'Coke was my number one choice because I thought that unlike other drugs it wasn't addictive,' recounted a well-off 35-year-old mother; 'I went on thinking this until I realized I was needing to snort 5 g. which were costing me £250 a day.' Yet a large number of other people reconcile the habit with otherwise normal social lives: 10 million Americans (including 1 million in the New York metropolitan area) now take cocaine at least once a month, compared with 4 million in 1982. Recent surveys in the USA reveal that 30 per cent of all college students, and 40 per cent of those aged twenty-seven have used cocaine. Each day an estimated 5,000 more Americans try it for the first time. Cocaine is increasingly popular because it lends users a welcome feeling that they are sharply creative, articulate, funny and original. Unlike older-established drugs such as cannabis, opiates or alcohol which offer people a deadening escape or oblivion, cocaine's special appeal lies in the positive option that it appears to offer: enhancing the user's reality rather than removing him from it, making him feel both more clear-headed and in greater control. Freud recalled that it gave him the same feeling as having dined so well 'that there is nothing at all one need bother about', but without robbing him of energy for exercise or work. Another man who experienced it said cocaine made him 'look down upon my normal fragmented condition with compassion, amusement . . . but on the return, as the effects wear off I plunge from the heights of heaven to the depths of the abyss: deep depression, mental bitterness'. Hence the reason why heavy users repeat their sniffing of lines of cocaine every twenty minutes – sometimes for hours at a time – in order to postpone return to earth and prosaic reality. Cocaine also acquires followers who believe it is a virility symbol and sexual enhancer, since it is a climax inhibitor for both males and females as well as a sensory stimulant.[7]

The drug's dependants, however, warn it is easy to delude yourself that cocaine is holding your life together while, without your realizing it, in truth it is tearing it apart. A London actress described how her step-son 'inherited a house full of good antiques but Hoovered the whole lot up his nose within eighteen months'; an heiress who at first was very pleased to switch from heroin to cocaine ('unlike with heroin, you actually want sex, and coke opens the pupils of your eyes so that no one sees you're pinned') found its addiction worse than heroin's and had to take up crime and prostitution to pay for her habit. One recovering addict recalled that, to begin with, 'It seemed to straighten me out, I felt 100 per cent in control. Then my life started to fall to bits around me, and I snorted more and more. I still felt it was the only answer to my problems; it wasn't until I came in for treatment months later that I realized really it was causing them.' Bobbie Kingham of the Charter Clinic advises, 'If weekends aren't the same without cocaine; if your decision about whether or not to go out is determined by whether there will be cocaine available; if the drug is starting to cause problems or you are using it as a means of coping, then the chances are that addiction has been established and that you should seek help for it.' The best method to use for coming off cocaine is abrupt withdrawal: the physical discomfort is less severe than breaking a caffeine habit. None the less, information for the public about cocaine is much sparser and generally less available than that about other drugs. 'There's very little literature on cocaine, a dearth of information. I can't think of one serious paper in this country on the subject in the last twenty years,' says Dr Ghodse, the consultant psychiatrist at St Thomas's Drug Dependency Unit. When Cocaine-800, a twenty-four-hour help-line service exclusively for cocaine addicts, started in 1983 in New Jersey, it received an average of 1,000 calls a day.

Dr Andrew Weil warns, 'I do not believe we are meant to put powerful drugs into our systems by the nasal route. When cocaine is sniffed, it rapidly and directly enters the bloodstream. Snorting is only one step down from intravenous injection. Like shooting, it bypasses many of the mechanisms our bodies have for protecting us from the adverse effects of foreign substances. When we put a drug in our stomach, we allow the body to decide how fast to admit it to the bloodstream and give the liver and kidneys time to work at metabolizing and eliminating it.' By contrast, in the Andes and Amazonia, coca leaf, which contains 0.5–1.5 per cent cocaine, has long been a sacred part of the inhabitants' culture and way of life: although the local children do not take it – not because it is prohibited by law, but because of social custom handed down by each generation of a family. 'Mama coca' (traditionally female: coke is 'girl' or 'lady' in New York where heroin is 'boy') is thought of as 'the gods' gift of food for the soul': for many centuries, adult peasants have employed it medically in over forty different ways, as well as regularly chewing it to dull hunger, cold and tiredness, without any adverse effects being recorded on their livers or health.[8] Bolivians, from the government downwards, offer visitors coca tea as a courtesy. Many families also depend on it economically: although the current export boom has caused land erosion in the Amazon basin, with forests cleared for a coca crop and then abandoned (the bushes being ready for harvesting a mere six months after planting). Although in 1978 the Peruvian government made a vain attempt to ban coca chewing in places below an altitude of 1,500 metres, 600,000 Bolivians are permanently employed in coca farming, and its profits exceed by more than ten times those of the country's next principal industry, tin mining.

Nevertheless, in Washington and at international conferences, voices from rich developed countries increasingly demand that the cocaine menace 'be eradicated at its root source', even though to date no herbicide has been found to act on coca as paraquat does on cannabis plants. Furthermore, for indigenous growers in some of the poorest countries in the world, coca eradication programmes look quite different from the way they appear to the US Congress or Drug Enforcement Administration. Local peasants feel that the problem of addiction in rich countries is a matter of responsibility, not for them, but for those so-called civilized nations whose inhabitants seem to have more money than sense. The Bolivian peasant leader José Vallegos argues: 'Why should we be made to pay for the inadequacies of the rich gringos? We are not responsible for the thousands who seek salvation in abusing drugs. We have used the products of nature for hundreds of years. They should look to the rot in their own societies before dictating to us how we should run ours.'

In 1983 Vallegos and other peasant organizers in the coca-producing areas of Chimore and Chapara placed advertisements in the national Press asking for a new and rational policy towards coca agriculture, based on its development into a modern pharmaceutical industry. They pointed to the Andean countries' annual expenditure of $150 million on synthetic anaesthetics, which are sold by wealthy drug companies originating from just those countries which are asking the poor to destroy their coca crops. Instead they proposed that with proper planning and capitalization, Bolivia and Colombia could develop national ranges of low-cost anaesthetics and concentrated nutritional aids besides soft-drinks ingredients, which would solve their economic problems at the same time as undermining the crime syndicates that thrive on the present situation. Eudora Barrientots drew up plans at a meeting of 700 delegates of coca growers' unions to wrest their crop from traffickers and channel it through a new locally-controlled industry to make coca-based biscuits. (The calcium in coca renders it particularly welcome for people on a milkless diet.) A number of large-scale coca producers see themselves as Robin Hood figures who are helping poor Latin Americans at the expense of spoilt gringos, and have gained local loyalties by making benefactions. The Bolivian intellectual Amado Canelas argues that 'cocaine is an instrument of historical vengeance' against not only the Conquistadores but also more recent white oppressors; more encouragingly for Washington, the Amerindian civil rights movement Consejo Regional Indigena del Cauca (CRIC) has proposed an alternative policy which aims: 'To conserve coca as part of Indian culture; for the purpose of shamanism and agricultural work, and as a medicine: it is necessary to stop trading coca with whites, because coca is a thing worthy of respect, and traders use it in a way which is not appropriate.'[9] In the eyes of Dr Timothy Plowman of the Chicago Field Museum's Department of Botany, to have the Latin American coca plantations physically burnt and poisoned seems to the local inhabitants to be 'a direct act of aggression and imperialism, fostered by the

United States and in many cases imposed upon these South American governments more or less by a kind of economic blackmail'. The US anthropologist William Carter has suggested that coca eradication may amount to a form of genocide; another American expert sees it in terms of a manichean psychodrama representing the struggle between good and evil in which the drug has been cast in the role of the devil.[10] Some peasants in Bolivia are turning from coca to drinking infinitely more harmful forms of intoxicant, distilled at local sugar-cane refineries with 89 per cent pure ethyl alcohol and described as 'if one were to take sudden death'.

Whether or not a beneficial indigenous coca industry or alternative labour-intensive agricultural projects can be developed, many growers and traders will continue to find the snowballing profits from cocaine irresistible. The Andean region is capable of growing around 150,000 metric tons of coca a year: about 15 per cent of this is used by local people for chewing or tea, plus another 5 per cent for pharmaceuticals; the rest is available for the illicit market. At present a farmer in Bolivia can sell 500 kg. of coca leaves for $2,000, from which 2.5 kg. of paste or 1 kilo of cocaine will be made in a Colombian laboratory, to be sold for $7,000. This kilo of cocaine can be resold by Colombian distributors for some $18,000 to a wholesaler in Canada, who markets it for around $100,000 to street pushers in Toronto. These are then able to retail it – in 75 per cent adulterated one gram amounts, for $200 each – making a total of $800,000 (more than six times the price of the same amount of gold, and a hundred times the profit from marijuana).[11] In Washington, Dr Turner says, 'We have an enormous problem budding, because past administrations thought "Don't worry about it, it's so expensive it will not become a problem."' And no longer is it just a problem for developed northern countries: as the US government strives to deter imports of cocaine, the excess production is unloaded at rock-bottom prices on to the streets of Latin America, causing devastation from Lima and Medallin to Mexico and La Paz. Several thousand teenagers addicted to 'bazuka' coca paste haunt the shanties of Bogota, where some addict urchins are forced to fight each other in a human version of a cock fight for the sake of rewards of coca paste.

Cocaine production spread throughout 'Narcolandia' – an area which closely mirrors the land of the pre-Columbian Inca empire – when the bottom fell out of its marijuana export market, due to the spectacular growth of domestic pot cultivation in the USA. Peruvian colonists who moved east of the Andes in search of quick riches found the only fortune they could readily make was in cocaine. Meanwhile political insurgents – left- and right-wing in Colombia, extreme left in Peru, and extreme right in Bolivia – are encouraging drug-dealers to operate in their areas in return for shared access to airfields, planes, weapons and hard currency. The $2 billion income of cocaine barons such as Bolivia's Roberto Suarez ('Su Sanctidad') – whose private army rules his fiefdom at Santa Cruz with the help of former Nazis – amounts to double his country's entire legitimate export earnings. Some 60,000 new users of coca paste in Bolivia itself have inflated the price of coca leaves beyond the purse of many of the poor traditional users. Peasant smallholders resent the fact that they are victimized by having their fields sprayed with Agent Orange whenever US congressmen arrive, while governments seem impotent to finger the really powerful syndicates. Especially in Colombia and Mexico, a nationalist feeling persists that drugs are primarily a North American worry, despite the spread of addiction among their own youth. Colombia (parts of which produce four crops a year) started to export drugs to the USA on a large scale in the mid-1970s to replace the Mexican crop that had been sprayed with paraquat: first marijuana, and then cocaine which they found less bulky and more profitable. The narco syndicates there are also the biggest source of Quaaludes and have now begun to grow opium poppies as well to add heroin to the range of exports.

Uniquely, in Colombia a black-market dollar is now worth less than the official one because so many 'narco dollars' are being illegally earned from drugs. (Bishop Dasio Castrillon of Colombia, who has admitted to receiving money from the traffickers 'to give to the poor', claimed: 'I warned them that, with this gesture, they would not be saved. I did it to prevent the money from being invested in brothels, the production of more drugs or any other crime.') A British ambassador who served in the area said that trying to stop the trade was doomed because the traffickers 'have enough money to buy several police forces and the relevant governments too'. In a number of Latin American countries, drug money has corrupted not just politicians, but also the police, judiciary and armed forces, as well as sportsmen, journalists, bankers and even churchmen. (At the lavish parties of a chief of Mexico City's police,

police waiters used to offer guests cocaine as an alternative to champagne.) The traffic is increasingly organized on a cross-frontier international basis: when Panama in 1984 belatedly seized the supplies of ether and acetone used for cocaine refining in Colombia, the trafficking network quickly switched to laboratories in Venezuela, Brazil, Argentina and within the USA itself. More and more cocaine is now being processed in the USA, where the ether needed is legally obtainable for $500 a barrel, compared with $8,000 a barrel in Colombia. Colombian and Cuban exile drug rings deploy modern planes linked to a web of landing strips throughout the Caribbean and the USA. Loyalty is enforced by a brutality so extreme that it elicits awe and fear from even hardened hoodlums: 'These people are animals,' one Mafia connoisseur protested.[12] 'We hardly ever get a Colombian to co-operate,' said a Florida police officer. 'They usually say, "I'd rather do the time and save my family's lives."' Colombian drug-dealer killers believe in leaving no witness: 'They kill the victim's maid, TV repairman, grandmother, child – anyone who is around. Then they finish by murdering the Minister of Justice too.' The North American police find it as difficult to infiltrate the Latin distribution networks as they do to penetrate the far-removed glitzy world of the coke-snorters' private parties. In the summer of 1986, warfare between gangs struggling to control the booming cocaine market reached the UK, led by a Jamaican syndicate who – trained by Cuban gangsters in Miami – shot six people in south London.

The steadily dropping price of cocaine in both the USA and Europe evidences that the drug syndicates are winning. Using the glut from over-production in Colombia, Bolivia and Peru, the major dealers plan to turn cocaine into a mass-selling cheap 'classless' drug, as cannabis was in the 1960s. Their strategy is to lower the price at first in order to build up a network of addicts, and then raise the price at will. In 1984 cocaine's street price fell to less than one-seventh of what it had been five years before; the profits, however, escalated exponentially, in a textbook demonstration of capitalist marketing. Police Lieutenant Lamont of Miami comments: 'If you took all the drug money out of south Florida, the economy would totally collapse.' Since 1981, when earnings from cocaine overtook those of marijuana by $11 billion, it has become the biggest illicit income-generator of any drug in the USA. In 1982 John De Lorean was headline news when he was charged (but later acquitted) with purchasing for resale 220 lb. of cocaine having a street value of £14 million. By 1985 the newspapers hardly noticed when the members of a San Diego-based gang were arrested and accused of having smuggled £10 billions' worth of cocaine into the USA the previous year; a receipt-book was found showing that they had successfully imported more than £630 millions' worth of the drug during the previous six months. The value of the consignment seized on one plane alone at Miami was £742 million. An American official attached to Interpol said that it had taken the coke barons only two years to sew up the USA market, so that Europe – with Britain especially targeted – is now 'a ripe plum' poised to fall to them. Cocaine supplies are being smuggled, force-fed in animals and parrots imported into Spain, impregnated in children's books via Frankfurt, and packed inside corpses or guitars. Most often consignments are borne internally by impoverished human 'mules' who 'swallow or stuff', several of whom die painfully each year when the powdered acid in cocaine eats through the full balloons they are carrying inside their bodies.

Detective Superintendent Derek Olley, recently with Scotland Yard's Central Drugs Intelligence Unit, warns: 'All available intelligence tells us we're on the threshold of a cocaine explosion.' British criminals who moved abroad to countries without extradition laws are financing European supply networks. In 1985 seizures of cocaine in West Germany and Spain for the first time overtook those of heroin. An American federal official at the Drug Enforcement Administration concedes that efforts against cocaine in the end amount to only a token performance: 'We feel like we're part of a spectator sport. We're not the answer. The answers are going to be found in your wallets, or your conscience. The only way to stop the trade is to stop the demand or the production; and we can't stop the source.' As an anti-drugs agent in Denver admitted, 'Coke's mystique, myths and respectability are all working against us – and hence against regard for the law generally.' Persuading people not to plunge nose-first into the 'white blizzard' will be much harder than warning them off heroin, because cocaine appears not only glamorous and beguiling to its users but also deceptively harmless. They remain loyal to cocaine because, as they point out, it does not put them to sleep, give them a hangover, smell or affect their speech or performance; they claim its use in moderation compares favourably with either alcohol or cannabis. Women, in particular, are increasingly attracted to it. Not only business and professional executives now use it as a routine aid, but people from every social category including blue-collar workers. What particularly worries the authorities is that 'It hurts and endangers society directly because, unlike heroin, it is used most by just those people who make the wheels turn,' in the words of one official. 'We can cope with heroin addicts because they tend to be the drop-outs anyway. What we can't afford to lose is the services of half a million skilled and productive people.' In the USA, where a gram of cocaine now costs less than an ounce of quality marijuana, there are demands for urine tests to verify that pilots, traffic controllers and train drivers are not high on coke. American officials warn that they began to perceive the existence of their cocaine epidemic much too late, and that Europe seems certain to follow exactly the same path, as has already happened in sections of society in Rome, London, Paris and Madrid.[13] For cocaine seduces by appearing to provide, at a price, enhanced performance in the roles most sought after in modern society: stimulation for work and sex; an apparently easy way for the shy to buy social confidence; a simply-acquired badge of glittery success; plus, at the same time, an illusion of power and self-control. It entices because it seems to offer a glamorous passport for those people who want a short-cut to pleasure, without guilt, effort or commitment – and who want to buy it instantly.

9

Routes to Paradise: LSD

'Truth is too naked; she does not inflame men.'

Jean Cocteau

'My suspicion is that the universe is not only queerer than we suppose, but queerer than we can suppose.'

J. B. S. Haldane, *Possible Worlds*

The history of LSD (lysergic acid diethylamine-25, also known as acid, dots, big D, cubes, Zen, sugar, the Chief, the handle, Black Star, California or orange sunshine, strawberry fields, white lightning or window pane)[1] began as the result of an accident. On the afternoon of Friday 16 April 1943, Dr Albert Hofmann was working in the Sandoz Laboratories at Basle in Switzerland on a derivative of ergot – a purple fungus which attacks mouldy rye. In medieval Europe, this had been prized by midwives as an aid in childbirth; however, people who ate bread made from such infected rye succumbed to epidemics of what they called St Anthony's Fire. Not only did victims' fingers and toes blacken with gangrene, but they began to see hallucinations of light and flames – which may explain some accounts of early religious and other visions. Ergot also happens to be the main natural source of lysergic acid; and Dr Hofmann in his laboratory unknowingly ingested four micrograms (millionths of a gram) of LSD – a minute amount but sufficient to produce, as he describes, the first recorded 'trip': 'I had to leave my work and go home because I felt strangely restless and dizzy. I lay down and sank into a not unpleasant delirium marked by an extreme degree of fantasy . . . accompanied by a kaleidoscopic play of intense colours swirling around me.' To confirm what he suspected was the cause, he next experimented by deliberately swallowing 250 further micrograms of LSD. After forty minutes, he wrote in his notebook, he felt an 'inability to concentrate, visual disturbance and uncontrollable laughter'. Prudently he asked his assistant to accompany him on his four-mile bicycle journey home, during which:

> I had the greatest difficulty speaking coherently and my field of vision fluctuated and was distorted like the reflections in an amusement park mirror. I also had the impression I was hardly moving, yet my assistant later told me I was pedalling fast . . . [later I felt] . . . a feeling of suffocation; confusion alternating with a clear appreciation of the situation; at times standing outside myself as a neutral observer and hearing myself muttering jargon or screaming half madly.

After a good night's rest he recorded that he felt 'completely well, but tired'.[2]

Hofmann had by chance happened upon an extraordinarily powerful drug. A quantity of LSD which is invisible to the naked eye is enough to cause a person to hallucinate. Weight for weight, LSD is 200 times as strong as other hallucinogens such as the psilocybin in Liberty Cap mushrooms, and 4,000 times stronger than the mescalin of the Mexican peyote cactus,[3] both of which had been used in Amerindian religious ceremonies for centuries. Reports of the potency of Hofmann's discovery excited governments with the fantastic idea – and also fear – that LSD might offer the supreme political prize: the key to control people's minds. The Pentagon and the CIA during the 1950s repeatedly pressed Hofmann to work for them, while the Chemical Division of the CIA's Technical Services Staff explored the possibilities of using LSD to brainwash or disorientate an enemy. Military chiefs argued that such temporarily incapacitating agents were not only the ultimate weapon, but, unlike nuclear weapons or poison gas, were also the most humane way of winning wars: countries conquered by such means would not be devastated, but could function normally again as soon as desired. Studies were made of the possibilities of aerial spraying of the drug from planes or rockets. The Pentagon, however, also uneasily contemplated the sobering thought that a mere 15 kg. of LSD – capable of being carried by a single man in a small suitcase – would provide enough for the KGB to slip 150 million doses into America's air or water. The Chiefs of Staff were warned that detection of LSD is virtually impossible; it even survives boiling, and Hofmann's experience showed that it can take effect when breathed in unwittingly. A CIA memorandum dated 5 August 1954 furthermore warned, 'The basic material from which LSD is prepared is ergot, and the Soviet bloc has an abundant supply of it.' A deal urgently needed to be struck with the manufacturers; Hofmann's employers, the Swiss pharmaceutical company Sandoz, agreed to sell the US government 100 g. a week indefinitely until further notice. Several other countries including the UK and China similarly began to lay in stockpiles. In America, a programme of secret official human experiments with the drug was started forthwith. Besides being administered to groups of CIA employees and soldiers, LSD was also tried on inmates of mental hospitals and prisons, sometimes coupled with an inducement of remission. These human guinea pigs included a number of unconsenting individuals who were unaware that they were being given the drug, sometimes with tragic consequences: in 1975 the Rockefeller Commission reported that two men who had no idea they had taken any LSD had died because of the CIA's inexperience. Experiments were carried out on animals as well: spiders were found to build more perfect webs under the influence of LSD, whereas when they were given mescalin the webs were more disarranged. Ironically, however, the main result of the US government bringing so much LSD into the country was that American students soon became aware of the serendipitous potential of the new drug: it was the CIA who funded the LSD research at Dr Timothy Leary's university.[4] Washington's attempt to harness the drug as a mind-control weapon escaped like a sorcerer's apprentice, fuelling an anti-government counter-culture which advocated that the nation's best and brightest youth should 'make love, not war'.

LSD's associations, through attempts to pervert it into a military weapon or due to the furore aroused by Leary's publicity, still makes calm evaluation difficult. Research has shown that its use

193

does not result in physical dependence or withdrawal symptoms, and that an LSD overdose has very rarely been known to cause a human's death. The Canadian government's Le Dain Commission of Inquiry into the Non-Medical Use of Drugs concluded that 'in terms of lethal toxicity, LSD must be considered one of the safest drugs known'. Laboratory experiments indicate that no new effect is caused from any dose above 1,000 micrograms. The risk of hazard is psychological rather than physical, being most likely to occur to somebody who already has existing psychological difficulties. Effects begin to be experienced between thirty and sixty minutes after taking LSD; they peak some two to six hours later, depending on the size of the dose, and fade away after about eight to twelve hours, usually having progressed through several intense and often dramatic phases. The fantasies a user has depend upon his own disposition, mood, sense of security and expectations, and also on the company and setting in which he takes the drug; LSD tends to accentuate and distort whatever was the taker's previous emotional and mental state. Small doses of 25–80 micrograms have an effect not dissimilar to that of cannabis; doses of 80–250 micrograms produce distortion or hallucination; larger doses often result in a sense of revelation. If a consumer uses illicit supplies, he finds it hard to know the drug's purity or strength – which is commonly weaker than claimed: since LSD has no colour, taste or smell it is easy for pushers to sell pieces of blotting paper or sugar that contain no trace of the drug. It is so unobtrusive that police or Customs officers also find it an almost impossible nightmare to detect. Two British servicemen, who in 1985 alleged that some of their colleagues took LSD whilst on patrol in Polaris nuclear submarines, said that Customs officials lacked the security clearance to search for drugs behind the reactor area.

The effects that LSD produces include vibrant kaleidoscopes of colour; the distortion of time, with the past and future merging into the present; and the disappearance of the user's ego with his viewpoint elevated to a position of detachment. One of the most extraordinary results Hofmann felt was that he was seeing music and hearing colours (the phenomenon known as synaesthesia). 'The effect is incredible and impossible to describe: it's like all your senses merge.' At its best, a taker of LSD can throw off his tensions, doubts and anxieties along with his self-consciousness. Analytical personalities, however, often find it more disturbing than do intuitive people, and some users become dissatisfied with the dullness of normal colours and sensations after the experience. Under the drug's influence, rational logic appears to be in abeyance; the user believes he can transmit and read thoughts – though the profound ideas he thinks he is uttering generally sound considerably less brilliant to other people: 'LSD makes people feel more creative, though it doesn't improve their creativity,' says Don des Jarlois in New York. Besides experiencing a new sense of their own identity, its users often report a feeling of oneness with art or the universe: the sense of depersonalization can approach what a Zen Buddhist seeks to achieve by meditation. On the other hand, as Aldous Huxley reported in his 1954 book, its doors of perception can open on to psychotic hell as well as transcendental heaven. Twinges of anxiety or jealousy can swell into unbearable traumas. What appears to one user as a transcendental vision can terrify another by seeming to be an indication that he is going mad. Panic frequently follows the user's discovery that he is unable to control the effects of the drug; reactions of paranoia – or even latent psychosis or schizophrenia – can be triggered off by the feeling that some strange power is succeeding in manipulating his mind. Disorientation from a bad trip is least likely if a dose is taken in secure and undisturbed surroundings, where the user feels at ease, preferably in the company of a totally trusted friend. It is dangerous to allow a trip – or flashbacks, which can occur for some considerable time afterwards – to coincide with any task that requires concentration, such as driving a car. The illusion of omnipotent indestructibility some users acquire can have fatal consequences. To give LSD to someone without warning by spiking their food or drink is obviously irresponsible in the extreme.

In the 1950s and early 1960s it was hoped that LSD might provide a tool to create a model psychosis to give insight into the biochemical processes of mental illness, including schizophrenia which ostensibly shares several similarities with the experiences produced by LSD. Attempts have also been made to treat drug addiction with LSD; in Canada doctors unsuccessfully tried to cure alcoholics by using it. Over 40,000 American patients volunteered to be given LSD therapeutically; among them was Cary Grant who warmly praises its effect.[5] It has been given as well to dying patients who requested it. (Aldous Huxley was so impressed by the spiritual benefits of mescalin that he asked for some on his death bed, and is reported to have ended his life gazing at his wife with an expression of love and happiness.) In a study of other terminal patients who were given LSD, none complained of feeling worse as a consequence and two-thirds reported some benefit; half of these said they experienced increased peace of mind, with reduced anxiety and depression, accompanied by diminished fear of their approaching death.[6]

No therapeutic use at all, however, is known to be made of LSD in the UK at the present time. Unfortunately, as Dr Michael Gossop says, 'Ever since its discovery, LSD has polarized attitudes and generated hysteria . . . The LSD crusades (both for and against the drug) have made it all but impossible to hold a rational discussion about the possible benefits.' Public furore eventually made Sandoz withdraw it from the clinical market altogether, closing off further research. In 1978, for example, the *Daily Mirror* reported: 'Takers have been known to . . . chew a hand down to the bone, believing it to be an orange . . . or truss and prepare a baby for roasting, believing it to be an oven-ready chicken.'[7] Today LSD has largely disappeared from the British headlines since the Operation Julie trial (described below), though its street price of only £2 for the amount needed for a trip indicates that it has not stopped being manufactured illicitly for recreational use. It is relatively simple for a chemist to produce LSD from ergot using industrial chemicals, making a tartrate salt which is soluble, often being soaked in a lump of sugar or 'microdots' of blotting paper. Usually it is swallowed, sometimes as a liquid, though it may also be sniffed or injected.

After the sensational publicity about bad LSD trips, recreational preference tended to move to more natural hallucinogenic substances. Although – as with most drug use – it is only the experiences of the untypically most literate users which are generally recorded, there is evidence that LSD may now quietly be being used by a wider section of society than its previous following amongst students and graduates. Hallucinogenics are generally taken with deliberate premeditation, but are rarely used regularly; and they are unlikely to gain converts by being spontaneously passed around at a party. Even so, approximately 5 per cent of the American and 1 per cent of the British population somewhat surprisingly admit or claim to have used it. Consumer opinion in fact does not accord with the media's shock-horror label. In one study of ostensibly 'normal' subjects who were given a single high dose of LSD or mescalin, as many as 78 per cent described it as the greatest thing that had ever happened to them, and several months afterwards still stated it had made them happier, less anxious and more able to love other people as well as understand themselves. On the other hand, the drug undeniably can entail some real dangers – such as lending an Icarus-like delusion to the user that he can fly. However, according to the UK Institute for the Study of Drug Dependence, luridly exaggerated tales about LSD, far from acting as a deterrent, tend to undermine the credibility of straight information amongst those who need such facts most – its users and potential users.[8]

There have been several intellectual advocates for hallucinogenic drugs, of whom the most persuasively eloquent was the writer Aldous Huxley.[9] Initially interested in pursuing the idea that the ancient Mexican psychedelic drug[10] mescalin might be chemically similar to adrenaline, he experimented with it in the hope that it would admit him to the inner world experienced by visionaries such as William Blake: 'If the doors of perception were cleansed, everything will appear to man as it is, infinite.' Huxley found the effect on himself was to help him recover 'some of the perpetual innocence of childhood, when the sensum is not immediately and automatically subordinated to the concept'. He hoped it might even be the solution to worse drug problems, arguing:

The problems raised by alcohol and tobacco cannot, it goes without saying, be solved by prohibition. The universal and ever-present urge to self-transcendence is not to be abolished by slamming the currently popular Doors in the Wall. The only reasonable policy is to open other, better doors in the hope of inducing men and women to exchange their old bad habits for new and less harmful ones. Some of these will be social and technological in nature, others religious or psychological, others dietetic, educational, athletic. But the need for frequent chemical vacations from intolerable selfhood and repulsive surroundings will undoubtedly remain.

Huxley went on to claim: 'Unlike alcohol, mescalin does not drive the taker into the kind of uninhibited action which results in brawls, crimes of violence, or traffic accidents. A man under the influence of mescalin quietly minds his own business. Moreover, the business he minds is an experience of the most enlightening kind, which does not have to be paid for (and this is surely important) by a compensatory hangover.' Huxley recognized, however, that: 'Although obviously superior to cocaine, opium, alcohol and tobacco, mescalin is not yet the ideal drug. Along with the happily transfigured majority of mescalin takers there is a minority that finds in the drug only hell or purgatory.' He hopefully suggested nevertheless that: 'Ideally, everyone should be able to find self-transcendence in some form of pure or applied religion . . . Christianity and alcohol do not and cannot mix. Christianity and mescalin seem to be much more compatible.' Robert Graves similarly commended the positive case for the psychedelic drug psilocybe:

Any use of hallucinogenic drugs, except for medical purposes, goes against civilized conscience; perhaps because, in this Christian world, only visions won by prayer and piety are ascribed to God, rather than the Devil. Because of my Protestant conditioning, I would never take cocaine, heroin, hashish, or marijuana, even experimentally; but the Mexican mushroom does not belong to this range of drugs, nor is it habit-forming. So far from stupefying the senses, it quickens them. An experimentalist's mind will stay conscious throughout – indeed supraconscious. This peculiar virtue, of enhancing reality, turns the Greek command 'know thyself!' into a practical precept; psilocybe illuminates the mind, re-educates sight and hearing.[11]

LSD was to give Paul McCartney a religious experience: he said, 'It opened my eyes to the fact there is a God.' A very senior banking executive, who discovered the study of psychedelic mushrooms to be more engrossing than the world of finance, believes that the mystical visions of the founders of many religions were due to botanical hallucination. Havelock Ellis found mescalin not only fired his intellectual energy but also provided him with coloured visions so like Monet's paintings that he gave some of the drug to Monet – who enjoyed similar visions under it, which were, however, followed by a nightmarish aftermath in reaction.[12] In 1910 the self-appointed satanist Aleister Crowley used peyote to 'turn on' audiences at his controversial meetings.

Mescalin exaggerates, rather than alters, reality, whereas LSD produces more complicated effects: the Gestapo, who experimented with mescalin on inmates at Dachau, naively noted that (not surprisingly) 'sentiments of hatred and revenge were exposed in every case'. Some people subjectively claim that either drug can act as a powerful aphrodisiac. Aldous Huxley advised Leary to keep this quiet: 'We've stirred up enough trouble suggesting that drugs can stimulate aesthetic and religious experiences. I strongly urge you not to let the sexual cat out of the bag.'[13] However, whereas mescalin and its raw material, the peyote cactus, are not easy to obtain in Europe and the eastern USA, LSD can be mass-produced in laboratories anywhere. Michael Hollingshead, a young English scientist from Oxford who was studying the effect of lysergic acid on web-spinning by spiders in the USA, mixed the drug into powdered sugar to attract the insects. As an afterthought he and a doctor colleague licked the spoon – and thus unwittingly ingested an unprecedented dose. The two researchers sat immobile and mesmerized for several hours; overwhelmed by their experience, they decided to abandon the spiders forthwith and switch to the study of LSD. It was Hollingshead who, while working for the British Council in 1961, introduced Timothy Leary to LSD – a move that was to have fateful consequences for the reputation both of Leary and of LSD. Dr Leary, a former West Point cadet who was at that time a highly promising assistant professor of clinical psychology at Harvard, immediately underwent total conversion and made plans to distribute free LSD throughout the USA.[14] This was too much even for Harvard, which dismissed him in 1963. Leary was undeterred. From mescalin he says he has realized 'that the brain is an underutilized biocomputer, containing billions of unaccessed neurons. I learned that normal consciousness is one drop in an ocean of intelligence. That consciousness and intelligence can be systematically expanded. That the brain can be reprogrammed. That knowledge of how the brain operates is the most pressing scientific issue of our time. I was beside myself with enthusiasm, convinced that we had found the key we had been looking for.'[15] A sponsor for his mission arrived in the form of William Mellon Hitchcock, a Wall Street broker and a scion of the immensely wealthy Mellon family, who gave Leary and his followers the use of Millbrook – a mansion with a 4,000-acre estate in upper New York state – which became the centre of the 'Tune in, turn on and drop out' reaction to America's war in Vietnam. Leary viewed the utopiate drug as a sacrament, and himself as its evangelist with a mission to change the world. The League of Spiritual Discovery was founded to spread with its help a religion of universal love and peace world-wide; this was succeeded by the Brotherhood of Eternal Love, a group which was given charitable status as a religious organization by the state of California. While LSD was still legal, among those who tried and favourably recommended it were not only Jack Nicholson and Andy Warhol but also Henry and Claire Luce. The adventures it brought Ken Kesey (the author of *One Flew Over the Cuckoo's Nest*) and his acid-freak Pranksters were recorded by Tom Wolfe in *The Electric Kool-aid Acid Test*.

However, the US government, alarmed that the spreading drug culture was in danger of turning on and into an anarchic revolution, banned LSD in 1967. In the same year Britain made its possession and distribution illegal – though, due to a loophole in the law, its manufacture remained legal until 1974. Gordon Liddy, later to be indicted as a Watergate burglar, was the FBI agent who raided Leary's LSD commune at Millbrook. Leary – according to taste, either a psychedelic Peter Pan or the Pied Piper of the acid revolution – was convicted, but was sprung from jail and spirited out of the USA by the Weathermen in return for $50,000 paid by the Brotherhood of Eternal Love. He went to live alongside Eldridge Cleaver in Algeria, but was kidnapped in a CIA sting inside Afghanistan and returned to prison in the USA. Meanwhile, the Weathermen started to use LSD to screen their new recruits, insisting that applicants should take it in group sessions designed to expose infiltrations; the very different Charles Manson also employed it to help indoctrinate his followers. The Brotherhood of Eternal Love continued as an underground movement, becoming, however, a less idealistic organization which distributed LSD to Hell's Angels and allegedly planned to put LSD in the water supply of cities. From 2.8 kg. of ergotamine tartrate imported from Europe for $14,000, the Brotherhood's talented chemist Owsley – described by a Washington official as 'the man who did for LSD what Henry Ford did for the motor car' – made 5.6 million dosage units which the organization sold for $5 million. By 1970 the Brotherhood had made $200 million from drug-trafficking; and considered buying Clipperton Island in the Pacific, with the intention of making it the world's first independent state founded on LSD. Although several of the leaders (who plotted some of their transactions in the unlikely setting of the Oxford and Cambridge Club in London) were arrested in 1972 and 1973, survivors from the group have recently diversified into arms-dealing as well as cocaine smuggling.[16]

The existence of a skilled LSD-producing organization in Britain, in touch with the Brotherhood, came as a major shock to the authorities when it was revealed in 1977 by Operation Julie. The British group, which was organized in a cell-like structure, had since 1970 been making some £20 millions' worth of LSD a year to distribute and sell throughout the world. The scale and productivity of this export enterprise astonished the UK government, which only three months previously had assured a WHO conference that no LSD was being manufactured in Britain. In 1975 the total of LSD seized throughout the whole world amounted to 80,000 dosage units; the Julie police found 18,000,000 dosage units hidden by a few young amateurs in Wales, Berkshire and Hampshire – which may provide some food for thought about the scale of other drug supplies as yet undetected. The syndicate was only unearthed due to thirteen months' work by one single-minded junior Thames Valley police officer, Detective Inspector Dick Lee, in the face of scepticism and even obstruction from Scotland Yard as well as several of his seniors. Customs officers were convinced that substantial bribes had been paid to certain Metropolitan policemen to protect the network, with the result that Lee's team were forced to keep their investigation secret even from the capital's police. Lee had noticed the exceptional amount and quality of the LSD which was available at his local Reading and Windsor pop festivals, and followed its trail to an isolated farmhouse near Lampeter in mid-Wales. Here a young chemist called Richard Kemp was living with Dr Christine Bott, ostensibly leading a simple rural life tending goats. A key clue came to light by chance when Kemp's Range Rover was involved in a fatal road accident; inside the damaged vehicle were found six tiny scraps of torn-up paper which, when fitted together, spelt out 'hydrazine hydrate', a major ingredient in making LSD. Beneath Kemp's kitchen floor, in a small plastic box less than a foot square, the police discovered 13 million dosage units of LSD crystal – then worth £65 million, reputedly at that time the largest drugs haul ever made.[17] Kemp, sentenced to thirteen years' imprisonment, is a highly intelligent honours graduate who lived modestly and gave away some of his huge profits to causes he supported; among his young partners who were also jailed were a law graduate of the London School of Economics, another graduate who was a schoolteacher, and the Cambridge graduate son of a retired police officer who held a Master's degree in chemistry at the University of East Anglia, in the laboratory of which he tested the purity of the LSD. Christine Bott, a GP who had been at university with Kemp and was sentenced to nine years' imprisonment, said: 'We weren't in it for the money . . . I felt it was my contribution to alter society . . . I feel that cannabis and acid if used properly lift the veil and one sees the truth . . . You feel at one with the world. You begin to appreciate everything surrounding you.' After the arrests the street price of a LSD microdot (a pill the size of a match-head) rose temporarily from £1 to £5, but it took only two weeks before another source of supply materialized to fill the demand. The comfortable Victorian house at Hampton Wick, west of London, where the Julie chemists had made LSD, was ordered to be demolished two years afterwards because experts believed that it was still impregnated with mind-bending fumes.

How dangerous in fact is LSD? Leary – who now appears as a double-act with Liddy on the lecture circuit – claims that 100,000 people took LSD at Woodstock without serious harm. He contrasts this with the results of alcohol:

> Most of my fractured friendships have unravelled under the influence of liquor. 90 per cent of the eruptions of vulgarity, insensitivity or aggression in my history have been triggered by mild to moderate doses of booze. (The remaining 10 per cent have been performed sober.) In the last twenty years I have ingested enormous quantities of psychedelic drugs (mainly cannabis and LSD). I find that these chemicals stimulate quiet, serene, humorous, sensual, reflective responses. They make me a better person. I have never done anything I regret while under the influence of these substances . . . Around 10 per cent of alcohol drinkers are abusers. Then as now booze casualties were epidemic, so the jaded Press paid no attention to the misadventures of one drunk. Their attitude was different with psychedelic drugs. Only one out of every thousand LSD users reported a negative experience, yet the Press dug up a thousand lurid stories. There was such an appetite for anti-LSD tales that many hoaxes developed . . . When a story was later exposed as a fraud, little attention was paid to the quiet retraction. Throughout the land anti-drug people – politi-

cians, police officials, institutional psychiatrists – popped up to denounce LSD and marijuana as the most dangerous threats confronted by the human race. This sort of propaganda was guaranteed to create mass hysteria and to sow the seeds of bad set and setting.

Authorities appear to feel particularly threatened by psychedelic drugs, perhaps because social order is usually founded on a consensus of what reality is, and conflicting perceptions undermine this consensus.[18] The tragic drug deaths of public media figures such as Brian Jones, Janis Joplin, William Holden, Natalie Wood, Jimi Hendrix, Keith Moon and Mama Cass were all due to alcohol being taken in combination with uppers or downers. By comparison, Dr Albert Hofmann, LSD's discoverer, testifies that to his knowledge there has not been a single fatality as a direct consequence of LSD poisoning, as distinct from mental disorientation due to LSD intoxication.[19] (When John Griggs, one of the founders of the Brotherhood, died in 1969 after taking psilocybin, it was later discovered that it had been laced with strychnine.) Hofmann expresses the hope that if LSD were used in the right conditions 'then in the future this problem child could become a wonder child'. Such conditions are obviously absent when LSD is being illegally imported – as it now is – from Amsterdam, impregnated on stamps or transfers of Superman, E. T. and Snoopy for young people to lick. Perhaps its use might be medically licensed, in order to learn more about it and to safeguard against its undoubted risks. Current medical advice is that nobody should take any psychedelic substance unless (i) they have a stable personality; (ii) the dose is pure and accurately measured; (iii) the setting is relaxed and free from interruption; (iv) there is expert, sympathetic and medically qualified supervision; and (v) antidotes are available at hand.[20]

Psychedelics cannot be 'disinvented'; indeed more new forms of them will inevitably be discovered. The latest to find fashion in America is 'Ecstasy' or XTC – a member of the phenethylamine family, related to both mescalin and amphetamines, and also known as 'Adam' or MDMA. At present it is still legal, but also untested, though a number of psychiatrists are using it in therapy to help patients explore their feelings. Unlike LSD, XTC is reputed to be safe and not to cause bad trips: it lacks the dangerous side effect which breaks down the user's ability to distinguish reality from fantasy, and is now the current drug of choice on campuses from Berkeley to Cambridge. It is the latest, but certainly far from the last, drug to have escaped from the laboratory into the streets.

10

Glue Sniffing and Solvent Abuse

'There are more spells than your commonplace magicians ever dreamed of.'

Joseph Conrad, *Victory*

A person who inhales the fumes of volatile hydrocarbon chemicals (such as are in some glues or solvents, especially those based on petroleum and natural gas) may become intoxicated in a way which is not unlike being drunk. Historically, the fashion for sniffing such vapours for pleasure recurs and recedes in scarcely predictable waves. Victorians sniffed ether and laughing gas to obtain a buzz as a fairground frolic, until these vapours – like smelling salts – went out of vogue of their own accord. Any 'high' effect reaches the sniffer's brain and liver very quickly from the lungs, although the sensation only lasts a few minutes unless it is prolonged by concentrating the vapour inside a bag.

Today, solvent vapour abuse usually occurs amongst bored young people between the ages of twelve and sixteen, almost all of whom try it for only a brief period before growing out of the habit naturally. It tends to be mainly a group activity amongst male teenagers – a substitute for their elders' visits to the pub – and often to centre round a particular school or housing estate. Instances were first reported during the 1950s in the USA; in Britain it is now most prevalent in depressed northern urban areas such as Tyneside, Clydeside and Merseyside, although cases have also occurred in isolated rural districts such as mid-Wales. As happened in the USA and Canada, young people's interest in the idea can be aroused by sensational Press stories that, telling how and which substances to use, alert them to a new way of shocking their elders – and one moreover for which they are safe from prosecution.

How much danger is involved in this way of rebelling? Solvent sniffing (which should be retermed solvent poisoning, since it is through the mouth that the vapour is often inhaled most deeply) can produce tolerance and psychological, but not physical, addiction. Among groups, its attraction is similar to that of alcohol: youngsters employ it to get merry and fool about together. The outward symptoms that users display include clumsiness, slurred speech and aggressiveness. Internally, the result can graduate from dizzy euphoria to nausea or hallucinations; the after-effects generally amount to a mild hangover for about a day but seldom any worse physical consequence.[1] In a 1985 survey nearly 17 per cent of British teenage schoolchildren admitted to having tried inhaling glue or solvents at least once.[2] About one in ten young experimenters – often an adolescent having underlying social or personality problems – continues as a 'lone sniffer'. In a few instances he may persist for hours each day, which can damage his brain and control of movement or affect his liver and kidneys. One man's consumption reached as much as a litre of glue a day. Serious or even fatal injury can result from three infrequent causes: firstly, suffocation – as a result of swallowed vomit, a person squirting gas directly into his throat, or inhaling with his head inside a plastic bag; secondly, by poisoning from aerosol gases (which are more harmful than glue); or thirdly, from accidents when a person who is 'high' on solvent catches fire, or launches himself into space or a canal under the delusion that he is indestructible. Intoxicated young people have been found wandering in busy traffic or along railway lines, or may go berserk: one sniffer said that when high, 'like Popeye with his spinach', he feels capable of anything. A Reading decorator in 1986 ran amok having become accidentally intoxicated from glue fumes when he was stripping wallpaper. In 1982, fifty-nine children under the age of eighteen died in Britain as a result of this type of abuse; recent fatalities included a 28-year-old games teacher and a former swimming champion aged thirteen. The total number of deaths attributed to solvent misuse in Britain, although still low, has moved upwards in recent years from twenty-nine in 1980 to eighty-one in 1984. Each such death is an unnecessary tragedy – though it may help to keep the problem in perspective if we remember that the total is less than one-thirtieth of the number of young people of the same age who die in road accidents.

To a youngster, the habit offers a 'kick' that is easy to obtain and quick to take effect, coupled with the excitement of a degree of risk The reasons users give range from the wish to counter anomie and depression, to a desire to copy friends and 'look big'. (And 'Because life is boring and frustrating'; 'It's something that parents and teachers don't like.') Several teenagers act out the stereotypes of 'tearaways', 'hooligans' or 'victims' which have been pinned on them by the media. In the shanty towns of Latin America, on the other hand, teenagers sniff to blot out feeling hunger and cold; Ricardo, who lives in a slum part of Santiago, told one Oxfam worker: 'When you're high, you don't feel the cold. But if you inhale very often, then you do feel it. When you sniff a lot, you feel like an old man.' The pull to conform with current crazes probably reaches its peak in adolescence: the cheapness of solvents renders them the drug most readily accessible to out-of work young people lacking money. The high visibility of the offensive challenge given to conventional society lends added attraction – heightened also by adult authorities' current uncertainty as to what, if anything, they can do about it. To most older people the practice appears not just unaesthetic and inexplicable, but alien and bizarre, like some invasion of the familiar world by new-wave zombies. (Along the banks of the River Swale near Richmond in Yorkshire, in some of the most beautiful woods in England, the only signs of twentieth-century human civilization are trails of discarded plastic bags containing mucus-like lumps of glue.) There is no doubt that the anguish caused for parents is real, when they see a loved teenager possessed by an incomprehensible daemon. Solvents can disrupt personal relationships with family and friends as much as alcoholism does. The London mother of D., one eighteen-year-old, told Harry Greenway, MP:

I felt sorry for my younger son P., because he is a good boy and he has to live with all the misery of his mother and brother. The last job D. did closed down at Christmas, and he hasn't even looked for a job since. He is probably on glue twenty-four hours a day. He takes it to bed with him and starts sniffing the minute he wakes up, so we have rows every morning and night now. I have told him to go out and not come back, but where can he go? We have no other family or friends. All D.'s mates have grown out of glue and ignore him now. I think he is always on his own. Last week the Careers Office phoned him and asked him to go and see them, and he came back and said he had an interview for a job in a big hotel in two days' time, but he had to wear black shoes and black trousers, which he didn't have because he always wears jeans and trainers. He was so enthusiastic about getting this job. I went out with him and spent my electric bill money on getting him a pair of black shoes and trousers which cost me nearly £40, but I was hoping he might get the job. He looked really smart, and I was just as disappointed as he was when he didn't get the job. So we are back to square one again. A few days ago, D. came home early and locked himself in the bathroom to glue sniff. He started shouting and swearing and saying he wished he was dead. He was sick of this life, and me, and this house, and his brother. I tried to speak calmly to him. I was scared he might try to kill himself, when my younger son came in and tried to break the bathroom door down. I phoned Carter Street Police Station and asked them, if there were any police passing, could they call here, because my son was a glue sniffer and he had locked himself in the bathroom and my other son was trying to break the door down trying to get him out. (No wonder nobody talks to us.) Five minutes later two officers called and they persuaded him to come out. One of the officers took him into his bedroom to have a talk and I helped the other one to find the tin of glue. He said he would take it away. They said it's a shame to see a young boy in such a state, there are so many kids on glue or drugs these days, but D. wasn't breaking the law, it's OK to sniff glue. They admired all his boxing trophies in the front room and asked him if he was still boxing. He said 'No', and they went. They also told me to phone up anytime we needed help. The next day D. was back on glue. When I think that there are so many places for drug addicts, so much help for alcoholics and even gamblers, but people don't realize that glue is dangerous. It's only if it is in your own family that you find out all the misery and upset it can cause. We are not a family any more.[3]

What then can be done? Since it is the vapours of only quick solvent-borne impact adhesives that are abused, one obvious solution would be to ban these types of glue. The trouble is that toluene – the solvent that affects the central nervous system of people who inhale it – is also found in many paints, paint thinners and plastic cement. There are in all no fewer than 700 different substances capable of being similarly misused, including many everyday necessities found in the broom-cupboard or garage of the average household. Such volatile chemicals include acetone (found in nail-varnish and removers), amyl acetate (in typing correction fluid), tetra-chloride and trichloroethane (in dry-cleaning fluids, industrial solvents and domestic cleaners), hexane (in plastic cement and carpet adhesives), methylene (in several dyes), butane (in bottled gas and gas-lighter fuel, the cause of almost as many deaths as glue), bromochlorodifluoromethane (in some fire-extinguishers) and benzene (in petrol). Different individuals are sensitive and allergic to different chemicals: the cause of one highly intelligent boy becoming disruptive and disturbed was traced to the formaldehyde (commonly used in photocopiers) present in the foam insulation of his new bedroom wall.

Cases of the deliberate inhalation of petrol fumes have been widely reported from different parts of the world: from among Australian aborigines, several areas of Africa, and the Indians of Canada's Arctic Manitoba.[4] Of rather greater potential danger are the halon or fluorocarbon propellant and refrigerant mixtures contained in aerosols such as hairsprays, pain-relief sprays, deodorants, cleaners, shaving-creams, de-icers, anti-insect and paint sprays; deaths have resulted from inhaling fluorocarbon gas, and sprays have also been known to cause suffocation by coating the inside of an inhaler's lungs.

Even if it is, therefore, scarcely practicable to withdraw from sale all potentially dangerous solvents (which would include, for example, bicycle puncture-mending kits), should not manufacturers at least be required to impregnate their products with a sufficiently off-putting smell in order to deter sniffing? Labels indicating the risks should also be mandatory – though not in the sensationalist way in which it was carried out in America. Information alone might not be enough: Professor Griffith Edwards, the Head of the Addiction Research Unit at the London Institute of Psychiatry, warns: 'There is very little evidence that factual education has ever affected any sort of drug habit' (although it is reasonable to assume it must have helped to reduce smoking). It would, nevertheless, be perfectly possible to replace solvent-based glues with slower-acting water-based – or comparably effective latex-based – substitutes. However, manufacturers at present are resisting doing so on the commercial grounds of consumer preference: they argue that the public – perhaps significantly – like the aroma of solvent in the glues they buy.[5] This is scarcely a sufficient reason for not saving lives: legislation should be passed urgently to forbid any dangerous solvent-based product which does not contain a deterrent additive.

The alternative course of action, to forbid the sale of all such items to young people – as is done for tobacco, alcohol and fireworks – would be less likely to work. Quite apart from the number of such substances readily accessible in most family homes, a survey found that 39 per cent of adolescents who abuse solvents obtain them by stealing, and a further 33 per cent by persuading someone older to make the purchases for them. Only 15 per cent bought their glue at a shop in person.[6] Petty pilfering of industrial or office solvents is not unknown and is also very difficult to prevent. Meanwhile some traders (including at least one in the Newcastle area who is well-known for operating on a tricycle) have been selling young people 'happy bags' – kits ready-made for sniffing, with dollops of glue already inserted in old crisp bags. Such deliberate profiteering in misuse has recently been made illegal in England and Wales by the 1985 Intoxicating Substances (Supplies) Act, a private member's bill introduced by Neville Trotter, MP.[7] In Scotland, unlike south of the border, such sellers could already have been convicted under the old common law offence of 'palpable and reckless' conduct that causes real injury to others: the Lord Justice General, Lord Emslie, ruled that this crime could apply to selling glue-sniffing kits – even though there was no statute law against this – because Scottish law states clearly that 'An old crime may be committed in a new way'.[8] In the particular case the judge was considering, two brothers who kept a newsagent's shop in Glasgow were jailed for three years for continuing to sell glue in crisp bags for 30p to children, despite appeals from neighbours and the police to stop doing so. Parents' demonstrations outside the shop equally were unavailing: the shopowners declared they were not breaking any law and refused to stop. When the police obtained a search warrant, they found four gallons of glue on the premises.

The law does not, however, prohibit the sale either of glue and plastic bags as separate items, or of the other solvents and aerosols that carry an even greater degree of risk. Banning all sales, however innocent, of products containing solvents to a particular age group, even were it feasible, might create a worse crime situation by making a profitable market for 'pushers' – besides lending such items the false glamour of forbidden contraband. Neither do those experts who have studied the problem believe that it would make any sense to forbid the act of glue sniffing itself by law. To do this would alienate more of the younger generation and give them a criminal identity, for the sake of a misguided juvenile aberration that the majority grow out of naturally. It would make them more secretive, driving the practice underground and away from help; it might also deter parents and friends from seeking assistance just when it is needed. Too many young people are already sucked into the criminal justice system when they are immature – to the long-term detriment of society as well as themselves. Superintendent Max Frood of the Strathclyde Police opposes glue sniffing being made a criminal offence: 'That would do no good at all. We're trying to help these children, not convict them. And for that we rely on information from families, friends and neighbours, which would just dry up if the youngsters were going to be taken to court.' Dr Ian Jones of Fife claims that the problem of solvent abuse has been blown out of all proportion: 'More people die in a day in Fife from the effects of tobacco and alcohol than die in Scotland in a whole year from solvent abuse.' The English Magistrates' Association, however, argues that the police need a statutory power to take a juvenile found sniffing to a place such as a hospital, police station or his home, in order to contact a parent, doctor or social worker.[9] The Justices' Clerks' Society indeed urges that such a power should be extended to allow the police to detain anyone intoxicated from any cause – liquor, drugs or solvents – in a public place. They do not believe that the Home Office's present official circular of advice on solvent misuse (number 30/84) goes far enough. This states:

> Solvent misuse is indulged in mainly by young people. For the majority it is merely a transient phase arising out of boredom or a desire to experiment. For the small minority of persistent misusers, it may be a manifestation of a more deeply rooted maladjustment. For these reasons it is generally considered that the criminal law would not be the most effective means of responding to the kind of educational and social problems which solvent misuse poses . . . In the majority of cases in which the police come across a person misusing solvents, the most appropriate course of action is likely to be the offer of advice or assistance. Since solvent misuse does not constitute an offence, a person who is offered advice or assistance is always free to refuse to co-operate. (A misuser who was clearly incapacitated could, however, normally be dealt with under existing arrangements for dealing with cases of illness in the street.) But where a misuser is prepared to co-operate, the informal approach will often be the most sensible and the most productive . . . There are various kinds of informal action which the police can take in dealing with juvenile misusers. In many cases, the helpful course of action will be to take them home and discuss the matter with their parents. In some forces, juvenile bureau officers make a point of visiting the homes of solvent misusers to talk to their parents . . . In suitable cases it may be possible to refer the misuser to other services with whom he has already come into contact (e.g. teachers, education welfare officers, school nurses, general practitioners, social workers, youth workers, probation officers), especially where an agreed referral system is in operation.

At present a person found intoxicated from inhaling glue or solvents – or from any other cause besides alcohol – cannot be charged with being drunk and disorderly, although a car driver who had inhaled glue has been convicted for driving while unfit through drink or drugs.[10]

There is always a danger that society, when faced with a difficulty, believes that if legislation has been passed then the problem is dealt with *ipso facto*. Mencken sagely remarked that there is usually a ready solution to most human problems: obvious, simple and wrong. No law by itself has the slightest chance of ending the misuse of solvents – any more than it has of solving the problems of any other drug. What is needed is a qualified team in each neighbourhood which will help to link the efforts of parents, schools, shopkeepers, the police, doctors and social workers; and also provide expert advice for families, teachers and youth workers so that they can recognize symptoms, explain dangers and seek help. Among the warning signs that may indicate solvent misuse are: a red rash or sores around the mouth or nose; plastic bags in a bedroom; a drunken appearance without any sign of alcohol; slurred speech, moody and vacant behaviour or glazed eyes. The mother of one son who started the habit advises from her experience: 'The way to tell if your kid is completely hooked is once he has reached the bag stage – that's when the glue is squirted into a plastic bag: the tell-tale sign, apart from the post-high glazed eyes, filthy temper and stagger, is a nasty rash of sores around the mouth where the bag has been sucked in.'

The UK Department of Health has made a highly praised educational film about solvent misuse called *Illusions* – but has decided not to show it to schoolchildren lest it encourages them to start experimenting. A number of social workers believe that persistent solvent misuse is a visible symptom of a young person who is avoiding deeper problems – for example, the inability to express aggressive or sexual feelings – and that it cannot be treated in isolation from his underlying emotional situation.

Since solvent misuse is so overwhelmingly a young person's habit, perhaps we should consult teenagers' views about it. The first is a boy who gets through 'one or two tins a day':

I go and do it outside so my parents won't smell the glue at home. I sniff shoe-polish, turps, but Evo-stick most. It's escapism – but no worse than going to the pub. The first time it's strongest – a feeling like falling down a hole. Then it passes the time . . . beautifully: you don't need to eat or smoke. But when my mate's all bagged up, you can't talk to him. We laugh a lot after sniffing – it's better than drinking. But if you want to stop and come off glue, it's easy.

By contrast, the opinion of Quincy, a fourteen-year-old girl at a London comprehensive school, is:

Glue sniffing can't as yet be described as an epidemic by comparison with other forms of drug abuse: alcoholic poisoning, for instance, claims thousands of deaths a year. But I heard of someone who became a totally different person while under the influence of glue – he became violent, vicious and selfish. After the effect had worn off he would start crying and apologizing. This is perhaps one of the saddest effects of all drugs – that they force people to do and say things which they are later bitterly ashamed of – or worse still, totally unaware of. I personally think that harmful organic solvents should only be sold for industrial purposes and not available over the counter, while research is carried out to find a substitute which doesn't have its devastating effects. There are many glues which aren't harmful on sale at the moment, so glue could still be purchased for normal purposes. I also think that the government should set up clinics to help glue and other addicts to stop their addiction, and not leave all the problem for the families. And perhaps money would be spent best of all in finding out (and changing) why so many young people find it necessary to escape from the 'real world'.

11

Pot or Not?

'There is no truth, there are only ways of seeing.'
Gustave Flaubert

'All laws which can be violated without doing anyone any injury
are laughed at . . . and men of leisure are never deficient of the
ingenuity needed to enable them to outwit laws framed to
regulate things which cannot entirely be forbidden.'
Benedictus de Spinoza

Cannabis is the most popular and widely used of all illegal drugs. Between 1 and 5 million people in Britain, some 56 million in the USA (of whom a third use it regularly) and a further 200 million people elsewhere in the world, many of them in Asia, the West Indies and Africa, are estimated to enjoy it. Some countries still tolerate its traditional use, particularly in regions where alcohol is prohibited. Cannabis can be sniffed or chewed; most often it is smoked (occasionally combined with tobacco) or its resin mixed in drinks or cakes and biscuits. It is not soluble and cannot be injected.

There are few warm areas of the world where *Cannabis sativa* (the Indian hemp plant), a relation of the hop, may not be grown easily: depending on the soil and climate, the bushy nettle-like weed can reach a height of from one to twenty feet. Local preparations of the mildly hallucinogenic drug obtained from the plant are known by scores of folk names, of which among the most common are:

marijuana, dope, pot, weed, tea, grass, herb, blow, hemp, smoke, boo, gage, shit, kif, dagga, bhang, greefa, ganja, puff, blim, bush, draw, Mary Jane, charge, loco-weed, hay, jive, rope and Texas tea. Consumers are called 'tokers', 'tea-heads' or 'heads', who 'blow' when they smoke cannabis, or 'get stoned'; cannabis cigarettes are called 'spliffs' (formerly 'reefers') and the stub is known as a 'roach'. The slightly stronger cannabis resin – hashish, charas, hash, Nepalese temple balls, Lebanese red, Acapulco, Moroccan or Colombian gold – is scraped from the flowering tops of the female plants. The drug's chemical formula is $C_{21}H_{30}O_2$; its potency depends on the amount plants contain of the psychoactive ingredient THC (tetrahydrocannabinol), which varies according to their place of origin.[1] Lately the most powerful form, cannabis oil – a liquid concentrate containing up to 60 per cent THC – has been appearing on the illicit market. Imported cannabis at present retails for around £40 an ounce (28 g.); resin for £80. A survey has found that the average user purchases about half an ounce of cannabis a month.

Cannabis acts as a sensitizer, which affects different people in a variety of ways, partly dictated by their mood, setting and expectations.[2] First-time users often complain of feeling either nothing or nausea. In the East it is known as the 'weed of illusion'. Whereas Westerners credit it with loosening inhibitions, Eastern monks take hashish to subdue their sexual appetites; some users value it as an energizer, others as a sedative: the truth is that it is a depressant which first acts like a stimulant. In the small amounts usually taken, it produces hazily relaxed feelings, stimulates appetites and alters perception of time, while generally reducing – but occasionally accentuating – anxiety. Many consumers describe experiencing peaceful sensations of amusement and sexual pleasure, frequently ending in deep sleep, though others report 'bad trips'. One guide comments: 'Like alcohol it can intensify your previous feeling of joy or depression, but, unlike alcohol, the effect is to make one inward-looking, passive and imaginative.'[3] Unlike many other drugs, cannabis usually assists sociability: shared in a group, it often produces mellowness or talkative hilarity. Larger doses are more intoxicating – reducing driving ability[4] as well as exaggerating senses and moods – or else can be wildly hallucinogenic for people who are 'stoned'. Théophile Gautier, despite the fact that it gave him nightmares, said: 'Never has greater beauty immersed me in its flood,' but Charles Baudelaire's verdict was: 'The brain and organism on which hashish operates will produce only the normal phenomena peculiar to that individual – increased, admittedly, in number and force, but always faithful to their origin. A man will never escape from his destined physical and moral temperament: hashish will be a mirror of his impressions and private thoughts – a magnifying mirror, it is true, but only a mirror.' The euphoric effect, which may last from one to six hours, can seductively enhance the enjoyment of music and colours, but weakens memory and concentration as well as intellectual or manual skills. (Jazz players frequently relish what were called 'naughty-type African Woodbines', though these may not always improve their performance.) The consequence is that cannabis is more of a recreational drug than cocaine, since it increases the pleasures of leisure, but on the other hand may impede work. Partisans claim that puritans attack cannabis for this very reason: because it is associated with pleasure, instead of forming, like pep pills, an adjunct of the work-ethic.

For youth in the 1960s, cannabis's prohibition lent it a street-cred mystical halo, a panacea removed from their reach. Its enigmatic nature came to be appreciated more slowly. Chemically, cannabis is extremely complex; it contains 421 separate components, of which sixty-one are cannabinoids and some of whose characteristics are still uncertain – which is why the results of research into its effects often remain equivocal and are still a matter of dispute and controversy. Certainly smoking it can lead to carcinogenic and respiratory damage in the same way as tobacco smoking does. It is also suspected of causing cerebral atrophy, and that it may be dangerous to accumulate THC in fats or the liver. Despite this, fatal overdoses of it are unknown, and it is not physically addictive, although it can produce tolerance and psychological dependence.[5] Expectant mothers should avoid it – like any other unnecessary drug – because of the risk to foetuses, especially in the early months of pregnancy. A few users have also suffered irreversible lung damage from using cannabis plants sprayed by law-enforcement authorities with a hazardous poison such as paraquat – which unfortunately is virtually undetectable, being invisible as well as tasteless and odourless.

The connection between long-term cannabis use and personality change is still the subject of vehement argument. The first full-scale inquiry, the British government's Indian Hemp Drugs Commission in 1893–4, was told it caused insanity; but scrutiny proved this evidence to be less than reliable, being based on the surmises of untrained policemen. It is not easy to determine how far any psychotic disorders of cannabis users are in fact rooted in pre-existing psychiatric difficulties or problems of personality. The same might be true of cannabis users diagnosed as lethargic or 'amotivational' and whose unaggressive personalities or lack of thrusting ambition could be drawn to, rather than caused by, the drug. On the other hand, Baudelaire declared, 'Wine exalts the will; hashish annihilates it', and that hashish is a 'chaotic devil' by comparison with opium which he described as a 'peaceful seducer'.

Official attitudes towards 'the weed' have always been chequered. Its earliest advocate was the legendary Emperor Shen Nung, who in 2737 BC allegedly recommended it for 'female weakness, gout, malaria, constipation and absent-mindedness'. In fifteenth-century BC China it was authoritatively valued as an anaesthetic. Herodotus described how the Scythians used to scatter cannabis seeds on hot stones and shout for joy in their vapour. The Crusaders brought the word 'Assassins' back to Europe from the Haschishiniyun they heard about in Syria – a fierce eleventh-century sect who reportedly took hashish to induce visions of the paradise of martyrdom before killing, as a religious duty, the sect's enemies. Marco Polo, on his way to China in the thirteenth century, likewise recorded tales of the drug's power to transport people into the gardens of paradise. In the England of Queen Elizabeth I, far from it being banned, it was in fact illegal for anyone with five or more acres of land not to grow cannabis; and her successor James I ordered his American colonists to cultivate the plant widely, because of its value in producing the hemp fibre used for the ropes and sails of the Royal Navy. Rabelais, who was a distinguished doctor as well as the greatest satirist of sixteenth-century France, described its use in *Gargantua and Pantagruel*. None the less, despite much talk about it by the intellectuals of the Club des Haschischins in mid-nineteenth-century Paris, cannabis did not become widely popular in Europe for another hundred years – and then mainly due to African and West Indian cultural influence. Some, though not all, Rastafarians of the Ethiopian Zion Coptic Church revere ganja as a sacramental herb (as distinct from drugs, which they define as tobacco and alcohol), identifying Jamaican cannabis as the 'herb for the service of man' in Psalm 104:14 and Genesis 3:18. Lee Perry, the reggae singer, says, 'I smoke ganja most of the time. Some call it a vice, but not I. I believe it is the herb of life; it is a very holy plant

given by God; it is the spirit of His son reincarnated in the soil.'
George Washington grew it, while Queen Victoria's physician, Dr
Reynolds, described cannabis as 'one of the most valuable medicines we possess'. But today, although hay-fever sufferers claim that
it gives them relief, its medical use is confined to the treatment of
glaucoma eye disease and cancer (where cannabinoids can counter
the nausea produced by chemotherapy). During Prohibition in the
USA, 'tea pads' – cannabis-smoking parlours – grew up as alternatives to speakeasies; by the early 1930s, New York City had some
500 of such places peddling dreams and other nostrums, as Amsterdam has today. However, when in 1932 H. J. Anslinger, committed
to a crusade to eradicate this 'lethal weed', was appointed the
US Federal Narcotics Bureau Commissioner, he imparted to the
League of Nations Opium Committee the adamantine benefit of his
invincible ignorance: 'The drug [marijuana] is adhering to its old-
world tradition of murder, assault, rape, physical demoralization
and mental breakdown . . . Bureau records prove that its use is
associated with insanity and crime. Therefore, from the stand-point
of police work, it is a more dangerous drug than heroin or cocaine.'[6]

As Dr Michael Gossop contends, the myth of the dope fiend
clearly satisfies a profound need in the public, and it was eagerly
exploited during this period by popular fiction of the Fu Manchu
genre. The film *Reefer Madness* portrayed cannabis turning virtuous
citizens into crazed criminals. And Sapper described a torture that
would have surprised the spaced-out hippies of Haight-Ashbury:

'That drug; what is that ghastly drug?' moaned the prisoner.
'Haven't they told you?' asked Veight. 'It is not a nice one,
Waldron, and its result in time is to send you mad. It is . . . a
Mexican drug called Marihuana . . . It instils such fear into the
mind of the taker that he ceases to be a man. He is mad with
terror over nothing at all; his brain refuses to function; his
willpower goes. And finally he finishes up in a suicide's grave or
a lunatic asylum.[7]

Tobacco companies, as well as distillers and brewers, have an
interest in keeping this competitor illegal. The movement for
international prohibition and control of cannabis was led by the
USA together with Egypt, who in 1925 overcame an initial reluctance from Britain, the Netherlands and India. The USA, impelled
by Anslinger, denounced marijuana as 'the worst of all narcotics –

far worse than morphine or cocaine; under its influence men become beasts'. In vain did a leading international expert, Dr Bouquet, advance his opinion that the prohibition of cannabis could result in increased addiction to other, far more dangerous drugs; in vain did the Mexican delegate point out that a ban on marijuana would lead to its replacement by alcohol, with much more harmful and violent results. It was never explained why policy on alcohol should be a matter for each nation's prerogative, whereas cannabis must be forbidden internationally. Some members of the International Commission on Narcotic Drugs were indeed impervious to scientific research or argument; the French delegate at the 1973 session declaring:

> The question of the relative harmfulness of different variants of cannabis, of taking the drug in small or large doses, etc., was doubtless of theoretical and clinical interest and the World Health Organization should certainly continue its investigations along those lines, but such investigations should not be allowed to influence international control measures in any way whatsoever.[8]

In the face of such an attitude – reminiscent of the judge who declared 'I know what I think; don't confuse me with the facts' – commission piled on committee has laboured to no avail. The Commission of Inquiry into Indian Hemp heard more than 1,000 (often contradictory) witnesses before reporting to the British government in 1894 that it was widely used as a social and religious drink, as a tonic for endurance and as a medicine; and that if used moderately its effect was:

> refreshing and stimulating, and alleviates fatigue, giving rise to pleasurable sensations all over the nervous system, so that the consumer is at peace with everybody – in a grand waking dream. He is able to concentrate his thoughts on one subject; it affords him pleasure, vigour, ready wit, capacity for hard work, and sharpness for business . . . Its moderate use has no physical, mental or moral ill-effects whatsoever.

The Commission recommended against a ban, and pronounced hemp preferable to alcohol, that would be likely to replace it. This benign verdict was echoed fifty years later by the New York Academy of Medicine which was asked by Major La Guardia for a scientific report on the issue. In 1944 the Academy concluded that cannabis was not addictive (as medically defined) and that it did not lead to the use of drugs such as morphine or cocaine; it had no effect on the user's underlying personality, and was not a cause of crime. The Academy's Report underlined that the then current hysterical publicity about the catastrophic effects of cannabis was completely unfounded.

In 1966, the Wootton Sub-Committee was set up to advise the British government on cannabis. Its Report, submitted in 1968, found no evidence that the use of cannabis led to crime or aggressive behaviour, nor that it caused psychotic states in otherwise normal users: 'Having reviewed all the material available to us we find ourselves in agreement with the conclusions reached by the Indian Hemp Drugs Commission . . . and the La Guardia Report, that the long-term consumption of cannabis in moderate doses has no harmful effects.' The Report nevertheless concluded that cannabis is a 'dangerous' drug, although a less physically dangerous one than amphetamines, barbiturates or alcohol.

The US Shafer Report of 1972 came next. Authorized by Nixon himself, it surprised and disappointed hardliners by its findings that cannabis causes no psychological deterioration, either in motivation or intellect; that it does not result in physical dependence, and that the 'overwhelming majority' of cannabis users do not escalate to other drugs. It unanimously recommended the ending of criminal penalties for private use, although it did not favour legalization. In the same year the comprehensively detailed report of the Le Dain Commission in Canada also concluded that cannabis is not addictive and that its short-term effects are of little clinical significance. However, the Le Dain Report (despite selective quotation from it by partisans) did not completely exonerate cannabis: 'What has come to our attention with respect to long-term effects is a matter for cautious concern rather than optimism.' The Commission did, however, warn: 'It is a grave error to indulge in deliberate distortion or exaggeration concerning the alleged dangers of a particular drug, or to base a programme of drug education upon a strategy of fear. It is no use playing "chicken" with young people; in nine cases out of ten they will accept the challenge . . . There is no doubt that the law on cannabis has created . . . disillusionment with law and legal institutions, as well as the processes of government generally.'[9] The Le Dain Commission's principal recommendation was:

Although research has not clearly established that cannabis has sufficiently harmful effects to justify the present legislative policy towards it, there are serious grounds for social concern about its use, and this concern calls for a continuing policy to discourage its use by means which involve a more acceptable cost than present policies, to the individual and to society.

In 1977 President Carter, whose Director of Drug Abuse Policy was then Dr Peter Bourne, proposed to Congress that possession of up to an ounce of marijuana for personal use should be dealt with by a fine rather than the stigma of imprisonment, which risked introducing many otherwise law-abiding people to professional criminal cultures. The 1961 International Single Convention on Narcotic Drugs obliges countries party to it to penalize for trafficking and possession, but not for use – though the Convention leaves each nation to decide on its own penalties.[10] The Le Dain Commission's recommendation had been that although trafficking should continue to be punishable, this should not apply to simple possession of cannabis. This view was in fact more liberal than that of the Wootton Sub-Committee, which, while advocating lower penalties than previously, recommended that possession should continue to be punished by a fine of £100 or four months' imprisonment.[11] Even this proposal, however, was rejected by the then Home Secretary, James Callaghan, who argued: 'To reduce the penalties for possession, sale or supply of cannabis would be bound to lead people to think that the government takes a less serious view of the effect of drug-taking . . . Because we have a number of social evils in this country at present, it would be sheer masochism to add to our evils by legislation to make it more easy for people to introduce another one.' It is easy to understand why the Royal Commission on the Non-Medical Use of Drugs in South Australia in 1978 complained:

The regulation of the non-medical use of cannabis has been the subject of many official inquiries. These inquiries have reached strikingly uniform conclusions on the effects of cannabis use, both on the user and the community as a whole. The failure of legislators . . . to accept these conclusions suggests that legislative responses are affected more by the perceived social status of users and the values and perhaps prejudices of powerful groups in the community, than by a careful evaluation of the pharmacological, medical and sociological evidence.

Predictably, this Commission's own recommendations were also ignored.

Too much of the debate about cannabis research recalls the dictum 'if you torture the data long enough, in the end it'll confess'. The sober Report of the Wootton Sub-Committee was reviled by conservatives for its permissiveness, but the full Advisory Committee, of which the Wootton Sub-Committee was part, concluded, 'We have no doubt that the wider use of cannabis should not be encouraged,' and the Report itself quoted the opinion of Professor Sir Aubrey Lewis's international review, that 'Observers with long experience concur in the opinion that continued excessive use of cannabis over a period of years leads to moral and social decay; countries from which such reports come are South Africa, Morocco, Algeria, Tunisia, Syria, Turkey, Astrakhan [sic] and India.' Lewis had found 1,750 reports and noted that 'almost every theme is beset with contradictory observations and opinions'; the Wootton Sub-Committee decided that 'the subjectivity of the mental effects of cannabis makes it particularly difficult to measure the total effect . . . We conclude, therefore, that in the interests of public health it is necessary to maintain restrictions on the availability and use of the drug'; but it emphasized above all the need for more research.[12]

The latest (1982) report by the British government's Advisory Council on the Misuse of Drugs is equally cautious but still inconclusive:

> Use can produce tolerance and withdrawal symptoms, but evidence in relation to other elements of possible dependence syndrome is scant. Nevertheless a dependence syndrome may exist. Use can give rise to acute and transient mental disturbance, and may lead to fall-off in social performance; but does not affect performance of simple routine tasks. The extent to which it can produce longer-term psychotic disorder remains open.[13]

Eleven US states now have laws permitting individuals to possess marijuana for their own use, though not to sell it. Other states have a fixed penalty or minimum sentences for possession. There are now indications that marijuana use in the USA and Canada has recently begun to level off. However, the US Public Health Service estimates that about one in four of the American population has used the drug – a thirty-fold increase over the past twenty years. Marijuana (led by the seedless *Sinsemilla* species, which is especially high in THC) is now reputed to be one of the USA's two largest cash crops – with a turnover of more than $17 billion a year, comfortably outstripping soya beans and even wheat. The lobby to legalize it is currently quieter, partly because of the boom profits illegal growers are enjoying: the business even supports its own trade journal, *Sinsemilla Tips*. Although what might be called the US Grass National Product's value has recently been overtaken by sales of cocaine, it is nevertheless still estimated to be the fourth biggest American business after Exxon and General Motors. California produces the most (worth more than $2 billion a year): no longer only in innocently Utopian window-boxes and smallholdings, but as the state's number one industry harvested on vast rolling plantations policed by private armed guards. An increasing quantity is being cultivated indoors in hydroponic warehouses or barns with controlled light and heat; crops also flourish in California's 'emerald triangle', often camouflaged and protected by guns and mines. Raids upon plantations in California and Oregon – by rival growers as much as the police – echo Prohibition Chicago. More and more farmers, hit by the agricultural recession, have spread cultivation to national parks and forests (by 1985, marijuana was being grown on no less than 946,000 acres of forest service land); and into other states all over the country, with Arkansas and the tobacco states of Virginia and Kentucky in the lead. The remaining half of America's supplies is imported from Colombia, Jamaica, Lebanon, Morocco's Rif mountains and Thailand; marijuana has now also become a major cash crop in Hawaii. Mexican brands, which supplied the bulk of the US market from the 1930s to the 1960s, suffered a dip in popularity in 1973 when the government there was persuaded by Washington to spray crops with herbicides such as paraquat. (Prior to Watergate, the man who went to Nixon's White House to help set up the Drug Enforcement agency, and organized the attempt to seal the US-Mexican entry points and paraquat-spraying was Gordon Liddy.) Latin Americans were quick to ask why Washington did not advocate herbicides for the USA's own fields of marijuana. Despite these measures, the rich prosperity of cities such as Barranquilla in Colombia continues to be built on a solid foundation of marijuana profits. And despite all the recent carnage and turmoil in the Lebanon, 2,000 tons a year – producing $500 million – continue to be grown in the Bekaa Valley near Ba'albek, the one industry in which different politics and religions still successfully demonstrate ecumenical co-operation.

Cannabis remains primarily a young person's drug, whether for reasons of escape, pleasure or protest. In Britain, which has the stiffest laws on personal consumption in Western Europe, three-quarters of those convicted of cannabis offences are under the age of thirty. More than half the US population between the ages of eighteen and twenty-five have used cannabis illegally, and 27 per cent continue to do so at least once a month. The New York police state that there are 800 shops selling marijuana, spread throughout all parts of the city. An American schoolchild who looks somnolent while saluting the flag or singing the national anthem is now liable to be marched off to be given a urine test. On the whole, though, most pot users' behaviour is not as conspicuous as alcohol users'. However, the Shafer Commission's survey in the USA found that 41 per cent of adults and 45 per cent of youths who had tried marijuana subsequently lost interest and gave it up; but that 2 per cent (500,000 people) continued to use it as much as several times a day. A contemporary separate study of US troops in Germany found that 46 per cent of troops had tried hashish resin at least once, and 16 per cent smoked it regularly (at least three times a week); and that, whereas moderate users suffered few mental or physical effects, heavy smokers (of seventeen or more cannabis cigarettes daily) suffered a 'chronic intoxicated state characterized by apathy, dullness and lethargy with mild to severe impairment of judgment, concentration and memory'.

The Polish authorities admit to there being at least 10,000 cannabis users in Warsaw. Surveys suggest that approximately 2 million people smoke cannabis daily,[14] of whom Sir William Paton estimates half a million smoke it so regularly that their health is at risk from by-products of the drug accumulating in their body.[15] Convictions for cannabis offences have continued to rise in the UK; as Table 4 (overleaf) demonstrates.

The rising rate of convictions in Britain is all the more striking in view of the fact that several police forces have lately adopted a policy of not prosecuting people found for the first time in possession of cannabis, in order to be able to concentrate on suppliers and more harmful drugs.[16] A 1985 editorial in the *Police Review* commented that use of the drug seems acceptable to large sections of the community – including a number of chief constables. The law is

Table 4: **Cannabis in the UK**

Year	Persons found guilty of or cautioned for cannabis offences	Kg. of cannabis seized	Kg. of cannabis resin seized
1974	9,517	1,980	5,782
1975	8,987	3,111	2,112
1976	9,946	3,169	1,923
1977	10,607	1,945	2,379
1978	11,572	3,161	3,480
1979	12,409	6,445	5,454
1980	14,910	18,419	7,752
1981	15,388	16,874	7,817
1982	17,410	12,995	4,413
1983	19,966	13,735	6,816
1984	20,529	17,723	11,293
1985	20,976	14,282	7,861

arbitrarily enforced in different areas; crack-downs against pot were blamed as part of the cause of recent urban riots. In other inner-city ghetto areas, Rastafarian cannabis dealers help the police to keep heroin out. Tony Judge of the Police Federation explained: 'The police do not have the resources to control possession of cannabis. The law on possession is fairly unenforceable and it points to a growing lack of conviction that it is a sensible law.'

Is it therefore time to consider changing this law? In the balance-sheet of arguments, the main reasons in favour of legalizing cannabis are as follows:

1 *Freedom for human beings to lead their own lives*. In the absence of overwhelming reasons otherwise, we should minimize laws and not forcibly restrict the right of others to decide how to live their lives – even if we warn them of risks and try to persuade them to abstain from potentially harmful practices. The clear onus of proof lies on those who seek to make any restrictive law.
2 *Pleasure*. Cannabis – called 'the herb that's superb' – certainly gives enjoyment to a large number of people.
3 *The damage which the present law can cause people*. Several thousands of often young and mainly otherwise law-abiding citizens capriciously acquire criminal records as a result of the ban. The experience adversely affects their view of, and rela-

tionship with, the police on other matters: searches for cannabis are a frequent cause of friction. A number of talented people's lives have been permanently blighted through their arrest and conviction; some people, such as teachers and doctors, have lost their whole career (one Glasgow doctor being sent to prison for six months), while other people have been subjected to black-mail. Over a thousand people are being imprisoned each year in Britain because of cannabis offences. As recently as 1970 a first conviction for selling marijuana in Georgia carried the penalty of life imprisonment, while a second offence could result in a death sentence.[17]

4 *The cost of the ban to society.* It increases the burden on our courts, probation service and overcrowded prisons, as well as the workload of our overstretched Customs and police officers. Many policemen consider the law – the prosecution rate of which must be derisory – arbitrary and unenforceable, and some think it also wrong.

5 *Disrespect for one unenforceable or undesirable law can weaken regard for the law in general*, as the experience of Prohibition in the USA showed.

6 *The effect on the control of drugs that are more dangerous.* Possession of cannabis now accounts for 88 per cent of all UK drug convictions, compared with only 43 per cent in 1967: if it were legal, a large amount of police and others' time and efforts could be redirected into deterring hard drugs. Many young people who have disregarded dire warnings against cannabis believe it is harmless, and are then less prepared to credit warnings against other, more dangerous drugs. People who smoke pot as a rebellious act of defiance might be less interested in doing so if it were legal. (Auberon Waugh suggests that it might only be available in church on Sundays.) Another result of the illegality of cannabis is that users are driven to criminal sources for their supplies, where they are liable to come into contact with hard drugs. (Due to its illegality, cannabis is no cheaper than heroin in many places.) Some unscrupulous pushers have been known to lace cannabis with more dangerous drugs, so as to cause clients to become addicted to these unwittingly. If there has to be a social drug, cannabis would be less harmful to offer at parties than alcohol or tobacco, besides the fact that it makes people less aggressive than does alcohol. A large

proportion of young people condemn as hypocritical any society in which parents, frequently reeking of booze and fags, moralize to them about pot.

7 *The loss of control and revenue through illegality.* Since much expert opinion considers moderate – though not excessive – cannabis use to be harmless, if it were legal an individual's intake might be controllable by prescription or rationing. Strength, purity and effects could then be properly monitored, which they cannot easily be at present. If it were a government monopoly, or a luxury tax or duty were placed on supplies, this could raise significant revenue (which some estimate at as much as £1 billion in the UK, and up to $10 billion a year in the USA) that is badly needed to help the health service or other public programmes. It is reported that some alcohol and tobacco companies have already in fact registered trade names for brands of cannabis against the day when the law is changed.

On the other hand, the arguments for 'Keep off the grass' and retaining the present prohibition are:

1 *Medical.* The most recent research raises some disturbing indications, especially concerning psychological dependency, damage to fertility and the long-term effect of heavy use. When in doubt, it is preferable to err on the side of caution: it took several generations before the devastating damage caused by tobacco was realized.

2 *A blinker to life.* Cannabis, like most drugs, puts an artificial gloss between users and reality, causing them to avoid the truths of life. A man who has smoked it with enthusiasm for fourteen years said: 'Cannabis does not kill people directly, and, in comparison with alcohol, seems gentle enough. And that is where the real danger lies. Cannabis is subtle – a truly subversive substance, which works directly on the will . . . My experience was that it was only during the two or three years while struggling to kick the habit that I gradually realized the horrifying extent to which I was in thrall and to acknowledge the probability of some kind of permanent damage.'

3 *Why add to our problems?* We are already paying a heavy price for previous complacency about tobacco and alcohol. Even

though cannabis may be preferable to either, that is no reason to legalize an additional drug which may cause more problems.

4 *Escalation*. It is often argued that cannabis leads users on to hard drugs. This may, however, be an example of the *post hoc propter hoc* fallacy. For example, the fact that most meths drinkers earlier in their lives drank tea proves nothing: the relationship is statistical rather than causal. Some cannabis users are indeed likely to try other drugs for the same reasons that they experimented with cannabis; but others, such as Paul McCartney, declare that they do not try other drugs precisely because they are satisfied with cannabis.

5 *International convention*. Legalizing would be contrary to the international obligations of the UN Single Convention.

There are two other alternatives besides prohibition or legalization. One is decriminalization, as recommended by the Shafer and Le Dain Commissions: whereby the possession of small amounts of cannabis for personal use ceases to be regarded as criminal. Cultivating small amounts for personal use or giving a modest amount to another person would be allowed, but other transactions, including the possession of larger amounts, or supplying for profit, would remain illegal. The aim of decriminalization would be to remove the stigma of criminality from individual cannabis use, while at the same time to prevent commercial exploitation. Some restrictions on personal use, such as when driving a vehicle, would remain necessary, as they are for alcohol. (Paul McCartney's view is: 'I personally think that decriminalization rather than legality is the answer. There is some sense in the idea that we are so messed up with one thing and another that we don't want to encourage or endorse the use of yet another stimulant.')

The other compromise option would be licensing. This would regulate use and at the same time raise revenue. In the case of cannabis, a licensing or regulatory system could enable its moderate use by adults while short-circuiting the illicit market by providing a legal source of supply. Such an approach is admittedly a pragmatic compromise, founded on many governments' experience that if people want something (such as alcohol) enough, it is virtually impossible to stop them getting it – as Prohibition proved in the USA.[18]

In recent years, the possession of small quantities has been decriminalized in Mexico, Italy, Spain and in some states of the USA. In France, people found in possession can be ordered to have compulsory medical treatment. Denmark, on the other hand, has simply allowed its legislation about possession of cannabis to fall into disuse: no one has been prosecuted for the offence since 1967. The city of Amsterdam (as described in Chapter 3) has tried to institutionalize the supply of cannabis, in order to separate its trade from that of heroin and opium, and it is reported that cannabis use there appears to have declined. In Britain, however, only the Green Party currently supports legalization. Although Lenny Bruce once predicted that 'Dope will be legal when all the law students who've smoked it at college grow up to be senators and congressmen,' most British MPs agree, 'There are no votes in pot.' American federal courts have ruled that members of the Ethiopian Zion Coptic Church should not be permitted ganja even for religious sac-ramental use.[19] (In Britain, by contrast, Sikhs have been granted on religious grounds exemption from the law that requires safety-helmets to be worn at work – a higher medical risk than the use of cannabis.) The one certainty is that we have not seen the last of commissions which will examine the issue: the only policy on which everyone agrees is the need for more research.

Part Three

What Is To Be Done?

12

Drug Misusers:
Who? Why? and Treatment

'Like diamonds, we are cut with our own dust.'
John Webster, *The Duchess of Malfi*

'Dreaming when Dawn's Left Hand was in the Sky
I heard a Voice within the Tavern cry,
"Awake, my Little ones, and fill the Cup
Before Life's Liquor in its Cup be dry."

'And, as the Cock crew, those who stood before
The Tavern shouted – "Open then the Door!
You know how little while we have to stay,
And, once departed, may return no more."'
The Rubáiyát of Omar Khayyám,
translated by Edward Fitzgerald

Before determining any response or solution to the problem it is first necessary to understand why people misuse drugs. The uncomfortable truth most critical studies of drug-takers shy away from facing is that many users' chief motivation is pleasurable enjoyment. 'Fifteen years ago, drug use was a political statement. Today the reason kids use drugs is they like the feeling,' said Robert Dupont, the former Director of the US National Institute for Drug Abuse. Equally it would be unrealistic to think that all drug addicts (or suppliers) are full of regret. The addicted young scion of one respected family in Sri Lanka said in an interview:

Actually, I suffered from loneliness throughout my schooldays. My parents were not at home most of the time. I was also not allowed to go out very often and these restrictions really frustrated me. It was one of my close friends who first

233

introduced me to drugs. I didn't worry much about it and took it without hesitation. Then I found that gradually I was able to forget all my problems. Now I don't suffer at all from my loneliness. I feel fantastic.

But you know that drugs can destroy your life altogether, don't you?

Maybe what you say is true, but I don't care. After all, no one has bothered about me before, so why the concern about me taking drugs? I think the best thing they can do for me now is to mind their own business.

Do you have any difficulty getting your stuff?

Not at all. It is available almost everywhere. I just have to go out on the streets outside this room. There's absolutely no shortage. There are a lot of great guys out there active in the business. I'm really grateful to them for their splendid service.[1]

No magic cure for addiction exists. The one certainty is that we should look for any key to dependency not in the drugs themselves, but in the people who misuse them. Many stable characters can handle opiates, whereas others fall apart; a person becomes addicted not to a drug, but to the experiences it gives him. Every misuser's reason for taking drugs is individually unique, although several, when asked for reasons, may parrot identical currently fashionable rationalizations. All generalizations lack validity (including this one): but when we look for reasons we must first distinguish those which lead to drug experimentation or occasional use from those that cause persistent misuse and dependency. Factors may include, on one hand, external social influences – such as a person's environment, lover or peer group; drug availability or culture; society's exaggerated dependence on chemicals; the media's treatment of drug issues; and/or on the other hand, the subjective needs and rewards individuals derive from their experience of drugs or the drug scene.[2] That a person's response to both sets of factors nevertheless depends on the evolution of his personal identity is shown by the fact that the majority of people subject to those pressures suggested as causes – whether demoralizing destitution, bored privilege, or emotional deprivation – still resist the temptation to misuse drugs. At the same time, socio-economic or emotional disadvantage certainly can aggravate any damaging effects of drugs, while wealthy and socially privileged people find it easier to disguise or to cushion the consequences.

What makes some users addicts and others not, out of those who face comparable temptations and stresses? Researchers have tried to isolate predisposing genetic factors; behaviourists to identify traits; social scientists, politicians and journalists have tended to concentrate on cultural reasons. What is discovered is often a result of what is sought. Inevitably it is misleading to group individual drug-users into crude categories; each personality has a unique mixture of reasons and pressures. (Preventative research should also usefully examine the motivation and make-up of non-users: one English survey showed that of young people who are offered an illegal drug, on average about half accept.)[3] Every society has culturally sanctioned drugs: some of which are legal, and some not. And we are almost all dependent personalities, in different ways. The principal motives for trying illegal drugs initially are curiosity or peer-group pressure. (Opportunity and availability are obviously *sine qua non*, whether for starting or continuing.) But it is important to remember that the majority of experimenters never go on to become regular users, and of those who continue most do so only occasionally – often recreationally, as alcohol is similarly used. Many of those who try a drug as an experiment decide to stop because they do not like the initial effects, or because they are afraid of either addiction or the law. Others may choose to continue as 'chippers' – casual or occasional users of drugs, perhaps only in social settings or at weekends – and do not become addicted; such controlled users manage to subjugate their drug use to their overall life, and not vice versa.

The problems begin when an individual's ability to handle his life is handicapped by his drug habit. On the other hand, few people who are dependent on drugs are studied before they become dependent. Correlations should not be confused with causes; and we should also distinguish between apparent causes and what are really effects. A further hurdle is that not all drug-users are willing, or able, to be truthful about their situation, while at the same time the majority of such users continue to be unknown and unstudied: research obviously is inevitably as incomplete as it is difficult. What data we have, however, indicates that most known drug-takers are: (a) *on average of no lower than median intelligence and ability*: they include talented and privileged people as well as unemployed drop-outs; (b) *male* (by three to one, males are more likely than females to use psychotropic drugs, except for tranquillizers or depressants)[4]; (c) *young*: most users start in their early teens, at an average age of fifteen. (The peak age for drug overdoses – where the sex ratio is much nearer equality – is 15–19 for females and 20–24 for males.) The age range of drug misuse, however, is widening: abuse by old-age pensioners as well as schoolchildren is increasing in areas like Merseyside. But recent research by Professor Denise Candell of Columbia University shows that if a person does not use tobacco, alcohol or any other potentially addictive substance by the age of twenty-two, he or she is highly unlikely ever to do so; (d) *from all social classes*: the cost barriers have fallen, though drop-out or derelict users remain more visible than those in other, more discreet occupations. In recent years in Iran drugs solaced all social categories, from beggars to members of the royal family. 'Some Americans think they can protect youngsters from problems by having them sent away to fine prep boarding schools,' said the Dean of Students at one New Hampshire college; 'but we all have the same problems with drugs and alcohol.'

Hardly anybody consciously decides to become a drug-addict. Every addict, when he started, believed that he would not be the one to succumb, just as criminals are sure that this time they will not be caught. Contrary to myth, it is not easy to become addicted: it takes repeated time and effort, as well as expense. Dependency is not a spell produced by magical chemistry: it is a logical consequence flowing from the balance of feelings a drug gives a particular person. William Burroughs believes that drugs frequently win by default: 'You become a narcotics addict because you do not have strong motivations in any other direction . . . I tried it as a matter of curiosity. I drifted along taking shots when I could score. I ended up hooked. Most addicts I have talked to report a similar experience. They did not start using drugs for any reason they can remember . . . Junk is not a kick. It is a way of life.'[5] Most often drug use is a symptom of other problems, though sometimes it is due to normally healthy people succumbing to peer-group pressure. A crucial chance event may convert casual use into dependency: De Quincey appears to have been turned from an occasional user of opium, originally for medical reasons – 'It was not for the purpose of creating pleasure, but of mitigating pain in the severest degree, that I first began'[6] – into an addict by the deep depression he felt as a result of the death of Kate Wordsworth.[7]

The factors most often suggested as the cause of drug abuse include:

1 *Biological*: controversially, several addicts alleged to me they had inherited a predisposition to drugs or alcohol, vaguely linking this with the body's own production of endorphine peptides. Such genetic determinism would of course free them from responsibility. There is, however, no firm scientific evidence to inculpate geneticism or heredity – although some illicit drug-users copy the drinking or licit drug use of their parents, and a high proportion of alcoholics themselves have at least one alcoholic parent. It is true, however, that many drug-takers are also heavy smokers and drinkers ('cross-addiction'), whereas people who do not smoke or drink are those least likely to take drugs.[8]

2 *Easy availability* – as, for example, in the medical professions. By 1984 there were over 4,000 doctors in the USA addicted to drugs – besides the one in every ten American doctors considered to be an alcoholic: the rate of addiction for US doctors is at least thirty times higher than in the general population.[9] Patients who are prescribed certain medical drugs can also acquire dependency, as happened to De Quincey.[10] The fall in the price of heroin and cocaine has greatly widened exposure to their availability. In the Wirral heroin now has the reputation of being 'cheaper than cannabis or six pints of beer'. William Burroughs's view is: 'Addiction is an illness of exposure. By and large, those become addicts who have access to junk. There is no more a pre-addict personality than there is a pre-malarial personality.'[11] Several subcultures are particularly likely to have contact with drugs: numbers of men allege they became addicted in prison, and a number of prostitutes report that they were given heroin and other drugs by their pimps on condition that they worked satisfactorily.

3 The most common environmental cause is *peer/social/cultural pressure* – 'Go on, don't be chicken' – in the same way as heavy drinkers and smokers frequently try to get others to join them. The overwhelming majority of users state they were originally

237

introduced to drugs – often on the spur of the moment – by so-called friends, not by pushers or 'fiends'. (One eleven-year-old Merseyside girl was inducted by her thirteen-year-old sister in the playground.) For young people who are shy or insecure, especially in class-conscious societies, drug-taking groups seem warmly welcoming. Just as alcoholics often resent non-drinkers, so heroin users in communes or at parties proselytize from psychological motives as well as in order to trade. The isolation of addicts can cause them to try to spread their habit, since an ambivalent uncertainty about their way of life can make them want their peers to share and approve it. One of the more tragic, if unusual, cases concerned the addiction in 1980 of Jay Tarver, a Houston policeman who previously had had an exemplary career. While serving undercover, posing as a cocaine buyer in order to infiltrate a ring of pushers, he was forced under threat of death by suspicious criminals to snort rows of cocaine in their presence. At first he found the drug gave him energy to cope with the tension of his assignment, but then began to feel more and more moody confusion as a result of the increasing obsession for cocaine he acquired. In 1981 he was arrested, tried and convicted, and now works as a drug counsellor.

4 *Experimentation*. In some circles drugs are a status symbol, the media having given them a nihilistic glamour of daring but fascinating forbidden fruit. Many users cite bravado or boredom – a quest for excitement and new sensation – as their reason for starting.

5 Subjective factors can include the *self-destructiveness* which is latent in most people. Apart from masochism, low self-valuation can lead to despair and overdosing – including nihilistic 'Russian roulette' gambling with suicide by taking large amounts of drugs which can be a disguised call for help: British male heroin addicts have a suicide rate which is more than fifty times that of the general population. Others use illicit drugs, including opiates, as ill-advised self-medication to counter depression and other forms of emotional illness.

6 As a way of expressing *aggression* against family, authority and materialist values, or as a protest against a society viewed as uncaring and unfair. The example of the hypocrisy of adults who

misuse licit drugs can be used as an excuse by adolescents to escape a stage in life they feel is a pointless intermission. Drugs, like sexual experiences, may invite by seeming to be a passport to adulthood; a way of being streetwise and beating the system. The attraction of bourgeois norms may lead to shocking immersion in the alternative life-style of drug-users. Yet, as G. V. Stimson found in his study of London addicts, although many illicit drug-users are critical of society, a large number start to take drugs not out of rebellion but the opposite: weak conformity to the social example set by attractive and streetsmart acquaintances or idols such as rock stars. Throughout different social classes, young people's initiation most often begins at parties, colleges, squats, pubs, discos or pop concerts, where neophytes are surprised to see drugs being used not by the wrecks they had expected from the Press's harrowing warnings but by users ostensibly able to handle, enjoy and recommend the experience.[12] (The users who are not so fortunate are less visible at social gatherings.) Rightly or wrongly, much of the rock and jazz scene is identified with drugs by young people; a number of fading show-business and pop-music stars turn to drugs or drink when their previous high of fame or adulation wanes.

7 *Escapism*: the wish to reduce anxiety, if not gloss over reality: out of unhappiness or despair due to loneliness, failure, unemployment, an unhappy relationship, homelessness, conflict with authority or other problems – whether psychological, emotional or social. Drugs can appear to offer a seductive way to avoid, or at least postpone, such stress or depression: a means of abdicating responsibilities and turning inwards into personal sensations, away from the world's worries. 'They never received any affection,' commented one agency worker about some of his clients, 'or else have given up because their life offers them nothing.' Emotional reaction against the adult world's authority may compound the alienation. Insensitive attempts at control are capable of driving people who temporarily suffer such moods further underground, and cement their solidarity against conventional society: in Stuttgart young Germans said they blame their addiction on the wish to escape from their elders' 'repressive society and jealous hatred of youth and happiness'.

When alienation and anomie generate a desire to drop out, opiates or depressant tranquillizers provide a self-fulfilling alibi for failure. (A Valium habit can be much more deeply ingrained than heroin dependency.) Drug abusers frequently place the blame for their habit on their home life and parents – accusing them of being anything from loveless to over-protective. A higher than average number of addicts seem to be the children of successful public figures: this may be due to their attracting more notice, or because their parents have been too busy to give them much care, or because such children feel failures by comparison, or because the sons and daughters of the rich are most easily able to afford drugs. Some experts point to the frequent incidence of drug use in those who have a close relationship with their mother, often coupled with an absentee or ineffective father. A high proportion of drug abusers come from 'problem' or broken homes, though many others from similarly deprived backgrounds do not turn to drugs. A striking number of abusers, however, seem depressed, immature and unstable, often with their emotional development arrested at the time they started their dependency. They appear to have felt cut off and have had difficulty in forming close relationships or expressing themselves – even prior to the effects of drug-taking; whereas by contrast, the experience of their relationship with drugs has appeared invitingly easy to achieve.

8   *Pleasure*: the purchase of a short-cut to instant euphoria, in place of society's traditional philosophy of deferred gratification and belief that pleasure must be earned. A number of people take drugs with the intention of heightening their sensory and aesthetic awareness: one said he wanted to explore 'truth, not reality'. The hidden number of stable users who consume drugs, generally in secret and alone, are not ostensibly members of any counter-culture and keep clear of the junkie milieu: they exercise careful self-discipline, and, even when taking heroin regularly, they generally succeed in retaining their jobs and family life.

9   A few believe taking an illegal drug helps their *work* or life-style. Speed or cocaine are usually the preferred choice: giving, for example, the film director Fassbinder energy – though at the cost of irritable impatience and unpredictability. Marcel Proust,

racked by asthma and neurasthenic debility as well as hypo-
chondria, resorted to alternate narcotic and stimulating drugs in
a desperate attempt to finish his writing.[13] For a number of other
users, the transcendental experience of drugs, with its attendant
ritual, may form a substitute for orthodox religion.

Deaths and injuries are not due to drugs themselves (any more than
to mountains or revolvers) but to those personalities who misuse
them self-destructively. Opiates – certainly initially – are not in-
herently attractive; the seed-bed for dependency is to be found in
those characteristics that make a person need drug-induced sensations to cope with existence.[14] This dependency frequently becomes
progressively all-embracing because drugs make it ever more difficult for the user to relate to the reality of his needs and problems,
hence forcing his sense of well-being to depend increasingly on
props of illusion. Most of us react to anxiety by some tactic of
avoidance, and like to take short-cuts in an attempt to determine
any pattern in the confusion of our lives. Many men and women
believe in magic, go to palmists, or follow horoscopes as alternative
flights from reality. Addicts are only some of the large number of
people in the world who do not learn   or prefer not – to engage
fully with life, and who seek diversionary comfort with the help of
repeating a ritual. Non-religious people would say something not
very different about priests. In an abuser's life, however, drugs'
primacy is likely to become self-generating: atrophying alternative
options for him as the addiction's supremacy grows, and his other
friendships, interests and skills deteriorate. The psychological
mechanism of a drug-addict's life, as he feels inadequate in a society
whose driving principles seem to be success and productivity, 'adds
up to a self-enclosed system where he is able to provide his own
pleasure . . . He isolates himself beyond the need for human help or
satisfaction. He is dependent on no other person.'[15] At the same
time he can postpone any feelings of guilt at what he is doing,
because the role of an addict – hustling, scoring, fixing – occupies
virtually every moment of his existence, and blot out his other
worries. Many users are excited by the challenge of scoring, and the
appeal of avoiding arrest as an outlaw. The person who takes drugs
or drink to evade difficulties, however, finds that in doing so he only
exacerbates them, and is caught in a vicious circle of needing yet
more drugs to escape again. Jock Young describes this spiral in

relation to an alcoholic, who 'attempts to drown his own inadequacy with the very substance that is making him more inadequate. Social reaction against illicit drug use can merely serve to inspire the drug-taker with a sense of gross injustice,' as well as increase his isolation.[16]

Not every drug-addict is a reliable witness – and some people who listen to them are also selective, hearing what they want to hear. Many abusers, such as the multi-drug consumers known to the American drug culture as 'garbage-heads', are genuinely extremely confused. Most addicts enjoy talking about themselves as much as possible (perhaps to reassume the identity and individuality which their dependency has expunged) – and can verge on the tedious in their self-absorbed fantasizing. Many tend to be self-justifying, blaming everyone and everything except themselves. As Anthony Storr has suggested about many homosexuals, they 'have a vested interest in affirming that their condition is an inborn abnormality rather than the result of circumstances; for any other explanation is bound to imply a criticism either of themselves or their families and usually of both'. Self-portrayal by drug-addicts of themselves as victims of a sickness, or determinist biological theories of an 'addictive personality' undermine any commitment to cure, and offer an alibi for relapse. (Yet this is what society so often seems to want to make drug-users feel.) Even if no longer designated a 'fiend', the label of being a 'junkie' and a 'problem' is very difficult to lose: 'Being told you're a nothing going nowhere, that you'll never do any good and you'll always be a burden.' And those who feel rejected by the present social system are most likely to reject it in turn: seeing yourself – or feeling yourself to be seen as – a social misfit, it is tempting to sink into a nihilistic way of life.

Many drug-users are worried and frightened less by loss of control, than by the opposite: boredom, loneliness and responsibility. They like to believe their drug is stronger than they are. Heroin is, in the words of one addict, 'like wrapping a warm duvet all around yourself and curling up with no thoughts or worries'. Another user described it as being 'like coming in by the fire after a long walk in the countryside: not a bit like Piccadilly lavatories'. The same images recur: 'Life inverts. You only feel normal when you're stoned; whereas you feel displaced and confused as the effects start to wear off.' 'I only feel integrated after a fix.' 'When I'm spaced out, it's marvellous not to be myself for a while.' A young prostitute said she relied on drugs to block out the degradation she feels: 'It makes it easier to live with yourself.' Others agreed: 'H blocks out all my emotional pain.' 'At the drop of a needle, you can either mask off feeling or else boost it: you can lose your identity, or find one.' For others, taking drugs can seem like 'revenge on the world': 'When I first started I thought it would be a glamorous way to die . . . I was miserable, so I thought I would see what junk's about . . . I wanted to be the centre of attention. I thought I wanted revenge on this boy, [who] spoiled all my illusions, disillusions . . . The more you take, the less you have to lose.' 'Everyone was talking about it, so I had to try it: it seemed the ultimate challenge.' 'It made me feel I could cope. Actually to other people I didn't appear confident, but I thought I was.' 'There's something about the mystique of giving oneself an injection, I think, that is terribly self-satisfying. H's, if you like, a subliminal sex thing . . . Drugs tend to, I find, take over from and take the part of sex. There have been a number of affairs I've had in my life, during which my drug-taking has decreased . . . It's a curious kind of almost homosexual experience, in a sort of monk-like way, I suppose, rather than in a perverted sort of way.' The daughter of a prime minister said: 'For me heroin was a very destructive love affair.' A nineteen-year old man in Kentish Town, who said all his friends were on smack, explained: 'It simplifies life: one just has one problem instead of lots of them.' A Washington girl described the Catch-22: 'It can be like a hundred orgasms – but when it wears off you need a regular fix to feel normal.' 'I love smack because it gives me protection. It's my life-raft: it makes me forget. The difficulty about coming off is not withdrawing, it's staying off without its support.' (As Mark Twain said, 'Giving up smoking is easy. I've done it dozens of times.') 'Coming off drugs, you feel raw and naked without them giving you confidence: that's what made me go back on.' Jane Christian, working at the Hungerford Project drop-in drug advice centre in London, says:

For these young people, the fear of no drugs is greater than that of drugs themselves: they're the only security they have. Drug-taking in general seems more self-destructive and angrier today than it used to be, as punk has replaced flower-power. A number of the addicts we see describe to us how they didn't get much attention as children – their parents were preoccupied with ambitious careers in politics or something; having lacked love, the kids find it hard to form loving relationships. Sexual problems also crop up constantly; many of the kids have difficulty with their orientation and identity.[17]

Lyn Perry of Release believes the basic problem stems from 'the lack of trust of adults by kids: we should stop lying to them'. In contrast, one mother accused young people of using drugs in order to manipulate and control their parents; particularly in affluent upper- and middle-class areas, the surest way for a maladjusted adolescent to dramatize his situation and obtain attention is to start taking heroin. Dee Halpin at the ROMA centre also blames some use on 'the wish to be different'; others suggest as a reason 'the loss of faith in politicians or religion'. A growing number of teenagers explore several varieties of drugs – no longer just speed to get up and barbiturates to come down: many who are predisposed to drug abuse will try whatever they can according to their mood and the fashion of their environment, limited only by availability and their pocket.

Since it is mainly personalities with emotional problems and a lack of self-esteem who become dependent on drugs, the best antidote is to try to treat the cause, rather than the symptom, by tackling these problems – difficult as that often is. The high proportion of US soldiers who had used heroin in Vietnam but who came off the habit on their return home shows that the removal of the factors causing stress is the most lasting form of cure. But the roots of drug abuse can at times resemble a Rorschach blot that fits almost any theory. A political interpretation might argue that when government policies increasingly polarize society and widen the gulf between rich and poor, both the bored rich and disaffected poor turn to drugs, for different reasons. At the outset of my research for this book one expert said:

It's no coincidence that Poland and the USA are the countries with the very worst problem. Poland, cut off from freedom, can only escape into drugs. In the USA many of those who fail by the yardsticks and hyped pressures of materialist consumerism drop out into heroin; even those who are successful bury in cocaine their failure to find happiness. The chimera of such drugs fits all too naturally into a society where health is seen as popping pills, live relationships are increasingly replaced by the ersatz images of videos and films of violence and porn (since

first-hand sex has been deterred by herpes and AIDS, the vogue
is to replace it with the fantasies of drugs or of telephone sex
talk).[18]

Today, however, it is necessary to explain the rising spread of drugs
in societies ranging from Pakistan to Peru as much as in Europe and
the USA. It is not only in North America that drug use can be
accused of being symptomatic of a culture which uses the technology of chemical substances to mask social and psychological
problems.[19] Drugs, their users claim, are the logical result of an
illogical world. But as long as society hides from its problems by
alternately resorting to pharmacology and blaming it as a scapegoat,
the basic issues go unattended. If the current crisis of drug use leads
to new thinking about serious social faults, and especially those that
concern youth, the angst and trauma it is causing may not be in
vain.

In large schools and colleges, as in ghettoes and housing-estates,
anonymity has engendered the creation of subcultures, where
experimenting with drugs may bring acceptance as a member.
Heroin users form a secret counter-society (though Jimmy Boyle
says, 'When I was young there was at least a certain nobility about
being in a gang. Heroin addicts don't even have that'). A broken
home or social marginality can result in a lack of counter-influences
or other anchors in life. In human individuals, Freud's hypothesis
was that aggression against the self and against others are recipro-
cally related, frequently being based in severe depression stemming
from difficulty in forming personal relations.[20] Life and history
provide plenty of examples of people who in fact are bent on their
own destruction, although their ostensible (and indeed conscious)
aim appears otherwise. It is fallacy, however, to imagine that most
drug-users fit the stereotype of dead-beat characters: in fact, they
are often people who expect the most from life, being imaginative,
adventurous and too sensitive to bear reality. One doctor reported a
number of his addict patients consider their syringe and needle
represents a breast (or for others, a penis), and he thought it
significant how many of them are the favourite son of a very close
mother. For the insecure and unconfident, or the aimless and
pessimistic, amphetamines – like cocaine – lend an illusion of well-
being and energy; while other drugs such as heroin assist those
who are unable to express their aggression and frustration, by

245

blotting out these feelings – for as long as they go on taking them.

The idea of having responsible control of one's own life – as an alternative to blaming drugs or the authorities as a scapegoat – can be frightening. Many drug-users are not unconforming rebels so much as fearful of life without chemical crutches. Stanton Peele suggests: '[An addict] is eager to rely on drugs (or medicines), on people, on institutions (like prisons and hospitals) . . . This readiness for submission is the keynote of addiction. Disbelieving his own adequacy, recoiling from challenge, the addict welcomes control from outside himself as the ideal state of affairs . . . Fear and feelings of inadequacy cause an addict to seek constancy of stimulation and setting rather than to chance the dangers of novel or unpredictable experience.'[21] Pointing to the mutual support and approval of addicts' group culture, Peele argues that *amour fou* lovers share a not dissimilar conspiracy: their increasing dependency becomes their main source of gratification. Whether or not, as some argue, anxiety is more widespread today because stable social structures and religious beliefs no longer provide a framework, the increased opportunities offered by contemporary life can frighten many individuals – if only because as a result there is less excuse for failure. Much of the hardest pressure falls on those who are too inexperienced to know how to cope with it, such as teenagers, often enticed by advertisers with pleasures they are frustrated from attaining. In many places in the world today, any present or future chance of finding work is minimal; amongst the consequent despair the expanding network of dealing in drugs provides unemployed youths not only with a substitute, but a profitable and undemanding way of life. The recent study of heroin misuse conducted by Andrew Irving Associates for the British government concluded that key circumstances contributing to its increase are 'mass youth unemployment and breakdown in family life leading to despair, alienation and personal and community depression' (though it also reported that among those 'less at risk' are discerning users of 'soft' drugs, including 'West Indians who, though displaying many characteristics of those "at risk" in terms of social and family conditions, consistently distinguished between soft drugs which were acceptable, and hard drugs – especially heroin – which were unacceptable, almost taboo'). A relationship with a drug can also offer an easy substitute for failure to find the romantic ideal in personal relationships. Dr Helen Nowlis's research led her to the conclusion that most of the reasons which draw young people to drugs form part of the difficulty of learning to become an adult. 'The nature and extent of these problems are closely related to the way in which a society defines and relates to young people . . . Most of the factors associated with destructive and deviant behaviour, including destructive drug use, can be traced through family, social, educational and economic mazes to lack of trust, lack of sense of worth, of being valued, and lack of a sense of accomplishment and ability to accomplish tasks of value to the individual and society.'[22] Countries such as Denmark and the Netherlands believe that the best antidote to drugs misuse lies in improving their policy towards youth problems in general, so as to avoid isolating and dramatizing drugs.

Among women drug misusers, a significant proportion have been drawn into heroin and other illicit drugs by their dependency on older men-friends or lovers: this explains why the average age of starting heroin is lower for females than for males, despite the fact that generally girls are kept under closer parental supervision. Individuals who may be vulnerable to drug dependency often become attracted to each other and form a couple. Other partners begin to use drugs from a wish to share or understand their lover's problem: it is lonely to try to be close to someone who is regularly on another plane of consciousness. But many women turn to drugs because of social and emotional pressures. 'Drugs, like smoking cigarettes, help me feel tough and better able to withstand the hassle of making myself sexually available,' said one woman. Feelings of rejection can set in from failure to find a job or a lover, or after one's family have left home. As with men, either socio-economic or psychological factors can be determinant.[23] Women's many simultaneous roles and disadvantages in modern society expose them to multiple stress, often coupled with lack of confidence and few opportunities for jobs with interest or satisfaction. These factors combined readily create feelings of low self-esteem which it is tempting to use drugs to alleviate; some women drug abusers and alcoholics can be harder to treat than men, because they find it almost impossible to believe in their own worth, having been conditioned by a life over which they have always had too little control or responsibility. Their family frequently reacts by being embarrassed by their problem, as well as reluctant to confront its root causes. A number of women abusers in turn seek to pin blame on their relatives, doctor or lover, and try to make them feel responsible and guilty. Many of the increasing number of women dealers have chosen to trade in drugs as an alternative to theft or prostitution as a way of supporting their habit. And, as we shall see, women users find it harder than men to find help or treatment.

Harder than stopping a drug itself, to stay off generally requires changing one's whole life-style. When dependent on drugs, the user's streetsmart image in a druggy subculture derives from his skill at deceiving doctors, straight friends and people in authority, at forging prescriptions or stealing from chemists. The drug network probably offers the only social group that readily accepts and esteems him, giving mutual support, understanding and recognition of identity to a person who feels excluded by society from other roles. The self-contained deviant life-style, with its own language and moral code, becomes the addict's human prop and emotional haven, providing a new status and self-image – but at the same time reinforcing the alienation and escape from reality that originally drew him to drugs. Initiation into a number of street gangs the world over requires youths to prove their mettle by stealing and using drugs. Although there is little freemasonry amongst most addicts (the demands of need are too paramount, and the chronic unreliability characteristic of many addicts does not make social friendships easy), the life-style of a modern outlaw undoubtedly forms part of the attraction for many a drug-user. Drugs' ability to shock and challenge the establishment offers a romantic appeal to the immature. Not for them the dilemmas of existential choice: their single obsession rules and regulates their life. The drug culture's scene is likely to persist in retaining an overwhelming emotional pull for those trying to come off drugs, just as addicts lacking their drug often seek nostalgic satisfaction by injecting themselves with milk or water. 'After you've had the habit a certain while, the only people you still know are those connected with drugs in some way,' said a man who had detoxified several times, explaining one of the reasons he found it so difficult to escape permanently. 'Junkies don't have friends, just fellow junkies,' confirmed a woman addict in Bristol. Addicts have been known to resent the cure of one of their number; one young man who had escaped was pursued by his circle until he was hooked again. People who dislike and fear the milieu of drug-users find it difficult to understand the attraction this alternative society offers. Its ranks include many young people who are unemployed – but to whom society has offered no new role instead. When those idealists among them rebel against what they see as the unfeeling inhumanity of the adults who hold power, only to find their protests (whether against the Bomb, or about poverty at home or in the Third World) ignored, many opt for escapism: they retreat into drugs, live in communes or join cult religions which appear to offer new spontaneity and spirituality – as well as the inducement of sensations which are closer to childhood. Older religions seem too establishment- and adult-orientated to satisfy the void in their lives. The classless fellowship of a hippy life-style, with its hedonistic defiance of conformity and repression, can appear welcome and humanistic by contrast with their parents' Protestant Ethic-dominated society, which seems based on work, snobbery and hypocrisy, characterized by inherited hierarchies and deferred gratification due to guilt about sex and pleasure. A number of those who opt out subsequently are drawn to cults as a more structured life, after they have experienced the chaotic dislocation of the drug culture. Drug-users and cultists share a faith in some magical escape from the materialist pressure and problems of present-day society:[24] Christopher Lasch has termed this tendency to turn inwards 'the new narcissism', involving 'the overthrow of "inhibitions" and the non-stop celebration of the self'.[25]

Families and friends

Parents of drug misusers can feel stunned by a mixture of shock, bewilderment, guilt and anger. Rightly or wrongly, they believe that at some level their offspring's involvement with drugs represents a failure by themselves. No parent can ever be perfect: there will always be some more attention we could have given our children. But many schools as well as parents show culpable innocence about what is happening in front of their noses, whereas several others choose to turn a blind eye to the evidence, sometimes refusing for years to face the reality that a child is drug-dependent. Others seek to hide what they see as a shameful stigma ('I wanted to keep it hush-hush. No parent wants to admit that their darling kid is a dirty drug-addict,' as one mother said); because they themselves view it as a dreadful secret, they fear their neighbours will shun them as contaminated or infectious if they find out. Some London parents recounted: 'Your initial reaction is to keep it covered, hidden, because people will stop associating with you because they're afraid and you're ashamed also . . . You swim in guilt. You think there must be something you've done.'

Inside a family the balance of power is often taken over by the addict child. The authority of any parental response to the crisis is frequently weakened because many parents admit that their children know more about illicit drugs than they do, which inhibits them from giving guidance or even being able to have a credible dialogue beyond saying 'don't'.[26] In many schools as well as families, drugs are 'the unmentionable issue' because of the nexus with criminality. One Birmingham parent reported: 'There's a great stigma attached to drug use which there isn't apparently with alcohol . . . so there aren't places where you can go for help. You can't chat about it in the same way.' Too many GPs continue to remain ignorant and unwilling to help or even offer support: 'My GP just talked religion, and said if we had lived the ways of the Lord, this would never have happened'; 'Our twenty-year-old son's doctor refused to speak to us even on the telephone, because medical etiquette forbids him to talk about his patient.' In Bristol, the parents of some heroin-dependent children were nervous about seeking help because, they recounted, 'A woman I know, her husband was a heroin addict and she had a letter from her doctor saying that as her husband was an addict, he was removing her and her children's names from the register.'

The burden of attempting to cope, as a loved one disintegrates in front of your eyes before his life has properly started, is more often shouldered by mothers than by fathers.[27] Often they are torn between on the one hand their instinctive wish to show love and concern for the drug-dependent child, and on the other finding that his chaotic behaviour disrupts the entire home, and disturbs their other children to whom they can give less attention, so that eventually their own health and sanity are undermined. 'It's an awful strain . . . you're split in two between the addict and the rest of the family'; 'If you're not careful, you start living their hell with them'; 'You get like your addict – secretive, deceitful, suspicious'. Individuals who are capable of assisting others' drug problems can become confused and helpless when it is a member of their own family who is affected: 'You yourself become ill through the situation. The whole family becomes twisted . . . the whole thing of the powerful parent being able to do something is false'; 'You cry, you pray, you wheedle'; 'You say good-bye to your daughter and hello drug-addict.' Most addicts are deceiving themselves, and become adept at deceiving others: 'You never trust them or believe them.' The drug-user frequently seeks to control his family, using weapons of manipulation, bargaining, guilt and blackmail: 'A family needs to protect its own right to survive, but an addict doesn't have relations, he has hostages'; 'Once somebody becomes a drug-addict they become a con-merchant, a liar. He's kicked the door down at six in the morning when he's needed money.' Exceptionally, one former-ly rich mother in north-west London said, 'When my daughter burgled all I had, I learnt a great benefit: it changed all my values, away from relying on material goods.' Some parents' marriages, however, often crack from the strain: 'He'll find a wedge and drive it between you'; 'His behaviour got worse and I thought I ought to give him more love, take him on holiday . . . thinking that would make him well. What actually happened was that he slowly got worse and worse'; 'She keeps asking us for money, saying she is being threatened by violent drug-suppliers and warning she'll have to take to crime if we don't give it her.' Many parents are shocked and distressed at the hatred they find they feel for their addicted child. The scars on a family can be permanent, because of persistent uncertainty about when the trouble will recur. This can easily produce despair: 'When you first start, you think that there's a way of getting them off. When you get to our stage you know there's no way,' said the Liverpool parent of one heroin-addicted child. Some couples are finally driven to abandon and cut themselves off from their child because they believe it is the only way to save themselves. Other parents whose children died from drugs, on the other hand, say they will do anything to help others facing the same crisis.

Drugs are no respecter of talent, merit, school or family: part of their attraction is that they are wholly lacking in class-consciousness. 'You never imagine it will be *your* problem, but it happens without warning, to anybody's children in any family,' said the upper-middle-class Cambridge graduate mother of one addict; 'You can only hope they tell you, and keep contact.' Other parents react differently. One father, who had formerly served in the police, handed his drug-using son over to the police, and – weeping him-self – opposed bail for him on his twenty-first birthday; whereas another parent bought over £1,000's worth of heroin for her son to try to get him away from crime. In France, however, a judge at Rodez recently heavily fined the parents of a young heroin addict, stating that they must have noticed and that parents are responsible for their children's actions until they are of age. On the other hand, one Hampstead girl said her parents were less worried about her having drugs than junk food. A tiny minority of parents themselves introduce their children to drugs – most often cannabis 'for experience' ('We relate real well when we're all high,' an American father claimed); a Rochdale mother gave her eleven-year-old son heroin to smoke when he caught her using it. Other parents pathetically join in their children's drug-taking so as to keep up with them – often succeeding only in losing their respect. However, in Bogota, where eight-year-olds are now using bazuka (unrefined cocaine paste), a group of parents showed the Colombian drug squad – at considerable personal risk – the houses of the traffickers; Dublin parents have formed vigilante groups to denounce and hunt out pushers; veiled Karachi mothers recently took to the streets with their young children to demand government action. The actor Paul Newman has started the Scott Newman Foundation to work against drug abuse after his son Scott died from an accidental overdose. Two determined Merseyside parents kept their drug-using children at home twenty-four hours a day for two months; a neighbour padlocked her son to his bed with a twenty-foot chain; and others organize 'minders' to keep their children away from any contact with pushers or other addicts.

For distraught relatives (spouses and siblings as well as parents), support groups like Families Anonymous (FA) exist to help them realize that their desperation is not unique – even when admitting, as several do, that they really hate their child: 'I'm such a nervous wreck, I've begun to say "Let him die, let him die"; I could now literally shoot my son,' said one businessman. The relief as well as the mutual support is of considerable help.[28] At meetings of a FA group, where first names only are used, participants exchange bruisedly frank accounts of their experience: 'I find the dangerous time's when he's feeling better. When he says he's fine, it's probably a sign he's thinking he can handle a fix. I've come to believe once a junkie, always a junkie'; 'The best thing would be if my son were picked up by the police and sentenced – but then he'll have a criminal record'; 'My daughter presses and presses and presses until she finds our weak spot.' The cathartic honesty is painful, at times shocking, but also heartening; there is no point in pretence. If any consensus emerges at an FA meeting, it is generally about the desirability of 'tough love': 'We've found it's fatal to give emotional support, let alone money'; 'Be there when they are trying, and withdraw when they are not.' Lists of advice are popular, such as the exculpating 'Three Cs' ('I didn't cause it, I can't control it and I can't cure it') and the quasi-revivalist 'Twelve Steps' (which include recommendations to 'Make a searching and fearless moral inventory of ourselves' and 'Humbly ask God to remove our shortcomings'). The predominantly middle-class parents and friends are advised to detach themselves emotionally and to take care of themselves first: 'Cease to be an enabler or protector.' Although addiction is seen as 'a spiritual, mental and physical illness', there is general agreement that until the addict reaches his or her 'rock bottom' and decides on self-motivated recovery, family or friends can do little or nothing. FA attenders are counselled: 'Don't accept guilt for another person's acts; don't nag, over-protect, cover up; do allow other people to accept their responsibilities; manage your anxieties one day at a time.' A mother of an addict was given the following 'Open Letter to My Family from Your User' by FA:

Don't solve my problems for me. This only makes me lose respect for you and for myself. Don't lecture, moralize, scold, blame or argue whether I'm stoned or sober. It may make you feel better but it only makes the situation worse. Don't accept my promises. The nature of my illness prevents my keeping them, even though I mean them at the time. Promises are only my way of postponing pain. And don't keep switching agreements: if an agreement is made, stick to it. Don't lose your temper with me. It will destroy you and any possibility of helping me. Don't let your anxiety for me make you do what I should do for myself. Don't believe everything I tell you. Often I don't even know the truth – let alone tell it. Don't cover up or try to spare me the consequences of my using. It may reduce the crises, but it will make my illness worse. Above all don't run away from reality as I do. Drug dependence, my illness, gets worse as my using continues. Start now to learn, to understand, to plan for recovery. Find Families Anonymous, whose group exists to help families in just your situation. I need help – from a doctor, a psychologist, a counsellor, from some people in a self-help programme who've recovered from a drug problem themselves – and from a Power greater than myself.

FA meetings usually start with the 'Serenity Prayer': 'God grant me to accept the things I cannot change; the courage to change the things I can; and the wisdom to know the difference.' Many people are profoundly grateful for the help FA has given them ('troubles shared are troubles halved'), though some non-religious new-comers have been deterred by details such as the opening prayer. FA states that it is not religious and that non-believers are welcome, although it agrees that it is 'based upon spiritual principles' and a belief in the help of a 'Higher Power' which can be, in addition to any God, the power of the Universe, Nature or the group itself: 'The idea is to gain strength to accomplish the difficult by turning to something greater than ourselves.' However, one London woman designer who has been going to FA for two years said, 'I nearly gave up at the first meeting because of the American ethos as well as the prayer and talk of a Higher Power: I know a few others were also put off and abandoned going altogether.' Another mother, a writer, said she did not wish to be characterized purely as an addict's parent. Nevertheless, increasing numbers are finding comfort and reassurance from such mutual support groups. Members urge that between ten and twenty is the best size for a group, and that groups should sub-divide if their success makes them too large, since the main value is in every participant having a chance to talk, and not just be talked to.

Symptoms that may indicate drug use

It is easy to draw wrong conclusions from teenagers' moodiness or their natural desire for privacy and independence. Contrariwise, several parents have optimistically but mistakenly interpreted their drug-taking adolescents' unusual new behaviour as the pangs of love. Too interfering a suspiciousness – as advocated by a few experts – [29] risks causing the very alienation which can easily lead to drug use. However, warning indications (besides obvious clues such as burnt tinfoil) that should trigger concern are: glazed eyes or dilated pupils; changes of mood and personality far exceeding a particular person's usual ups and downs; furtiveness, lying, locked doors and unexplained absences; loss of appetite, sometimes combined with vomiting and loss of weight; a derelict life-style or abandonment of interest in personal appearance; falling asleep at meals, lethargy, loss of memory or enthusiasm, sometimes together with slurred, slow or halting speech; needle-marks, which may be hidden by wearing long sleeves; frequent secret phone calls, and a new set of friends who are never brought home; the use of strong new cigarettes or scent to hide smells; unexplained borrowing and debts or the disappearance of money and items from home.

While many problems underlying drug misuse begin in the family, and can also be treated in a family setting, adults as well as children often start to abuse alcohol or other drugs because of problems about which their relatives and friends are not aware. A woman pointed out one indication she had found: 'When a man is addicted to heroin, he cannot function sexually; he not only finds it difficult to get an erection but doesn't care anyway.' Women on drugs similarly are likely to lose their sexual urge – though this may be due to many other reasons. Some wives and husbands have been known to make themselves as helpless as a child on alcohol and drugs, believing this will prevent their spouse leaving them; other partners, however, can be jealous of concern and treatment, because this means they receive less attention. A number of marriages and relationships break up once a cure is achieved, because the drugs or alcoholism masked or were only a symptom of other problems.

It can be a difficult dilemma whether to tell anybody (and if so whom) when you discover that someone is using hard drugs. Parents feel angry and betrayed at the fact that friends of their son or daughter did not inform them he or she started to use hard drugs (generational solidarity is very strong), or that a doctor had not informed them when he found drug symptoms, because of the confidentiality required by medical ethics. In the shock of discovery, people's feelings often run a gamut from scapegoating and denial to resentment, rejection and despair. They are bewildered that there is no magic solution, and that doctors and experts disagree with each other concerning the subject. Some very good advice is offered by the mother of one ex-addict: 'Talk *before* they ever get near drugs, so that they will be able to handle the situation when they do . . . Perhaps the most important thing a parent can do is to leave the door open: if they ask for help, that could be the beginning of a cure.' One former addict said of her parents: 'They used to put the phone down on me; now they can't keep off it.' It is a field where no rule is immutable: a senior London lawyer believes that he won the battle to wean his children off drugs by giving them just that unwavering love, support and attention which FA meetings counsel against. A probation officer advised:

> Don't panic. Try always in any event to keep an open relationship with your son and daughter. Discuss, not only drugs, but any other major problems in the family. Many cases of drug abuse I've seen have been due to young people having parents who were not interested in, or undervalued, them – or else have parents who are so ambitious for them that they couldn't cope and felt they were inadequate failures.

The headmaster of a Hertfordshire boys' school declared, 'Everybody will be offered illegal drugs sooner or later, so I advise the children to prepare their reply in advance – preferably a negative one – so as not to leave them open to a chance impulse.' (The chaplain at the same school blamed the contemporary appeal of drugs on modern advertising which leads young people to expect life to be continually exciting and glamorous.) But a teacher at another, public, school regretted that: 'Many schools like this one won't ever mention the drug incidence – obviously it's against its business interests.' Encouraging children or friends to talk openly – listening to their silences as well as what they say – may help you notice early any signs of new problems, and be less likely to be caught unaware when emergency action is required. Attempts to change any young person's habits or acquaintances have to be approached carefully – and the degree of success ultimately depends upon his or her accepting the need for the change. Whichever plan is eventually worked out to deal with a case of drug-taking, parents and friends should show confidence in the ability of the user to win through: every comment should continue to demonstrate this faith – which is not the same as ignoring any slip-ups which may occur en route. Coercion is unlikely to work for long: when one English mother locked up her eighteen-year-old son whose heroin habit she had discovered, he 'dressed up as a woman to get out of my house. So brilliant was the disguise that I did not recognize him immediately, and it was all done so quickly that I was just left wondering who'd walked out of the front door. He then rang me from a call-box to say he disowned me as his mother and I was the foulest and most horrible creature ever yet born.' (At least he cared enough to tell her this.) In fact, no solution to a drugs problem is likely to succeed permanently without the co-operation and commitment of the user. And to achieve this a positive approach has much the most likely chance of persuading him to change course:

> It is difficult not to dwell on the weaknesses of someone involved with drug misuse. The idea seems to be that if the weakness can somehow be removed all will be well. An alternative approach is to build a picture of the strengths possessed by the child. What are his talents, his achievements, the quality of his relationships? . . . In the process of finding and fostering strengths, parents will be showing their faith in, and acceptance of, the child as he is . . .[30]

It is almost irresistible for most parents – like many friends – to attempt to make a person conform to their own ideas because they are reluctant to accept the differences in his personality: 'Children never turn out exactly as their parents had hoped or imagined, simply because they are individual beings . . . This inflicts a sense of guilt on the child and decreases the self-esteem which is so necessary to him, especially during the difficult period of adolescence.'[31] (It was Oscar Wilde who said that children begin by loving their parents; then they judge them; sometimes they forgive them.) Nevertheless, even if parents ostensibly succeed by means of authoritarian measures, the likely cost is that the child's personality will remain fixedly child-like – one of the most likely seed-beds for the propagation of drug-dependency.

Self-help

SHADA – Support, Help and Advice on Drug Addiction – was set up in October 1982 by residents in Muirhouse, a desolate housing-estate in Edinburgh which currently has a very serious opiate epidemic, with some one in ten of its young people on heroin and several drug deaths a year. Jimmy and Sarah Boyle were among the prime movers in starting the organization, which serves as a drop-in centre and pressure group as well as a support body; the crowded twice-weekly meetings, held in a small pre-fabricated hut, draw current addicts and former addicts as well as families and friends. At the meetings, speakers articulate their angry desperation, often voicing suspicion of professionals as well as the police. SHADA has given many residents a new sense of community and ways in which they can help each other, though there have been set-backs such as when one of its main founders, who had detoxified after being an addict for ten years, reverted to heroin and resigned. Parents at another self-help group on Merseyside angrily demanded: 'Are our children dying to help Pakistan's corrupt economy or to finance the Afghan war?', and were only narrowly dissuaded from setting fire to a Pakistan ship docked at Liverpool that was found to have heroin aboard. (But, as Alan Parry of Hope House points out, the major drug and health problem on Merseyside is alcohol abuse, and adults have yet to be seen to attack pubs which sell drink to under-age children.) It is notable that working-class communities display much more initiative and solidarity against drug-dealers than middle-class areas do: there is no sign of people in SW3 or NW3 combining to drive pushers out of the King's Road or Camden pubs, despite the high proportion of young people in those areas being at risk.

Other groups of mutual support organizations concentrate on helping former users. The oldest and largest is Alcoholics Anonymous; its parallel body for ex-addicts of other drugs is Narcotics Anonymous (NA). NA's meetings usually start with one of its members recounting their own history for twenty or thirty minutes. Most of the unselfconscious speakers seem to be young and upper or middle class; the minority of working class and older attenders tend to sit at the back of meetings and are less articulate. At one meeting, the woman who spoke first began: 'I'm Caroline. I was an addict for six years. Just as I didn't become an addict overnight, I won't be cured in one evening. I find I need to come to NA meetings five times a week.' The son of a Privy Councillor said that he liked the 'pleasing anarchy' of NA, which (like AA) has no bureaucracy or subsidy; any two or more people can start a new group. So keen is AA to maintain its financial independence that in the UK it obtained a special Act of Parliament in 1986 to give it the right to decline gifts – the first charity ever to do this. Those people for whom NA and AA are suited, swear by them. AA and NA believe a person can never claim to be cured permanently; some members continue to attend meetings for nine or more years after they are 'clean', partly for the friendship, but mainly for the support they feel they still need. (This suggests that NA and AA may provide substitute dependency, if a much less harmful one.) Both organizations cost nothing – except for commitment and time – and have no waiting list.

The atmosphere at meetings is generally positive and serious, but uncensorious – at times more like a successful if sober party than a group casework meeting. There is no shortage of participants anxious to share their insecurities, sometimes at substantial length. At an NA meeting a good-looking 27-year-old man confesses: 'I used to smoke heroin before any social occasion, otherwise I thought people wouldn't consider me interesting. I come from a very privileged background and home, but it was ten years before my parents, whom I saw most weekends, realized I was on heroin – some families are the last people who recognize or admit what is happening . . . I myself didn't realize until quite recently when I'd finished at the treatment centre just how *boring* I was when I was on drugs.' His neighbour, a woman of about the same age, with long hair framing a thin pale face, joins in: 'Yes, I also started by taking coke along to parties so that people would be glad to see me and come up and talk to me.' A more socially-consious and confident woman comments: 'The trouble is we middle class don't actually have many real problems. So we get bored and create our own problems.'

NA and AA members are required to maintain total abstinence, from alcohol as well as any other drug. Dr Meg Patterson believes that, while support is vital, the organizations' approach is not ideal for everyone, because they focus on negative aspects which keep drugs and alcohol in the forefront of members' minds, instead of replacing them with positive new ideas. However, part of their success is because participants, in addition to receiving support, feel they are playing a caring role themselves. Another reason is because, as an ex-user said, 'Having been amoral when you were an addict, you've no moral structure when you come out. But it's hard to con another junkie – they can see right through you.' One NA member, the son of a former government minister, recounted: 'I was one of the more honest junkies – I only drove get-away cars of cheque-bouncers. I was attracted to junkies' laid-back style. Now they seem exceptionally dull: as a junkie you have to keep lying to everybody, including yourself. You can't communicate at all, because of the continual bullshit about "I'll give up next week", etc. When you go straight, you lose all your previous friends, and NA is very useful to fill the gap.' Another member added: 'The silences can be very useful to bring out the shy. One can hate oneself; at a NA meeting you will find friends prepared to help because they've all been through it too. It's a bridge to normal living – I went to ninety meetings in ninety days to start with.' A member educated at a public school said, 'Admitting one's own vulnerability and loncliness makes one much more understanding of others. All my life I'd been taught not to speak of my feelings. Now, saying how I felt was a breakthrough. Honesty breeds honesty. I've begun to be able to talk of my emotions outside NA too.' A high proportion of NA members are graduates of Broadway Lodge or other fashionable clinics. Until now, such groups have flourished almost entirely in middle-class areas; the slum districts of greatest need have fewest of them. For the great majority of drug-users, who live in rural and other areas a long way from West London or Sunset Boulevard, where the absence of public transport or lack of money makes it impossible for them to get to meetings of NA or other self-help groups, telephone-linked networks should be set up to provide basic support and advice.

Treatment: What is wrong?

'Society', Sir Bernard Braine MP says, 'does not want to know about the problems of drug addiction.' However, help for people to give up drug misuse benefits society as much as the individuals themselves. It is not only the surest way to reduce the demand for drugs, but also their spread, since the most frequent introduction to illicit drugs originates from a friend or acquaintance already misusing. Those doctors and members of the public who argue that drug-sufferers have inflicted their unnecessary malaise on themselves and should be left to stew in the consequences, should reflect that society does not refuse treatment to people whose lungs are damaged because they have smoked despite warnings, or to heart patients disabled as a result of over-indulgence. Nevertheless the medical profession has generally given low priority to drug cases, perhaps because of various stigmas attached to them. Drug dependants are notoriously unpopular in hospital casualty departments.

Addicts are demanding and equivocal, not the humble and deferential clients professional people prefer: they do not fit easily into conventional structures – often because of the same reasons they become addicts. A minority of doctors may enjoy the power they exercise over addicts, but many complain, 'They don't keep their appointments' or 'They're only voluntarily ill – I've plenty of other involuntarily ill cases I haven't time to see.' It is quicker and simpler for a doctor to prescribe maintenance or pills (just as it is for a depressed person to take a drug or a drink) than to embark on the much more lengthy process of unravelling underlying causes and personal problems. Social workers, as well as GPs, feel they have more 'deserving' cases; and not every older professional person remembers what adolescent depression can be like.

Many economically-stretched local health authorities resent spending any money at all on drug cases. To cope with heroin cases alone, which now number some 100,000, the NHS out-patient capacity in the whole of Britain scarcely totals 2,000. In-patient beds, mainly occupied by alcoholics, number less than 300. Half the counties in Britain still possess no specialist drug service; in 1984, there were only twelve beds reserved for drug rehabilitation north of Oxford, with none at all in Scotland. Dr Strang in Manchester is the only full-time NHS drug consultant in the UK outside London; though, even in the London area, treatment facilities remain inadequate in half the boroughs.[32] The House of Commons all-party Social Services Select Committee in June 1985 castigated Britain's facilities (despite the government's recent injection of £12 million – a sum probably less than traffickers make in a single week) as being 'woefully inadequate':

> Treatment facilities are few, underfunded, often inaccessible and always with long waiting lists. Rehabilitation is provided, if at all, by voluntary organizations unable to plan ahead for lack of secure funding. Experienced staff are in very short supply. Drug misusers and their families do not know where to turn for help. General medical and social services are too often unable or unwilling to become involved. Many drug-users end up in prison where they are likely to receive no help at all.[33]

Nor is the crisis in treatment confined to Britain. The USA actually reduced expenditure on drug treatment and education from $458 million in 1980 to $206 million in 1983. The requirements of treatment and rehabilitation services range from detoxification and counselling to emergency medical provision to deal with overdoses or infection from needles; on the other hand, any exclusively medical concept which views alcoholism or drug addiction as a disease, risks encouraging the user to disown responsibility for controlling his habit or introducing it to others. David Turner of SCODA (the Standing Conference on Drug Abuse) points out that it was a lack of recognition of the multiple causes and problems involved in drug misuse which led to the overall failure of the ill-prepared British clinics in the 1960s. The initial policy aimed at control (by methadone maintenance) more than cure; the plan was for these clinics to attract misusers and establish contact by providing free drugs which would otherwise have had to have been obtained illicitly – though one unlooked-for result was that some occasional takers graduated to becoming regular users. Dr Ann Dally blames clinics for mystifying the subject: 'The public, doctors and journalists believe addicts are revolting untouchables who should only be dealt with by specialists. But I know addicts who are accountants, publishers, civil servants, skilled workers: far from social misfits.' A great number of clinics and doctors today still remain uncertain whether their policy should be maintenance or withdrawal: recently, under the pressure of escalating waiting lists and disillusionment with methadone maintenance, there has been a firm move towards a more interventionist and confrontational approach. Methadone is now being dropped on the grounds that it only perpetuates drug-taking, despite its supporters' claim that it provides crime-free stability.[34] However, there remains the problem that clinics which refuse to supply maintenance drugs are ostracized by many addicts who turn instead to those GPs who will do so; in the USA, particularly on the West Coast, certain doctors are known as 'script mills' because of their generosity – at a price – in grinding out drug prescriptions.

Recent years have seen a huge increase in the number of people with drug problems who are being admitted to mental hospitals, though this has been criticized as being as unsatisfactory for the addicts as it is for other patients there. Ian Ward-Baskin, who runs the acupuncture Institute of Biophysical Medicine on Merseyside, says: 'Addicts are nice, pleasant, intelligent people: anybody's son and daughter. For some reason, it is given over to psychiatrists to treat drug addiction, but very few addicts are mentally ill.' However, 'addicts who can only be given an appointment by a NHS clinic ten weeks ahead,' as David Turner says, 'tend not to come back.' In the Wirral, the waiting list runs to a catastrophic six months. Many clinics can see a patient only for a maximum of an hour a week. For alcoholics, the only treatment the NHS can generally afford to offer is group therapy, although most cases of psychological dependence are complex and require careful individual investigation. The central UK government wrings its hands and laments the shortage of clinics, but says it does not control the regional health authorities, who have different priorities. The only way to avoid a long wait for National Health treatment is to go private: but private treatment such as is available at the profit-making Charter Clinics in Chelsea and Hampstead can cost over £4,000 for six weeks; Ticehurst in Sussex and the Priory at Roehampton cost a minimum of £1,000 a week; while many US drug clinics charge more than $1,000 a day. Dr Martin Mitcheson condemns the inequalities between the private and public treatment as 'ethically objectionable. The answer must be to produce a dramatic improvement in the NHS facilities.' A considerable number of drug-addicts switched to private doctors when at the end of the 1970s the clinics stopped supplying injectable opiates and only offered oral substitutes. Some private prescriptions, however, are so large that they enable addicts to sell enough of the surplus drugs to make a profit as well as pay the doctor's fees. Turner in fact suspects that treatment to phase out drug dependency can be fundamentally incompatible with 'commercial medical practice, which is geared to provide a service demanded by the customer, provided he or she can pay for it'. Some private practitioners in the Harley Street area of London, who notoriously provide more generous quantities of drugs than any clinic does, are reported to be earning £100,000 a year from the trade. Even ethical private doctors are worried by addict patients who tell them, 'If you won't give me my drug, I'll go to your less reputable colleagues who will.' H. B. Spear at the Home Office states, 'We are at a crossroads. Doctors must decide whether they are solely patient-orientated, or whether they have a function in social control.' One solution would be to prohibit private doctors from profiting in future from the supply of any addictive drug.

Probably some nine out of ten drug dependants, however, are unable or unwilling to go near a clinic, not all of which are welcoming and 'user-friendly', or as unembarrassing to visit as the

Cocaine Clinic in New York that intentionally is sited in part of an unmarked office block. Too many are housed in depressing, austerely deterrent premises – 'a social disease to be hidden at the backs of hospitals,' as Martin Mitcheson describes them. Addicts shun some clinics because of the stigma from their being attached to psychiatric hospitals. A civil servant, who became addicted to heroin at university fourteen years ago, also criticizes many British clinics for being inflexibly regimented; whereas in the USA, too many reveal a fundamentalist or salvationist cast. Patrick Monahan, a consultant surgeon in Swindon with experience of a heroin addict in his own family, started the support group ADFAM because of the lack of help available; he believes that GPs remain the best people to treat addicts, since they are close at hand, may possibly know the addict's history and family and are able to treat him in his own surroundings. Unfortunately, many GPs are extremely reluctant to undertake any such role – although attitudes may change as addiction affects more doctors' families. Dr Ann Dally, a Devonshire Place psychiatrist who formed the Association of Independent Doctors in Addiction, has proposed that family doctors should be given an annual bonus of, say, £200 a patient to help overcome their hesitation, and argues that this would be cheaper than new specialist clinics. GPs, however, fear that if they take no more than a very few addicts, these will take over their practice. Spear suggests that ten to fifteen addicts may be the most an individual doctor can handle; and that if every GP treated addicts, there would be an average of only two on each list. Among GPs who do treat addicts, complaints of deviousness and tough bargaining are common: one increasingly used method is to draw up a written contract with the patient specifying a period of four to ten weeks in which he will phase out his dose of opiate substitute.[35] A doctor at Shepherd's Bush said: 'I still see addicts but I tell them never to mention their addiction to me. Once you get a name for prescribing anything, your life becomes very difficult . . . addicts are very manipulative people; they create mayhem in the waiting room, they say they've lost their prescription . . . I don't have the time for addicts, or the will.' Another reported that addicts pretend to stranger GPs they have cancer in order to obtain heroin and morphine; since addicts have only one obsession whereas doctors have many things to think about, he concluded that addicts will always win in time. Some doctors believe a urine test twice a week is the only way to stop addicts lying (though samples of purified urine have been known to be sold). Addicts exchange lists of GPs who are 'soft touches', and employ tricks like trying to register with two or more doctors, or giving their GP a phone number where a friend is waiting to impersonate another doctor who will confirm their story. Dr K. Sathananthan is now one of only two doctors in England licensed by the Home Office to prescribe heroin privately for addicts: indefinitely if necessary, although his patients have a cure rate of 15 per cent. However, Dr Elizabeth Scott, a GP who practises in Edinburgh, argues against the desirability of any such role:

It is time that the government and the public stopped looking to the general practitioner to treat drug-addicts, alcohol abusers and smokers. We have no time, inappropriate training and no facilities. The successful way to treat these three categories of people is first to remove them from the environment that fosters their addiction. Once isolated, they need to be allowed to follow a programme of physical exercise and mental stimulation to enable them to stand up to the temptations of their friends to resume their addiction when they return to their own society. The facile idea that a few words from their family doctor will put them back on the right path is manifest rubbish . . . To prescribe their addiction for them in a different form, be it methadone, diazepam or nicotine gum, is to prolong their habit and to waste NHS money. To cure addicts we need residential treatment centres, sited outside the cities, where addicts may go voluntarily to be isolated from their addiction and the society that has forced them to it . . . Isolation of patients from the community is not a new concept in treatment. Other than in the examination and treatment of physical and mental disease arising in an addict, doctors have no part to play in curing an addict of his habit. It is a specialist job for non-medically trained carers who can give twenty-four-hour care to their clients – this is why monasteries and communities run by ex-addicts have the best figures for curing addiction.[36]

The majority of addicts, with their own self-sufficient street networks, feel they have little reason or incentive to seek treatment when their habit is going well: they usually only approach doctors or agencies after something has gone wrong. Many drug abusers utterly refuse to see themselves as sick or in need of help. Some only detoxify in order to revert to a smaller effective dose and so reduce its cost. The present services in Britain or the USA, moreover, would be totally unable to cope if even a quarter of the current number of addicts were to seek treatment.

Some specialist doctors believe addiction has a physiological root, and should be tackled by research into the biochemical structure of the brain; others disagree, believing that its origins are socio-psychological. Indeed, is drug misuse a medical problem at all? Might not the fact that so few drug misusers even attempt treatment (and that only a minority of these succeed in coming off drugs: at present a mere one in three heroin addicts who are treated manage to stay off for five years) mean that other factors underpin their dependency: social or emotional problems, homelessness, unemployment, family crises – and these are not being tackled? Most abusers need the help of trained advice, while some require therapy and others, practical help. Many, even if they are rehabilitated, have no stable life-style or job to return to. Addiction is always easier to deplore than to cure: simplistic solutions are as delusory as the simplistic drug habits with which they try to deal. 'Our primary aim', says Giampi Alhadeff, the Director of the City Roads Crisis Intervention Centre in London, where addicts can stay for three weeks, 'is to keep people alive. If we help them to live a drug-free life, it's a bonus.' A twenty-four-hour telephone service is needed in every country, which could give emergency advice as well as helping overdose cases until a doctor arrives. Some American experts, however, still believe the only way to reach three-quarters of heroin addicts is to offer free opiate maintenance – a suggestion that angers black leaders in New York who have termed it 'a recipe for wholesale genocide'. Such an experiment has been attempted in Amsterdam, in the hope that decriminalizing the supply will demystify heroin and so encourage cultural controls. Nevertheless, any clinic and doctor running such programmes should insist on addicts taking their dose in their presence, so that they cannot sell any surplus. Dr John Strang of Manchester, however, argues that any maintenance policy is as sensible as treating problem drinkers by providing them with a daily bottle of vodka on the NHS. Furthermore, Dr William Martin (the recent Head of the US National Institute of Mental Health's addiction research centre) believes there is a danger that heroin addiction produces permanent metabolic changes that will preserve a craving indefinitely. France, unlike Switzerland, has no methadone maintenance programme, and Dr Olievenstein, the founder of Paris's renowned Marmottan Centre, criticizes any idea of a free opiate policy as being 'pragmatic but unethical . . . methadone maintenance is catastrophic when erected into a system'.[37] 'The most common mistake', in the view of Stanton Peele, 'is for a treatment programme to substitute one addiction for another, just as we ourselves do when we start smoking heavily to keep from overeating, say, or after the break-up of a relationship . . . Something akin to this substitution can take place in drug rehabilitation programmes, even those which are otherwise constructive, when an addict is allowed to become so dependent on the support of the group that he transfers his addiction from the drug to it.'

What hope?

Fortunately, 40–50 per cent of addicts succeed in 'curing' themselves, despite the current vogue for self-fulfilling pessimism about heroin. Many, in the American phrase, 'mature out' in their thirties, perhaps giving up experimentation or occasional use as they change to married security or parenthood. Experts can claim credit for only a small proportion of the successes (private clinics' statistics have to be viewed against the fact that most of their clients are highly self-selected and motivated, possessing a strong financial incentive or firm backing from their family). As with alcoholics, the reason a substantial number of drug-users change their behaviour is because of another pressure or dependency that becomes more meaningful to them than the drug's: the influence of a sexual or work partner ('I'll have to leave or throw you out if you don't give up'), a support group or a new positive motivation, whether a valued relationship, marriage, or job; a new interest, life-style or emotional maturity; perhaps a move away from the previous setting; or the shock of an overdose, bad trip, car accident or arrest. Unfortunately, far too little vocational rehabilitation or work for ex-addicts is available. People with the greatest social and other support have the most favourable chance; those with serious mental and psychological problems face greater difficulties.[38] Ex-addicts' views confirm this: 'Drugs need to be replaced by something just as good – like people who care'; 'You become a junkie because you are lonely: what you need is love and reliability'; 'My hatred for myself began to turn into hatred for the drugs – I began to believe in myself as an ex-addict'; 'When I wanted to take heroin I'd force myself to play the guitar, write, paint, cycle. Eventually, I didn't have to force myself so hard to do something else – I actually wanted to'. One of the most famous of contemporary former drug abusers says he resolved to kick the habit after staring at his big toe in Tangier for eight days and deciding that this was a waste of life. Others said: 'The best reason for giving up drugs is because you want to do something else more'; 'You need a less harmful substitute.' (Though a nineteen-year-old undergraduate on heroin commented: 'I wouldn't get off it from anything officialdom has to offer – but maybe if I were offered a lot of pleasure, like a lot of pot.') Dr Mike Williams, a paediatrician at St Mary's Hospital, Paddington, says, 'Often a junkie couple will see a baby as a way out to normal life. Sadly, it isn't so.' A few come off the hard way: in prison (where an even higher proportion would do so if proper treatment facilities were available to prisoners). A doctor, who had himself been a heroin addict, related that an addict's successive mental stages prior to a decision to come off can parallel a bereaved person coming to terms with grief: first incredulity and denial of the problem, then anger and depression, and finally acceptance.

One new avenue of treatment may result from the recent development of Naltrexone, which is believed to stop the craving for heroin without (as methadone does) creating new addiction, by blocking the receptor sites in the brain which react to opiates: taken orally twice daily by a person motivated to give up, it is claimed to free him or her from heroin dependence within six to eighteen months.[39] Several people have been helped to withdraw from heroin by acupuncture. (Stimulating key areas of the body by acupuncture or minute electrical pulses can produce endorphins, the natural equivalent of opiates.) In Singapore a new laser variant of acupuncture for curing smokers is claimed to be cheap, painless and quick. Pete Townshend, Keith Richards, Eric Clapton and other pop-stars swear by the effect of the neuro-electric therapy of Dr Meg Patterson which, originally developed in Hong Kong, can help addicts of any drug to detoxify. Fashions in other 'miracle' cures tend to wax and wane in the way that cures for cancer do: for a believer, these may have the potency of faith healing. Meanwhile, another, current pop megastar legendarily goes to a private clinic in

Switzerland each year to have all his blood changed, so that he can continue to enjoy heroin with a lower tolerance.

A minority of drug-takers turn to treatment agencies and clinics, generally as a result of pressure from families, sexual partners or friends; sometimes under the threat of illness or an impending court appearance. An addict is best helped by someone he knows and trusts – perhaps by transferring his dependency to them. Eric Blakeborough, Director of the Kaleidoscope Project in Surrey, believes that the key starting-point, 'the most difficult part of dealing with drug abusers, is to establish a relationship, from which the individual's difficulties can be explored'. A few doctors and agency workers indeed become victims rather than saviours of addicts, adopting their jargon and identifying so totally with them that the addicts tell them what dose they need rather than vice versa. Many barbiturate dependants are even harder to communicate with than opiate addicts. Overall, drug-addicts must be among the most difficult and demanding of any people to work with; many agencies' staff feel burnt out after three or four years. When I asked some agency workers what motivates them, they replied: 'Many of us find drug-users fascinating – a few perhaps in a somewhat voyeuristic way – and the battle of wits with them is a perpetual challenge. Some of us I suppose are lay missionaries: though it's pretty rare that one gets the satisfaction of seeing the successful cases, like teachers do, to make up for all the failures.' Lyn Perry at Release used to be a librarian, but finds her present work 'more real'. The impersonality of many hospital clinics does not offer much chance of developing the personal relationship needed by suspicious drug-takers; rootless addicts much more readily trust the informality of accessible street agencies such as Release or the Hungerford and Blenheim Projects in London. (Release would collapse financially without the Home Office's support but, contrary to initial fears, this has never affected its independence.) Manchester's Lifeline also offers practical advice from qualified but sympathetic young staff able to relate to people conditioned to steer clear of anyone who smacks of authority. Brian Arbery of Turning Point says: 'A good case-worker doesn't have fixed ideas or make judgments. He needs endless resilience, and to recognize that the only person who can decide on a cure is the client.' Alan Parry, working in Merseyside, urges that ideally addicts should feel a sense of involvement and achievement in their own cure, not just 'have things done to them'.

Drug agencies and clinics lie in the front-line of conflict between social control and therapy. (If there is too much control, many patients will no longer attend.) By and large, most clinics are fully occupied with the relatively settled old timers: usefully so, but hardly touching the crucial mass of new users. In Britain the 'voluntary sector' of help with addiction developed out of the alternative information centres and arts-labs of the 1960s; or else from religious missions. Until now, it has lived from hand-to-mouth on donations or local funding – parlously, since financial crises have coincided with the rise in addiction. Lifeline, the main centre for helping drug-users outside London, three times lost a potential site for residential rehabilitation through refusal of planning permission; in 1976 it faced financial closure, but was saved by NACRO and SCODA. Under Dr Eugenie Cheesmond and today Rowdy Yates, Lifeline rejects the stereotypes which addicts themselves often cling to, and negotiates realistic contracts regulating the behaviour, goals and needs of each attender. But in 1980 both Lifeline and the Blenheim Project had to reduce staff through cuts in funds; the next year, City Roads' funding was officially terminated, the Pharmakon Clinic closed completely with the loss of thirty beds, and the New Life Foundation had to shut two rehabilitation houses, losing a further fifty beds.

An ideal agency offers multidisciplinary help for the underlying problems that withdrawal exposes – when, as an ex-addict said, 'One comes to realize one's just been sedating those feelings, and that sticking a needle in isn't going to make them go away.' 'There are people', Philippa Smith of SCODA points out, 'who've been neglecting themselves for so long that the actual withdrawal will reveal other serious health problems.' Above all, the addict must be viewed as a whole person, not just a drug problem. ROMA, under the auspices of the Rev. Terence Tanner (who said 'Addicts are the scapegoats of our age'), pioneered the provision of housing for them. A new clinic in Cambridge aims to provide a co-ordinated package of services: medical treatment and a place on a job-training scheme, together with collateral family therapy; Bermondsey's Committee against Drug Dependency aims to 'take the care of addicts out into the community'; while agencies such as Blenheim specialize in helping the problems which follow detoxification. Not every drug-taker, of course, is a problem case, but early intervention can often save more serious complications. The spectrum of related problems requires a mixed range of treatment strategies, though rehabilitation in general has been made much harder by unemployment and economic recession. Dismissal from work, school or college can convert occasional chipping into chronic drug use, although most people who take drugs regularly find it hard to hold down a job because of unpunctuality and unreliability. The stereotyped view of drug-takers held by the public unfortunately makes it very difficult for addicts to re-enter society or find work, and the more they are isolated, the less likely they are to respond to informal social controls. Brian Arbery believes that many drug-users are also deterred from seeking help by fear of having their name on any file (although, as in the USA, treatment data are not meant to be used for law-enforcement), and that we must also accept that a large number have no wish to come off drugs in the first place. Some addicts resent 'treatment', regarding it as a middle-class, puritanical concept. Nevertheless, more day rehabilitation centres are badly needed (many misusers require help in their home setting), with family psychotherapy as well as rehabilitative jobs, in addition to further drop-in advice centres for young people. Disabled drug-users require special provision. Above all, there is a particularly urgent need for better facilities to help the increasing number of female addicts: very few clinics or hostels have a crèche for young children. Deaths among female addicts are higher than among males. Women users are more hesitant to seek help, and also have specific needs: they often abuse tranquillizers and barbiturates, whereas most clinics are opiate-orientated. Mothers using drugs are terrified lest their children be taken away from them; and not all women are able to discuss their problems at meetings with males, so there should be special women-only agencies (with child-care help). At present there are only twenty-five beds reserved specifically for women in rehabilitation houses throughout the whole of Britain. Women in the USA are similarly under-represented in treatment, forming over 40 per cent of the known abusers in New York, but only 31 per cent of those receiving treatment. There are also conspicuously few non-white clients, even though it is possible that in some cases extended families provide their own support systems.

In the USA there are in all over 300 therapeutic communities, containing more than 9,000 residents. Britain by contrast has only twenty-five residential drug-free treatment hostels – almost all concentrated in south-east England. These divide into three broad categories:

(a)   *Concept-based therapeutic communities* (such as the Ley Community and Alpha House), started in 1968 on the lines of Phoenix House and Daytop Village in the USA. These had originally been developed from Synanon, a tough puritanical commune in California that forbade money and flour as well as any alcohol, smoking or drug. (Synanon's name probably derived from 'seminar', an early name for an encounter group. Its regime became increasingly brutal; in 1977 its charismatic ex-alcoholic leader, Chuck Dederich, was arrested for attempted murder.) At their worst, such institutions remove residents' self-confidence, forcefully persuading them of their degeneracy in a manner not dissimilar to the earlier witch-hunts of Salem. Recently, at San Patrignano in Italy, the inmates of one institution were confined by chains in small coops – often with their consent. Characteristically, such houses possess a hierarchical structure – often strictly authoritarian – in which a new resident earns successive privileges dependent on his behaviour, attitude and work; responsibility is placed squarely on him both for his previous difficulties and for achieving the necessary changes in himself. Brian Donnellan, the Director of Ley (near Oxford), likens this to 'the experience of a young adult leaving home for the first time and finding out about the real world', though critics cite it as 'the enforcement of middle-class control'. At many houses, peer-pressure in group meetings and penalties are – as in communist societies – employed to confront and challenge 'anti-social' attitudes (for example, to make an addict see himself as a pathetic bore rather than a tragic hero).[40] On the street, myths are rife about the harshness of different regimes. Alpha House was described by a doctor as 'run like an old-fashioned public school': indeed a public-school-educated woman who had been a long-term resident at another house said: 'Those people who've been at boarding school, in prison or the armed forces accept this type of institutional life most easily.' Loner drug-users who are allergic to group living require individual counselling and psychotherapy, which are both hard to find and expensive. A steady number opt out early (unless they are on bail or probation, when the overhanging threat of prison may impel them to remain), but residents who complete a nine-month course of treatment have a good chance of remaining free from drugs subsequently. Phoenix House aims to restore residents' self-discipline and self-respect; its work in both the USA and Britain is often praised by local authorities – with the proviso 'as long as you don't start one in our neighbourhood'. Critics of concept houses allege they often try to 'make the client fit the house, rather than meet his particular needs – so that many of them run away and relapse'. However, many people admire the distinctive way in which residents care for each other, a feeling which frequently continues after leaving (graduates of Phoenix House and Broadway Lodge are renowned for evangelizing) – a constructive means of losing the sense of stigma felt as an addict. Many of the centres' staff are themselves ex-addicts; Phoenix House in London is wholly run by its fifty inmates. Therapeutic communities offer a 24-hour-a-day alternative subculture to that of junkies – by comparison, one hour a week in a clinic offers little competition. The Betty Ford Centre for drugs and drink cases at Palm Springs insists on patients' families also spending a week there. Broadway Lodge – in a former convent once called Totterdown Hall outside Weston-super-Mare – is not a concept house, but is based on the Minnesota Method programme which was developed in 1949 by the Hazleden Foundation in the USA.[41] Its fees are £100 a day, for alcohol or drug cases, though it also takes some poorer patients. Much of the Minnesota treatment – which requires total abstinence as well as a new morality – is predicated on a theory (as yet unaccepted in most of Europe) that addiction is a disease with no cure, caused by a substance called THIQ found at the base of the cerebellum of that 7 per cent of the population who alone are liable to become addicts.

(b) *Christian-based houses* (such as Deliverance International or the Coke Hole Trust) were the first to be established in the UK during the 1960s. Iden Manor treats people with non-opiate dependency; Still Waters is one of the few which accept married couples with children. Many rehabilitation centres believe in the therapeutic value of exercise and keeping busy. Although religious conversion is not insisted upon as essential for cure, there is often a strong emphasis on the power of the Bible and Christianity to change lives. Sceptics are 'doubtful about the value of substituting one form of brain-washing for another', and argue that the focus on God's intercession may lead to the addict abdicating responsibility for himself. A former resident of Coke Hole said, 'The trouble is that a lot of ex-addicts swap drugs for Jesus and in fact are just swapping crutches. I want to find a better reason for living . . . but I find trusting people ends up with being hurt.' A wider difficulty for the client of isolated rehabilitation houses, as well as hospital in-patient units, is that their detached environment fails to deal with the social pressures facing the patient when he returns home. After having been protectively insulated, he is unprepared for coping with life outside. This is an argument for the third group:

(c) *Community-based houses*, whose therapy is aimed to achieve rapid re-integration within the community. They use local resources as much as possible to provide their clients with educational, employment, housing and recreational opportunities. Although these houses tend to be more selective in their admissions, they have the highest retention rates. Approaches are flexible: while ROMA offers a wide range of services, and City Roads takes in addicts when they have nowhere else to go, aiming to help them with longer-term rehabilitation, at Earls Court House residents are encouraged to go out to work as soon as possible, and at the Bedford Centre clients go home at night. The Marmottan Centre in Paris offers an eight-day contract of withdrawal; after which the client is placed in one of twenty houses each with a different character, and finally is either sent back to his family, or installed in a sheltered apartment or with a foster-family, accompanied by psychotherapy.[42]

One woman ex-addict (her face scarred from burning imaginary spiders with lighted cigarettes during the time she had been on drugs) reflected: 'Just because things or people are not formulated and tidy does not mean they are not worthwhile or worthy of God's attention.' However, as a sympathetic member of a local council said, 'Not only are there no votes in starting a new drug hostel in a neighbourhood, it's just the opposite.' One result of recent government campaigns to raise public fear about drugs seems to be an increased fear of drug-users. When Turning Point recently tried to start a new rehabilitation centre at West Bromsgrove, one of its senior employees was assaulted and the house fire-bombed. Dr Washton, the Director of Substance Abuse Research at a private New York hospital, argues: 'The average cocaine user is making over $30,000 a year and spending $500 a week on the drug. Why should you and I have to pay for his treatment?' Achieving the total recovery of opiate addicts can be a long, expensive and frustrating business (patients at the Corona institution, Los Angeles, are required to spend three years in its clinic before release, and even thereafter are required to be regularly tested as out-patients). None the less, the cost to society of refusing treatment is likely to be considerably higher. Dr Mitchell Rosenthal of New York proposes that there ought to be universal health insurance to cover drug abuse treatment; but recently Britain's second biggest private health insurer announced that treatment for drug or alcohol abuse will in future be excluded from its cover. Anybody who becomes dysfunctional because of drugs is likely to become a burden on others; the cost per patient in a rehabilitation centre, however, is only a fraction of that for a person in prison.[43] And, as Griffith Edwards adds, whereas the inmates of therapeutic communities often progress to staff positions as a reflection of the change in their attitude, who can say that of any prison?

Compulsory treatment?

At the opposite pole from the Washington judge William Bryant, who in 1984 suggested the answer for drug-addicts is to legalize heroin and 'just let them kill themselves', are those who advocate mandatory treatment. The only recommendation of the second Brain Report not to be implemented (partly on grounds of cost) was compulsory treatment specifically for addicts in withdrawal who seek to discharge themselves. Towards the end of the last century in Europe and North America, weighty medical opinion favoured locking up chronic inebriates; similarly, Dr Branthwaite told the Rolleston Committee:

> Drug cases are so difficult to control that they cannot be treated satisfactorily on any voluntary basis. They are so unreliable and untrustworthy that their word cannot possibly be taken, and under these circumstances I feel that cases of addiction should be dealt with in very much the same manner as persons of unsound mind.

The law already contains an element of such compulsion, when a sentence of imprisonment or conditional probation is given for drug offences, or when a juvenile is made the subject of a 'care and protection' order.[44] It has also been suggested that drug dependence, by being included in the definition of mental disorder, might be brought within the mandatory provision of the Mental Health Act.[45] William Deedes argues: 'The addict is not a free man. He has only sought to free himself, at fearful cost, from his own fears. He may well deprive others of their freedom. We should not have recourse to criminal law, but we should seek to extend our powers so that, in appropriate cases and with proper safeguards, patients may be given a chance to escape from themselves.'[46] The parents of an addicted son who recently died at St Helens in Lancashire agree: 'A law is needed that permits an addict to be forcibly committed with his parents' and doctor's consent where it is thought to be in the interest of his own safety.' The Magistrates' Association likewise has urged in a report:

> Drug dependence is an illness requiring treatment. It is a contagious illness, from which society needs protection. There is existing legislation providing for the compulsory removal to hospital of persons suffering from smallpox and other notifiable diseases for the protection of others (under the Public Health Act 1936, ss.169 and 170) . . . Hence compulsory powers already exist for the treatment of contagious, mental and other illnesses, and there appears to be no ethical reason why the illness of drug dependence should not be treated compulsorily. We feel that in many cases compulsion is necessary, particularly to support the patient when his motivation for cure vacillates. Accordingly we urge the establishment of centres for the treatment of drug dependence having a secure perimeter and a liberal hospital regime within this perimeter. The security should be such as to prevent absconding and the smuggling of drugs into the centre.[47]

More recently, there have been proposals that addicts should be isolated on islands such as the Hebrides so that they do not convert others.

Currently, an increasing number of addicts (1,200 in Britain in 1984) are only identified upon their remand to prison. A prison sentence offers one opportunity to provide medical treatment or counselling; but at present there is virtually none of this because of financial pressures – although it is likely to cost society considerably more in the long run to finance repeated processing of these individuals through the criminal justice and penal systems. For heroin addicts, it has been estimated that the probability of abstinence after being imprisoned for more than eight months, followed by compulsory supervision, is fifteen times greater than after voluntary supervision.[48] On the other hand, a spell in prison is liable to exacerbate many of the problems which led to addiction in the first place. The 1970 French Act 70.1320, which made it a criminal offence to abuse hard or soft drugs even in private, empowered judges to order convicted drug-takers to undergo medical treatment, with or without their consent. In the USA, New York is just one of the states which have resorted to the 'civil commitment' (as it is euphemistically termed) of some unconvicted addicts – though the results have not been encouraging. Other nations have been tougher. In the USSR, Malaysia and Singapore, treatment is compulsory. The latter has established 4,000-bed-capacity rehabilitation centres where medically-diagnosed abusers are mandatorily detained for between six and thirty-six months; detoxification is invariably 'cold turkey', and aftercare includes random urine tests to detect relapse. In the USSR, drug-addicts and alcoholics are viewed as a danger to themselves and to others; debating an issue that George Orwell might have relished, Edward Babayan, the Chairman of the USSR Ministry for Health's Standing Drug Control Committee, argues: 'Exclamations have been lately heard in the West that compulsory treatment of alcoholics and drug-addicts violates their human rights. The problem may be viewed from two standpoints. One, non-violation of the patient's private life, makes doctors leave him to the mercy of fate. The other is to save him, even against his wish, from decay and eventual death. We hold the latter is the more humane if more difficult way, justified medically, psychologically and legally.' Soviet doctors deny that a patient's co-operation is an essential prerequisite for successful rehabilitation. But opponents of compulsory treatment criticize it on the grounds that it is based on a fallacious analogy with disease, and is liable to fail to address those very problems that instigated the dependency. John Stuart Mill rejected the whole concept of compulsory treatment as a violation of personal civil liberty, except in the case of dangerously contagious diseases: the argument hinges upon whether the spread of drug addiction can qualify as such. There is also a very real practical objection that the threat would deter people from seeking help at an early stage. Griffith Edwards has suggested that a more humane way to try to stem the epidemic would be to develop outreach work, by sending trained social workers and counsellors out into the community to contact and offer addicts help: the more drug-users who can be brought into treatment, the fewer there will then be to initiate new people into drug-taking.[49] Such a hoped-for situation, however, may not be assisted by arrests like that of the pop singer Boy George at a clinic in 1986, which Dr Meg Patterson said she feared might deter other heroin addicts from seeking treatment.[50]

The argument over compulsory treatment is one fulcrum of the conflict that drug issues raise between the rights of an individual and their possible consequences for the rest of society. (AIDS is providing similar dilemmas.) Other alternative control options are examined next, before some forecasts about the future and concluding recommendations.

13

Trying to Stem the Rising Tide

'Gesetz ist mächtig, mächtiger ist die Not' ('Law is mighty, mightier is need').

Anon

'Nous avons tous assez de force pour supporter les maux d'autrui' ('We all have the strength to endure the misfortunes of others').
La Rochefoucauld, *Maxims*

'If you ever like something
They will tell you that
It's immoral, illegal,
Or it makes you fat.'

(Calypso)

Until very recently, the 'war against drugs' was being waged more with words than with actual resources. Several of the law agencies concerned are still mutually jealous, and belated recognition of the reality of the situation has also made them increasingly pessimistic. Although the amount of illegal heroin annually seized in the UK rose more than a hundred-fold in the decade up to 1984, its street price – the indicator of its increasing availability – continued to fall steadily, from £80 a gram in 1981 to only £60 for the same amount a year later.[1] (A very senior police officer recently admitted to a meeting of Chief Constables, 'Even allowing for the reduced level of inflation over the past few years, I am unaware of any commodity which has become so significantly cheaper.') During the same twelve months, the average recorded purity of illegal heroin in Britain actually increased from 34 per cent to 44.5 per cent. A growing number of the ablest criminals have switched to drug-dealing, it being safer as well as more profitable than any other crime, including robbing banks; Leon Brittan, when Home Secretary, pointed to the rare attraction possessed by drugs stolen from pharmacies and doctors: 'For, in contrast to most other stolen goods, the street value of drugs on the black market is much greater than their normal commercial value.'[2] In 1984 the UK government tentatively began to take some long-overdue steps. It doubled its contribution to the UN Fund for Drug Abuse Control (UNFDAC) – but, even then, this only amounted to £100,000. 'No sooner one stamps on one area, another emerges,' David Mellor, the Home Office minister in charge of measures against drug abuse, is realistic enough to admit; 'we are more often in the business of containment.' He concedes frankly that stopping the flow of heroin into Britain is 'enormously difficult', and that attempting to intercept it at airports and docks 'is like looking for a needle in a haystack'.[3] The quantity of heroin required to meet Britain's daily illegal needs – in value, a coup for a criminal equivalent to a comfortable annuity for life – can be imported inside a single shopping bag. Even if several couriers are arrested, this does not hurt the big traffickers – rather the reverse, for it temporarily raises the street prices they can command – and their profits are so enormous they can afford to finance unlimited waves of expendable couriers.

In the USA – which experienced its drugs crisis a decade before Europe, but has yet to find a solution to offer other countries – political rhetoric has gradually been overtaken by a realization of the size of the dilemma. Despite the setting up of 'federal task forces' (including in the epicentre, Florida), the prices of cocaine, heroin and marijuana all continue to fall, which demonstrates not only their increased availability but also that inevitably they are becoming more accessible to all income groups.[4] The US General Accounting Office's audit of the southern Florida anti-drug task force, set up at an annual cost of $70 million, characterized it as lacking in co-ordination, causing antagonisms between the participating agencies, and failing to prosecute drug-traffickers it arrested (with, in other cases, more than one agency counting the same arrests). 'Turf-war' tension, spilling over into animosity, has long existed between the fourteen agencies involved against traffickers, including the Federal Bureau of Investigation (FBI), the Drug Enforcement Administration (DEA), the armed forces, the

Central Intelligence Agency (CIA), the Justice Department, the Internal Revenue, and front-line organizations such as the Coast-guard and Customs services. The DEA has kept its independence by refusing to provide cover for agents of the CIA, whom it suspects of having had close links with drug producers in Asia. The anti-drug industry is indeed growing; sometimes, however, one of its members arrests another's agents, and jealous in-fighting has continually stymied the establishment of an overall command. A proposal for a Cabinet-level 'tsar' who would co-ordinate anti-drug work and end 'turf-wars' was in fact passed by both houses of Congress in 1983 but was vetoed by President Reagan. In that year, the Customs estimated that they probably intercepted only one smuggling flight in every hundred; even when a smuggler aircraft was detected, less than a quarter of the Customs planes were fast enough to have any hope of catching it. One congressman in October 1985 described well over half the Customs' seventy planes as still being aged 'junk',[5] and officials admit there are gaps, through which smugglers regularly escape detection, in the radar coverage even of the crucial Gulf coast and Mexican border. Whereas many of the smuggling aircraft fly low up mountain valleys, much of the military radar – intended to detect incoming missiles, not planes – starts only above an altitude of 14,000 feet (4,275 metres). The millionaire organizers of the trafficking syndicates – who are rarely identified, let alone caught – by comparison have more modern aircraft and boats, as well as highly paid lawyers and financial advisers for laundering their profits through tax-havens such as the Bahamas and the Cayman Islands. When an organization of Florida smugglers was raided in October 1985, it was found to possess the federal agencies' radio codes. A Thai critic ruefully asked, 'If the US's defence system can't track planeloads of drugs from South America, one wonders how well it will perform in locating enemy nuclear weapons?' Charles Hefferman, the Chief of the Narcotics Bureau at the New York District Attorney's office, described concentrating on Florida to me as 'like squeezing a toothpaste tube for the rest of the USA . . . These new cocaine dealers are no longer criminal stereotypes, but physicians, lawyers, even former FBI men, in it for the huge profits. The Cosa Nostra are now major drug traders, although they don't tolerate addicts themselves in their organization because they are unreliable. The situation's worse than Prohibition – at least the schoolchildren then weren't buyers.'

Over half the 12,000 lb. of illegal heroin annually entering the USA is smuggled in through New York, yet the Narcotics Division of the New York City Police was reduced by budget cuts from 490 men in 1974 to 380 ten years later. Robert Morgenthau, the New York City District Attorney, says: 'We lack sufficient commitment – both budgetary and from public opinion. The DEA has 240 agents for the whole New York area – it could use at least 1,000. The trouble is too many people now think nothing's going to help, so there is no more funding. But if we can spend $350 million to recommission the USS *New Jersey*, surely we can find $10 million for the drug problem in New York?'[6]

At least attempts to control heroin trafficking are no longer denounced as racist discrimination. It used to be resented that heroin, which a few blacks use, was suppressed much more firmly than the cocaine which whites preferred; but some of the most eloquently vociferous demands for action today come from minority leaders in Harlem as well as black Rastafarians in Britain. The main centre for heroin trading in New York is now the Lower East Side of the city, where drug-houses proliferate and are booby-trapped as well as steel armour-plated against the police. Any dealers arrested are almost invariably the 'cop-men' or 'jugglers' – the smallest fry at the bottom of the pyramid, making perhaps $200 a day from selling $10 packets – along with the 'steerers' or 'Sherpas' who direct customers to supplies. Because the city's court system and jails are choked (a courtroom's daily calendar often lists 200 cases), the majority of those convicted are merely fined $50 and revert immediately to dealing, especially since many themselves are addicts. Inspector Thomas Gallagher says, 'We have some people arrested eighteen or twenty times, and they're back out there on the streets.' Two out of every three people arrested on felony charges of the sale or possession of substantial amounts of narcotics in New York City in 1985 were not indicted, and due to shortage of time and resources the courts in that year were able to try less than 0.5 per cent of their cases. The dealers centred on Third and Fourth Streets have recently switched to using children, including small girls, as their couriers, calculating they are less likely to be punished if caught. 'If the police made ten times as many arrests and we had ten times as many prosecutors, it would still be the same,' said Sterling Johnson, a New York prosecutor. 'The more you arrest, the more they come back. It's like digging a hole in the ocean.' On the other hand, 'Despite the frustration,' another prosecutor explained, 'we have to keep the pressure on, because there's a million kids out there who are probably willing to make that kind of money by selling bags on the street.' In Detroit, one fifteen-year-old boy bought a Mercedes with $62,000 in notes he had made from being a runner for drug syndicates who have organized teams comprising over 300 teenagers to work for them in the city. The big traffickers, however, almost invariably succeed in eluding the law. In 1985 a cocaine laboratory was accidently discovered near Albany, New York, with a capacity of 1,000 lb. a week – one-third of the USA's total supply. Enforcement agents have found the major Colombian cocaine 'families' so far impossible to infiltrate: twelve of these are entrenched in the borough of Queens, each of whom the DEA estimates annually sells some $65 millions' worth of cocaine to wholesale middlemen, accruing a total profit in excess of $1 billion a year.[7] The head organizers remain safely out of sight; they dispatch perhaps twenty courier 'mules' on a single day, so that even if two are caught, eighteen get through. Policemen are routinely offered several thousands of dollars in bribes; following the scandal of corruption in the Serpico case (when thirty-nine members of 'New York's finest' resigned), all New York narcotics officers are now automatically transferred after a maximum of three years, despite the resulting loss of experience and contacts. Bruce Jensen, in charge of the DEA in New York, says, 'To stop all the drugs coming into New York, I'd need at least a Marine division'; the Reagan administration has, however, sharply cut back expenditure on drugs prevention from the budget as it was under Carter or Nixon (the DEA's eradication budget being reduced by $500,000 in 1985), emphasizing instead less costly items such as parents' groups. In the USA, as in Europe, there is growing unanimity that the only hope of controlling drugs will be to restrain the demand – but in the last two years the federal support for drug rehabilitation in the state of New York has also been drastically cut, from $34.3 million to $19.4 million.

Drugs' effect on crime

The nature and extent of the direct or indirect connections between drugs and crime remains a matter of controversy. Hypotheses and statistics require a careful approach (it is, after all, true that most murders are committed by men who drink tea . . .). No drug, of course, inevitably causes crime, though the one which most often indirectly does is undoubtedly alcohol. In the USA, a national survey found that one-third of prison inmates had been under the influence of alcohol and/or of an illegal drug immediately before committing the crime for which they were incarcerated. However, this recent finding of the Department of Justice does not prove that drugs or drink played a part in the motive or propensity for committing the crimes – they may merely contribute to the likelihood of these particular offenders being caught. Apart from alcohol's major contribution to violence, American research links drug-trafficking with more than a quarter of urban homicides, and suggests that up to 55 per cent of the robberies now occurring may be being committed by addicts seeking money for their drug supplies. In all, some form of drug-related crime is now estimated to affect one in three of American households each year. One recent study of known daily heroin users found they committed an average of 209 non-drug crimes a year, gaining $32,000 in stolen goods, in addition to distributing $26,000's worth of illegal drugs annually, on which they made a 40 per cent profit.

In Britain, illegal heroin addicts need at least £8,000 a year to pay for their habit, though only a minority of them are able to keep a job. A 1986 Home Office study found that half the males and two-thirds of females notified as drug-addicts had not been convicted before the age of twenty-eight; but that those who are drug-addicts are three times as likely to have been convicted as others of the same age. One addict from a rich establishment family told me, 'You've got to be a thief to be a junkie,' and a BBC survey found that nearly half of all users of speed had also committed serious crimes. A former state torturer in El Salvador said his colleagues often used LSD or marijuana when at their work. Drugs are used by many professional criminals, although analysis of the records of criminal addicts shows that a high proportion of them had a significant criminal history prior to their drug abuse. The Metropolitan London police now estimate that 32 per cent of targeted criminals in their area are involved in hard drugs – a few of them investing part of the profits in enterprises benefiting the community, as a sop for their consciences. One of the latest schemes of villains (as policemen call them) is to carry out a raid on addicts' homes, pretending to be plain-clothes police officers, and 'confiscating' any drugs they find. Several recent killings — in the Holborn, Holland Park, Fulham and Brixton districts of London – have been connected with drug-trafficking, and the police believe these mark the arrival of Mafia-style struggles for the lucrative drugs market in Britain. The implications of this are sobering. In Los Angeles, fighting between rival cocaine gangs for control of the several score of fortified 'rock houses' in the centre and south of the city resulted in twelve murders within a recent single fortnight. A number of the leading US franchise contenders, who compete for control of the underground drug industry from inside jails, use gang members aged as young as thirteen as salesmen and hired killers. The most successful syndicates now maintain their own security force as well as teams of hit-men to extort debts and execute or frighten away any competitors. Traditionally, informant addicts are dosed with a 'hot-shot', customarily composed of strychnine since this looks and tastes remarkably like heroin. (The extremities of violence resulting from drug-trafficking in Latin America are described in Chapter 14: the storming by guerrilla terrorists of Bogota's Court of Justice in November 1985 – which caused ninety-five deaths, including those of twelve Supreme Court Judges – was reported to have been financed by *narcotraficantes* intent on having the files of their deportation cases destroyed.) Even when a drug baron is convicted, prison is not necessarily any bar to his activities. Whereas prisoners once sold their clothes and food to obtain tobacco, British prison officers today report that drugs have replaced tobacco as prison currency, and claim that not just cannabis, but cocaine, heroin and Seconal are frequently more readily available inside prison than out. Three inmates recently died from drug abuse within twelve months at Wandsworth. A 1985 UK Parliamentary committee reported that a number of heroin users in Brixton prison had declined to go to hospital for treatment 'since in the main part of the prison they can readily obtain heroin and the means to inject it'. Some prison officers are alleged to prefer that their charges dope themselves rather than have the energy to cause trouble. In any event, the result is that increasing numbers of professional criminals, having learnt about drugs when in jail, take up dealing when they come out. In Lima's prisons in Peru, cocaine syndicates amongst the armed prisoners frequently fight for supremacy; and many US jails are run by drug gangs – often organized on ethnic lines, such as the white 'Aryan Brotherhood', the 'Black Guerrilla Family' or the 'Mexican Mafia'. Italian drug-pushers catapulted packets of heroin over the wall to prisoners in Genoa's Marassi jail, while the inmates of a US prison supplied themselves by means of a fleet of 240 carrier pigeons. One new form of record was established in May 1980 when five Washington heroin dealers broke *into* a Virginia prison to kill a rival heroin dealer who was imprisoned inside.

In the UK until very recently, drug cases have not been given high priority by the police, who felt that 'real villains' were more worthy of their attention. Drug arrests did not attract merit points, and few officers saw much purpose in devoting their resources to cases which were time-consuming and seldom productive of much job-satisfaction. A number of detectives investigating other crimes have a technique of keeping drug-addicts in custody without drugs, in order to force them to give information under pressure of the discomfort of withdrawal. However, since two Scottish officers recently contracted hepatitis B after being bitten by drug-addicts – users who share syringes are at high risk from AIDS – threats by them to bite are now taken doubly seriously. Three London officers nearly suffered serious injury when a large bag of heroin burst over them as it was being thrown by a dealer they were arresting. In theory, one police officer said, 'To catch a dealer should be as easy as arresting an unregistered hot-dog seller: they both, of necessity, have to be public and in the market place, with their whereabouts known to customers.' However, any addict-pusher whom they arrest is most unlikely to help with their inquiries and inform on the main dealers, because – even if not too frightened – he depends on them for his future supplies. However, rank and file police officers retain an entrenched distaste for the whole drug demi-monde's absence of order and discipline, and given a choice strongly prefer work involving conventional villains to whose values they can relate and who 'know the rules'.[8] In addition the police find it disconcerting that almost all drug offences are carried out in private between consenting parties: the normal complainant or victim of a crime being absent, officers frequently have to resort to entrapment. Middle-class people, including MPs, who used to urge the police to 'crackdown' on the use of pot in the West Indian community, were nonplussed when increasingly it began to be their own sons and daughters who were arrested. On the other hand, fears have been expressed that the law inculpates innocent people whose premises are used for drug-taking (one MP suggested that the Queen herself might have been held liable for an offence when John Lennon smoked cannabis in the lavatory at Buckingham Palace before his investiture – although the law in fact states that 'knowingly' is a requirement for guilt).

In the whole of the UK there was a total of 550 officers in drugs squads in 1984 – an increase of only a tenth on the strength six years earlier. Most senior police outside London used to hold the view that drugs were a problem confined almost exclusively to the central metropolis, and some of them believed 'If you don't have a drugs squad, then you don't have a drugs problem'. Until very recently large police forces close to London, covering areas such as Essex and Hertfordshire, did not have a drugs squad at all. In 1985 even the central Scotland Yard Metropolitan drugs squad, culpably, still could muster a pitiful total of only thirty-eight men (compared with, for example, Oslo's seventy-eight), and the Yard's force had not been strengthened for more than seven years during which time drug abuse had soared.[9] At the start of 1986 plans for regional teams of detectives to handle drug cases had to be delayed yet again because of financial arguments.

Added to the shortage of resources, a number of divisional officers still dislike their men investigating drug cases, because of the high likelihood of corruption, and because they consider that drug abuse is more of a social than a legal problem. Some senior Yard officers believe that international trafficking is a matter which only Customs and Excise officers should investigate. However, the Customs service, which has always had a reputation for exemplary honesty, used to feel (as it was delicately expressed to me) 'they could not always co-operate with the police'. Less tactfully stated, the reason was the considerable amount of corruption existing in the Metropolitan Drugs Squad prior to 1980. Temptation accrues not just from the enormous bribes (sometimes the equivalent of a lifetime's earnings for the policemen who have succumbed – in 1985 one FBI Miami agent pleaded guilty to accepting $850,000); the absence of a conventional victim also means that any dealer caught with 100 g. of drugs is unlikely to complain if the police allege in court that he had only 5 g. when they arrested him. Drugs can corrode public life as much as they harm private health. In the 1970s the Home Office became concerned at increasing reports that informants were being paid in drugs by some members of the Metropolitan Police's Drugs Squad, then under the command of Detective Chief Inspector Kelaher. Official alarm mounted following further allegations that policemen were not only unofficially licensing certain dealers to operate with impunity in return for information (a technique imported from the US Bureau of Narcotics), but that quantities of illicit substances were, after drug raids, regularly being auctioned at certain central London police stations. Recently, in December 1985, a further police inspector from West End Central station was jailed for stealing drugs. Nor is such corruption unique to Britain. The Knapp Commission named a number of New York police officers who were financing drugs deals and trading in heroin. The head of Belgium's élite drugs squad was arrested in 1980 in company with an American DEA agent and several other police officers, all of whom were accused of trading in a drugs ring for motives not solely in order to penetrate its network; shortly afterwards, $60,000 worth of heroin was stolen from a Hamburg vault to which only the police had access. Florida and Chicago syndicates of police have been convicted of protecting dealers and extorting drug debts on their behalf; and in December 1985 Zimbabwe's Police Commissioner himself was sacked for corruptly disposing of seized drugs. (It was Shakespeare's constable Dogberry who said: 'I think they that touch pitch will be defiled.')[10] The Police Chief of Henry County, Georgia, was accused of forming a drugs ring in concert with a sheriff and a probate judge; a lieutenant in charge of the Palm Beach sheriff's chopper was arrested for importing marijuana by helicopter; the distinguished-looking man detained soon afterwards with 100 lb. of marijuana in his private plane turned out to be a circuit judge from Alabama. A Hong Kong police superintendent said during the 1960s that much of the drug trade there was being licensed by corrupt members of the CID; in the next decade, a good forty of the colony's police officers fled into exile taking with them $80 million in cash. Seven of the suspects arrested for the Mexican abduction and killing of a US DEA agent in 1985 were themselves policemen, including at least one cocaine addict who was accused of being on the payroll of traffickers. In Illinois, a Cook County judge was forced to act as an undercover agent in order to penetrate the corruption. The likelihood of official malpractice surviving undetected is helped by the fact that a substantial segment of the population interested in such matters disagrees with the present stance of the drug laws; this ambivalence is easily capable of breeding reciprocal cynicism in some of the policemen expected to enforce such a code. Drugs are extremely easy to 'plant' on suspects. Because of the risk of corruption, every Metropolitan Drugs Squad member until recently was transferred elsewhere within two years: the maximum period is now three years, but this still truncates honest officers' effectiveness at a stage when they have accumulated expertise. One officer complained: 'Whenever the Yard have had bright people working on this, they've moved them on. And too many officers are targeted against cannabis, because this is an easy bust – whereas heroin dealers are harder to catch than armed robbers . . . It is the ultimate in detective work; almost no one gives you any information.'

A number of undercover officers, as in America, have themselves been sucked into using drugs.[11] A surprisingly large proportion of police officers wink at moderate cannabis use – occasionally because they like it themselves, sometimes because they think the prohibition against it is unrealistic; even because they consider the weed, as a pacifier, keeps alienated people from behaving in more actively anti-social ways. UK Customs officers have now been instructed not to prosecute first-time offenders carrying small amounts of cannabis into the country, but instead to levy an on-the-spot financial penalty, since too much of their time was being taken up by such minor cases in the courts. (The strength of the British Customs having been reduced by the present government, it is doubtful whether even 10 per cent of drugs imported at present are being intercepted: by 1984 it was officially estimated that £6 millions' worth of heroin was entering the UK each week through Heathrow and Dover.) The implications of this pragmatic move, however, causes anomalies, as a senior Customs officer pointed out: 'In effect, possession of cannabis on a small scale has been decriminalized so long as the offence is discovered at a port or an airport. Parliament has never decided that, but it is now the reality because the Customs service is so hard-pressed.'

While a person arrested in some inland areas for possessing even a small amount of cannabis can suffer imprisonment with the conviction imprinted on his record (Nottingham police have been issued with binoculars to try to see whose window-boxes are growing pot), police forces in other parts of the country now have a policy only to caution personal cannabis users. By contrast, US federal enforcement officials in Georgia are spraying marijuana plants with paraquat – a policy the *New York Times* described as being as extreme as 'laying land-mines in no-parking zones'. Conflicting attitudes towards police enforcement of the drug laws have been blamed as an aggravating factor in recent urban riots in Britain, and Lord Scarman's excellent concept of community policing fell victim to friction between traditions of local toleration and central government demands for crackdowns, although in Birmingham's Handsworth, an informal coalition developed between the police and Rastafarians (who venerate cannabis, but are firmly puritanical in their opposition to other drugs) against heroin dealers from Pakistan. Several other gangs of youths also strongly oppose drugs and enforce internal sanctions against any use of them.

One police officer in Costa Rica described to me how work in a drugs squad itself becomes addictive, and this is particularly true of the plain-clothed agents who lead a fast-paced and dangerous life. Agents who spend long periods undercover find it difficult to abandon their role when off-duty, and a high proportion of their marriages collapse. (The dangers of such work are increasing: in November 1985, twenty-one Mexican policemen were killed in a single incident by marijuana traffickers; and one of the Operation Julie officers had a £10,000 contract taken out on his life by a Stuttgart businessman.) Covert drugs squad officers have been required to live underground – sometimes for months at a time – assuming a new life-style, thinking and speaking the cult argot, and smoking pot as they hang out in the clubs and pubs where drugs are sold. (Not all of them find it as easy as Philby did to keep up their cover when having to drink heavily in order to penetrate such circles.) In a 'sting' operation in Miami, an agent was provided with an ersatz wife, servants, beach house, plane, cocaine laboratory and $9 million in cash, with which to receive a dealer from Bolivia. Sometimes a criminal record of drug offences is provided for an undercover officer in case a corrupt official checks this. One FBI agent lived in a criminal family for six years in order to gain credibility; another agent was placed so deep undercover that he was forgotten totally.

Whereas many officers regard pushers as the lowest form of human life, when dealing with addicts they frequently see themselves more as welfare workers than policemen, taking them to hospital and sometimes trying to find them flats and jobs. In May 1985 the Dorset police, for the first time in Britain, offered an amnesty to drug-users who were prepared to give information leading to pushers. A policeman in South Wales, however, said the problem was that: 'Drug-addicts don't believe they're committing a crime; they think all drugs should be legalized. They don't see they're harming anyone but themselves; and they'll always protect their own supplier.' Inspector Reg Gale says all of us, police and public, have 'got to learn what the drug problem is really about . . . there should be no sitting back and leaving it to the drugs squads'. Greater knowledge about the subject should become part of every policeman's training. Lately more police have somewhat reluctantly begun to give drugs higher priority, in the wake of many leading criminals moving into drug-dealing. Such traffickers operate across police boundaries (one, a legendarily successful Balliol graduate, channelled his bulk supplies of cannabis into England through entrepôts ranging from Ireland to the Hebrides). A national drugs squad – like a national fraud squad, and also an international UN police agency – is long overdue. However, a national organization was long resisted by many chief constables, partly because of sensitivity that it would be a step towards the logic of a national police service, and partly due to memories of the recent London corruption, since such a supreme unit would inevitably have to be based at Scotland Yard. There is a similar explanation behind Customs officers' opposition to merging their intelligence centre with the police's. The need for central co-ordination was nevertheless demonstrated beyond argument by Operation Julie, which only succeeded because an *ad hoc* inter-force team had been formed with great difficulty, only to be later disbanded; the LSD ring it unearthed had been flourishing and trading for six years in Britain, untroubled. Detective Inspector Dick Lee, the hero and organizer of the Operation, resigned from the police shortly after its successful outcome in disagreement at the disbandment. Even regional drug squads were not planned until 1985, when the formation of an equally long-overdue national drugs intelligence unit was at last also announced.

How can efforts to control the supply of drugs be made more effective? In 1984 police leaders protested that Britain was the only country in Europe where the law did not allow intimate body-searches to be made of people suspected of carrying Class B drugs, although the US Supreme Court under Frankfurter drew the line against the search of a suspect's stomach by means of a pump.[12] Trained dogs are being used in attempts to locate drugs in prisons as well as at airports – though it has been found in the Philippines that dogs can become addicted to heroin within a year and then have to be destroyed. A machine designed to sniff out drugs which are hidden on people (even those wrapped in several sealed layers), which is under trial at Heathrow, is reported still to find difficulty in distinguishing heroin vapour from orange juice. Enforcement officers were also set back by a London judge's ruling at a trial for drug-dealing in October 1985 which excludes any surveillance evidence unless police reveal their observation places – the owners of which fear reprisals. European Customs officers are concerned that the EEC's plans to abolish passport and Customs controls between member countries will seriously handicap attempts to stop trafficking; already the borders between the EEC and, for example, Switzerland can be easily penetrated in several hundred places by a smuggler on foot. The US Bureau of Narcotics in frustrated desperation at one time seriously considered forming a hit-squad to assassinate the key 150 traffickers, whose identities they know but against whom they are unable to obtain enough proof for a court of law.[13] More success has been obtained in the USA and Britain by means of twenty-four-hour telephone 'hotlines', on which the public can give anonymous information about dealers as well as obtain advice about drugs.[14] (It has been suggested that offering massive rewards might produce further leads to the top traffickers.) Visitors to the USA, however, continue to be surprised that, amongst all the official rhetoric against drugs, 'head shops' openly continue to sell to the public paraphernalia for illicit drug use, together with magazines like *High Times*, *Head* and *Hi Life* which unashamedly champion the enjoyment of drugs. Freedom to publish is protected by the First Amendment of the US Constitution, although the US government during the Prohibition era banned the equipment necessary for moonshining alcohol. DEA agents, however, have adopted a tactic of setting up bogus chemical companies which advertise components to make drugs in magazines such as *High Times*, in order to arrest customers who make contact.

In 1985, the British House of Commons' Home Affairs Committee urged that it was time to enlist the armed forces to counter drug-trafficking – arguing that there could be no objection in principle, since the armed services already carry out civilian roles such as fisheries protection and air-sea rescue. In May of the same year a US Senate amendment, over-riding the opposition of the Defence Secretary Caspar Weinberger, for the first time in peacetime authorized the American armed forces to intercept (but not to arrest) drug-smugglers. The web of international trafficking networks is being cross-tabulated by agents for analysis on computers; meanwhile scientists are researching into measuring brainwaves or biochips (microchips linking electronics to living cells) in order to detect which people are carrying chemicals, and are also investigating the feasibility of using a microbiological bacillus to trace people who handle drug money; the UN Fund for Drug Abuse Control is financing research into insects which will eat opium poppy and cannabis plants; Brazil's government is trying to perfect the culture of coca-specific fungi; and in the UK researchers at Aldermaston have developed a method of detecting cannabinol on the skin of users. The USA, which has built a computer complex for the DEA at El Paso in Texas, is concentrating on trying to improve methods of detection (including satellites and sensor balloons). However, the efficacy of these measures is at present open to doubt, if the vast marijuana plantations in the USA itself are any guide; and a further problem is that recently harvested coca bushes show up from the air only as bare fields.

In 1986 the US President's Commission of Organized Crime recommended that all federal employees should be tested for drug use, and that furthermore no federal contract should be awarded to any private employer who did not institute drug tests. Although the US courts have so far ruled that compulsory urine tests on teenage schoolchildren are unconstitutional, about 125 of the 500 leading US companies now use some form of drug screening, and random tests are increasingly being applied on grounds of safety and efficiency to civilian employees as well as in the armed forces.[15] The overall threat to civil liberties capable of resulting from panic about drugs, however, raises some disquieting echoes of Orwell's *1984*. (It is after all rare in history that any government ever relinquishes additional power it has acquired.) In the final analysis, this could be the most serious of all the damage caused to society by drugs. It is all the more striking because it occurs in a field of human activity which several responsible voices argue should be decriminalized altogether. In 1986 an innocent Devon woman suffered the confiscation (later rescinded) by Customs of her car in which, unknown to her, some strangers had hidden some cannabis – an official declaring: 'Any vehicle is liable to be seized if it is used in smuggling. It does not matter if the owner was unaware the vehicle was carrying the goods.' In June of the same year, the House of Lords upheld the conviction of a chemist who had dispensed drugs on a prescription which he was unaware was forged. Several countries' police forces operate 'no warrant' methods in drug inquiries that they are forbidden to employ even in murder investigations. The panic has even caused the clock to be put back many years through the reintroduction of literary censorship: in Britain the police have seized books which discuss drugs by writers ranging from Baudelaire to Tom Wolfe and Aldous Huxley, together with learned anthropological and scientific volumes published by university presses. (Volumes extolling tobacco and alcohol have, on the other hand, naturally been ignored. Eric Korn comments that it is only luck that *The Grass is Singing, Snow White*, and *The Coke, Anthracite and Allied Industries' Yearbook* managed to escape.) Confusion reigns: one Highbury magistrate decided that *The Guide to British Psilocybin Mushrooms* was not obscene, within a few days of a Marylebone magistrate ruling that it was. As Geoffrey Robertson, defending in a case against such books brought under the Obscene Publications Act, warns: 'You cannot save anyone from anything by censorship . . . and so beware of any attempt to suppress facts that are not convenient . . . Let us tackle the problem of drugs in the most honest way we can.' Censorship – as always – can only be an admission of failure.

Until recently, public opinion resented drug-testing as an invasion of privacy, but the national mood has shifted and Republican and Democratic party leaders are now competing to upstage each other with proposals for anti-drug 'crusades'. In August 1986 President Reagan and his staff took drug tests. Workers in civilian companies who fail such tests are usually offered treatment rather than being fired, but any job applicant who does so is unlikely to be hired. Opponents of such testing criticize that it is liable to have a 10 per cent rate of error, and cannot distinguish between drug abusers and occasional users.

It was unease at the idea of reversing the presumption of innocence until proof of guilt that for several years inhibited the UK government's desire to strip drug-traffickers of their gains – a scruple now jettisoned. In a separate step, the Inland Revenue has recently broken new ground by demanding income tax from an unconvicted Englishman they believe has made £1.5 million from smuggling cannabis. Hitherto, it had not been thought right to levy tax on any criminal or immoral earnings, lest sharing in the profit should be seen as condonation; but almost £1 million in retrospective tax has been demanded from a colourful figure who was acquitted in a dramatic trial at the Old Bailey in 1981 of a charge of smuggling 15 tons of cannabis into Britain (through a plea that he was working for MI6). Stating that it rejects the jury's verdict in that case, the Inland Revenue argues that it can work to the civil standard of proof of 'a balance of probabilities', which is lower than the criminal proof of 'beyond a reasonable doubt'.[16] The authorities' indignant frustration at the inability of the courts to seize the illegal profits of even convicted drug-dealers came to a head in the Operation Julie case in 1977, when although the police traced £750,000 of the LSD makers' profits to bank accounts in Switzerland and France, the House of Lords on appeal ruled that the courts had no power to order the forfeiture of most of the money. Other major traffickers have taken care to launder their vast profits beyond the reach of the police. The richest trafficker convicted to date in Britain (Terrence Clark, described in Chapter 4) died with the police having been unable to lay their hands on any of the £50 million fortune he is believed to have made from drugs. In the USA courts regularly order the forfeiture and sale of convicted smugglers' planes, cars and boats, which are then auctioned to defray some of the costs of enforcement – just as earlier judges ordered the seizure of vessels used for slavery, bootlegging or piracy. Of the Miami DEA's fleet of 200 cars, 119 were seized from drug-dealers. US enforcement agencies in 1984 seized some $420 million in drug-traffickers' assets – but only $20 million of that was given to the agencies to help their work. The New York City special narcotics prosecutor declared: 'The drug-trafficker is like a hydra; you cut a head off and another will grow back . . . If you really want to hurt a person, you hit him in the pocketbook.' In American courts, traffickers have been known to bargain for a twenty-year sentence rather than have their assets seized. Under the earliest Common Law, people convicted of felony were held to be in a state of attainder and forfeited all their property, but modern opinion has considered it wrong to add a second penalty on top of a court sentence.[17] However, the British government – having already increased the penalty for cocaine and heroin trafficking to life imprisonment – announced at the end of 1985 that in future: (a) there would be a new offence of handling drug proceeds, punishable by fourteen years' imprisonment, when the police or Customs may obtain an order freezing the assets of a person charged on suspicion of drug-dealing (i.e. before he or she is convicted); (b) all the income and property of anyone convicted is deemed to be the proceeds of drug-trafficking unless he can prove the contrary (i.e. reversing the state's usual burden of proof); (c) even lawfully acquired assets may be confiscated, equal to the proceeds of the whole of an offender's trafficking, and not just the offence of which he is convicted.[18] If, however, such measures to seize criminals' profits are right, why are they not used in other cases of serious crime such as armed robbery? Why, too, is the penalty for the illegal possession of a drug many times greater than for the illegal possession of firearms – which are much more likely to hurt other people? In short, what is it about drugs that is so uniquely frightening to the authorities?

Some magistrates nevertheless display endemic credulity in granting bail to people charged with importing and supplying drugs: almost half the arrest warrants issued at Reading Crown Court – which covers many Heathrow cases – are due to the non-appearance of alleged drug importers.[19] At present, one person out of every six convicted in Britain of possessing controlled drugs receives a custodial sentence (including one in eight of those convicted of growing a cannabis plant), together with more than half of those convicted of trafficking. There are, however, wide regional differences in courts' attitudes: those in the Lake District look on possession leniently, compared with courts in the Channel Islands which often impose a six-month jail sentence for this offence. The Lord Chief Justice, Lord Lane, in December 1982 outlined guidelines for the sentences he thought appropriate for drug importers, when delivering judgment in the case of R. v. Aramah: 'It will seldom be that an importer of any appreciable amount of the drug will deserve less than four years.' For pushers, he said it was seldom that less than three years' imprisonment was justified, depending on the amount and degree of involvement, recommending sentences of seven or more years where hard drugs of a street value of £100,000 were involved, and twelve to fourteen years for quantities valued at £1 million or more. He said that the only case when it would be appropriate substantially to lighten such sentences would be for an offender who pleaded guilty and helped the police. (Nevertheless, a Saudi prince convicted in 1986 of dealing in drugs in London was jailed for only three months.) Subsequently government ministers have declared that hard-drug dealers should be treated as 'premeditated murderers' and jailed for life – although many police representatives believe that this would only drive traffickers towards bigger consignments of drugs, since the penalty will be the same. Lord Lane's personal view is: 'If anyone deserves to be hanged it would, to my mind, not be the murderer, who is often inoffensive, but those who import and distribute heroin and similar drugs.' Another peer, Earl Attlee, has suggested that the penalty for a pusher should be for him to be mainlined with heroin and left to die.

In California, on the other hand, the penalty for conspiracy to distribute cocaine is a maximum of five years in prison: 'If you come out a millionaire,' said Robert Schirn of the Los Angeles District Attorney's Office, 'that doesn't seem so bad.' The US government, however, when recently investigating an allegation that a city's mayor was using drugs, stated that, although it was rare to prosecute individual users, public officials should be held accountable to higher standards than ordinary citizens. Writers of books about drugs should perhaps heed the case of Richard Lowell Stratton who in 1983 was sentenced to the maximum term of fifteen years' jail, in spite of his claim that he had associated with drug-dealers only in order to do investigative research for his writing (and despite Norman Mailer's appearance as a witness for the defence). The British Appeal Court has held that a journalist of previous good character, who naïvely smuggled some lettuce under the illusion it was heroin, was none the less guilty of attempting to harbour and deal in drugs and sent to prison for two years.[20] But such a sentence would be regarded as permissive leniency in other countries: one British subject is at present serving thirty years in prison in Turkey for smuggling cannabis; another was given a sentence of thirty-five years in Thailand for possessing half an ounce of heroin for his own use; Pakistan has raised the penalty for possessing more than 0.35 ounces of heroin or cocaine to a flogging in addition to life imprisonment; China, Malaysia and Singapore enforce a death penalty; while Iran has executed several hundred people for trading in

297

drugs, including pregnant women and youths under the age of eighteen.

An unusual, though understandable, American law prescribes double the normal term of prison for anyone aged over eighteen who is convicted of pushing drugs to a person under eighteen and at least three years younger than the pusher. Several of the most difficult cases in modern law have involved issues raised by drugs. In 1962 the US Supreme Court ruled that any laws which punished addiction as a crime were unconstitutional, being a 'cruel and unusual' punishment in violation of the 8th Amendment to the Constitution. The Court has ruled, however, that the use of heroin, even by an addict, can be punished. Since the police observe few people in the act of chasing the dragon, this involves enforcement of the law in areas difficult of proof – the search for which can often violate a person's right to the privacy of his body. To meet this problem, a number of US states have adopted laws that prohibit 'being under the influence' of heroin – an increasingly common charge in, for example, Los Angeles, where the mandatory minimum punishment is ninety days in prison.[21] By contrast in nearby San Francisco, the parents of a motor-cyclist who crashed and suffered permanent brain damage in 1985 sued a policeman because he had not arrested their son for drunken driving; and in England the parents of a man who died from a drugs overdose mounted a successful prosecution for manslaughter in 1986 against the friend who supplied him.

International control

Since a large part of trafficking is organized on an international basis, attempts to control it (like preventive policies) will have to follow suit. Measures to pursue traffickers' assets are also unlikely to succeed unless agreement is reached to adopt them internationally. At least one-third of Interpol's anti-crime work is now taken up with drugs. Interpol's role, however, is only to collate information, not to act operationally;[22] the total strength of its drugs sub-division is a mere twenty-five, and it even lacks nominal index computer support. Detective Chief Superintendent Penrose, Head of London's drugs squad, emphasized that it is useless to wait until floods of drugs reach this country; trained officers must be stationed at their source in the principal countries of origin, to gain intelligence about not only the smugglers planning to arrive but, even more importantly, the organizers behind the trade.[23] Until as late as 1983 Britain did not have a single such officer abroad,[24] although Canada, Australia, the USA and Norway already had investigators stationed in London – and Australia, for example, now has men based in Bangkok, Los Angeles, Paris, Kuala Lumpur, Jakarta, Wellington, Ottawa, Washington, Singapore, Rome, Manila, Hong Kong and Islamabad, while the Scandinavian countries also have officers in Athens, The Hague, Lima, and Wiesbaden, besides Pakistan.

At present the plain position is that drug-dealers are better organized, equipped and financed, more ruthlessly determined, and co-operate more closely transnationally, than the inter-governmental efforts. Although President Alan García of Peru recently described drug-trafficking as 'the only successful multinational business in Latin America', extradition arrangements everywhere remain patchy. The USSR is not even a member of the Customs Co-operation Council, or of Interpol – though now it has been officially admitted that the Soviet Union is not immune to the problem of drug addiction, international co-operation should improve. The UN Narcotics Division, with its HQ in Vienna, has to struggle in its efforts to monitor and improve the world's control of drugs with a total staff of only thirty-four and a regular annual budget of less than £1 million – a smaller sum than a trafficker can make from carrying a single suitcase of heroin from Karachi to Washington. A senior UN official assessed the WHO as 'disappointingly uninterested as a whole' in the issue, alleged that UNESCO does 'too little apart from one or two good education booklets', and wished that the International Labour Office would press for the retraining and employment of ex-addicts. The combined budget of the main agencies fighting the multi-billion-dollar drug boom amounts to less than US $10 million a year.

Political sensitivities continue to bedevil any coherent strategy. While the USA emphasizes the need to destroy poppy, coca and cannabis crops in the growing countries, the developing nations in turn resent the increasing penetration of their population by drugs – including some banned domestically – from the giant Western pharmaceutical companies. The first attempt at international regulation, the 1912 Hague Convention, needed in order to make it even partly effective a further convention in 1931 at Geneva, where agreement was reached due to the vigour of T. W. Russell ('Russell Pasha') who was appalled by the damage he had seen caused by heroin, even more than by hashish, in Egypt. This new measure pledged a ban on exports of heroin, and required each subscribing country to submit advance estimates of the amount of opiates needed for medical and scientific purposes; but the initiative ran into the sands because it was based only on voluntary compliance, and those countries which refused to ratify it continued to supply the illicit market without fear of sanction. Indeed, meetings of the international Opium Advisory Committee became known as 'the Smugglers' Reunions'. After the Second World War, the wider authority given to the United Nations opened the way to the adoption in 1961 of the UN Single Convention on Narcotic Drugs which (amended in 1972) provided for controls on opiates, cocaine and cannabis. Only a few countries such as Turkey, India and Poland are now permitted to export opium legally to supply morphine and codeine for pharmaceutical products. Synthetic stimulants and sedatives, however, as well as hallucinogens like LSD, were not covered because of opposition from Western companies until the 1971 UN Convention on Psychotropic Substances – and even then the UK did not agree to ratify this until 1985.[25] Less remembered is the fact that each convention requires its signatory nations to develop comprehensive treatment and rehabilitation programmes. The WHO has recently drawn up guidelines for national laws which would remove dependent people from the criminal justice system at all stages of arraignment, trial and sentence. International meetings, however, are dominated by the advocates of control: Dutch suggestions to consider the pros and cons of other alternatives such as liberalization have been firmly resisted, especially by the Germans and Swedes. Many developing countries – certainly until addiction spreads to their own populations – have felt resentment that the international drug control system has been dominated by Western (and especially US) interests: they pointedly ask why restrictions on the pushing of alcohol have never been considered, and why the destructive effects and trading of alcohol are ruled to be a purely national issue, whereas those of the less harmful cannabis are a matter of international control.[26]

Venezuela at the 1984 UN General Assembly proposed the need

for a new convention on drug-trafficking, which is now being discussed by the UN Commission on Narcotic Drugs. Its terms could co-ordinate different national legislation for tracing and seizing the proceeds of drug crimes; regulate the extradition of drug-traffickers, together with the searching of suspect boats in international waters; and make trafficking, like piracy, an international crime, so that it is a prosecutable offence anywhere, irrespective of the country in which it is committed. None the less, a further proposal that the UN should declare an International Year against Drug Abuse was dropped for fear that 'the publicity would generate more curiosity than opposition'.

Crop eradication and substitution

With official pessimism spreading as regards the practicability of ever preventing the smuggling of drugs (see Chapter 14), hopes have now turned to trying to cut the chain of supply at its source, by staunching illicit production. The fact that all the powerful resources of the USA are failing to prevent sizeable plantations of marijuana being grown within its own borders is evidence that the task will not be easy: the record US marijuana crop of 1985 is estimated to have been at least three times as big as that of much-criticized Mexico. The problems of operating in producer nations which are poor but none the less sovereign are immeasurably greater, especially since most illicit opium and coca grows in areas which are politically and economically unstable, and over which the relevant central governments themselves barely have nominal control. On the Afghan-Pakistan border and in the Thai-Lao-Burmese triangle, no writ of law enforcement runs. The culture of poppies and coca, often on marginal land by poor people, has long been crucially important for tens of thousands of local farmers, not only for their own traditional use but also as a cash crop (as many as two out of every five Turkish farmers were cultivating poppies in 1971) – so that total weaning, if it ever occurs, is unlikely for many years.[27] A British Conservative MP, Sir Bernard Braine, commented that this is part of the price we are having to pay for inadequately responding to the need for development aid in such countries, and 'it is high time that Western leaders understood' this.[28] Large parts of growers' land are unsuitable for other cash crops: in the Thai and Afghan uplands, opium poppies remain many times more profitable than any alternative (even when the grower receives less than 1 per cent of the street price). In Latin America, the USA is offering $360 a hectare to coca farmers who destroy their crop, but cocaine dealers offer them $12,000 a hectare for the leaves. Most daunting of all is the prospect that, even were the richer nations willing to subsidize the present producers to encourage them to desist, there are several hundred million alternative square miles in numerous countries admirably suited to growing illicit drug crops. Several areas of Africa are poised to produce opium if eradication in Asia were ever to succeed. Indeed some of the highest quality opium poppies have flourished in Europe and the USA, as well as there being excellent crops in the Sudan and Latin America – and they are being grown legally in countries ranging from France, Denmark and Poland to Turkey, India and Australia, so the world's potential crop is limitless. The entire current illegal heroin market of North America can in fact be supplied from the cultivation of less than thirty-five square miles. Furthermore, an increasing number of farmers in both south-east and south-west Asia are learning the lesson that, as one Pakistani told me, 'If you grow opium poppies, you receive visits from a nice rich Western man in a suit who offers you a new irrigation scheme; whereas if you don't grow poppies, nobody could care less if you and your family starve. So there is only one moral being drawn . . . '

Since the bottom fell out of the tin market, more Bolivians have turned to growing coca out of economic desperation. On the slopes of the Andes, the population has always been undernourished. Lately the traditional diet has been further impoverished because many local farmers have been persuaded to grow coca commercially for cocaine in place of food; an additional result is that the local people themselves have become much heavier consumers of coca paste, spending their limited cash on this instead of food. As in the USA and Europe, it is frequently the most vulnerable who are affected worst by drugs.

Since addiction and enforcement are costing the rich countries so much, it might seem a sensible plan for them to buy up and destroy the entire drug crop. Unfortunately – as recurs regularly in most plans to tackle drug problems – this seemingly attractive solution is fatally flawed: the guaranteed market would (as with EEC food) only encourage more to be grown, while criminal dealers would in any event always be able to outbid legitimate governments because of their premium profit as long as a drug remains illegal. Anyone who has seen a field of opium poppies in full bloom must marvel at mankind's capacity to derive tragedy out of such natural beauty. UNFDAC (the UN Fund for Drug Abuse Control), the international agency mandated to help poppy cultivators to switch to other crops – and probably the last UN body President Reagan will withdraw from – has never received even a tithe of the funding it needs to carry out its mandate. (France and Switzerland are examples of several countries which have made only tiny contributions.) It has achieved success in specific projects such as its $6 million showpiece, the Buner Valley on Pakistan's north-west frontier. Until 1975, Buner's 14,000 predominantly Pathan farmers produced one-third of Pakistan's opium poppies; nine years later it is claimed that none is being grown there. The UK in 1985 offered £3.4 million for a similar project in the Dir province of Pakistan, whose 12 annual tons of opium produce more than enough heroin to supply all of Britain's addicts. Michael Meacher MP has urged that Britain should spend at least four times as much on such projects as it does at present; although, so long as many major poppy-growing areas lie outside central government control, suppression in one area often only leads to increased production elsewhere. This syndrome is known as 'the balloon effect' – since if you squeeze one part of a balloon, it will inevitably expand elsewhere.

Many of the main drug-producing countries – Pakistan, Thailand, Jamaica, Turkey and in Latin America – happen to be particularly susceptible to US economic diplomacy; impelled by the increasingly firm conditions attached by Congress to US aid, the Thai, Pakistan and Mexican governments claim recently to have destroyed more opium poppies than ever before – but their drug production too is nevertheless achieving new records. The US State Department reported that, despite their receiving US aid, in 1984 Mexico, Bolivia, Thailand, Peru, Belize, Burma and Jamaica all increased their drug-producing crops – and Ecuador has recently joined them as a major coca grower. The critics of efforts at 'anti-drug diplomacy' argue that these only arouse internal political antagonism likely to endanger ally governments, and that in any event such pressure is incapable of application in the case of many relevant countries where the West has no leverage. The US government faces a particularly difficult dilemma because a great number of the Afghan guerrillas finance their fighting from heroin, and also from the fact that the drug producers in several other areas are anti-communist marauders whom the CIA is not over-anxious to hurt. On the other hand, when Washington recently allocated $18 million for drug eradication in Peru's Upper Huallaga Valley (the source of perhaps a fifth of the world's coca leaf), the programme aroused so much support for the Sendero Luminoso guerrillas who were co-ordinating resistance among the resentful local *campesinos*, that the US Agency for International Development hurriedly had to abandon its headquarters at Aucayacu, and twenty-one members of the anti-cocaine team were massacred in a particularly brutal way. When a similar programme was attempted by the Bolivian government in its coca-growing district of Chapare (as a result of firmly-couched offers from Washington that La Paz could not refuse), the farmers rose in revolt and the government itself fell soon afterwards. Bolivia's failure to eradicate 'even one' coca plant in 1984 – despite large-scale assistance from the USA – has been described as 'a major disappointment' by the State Department; but local anti-American political feelings were exacerbated when in 1986 the news emerged that armed US army soldiers and helicopters were secretly being used inside Bolivia to transport men to attack cocaine laboratories. (US lawyers questioned whether such use of armed force abroad in support of law enforcement was constitutional; President Reagan justified it by claiming that the drug trade now represents a threat to the USA's national security.) Turkish poppy farmers in the villages round the city of Afyonkarahisar, whose name means 'the black castle of opium', similarly deeply resent the US policy of forcing their government to destroy their traditional way of life. (Indeed, how would Britain react if a Muslim country told us to close down our whisky industry because their own inhabitants were drinking?) When the *Guardian* suggested that 'the international community should threaten Pakistan with sanctions unless it cleans up its heroin trade', a diplomat replied that to threaten a Third World country because of the follies of the rich, heroin-consuming West is as unfair and impractical as threatening the 'heroin-consuming countries with sanctions unless they eliminate drug-addiction'. Another Pakistani man in Karachi suggested that the West 'should learn to live with the heinous exports of cocaine and heroin from the Third World, as we over the centuries have learned to live with the evils of tobacco and whisky'.

In Thailand, eradication projects have been given finance by the UN, Western Germany, the USA, the Netherlands, the UK, Australia and Canada; but, despite the personal backing of the Thai King, results are constricted by endemic corruption and the lack of government control over the highland border areas. Neither the Thai nor the Pakistani government is anxious to alienate its border tribes lest they take up arms. The problem hence develops a self-reinforcing cycle: drug-crop profits are used to purchase arms and these arms buttress the independence which allows the tribesmen to grow more opium poppies. New crops, sown as soon as the government's soldiers move elsewhere, are popular because they offer much employment. Tribal poppy growers use a slash-and-burn technique, moving every two years (and denuding the ecology) – whereas coffee plants take four years to produce a crop and fruit trees even longer. The tribes therefore are being asked not only to change their traditional crops but also to abandon their nomadic life-style and settle down. This requires new villages and integrated rural development: hence the work of UNFDAC would be more successful if it were part of the UN Development Programme. Yugoslavia was successful in phasing out opium production naturally as part of its economic development. China is the only example to date of a country which has achieved the planned replacement of opium by other crops. It will certainly be many years, if ever, before any such policy could hope to succeed in the unpoliced Golden Triangle.[29]

Some critics oppose giving funds for drug-crop growers to diversify their sources of income on the grounds that it would be the equivalent of paying protection money to the Mafia. Others denigrate it as being like pouring wine into an ever-leaking bottle: despite all efforts at reduction, the world production of opium increased by 14 per cent in 1985.[30] A UN official in Islamabad, however, asks: 'Can you afford not to spend the money?' On the other hand, André McNicoll comments: 'One is led to the inescapable impression that supply suppression has been easier to push because it usually implies intervention in the societies of less powerful nations in the Third World, while an internationally-sponsored attack on demand would imply major scrutiny and intervention in the societies of the richest nations.'[31] Nevertheless, it must equally be in the long-term interests of developing nations, at several levels, to divert their land-use from producing drug crops (few of whose profits anyway accrue to the farmers) to the growing of food.

An overall analysis of the hopes for dealing with the drug crisis by methods of control, carried out by the Rand Corporation, is bleak. It states:

> The poor prospects for controlling the production level are illustrated by past efforts to reduce opium poppy cultivation in many different countries. These efforts have failed to make a lasting effect on the US market, for reasons that also apply to marijuana and cocaine: (1) drug crops are more lucrative than most other crops, and hence small farmers have a strong economic incentive to continue production despite government pressure; (2) governments are often weak in the growing areas, which are typically remote and sometimes controlled by ethnic groups not responsive to the central political power; (3) many governments are unconcerned about the US drug problem or unsympathetic with US interests; (4) all drugs have several source countries; for marijuana and opium, the number of producers is almost limitless since the crop grows in many climates; when one country's production is curtailed, other producers step in to fill the gap; (5) because local cultural conditions often allow or encourage a legitimate market in drugs and derivative products, it is difficult to prevent diversion to the illicit market; and (6) in many countries, drug cultivation is a traditional economic activity; substitution of other crops is generally not feasible because it would require very costly long-term development to upgrade farmers' skills, provide roads for shipping new crops, and so on. For all these reasons, it would be unrealistic to expect that greater diplomatic or international efforts could significantly constrain the overseas supply of illegal drugs, at least in the foreseeable future.

The Rand Corporation's assessment of the likelihood of control through internal policing is equally discouraging:

> In the illicit market, each dealer faces many risks and therefore sells to only a few customers to maintain secrecy. This means there is an enormous number of retail dealers – probably over

half a million to service the marijuana market alone (which has at least 20 million regular users). Local police make only about 50,000 arrests for marijuana sale each year, and few of those arrests result in imprisonment. We calculate that the probability of imprisonment is probably far less than 1 per cent for a year's dealing in marijuana. Similar conclusions apply to cocaine . . . As a result, we find that even doubling the quantity of cocaine seized would raise the price by no more than 4 per cent. For marijuana, which is marked up less than cocaine, doubling the seizure rate might increase the retail price by as much as 12 per cent; but since a marijuana cigarette sells for about 75 cents at retail, that increase would imply only a 9-cent rise in the price, hardly enough to discourage much consumption. It has been argued that federal agencies should imprison more couriers who smuggle drugs into the country, but we doubt that doing so would do much to raise retail drug prices. Many South American sailors are willing to engage in smuggling for modest wages. Even if their risks of imprisonment were greatly increased, the additional amount required to compensate them would probably represent less than 1 per cent of the drug's retail price. Finally, federal agencies strive to imprison high-level drug distributors and seize their assets. However, the value of assets seized is trivial in relation to the retail value of drugs . . . A large expansion in investigative effort would be costly . . . We do not thereby mean to imply that enforcement against drug-dealers should be abandoned. Enforcement has certainly made drug-dealing more risky, and it may make it more difficult for novice users to find dealers. Its effectiveness might be improved by rearranging priorities; for example, the effects of the current large expenditures on interdiction should be weighed against the possible effects of allocating those resources to other purposes, such as investigating high-level dealers . . . [32]

It is these dealers who are examined next.

14

The Global Connection: Smugglers, Multinational Trafficking and the Mafia

'What nature requires is obtainable, and within easy reach. It's for the superfluous we sweat.'

Seneca, *Epistles*

'Property is not theft, but a good deal of theft becomes property.'

R. H. Tawney, *The Acquisitive Society*

'We love the criminal and take a burning interest in him, because the devil makes us forget the beam in our own eye when observing the mote in our brother's, and in that way outwits us.'

C. G. Jung

A police officer is giving a talk on drugs at a Leeds school. The first question is from a mother: 'Why don't you stop it coming into this country?'

The attempts to do so unfortunately seem like trying to trap the wind with nets. 'We only catch a few of the very stupidest smugglers,' a senior Customs authority admitted; 'mainly, some of those unimaginative enough to go through Dover, Gatwick or Heathrow.' The cells at Gatwick are regularly full of such unimaginative passengers – currently, many of them Nigerians en route to the USA, since the 'Lagos connection' in 1985 became a key route for heroin from south-west Asia. On the other hand, women cannot be compelled to submit to internal examinations in countries such as Spain, while 200 g. of heroin (with a street value of £20,000) can be hidden in a vagina . . . and furthermore pregnant women cannot be X-rayed at airports because of the danger to the foetus, so it is not surprising that several drug rings now use expectant mothers (real or otherwise) as couriers. Any substance carried inside imported farm animals or carcasses is even less likely to be detected.

Extraordinary human ingenuity and imaginative talent is channelled into drug-smuggling.[1] I restrict myself, for obvious reasons, to describing only those methods which have already been publicly made known. None the less, Miami Customs officers have found cocaine hidden inside virtually everything from the transmissions of cars (which can each take several hours to dismantle, causing angry hold-ups at borders) to both live and stuffed birds. Consignments of heroin have elsewhere been discovered concealed in cricket and tennis balls, drums of paint, ikons, car-tyres, a false hunchback, the hollow heels of shoes, girdles worn by female models, planks of wood, toothpaste tubes, tennis-racquet handles, babies' bottles, ice-hockey gloves, Buddhas, teddy bears, coffee-machines, tombstones, guitars, tins of anchovies and strings of onions (to confuse sniffer-dogs). Drugs have also been discovered amongst the packing round genuine antique Cypriot statues; inside elaborate hair-styles, scooped-out fruit, consignments of flowers, sanitary towels, car-batteries, and wine bottles (just as Westerners flying to Saudi Arabia take their whisky in bottles labelled medicine).[2] Drugs recently imported into the UK from India via Amsterdam had been hidden in barrels of sheep's intestines carried in refrigerated lorries. 'Lucky' Luciano's speciality was wax oranges filled by a syringe with heroin and then concealed in crates of fruit; the Mafia also own a number of garages in Palermo and Turin that specialize in building pockets for drugs inside the bodywork of cars, which are then shipped with legitimate papers of sale to the USA or UK. Occasionally the Customs authorities have a triumph: in April 1986 a keen-nosed officer at Heathrow smelt the glue which two Iranians had used to fit a false bottom in a suitcase. Two other empty suitcases were found on analysis themselves to be constructed of heroin-coated fibre; in another, sad case fifteen months earlier, a disabled man crippled by paralysis in his arms and legs had been jailed for six years in Scotland for smuggling 23 kg. of cannabis in the cushion of his wheel-chair.

The $600 millions' worth of cocaine recently found hidden in a Colombian 747 airliner amounted to five times the value of the aircraft itself. Professional criminals today prefer to import-export the white powder of heroin and cocaine rather than cannabis, not only because of its higher profit but also because it is less bulky and therefore more difficult to detect – though a few criminals refuse on principle to deal in hard drugs. One successful recent smuggler who insisted on handling only cannabis made a fortune with professional and graduate friends, through importing several tons into Britain and the USA from the Near East, mainly via Shannon Airport. The consignments were hidden in rock-bands' equipment, often vacuum sealed and washed in petrol to disguise their smell from sniffer-dogs; though one large cargo was lost through inadvertently being eaten by goats on a Greek island while en route through the Mediterranean from Lebanon, and another lorry carrying twenty-one tea-chests full of Thai sticks had the misfortune to be blown up outside Dublin by Irish soldiers who suspected it of carrying IRA explosives.[3] Three packets of drugs, recently found by chance in the New Covent Garden fruit market among 124 crates of pineapples from Ghana, make the police wonder how many needles in other haystacks daily go undiscovered; as one Welshman, who smuggled two tons of cannabis in tins of Kenyan jam and cashew nuts, wrote in a letter to his wife, 'The way I am bringing it in, it is impossible to find.'

Table 5 shows the figures published by the UN Division of Narcotic Drugs for seizures of heroin and cocaine throughout the world:

Table 5: **World Seizures of Heroin and Cocaine**

		Heroin (kg.)	Cocaine (kg.)
1947–66	annual	187	41
1967–74	averages	953	625
1975		1,708	2,406
1976		2,586	2,419
1977		2,377	3,977
1978		2,441	5,391
1979		2,070	8,365
1980		2,510	11,820
1981		5,613	9,541
1982		6,210	12,113
1983		11,827	40,991
1984		10,643	58,737

Enforcement agencies, in order to justify their efforts and budgets, often announce details of 'record drug hauls' they have seized – which probably have the reverse of any deterrent effect when publicized with an astronomic sum as their street value. Officials are aware that large quantities continually enter unobtrusively: the 10 kg. of heroin annually found in postal items entering Britain must be only a fraction of the amount being dispatched (often to accommodation addresses or 'safe houses') in letters, between pages of newspapers and magazines and even hollowed-out picture postcards – particularly since the proliferation of heroin refining in Pakistan and India. One consignment of bibles which happened to be examined by an especially vigilant officer was found to have the Acts of the Apostles in each copy replaced by cocaine. Paper and cardboard itself impregnated with heroin is the most recent method of transit; another technique which is very difficult to detect is for travellers to impregnate angora sweaters with cocaine, and then boil them to recover the drug once they have passed Customs.

Anything that can be moved across a border is used. An Egyptian woman travelling as a nun was detained suckling a dummy baby stuffed with cannabis ('She forgot that not many nuns have children'), and French officials found that one corpse in a zinc-lined coffin from Lebanon was packed in heroin that would have been recovered by disinternment after the funeral. At Kai Tak women have taken dead babies filled with heroin over the border. In parts of the Middle East it is necessary for Customs to pat camels in a certain way: caravans of the animals are given packets of drugs to swallow which are retrieved on the other side of the frontier. Street-pushers often wrap their drugs in cling-film and carry it in the palm of their hand, so that it can either be quickly swallowed (for later recovery) if they see the police, or else they can transport it in their anus. Drug ring organizers try to select human smugglers who are most likely to appeal to the sympathies of the courts – such as frail elderly grandmothers or, in one case, the mother of a child with a hole in its heart – and who have the best chance of being able to abscond if given bail after they are caught. Among favourite tricks are for 'smotherers' to distract attention, or for 'bait' to be sacrificed: a syndicate sends several couriers on one plane and tips off the authorities about the least important of them, so that the main smugglers are able to slip through during the confusion of an arrest.

(No less than twenty-nine different passengers on one commercial flight at Brussels were found to be heroin couriers.) Children are often used as cover or decoys. Illegal immigrants or hopelessly indebted gamblers are frequently blackmailed into being couriers in Hong Kong. Certain film and rock stars, by contrast, are well known for getting their bodyguards ('beef') or secretaries to carry their personal drugs through Customs. Drug-dependent people often act as couriers, having a personal interest in seeing that supplies get through: Terrence Clark's organization (the best-known of six main ones in post-war Australia) used teams of women who were mainly addicts or prostitutes to import heroin on flights from Bangkok. They carried either cassette-recorders and typewriters with part of their insides removed, or specially made suitcases holding twenty-four bags each containing 8 kg. of heroin secreted in false compartments in their sides and base. The bags were covered with talcum powder, latex paint, hot wax or fibreglass to defeat sniffer-dogs, and the couriers were told to pack the suitcases with mothballs and dirty clothing, together with broken children's toys that would attract the sympathy of a Customs officer who might look inside.[4] Each courier was given, besides Australian $1,000 plus a further $9,000 on delivery, 10 mg. of Valium to take just before arrival so that she would not show signs of nervousness. Unknown to the couriers, one of the syndicate's organizers travelled separately on each flight in order to watch; if a courier was arrested, the organizer called an experienced lawyer and, provided the courier gave no information to the police, she had all her legal costs paid together with $10,000 deposited in her bank account. The prize for the most ingenious *chutzpah* must go to the smuggler from Minnesota who successfully passed through Los Angeles from Peru with 2 kg. of cocaine taped to his legs and torso, using a note he carried in his passport that stated: 'I am a federal narcotics officer and am travelling without identification. I'm following the dark-haired suspect with the big purse. Please expedite my clearance.' In 1984 two drug couriers who were the worse for drink were arrested at Heathrow only because they began quarrelling when one of them removed her corset which contained several packets of heroin, complaining that it (like her) was too tight. Nevertheless, each smuggler caught in the USA costs $35,000 a year to keep in prison – and receives better food there than at home in Colombia or Bolivia.

Whenever a head of the hydra is cut off, several more appear.

Historically, drug-trading used to follow certain traditional routes, with the UK, for example, obtaining its heroin from Pakistan and cannabis from Lebanon or black Africa, while Morocco's cannabis went to France and Spain. Today, however, the traffic of the global connection has become multi-directional, as drug-habits in producer and transit countries rival the traditional areas of demand. As soon as one smuggling method or route is known to be under observation, the planners switch to new ways. On one run, for instance, a courier flying to Spain – the 'trampoline' entrepôt to Europe for South American cocaine – joins up with a package tour homeward-bound from Majorca, arriving at Luton Airport inconspicuous as one of a sunburnt straw-hatted crowd; while the next week his colleagues will travel circuitously so as to arrive from unsuspected places: those on the Bogota to Boston run will not fly direct, but via Copenhagen and Shannon or the Channel Islands. (Transit points soon develop as new markets for drugs themselves.) One of the popular final legs into Britain is mingling with the cross-Channel day-trippers from Calais, Boulogne or Ostend. At Dover and other car ports, smugglers sometimes attach magnetic boxes containing drugs to totally innocent cars for retrieval after they have cleared Customs. Skiers carry drugs easily into and out of Switzerland over its many hundred kilometres of unguarded mountain frontier.[5] Unmanned midget submarines are used as well as parachutes and hang-gliders, and even radio-controlled model aircraft launched from boats lying offshore. Consignments of drugs arrive chained beneath ships, or welded into their holds (crew members have weeks of leisure during a voyage to hide drugs, and know the crevices of their ship much better than any Customs officer ever can). Other consignments have been hidden in plastic bags underwater, tagged with homing devices or marker buoys, to be later retrieved by divers in frogmen suits. But is such ingenuity really necessary? Every country has ports or airstrips where there is no Customs presence at all. Private aircraft, yachts or fishing-boats can land deliveries with virtual impunity. The Colombian drug syndicates have their own fleets of DC-3, DC-7, C-46 and Beechcraft aircraft, backed by sea-planes. 'Mother' or 'cooper' ships regularly lie outside national sea limits offshore, waiting to send in drugs by motor-boat to rendezvous on deserted beaches. (At the time of the slave trade, international interception was permitted, but not today; Soviet electronic trawlers, for example, would never agree to this.) Some smuggling ships carry communications equipment sophisticated enough to detect any movement by coastguard vessels.[6]

William Mitchell, an American millionaire who pleaded guilty in 1983 to being the ringleader of a cocaine smuggling syndicate (three attempts were made on his life to stop him naming his associates), delivered the verdict: 'Britain has lost and doesn't have a chance.' Many British people expressed angry amazement when their current government – professedly exponents of law and order – in the face of the rising flood of drugs entering the country between 1979 and 1984 actually cut the already modest strength of the Customs authorities by 3,600 – 1,000 of them front-line control staff. A very senior figure ruefully explained to me: 'The Customs were axed because they come under the Treasury, and when it was imposing across-the-board public service cuts, the Treasury didn't like to be seen exempting itself. This is now recognized to have been idiotic folly.' It is true that much the most cost-effective Customs results are obtained from intelligence work rather than relying solely on the uniformed 'thin blue line'. Unlike in most other countries, the UK Customs do not confine themselves to manning frontiers, but pursue smugglers inland down to the level of street distribution – including using the technique of 'controlled delivery', by which couriers, instead of being arrested, are kept under surveillance in the hope that they will provide leads to the main organizers of drug rings. Nevertheless, the diminished likelihood of any traveller being stopped even at Heathrow (where Customs net two-thirds of all the heroin they seize) can produce only one result. When the Green 'nothing to declare' channel system was first started, Customs stopped and questioned 30 per cent of passengers; by 1984, only one in 100 passengers arriving at Dover and Heathrow was being questioned – at peak times only one in 300 or 400, and during an arrest or at meal-times less than one in 1,000.[7] (If a suspect is caught, at least two men are lost to the line: one who is the arresting officer, and one or more as witnesses.) Meanwhile the annual number of travellers entering the UK during the same period rose by 10 per cent to 36 million. At the port of Dover, officers in the Green lane have an average of forty-five seconds to deal with each car; since it can take more than an hour to search a car thoroughly (even without dismantling it), even one occasional check can cause a huge backlog. It is cargo, however, which remains the chief conduit for smuggled drugs. A senior Customs man warned in 1986 that the future flow of freight through the Channel Tunnel is likely to increase drug imports sharply. Even now, 90 per cent of the freight coming into the UK eludes Customs' scrutiny; consignments from the EEC – including those from the major drugs warehouses in the entrepôt of Amsterdam – are subject to only a 2 per cent random sample check. Another weakness in control is considered to be the TIR convention, whereby lorries are subject to Customs inspection only in their country of departure – whose standards may not be as high as those of the importing country. Of 500 ships entering the busy port of Felixstowe recently, Customs were able to search barely one. There are now only three Customs officers on night duty for the whole of Scotland's east coast, two for south Wales, and often but a single person covering the entire 500 miles' coastline of Devon and Cornwall. Smuggling is made even more simple because yachts are subject only to voluntary Customs control: skippers are supposed to notify their own arrival, but nobody knows how many do this – or how many unload drugs or other contraband first.[8]

The USA's predicament is similar. Some 250 million people cross the country's borders annually; any thorough searching of cars, vessels or planes would bring travel and commerce to a halt. There are hundreds of airfields (six on Long Island alone) without any guard at night. 'The American public is not prepared to pay the price to stop drugs, which would include body-searches at JFK,' said Bruce Jensen of the DEA in New York. Dr M. Rosenthal added: 'Even if you managed to keep heroin and cocaine out, there are enough other drugs available in New York to supply everyone's needs.'[9] Customs men have been given some new help: dogs trained to detect drugs now sniff hand-baggage – though not travellers, which is forbidden. Most nations use Alsatians for this work, though the British retain an affection for labradors or spaniels, which are not so resilient. Different dogs are trained to detect the scent of cannabis, heroin or cocaine (though the Germans are experimenting by using a wild boar); smugglers retaliate by using fish and pepper as disguises or the smell of cats or a bitch on heat as a diversion. Other screening devices using X-rays, video, thermal neutron activators or gas-chromatography are being refined. However, the major hurdle the Customs authorities face is that a large proportion of the drugs coming in by land, air or sea never go near any official channel at all. The huge profits of trafficking – when heroin bought for £3,000 at Bara Bazaar in Pakistan can fetch £150,000 wholesale and have a street value of £1 million in London – provide a wide margin out of which to afford bribes: £5,000 is the going rate for one suitcase to be moved outside the Customs area. Airport and dock employees are frequent targets, since they know their area's system intimately and are easily able to identify its exploitable links. Some Customs officials, not only in Asia and Africa, earn many times more from not looking at luggage than they do from inspecting it. Ground staff and unloaders employed by airlines 'misroute' certain marked items of baggage, while pre-arranged cleaners collect packets hidden behind panels in the lavatories or oxygen compartments of aircraft and remove them from the airport in rubbish bags aboard refuse trucks. A number of Pakistan's corrupt airport security and other officials are reported themselves to be drug-addicts.[10] Even those drug consignments which are seized are not necessarily safe: the attempted robbery of several million pounds' worth of drugs at the main Customs warehouse at Heathrow in 1983 came within an ace of success. In America, the DEA is the somewhat apprehensive guardian of stocks of cocaine and heroin which command a street value of $10 billion – almost twice the official value of the USA's reserves of gold stored at Fort Knox – because drug exhibits have to be retained until interminably protracted court proceedings are completed.

Neither appearance nor status is any guide as to whom to suspect. Diplomats, lawyers, magistrates, beauty queens, philanthropists, politicians, policemen, airline pilots, a Prime Minister and the families of heads of states are among those arrested in recent months for smuggling drugs. The sleek drug-dealers seen at Hollywood and New York parties often keep their lawyers and bail-bondsmen permanently by their side. (When two Colombians absconded and forfeited their $400,000 bail in Anguilla in 1984, there was a local celebration: the sum provided nearly a quarter of the island's entire annual budget.) Some traffickers fly the world like multinational executives; a regular courier delivering heroin to New York testified he used Concorde 'because you get VIP treatment at Customs'. 'I travel so much that I wake up in the morning not knowing where I am,' one American international heroin dealer said, 'I go to Lima, La Paz, Santiago, Bogota, Tokyo and wind up through Vegas before heading home to New York.'[11] Drugs are used as an international currency by migrants, criminals and arms-dealers, as an easily-realizable asset that short-circuits exchange controls when crossing national boundaries. Four Mauritian MPs were accused of smuggling heroin in Holland in December 1985; a number of very senior Zambian political and diplomatic figures were detained three months earlier, on charges of smuggling con-signments of Mandrax pills (which, in large doses, have a heroin-like effect) from India to apartheid South Africa. Diplomatic bags – notably in New York, Geneva, Brussels and London – remain a continual loophole in every country's attempt to exclude drugs. Under the 1961 Vienna Diplomatic Convention, such bags may never be opened – although many countries privately X-ray them, even if they deny this. In April 1986 Italy expelled three Syrian diplomats for smuggling large amounts of heroin into Rome; a Belgian diplomat was recently arrested trying to sell $22 millions' worth of heroin to an undercover New York FBI agent. (Certain countries will sell one of their diplomatic passports for £12,000.) A Moroccan envoy's crate split when it 'happened to fall off' a forklift truck at Harwich, to reveal a third of a ton of cannabis (although diplomatic immunity prevented any prosecution), and another dip-lomatic crate from Zaire fortuitously was also dropped at Brussels, spilling 228 kg. of cannabis on the tarmac. A senior Nigerian diplomat accredited to Pakistan was given ten years' jail in Britain for smuggling heroin; twelve months later in 1985 another smuggler alleged to the British police that heroin was 'imported into the UK on virtually every flight from Pakistan, concealed in diplomatic bags'. The most overt concerted diplomatic traffic in illicit drugs was ordered by the North Korean government during the mid-1970s in an effort to acquire foreign exchange to pay for a massive advertis-ing campaign in the world Press extolling their President, with the consequence that the entire staff of North Korea's embassies in Denmark, Finland, Norway and Sweden (together with other diplo-mats, even in Moscow) were expelled. Many other envoys, how-ever, invoke diplomatic immunity to escape prosecution, although the USA has jailed a number of Latin American diplomats for drug-smuggling, and President Kaunda of Zambia commendably makes it his policy to waive immunity in all such cases.

One Gambian visitor to Belgium on the other hand found that honesty is not necessarily a better policy: Manju Turay who, when he was asked by Customs if he had anything to declare, replied 'Yes, 55 lb. of cannabis,' received three years' jail as his reward. Two brothers from Belfast bringing back what they thought was heroin from Pakistan, only to find they had been sold whitewash powder, were none the less jailed in 1985 for conspiring to smuggle. Two Nigerians, offered help at Kennedy Airport because they were limping, were found to have $2 millions' worth of heroin concealed in their deep-heeled shoes. Another smuggler was surprised to be detained at London Airport when he gave as the reason for his journey that he was taking his 'son back to school at Roedean'. A recent regular smuggler, who carried £10 millions' worth of heroin through Heathrow in twelve months, was a Japanese who travelled in boy-scout uniform, using a North Korean diplomatic passport which his backers had bought him. However, the couriers who run a double risk, from death as well as arrest, are the body-packers. One young woman, who tied a piece of cotton to her teeth attached to the heroin-filled condom she had swallowed, died in convulsive agony when the acid in her stomach dissolved a hole in the sheath. In a British hospital, another courier recently passed fifteen of such condoms in his bowel movements, but died with another forty still inside him. Body-packers are selected by drug organizers because they have no previous criminal record, and they receive rehearsal training for a fortnight beforehand at camps in Latin America, practising swallowing whole grapes as well as bulk antacid to coat their stomach linings. (The known record to date is one woman who kept inside her for five days 6,000 morphine tablets in 180 packages which had been made from the fingers of surgical gloves.) There is a limitless supply of poor slum dwellers from Bogota, Bangkok or among Turkish migrant-workers who are prepared to run such risks.[12] Some are caught because they sweat nervously when they reach Customs. Couriers suspected of having swallowed drugs are invited to secure quarters with a special lavatory where they are kept under continuous surveillance (some have been known to reswallow the drugs). However, in Britain, even under the latest Criminal Justice Act, suspects may only be detained for ninety-six hours; in Spain the limit is seventy-two hours, which Customs men say is not always adequate for solving such cases. Taking an X-ray without a court order can be an illegal assault.[13] Other, more prudent smugglers employ involuntary species as their carriers: one Sri Lankan used to feed dead rats containing packets of heroin to snakes, which he then exported to the zoo in Britain where his brother was working in the reptile house so that he was able to collect the packets as they passed through the snakes' digestive system.

In February 1983 officials seized a 926-lb. consignment of heroin at Jamrud, 120 miles north of Islamabad – though no prosecution followed; less than three months earlier, another 871 lb. had been impounded nearby. So large is the quantity of drugs currently being discovered, that the UN Narcotic Drugs Division recently ordered a re-check of all its recent data to make sure that its computer is still functioning accurately. Police and Customs alike frankly concede that they are fighting a losing campaign against the main drug-suppliers, many of whom possess superiority in organization and finance. The successful traffickers and methods are precisely those we know nothing about – just as the most skilful criminals are rarely the ones in prison. The biggest heroin supplier in Pakistan, reputed to be a billionaire well known in Karachi, who has an international network with its European headquarters in Amsterdam, takes care never to be in the same country as his consignments of drugs. When smaller traders are occasionally caught, they are almost always too frightened to give information about the big dealers – most of whom take care that street-level pushers (often also users themselves) never learn their real identity. Although the police put a variety of pressures on users to reveal their sources, many of them know that informers have been knee-capped or disfigured with a blow-torch. At present the Customs authorities in the UK – which, as an island, has in theory a frontier more easily controlled than most other nations – seize an average of less than 1 kg. of heroin a day, whereas the nation's illicit consumption is conservatively calculated to be several times that amount. It is significant that today even the largest seizures no longer have any apparent effect on retail prices in the illegal drug market. (Seizures of cocaine by the UK Customs in fact went down in 1984 from the previous year, whereas nobody believes the amount coming into the country diminished.) Customs officers in the USA as well as Britain privately doubt whether they are stopping even 5 to 10 per cent – possibly as little as 3 per cent – of the illegal drugs that are entering; each intensification of control is countered by more resourceful strategies on the part of traffickers. Few free populations will put up with continual toothcomb searches of their possessions, let alone their persons. No country, and certainly no liberal democracy, can be hermetically sealed. This does not mean, as is sometimes argued, that the attempt should be abandoned as hopeless: for Customs' efforts undeniably deter even larger amounts of drugs from entering in quantities that would reduce prices and thus make them accessible to yet more people. What it does mean, however, is that the only hope of solving the problem definitively is to tackle it at the demand end, and not at the supply.

The multinational traffickers

Who are the chief organizers of the drug trade, for whom the couriers are no more than expendable pawns on a chess-board? The *New York Times* has described the drug-traffic as the world's prime example of unrestrained, savage capitalism. As Don Aitken points out, it is one of the few remaining fields where individuals today may establish themselves in a classical system of laissez-faire capitalism, unencumbered by any government regulation. The captains of this growth industry do not see themselves as 'merchants of death' or as an 'evil organization conspiring to corrupt youth', but as paradigms of entrepreneurs and merchant-venturers speculating for monopolies in highly lucrative commodity-trading – backed by their own teams of lawyers, chemists, accountants, pilots and bankers. Collateral investors deal in futures, taking shares in large high-risk high-reward enterprises as their predecessors did in Sir Francis Drake's voyages of piracy and trading. Uniquely among trading markets, the drug business – although uninsurable – has the advantage of being recession-proof: economic, like personal, depression is likely to have the overall effect of only swelling the ranks of its consumers. It constitutes an archetypal sellers' market: demand exceeds supply at every level; so that buyers seek out sellers, rather than vice versa. Addicts' demand forms a classic 'captive market' for a perfect 'consumer product'. 'It's not just the incredible amounts of money that attract many of these people,' said a New York attorney. 'It's the fact they might make it instantaneously – as well as tax-free: they see drugs as a source of instant wealth. The big dealers then launder the profits several times over, buying into legitimate business investments and respected social status.'[14] (One of the leading Colombians who control the New York cocaine trade, a 35-year-old logistical genius, coolly masterminded his fleets of planes, boats and lorries with computers when he was in a rehabilitation centre; several others continue to run their organizations from inside prisons.) Some of the biggest traffickers have safeguarded their fortunes by putting them in the names of their children and their wives, whom they nominally divorce.[15] The drug overlords' mansions in Barranquilla in Colombia are fortified like bank vaults and guarded by private armies with better equipment than the government's forces possess. Their finances indeed rival those of banks: by 1982 New York City's illegal drug trade was estimated to gross $45 billion a year – comfortably ahead of any other business in the city, including retail trade ($24.5 billion) or manufacturing ($14.6 billion). Heroin and cocaine pushers continually develop profitable new veins to expand their clientele, while improving the organization of their operations: even some street-pushers now carry Citizens' Band radios. Some syndicates tip off the police about rivals in order to win hegemony and operate a price monopoly; price wars between competing organizations can result in bloodshed as well as low-price dumping – although unlike in much marketing, an increase in drug supply in fact creates new demand rather than vice versa.

Overall, the international co-operation of traffickers with differing politics, religion and nationality throws into stark contrast the lack of it amongst governments. Mathea Falco, formerly the US Assistant Secretary of State for Narcotics Matters, comments:

> The multinational, multi-billion-dollar drug-traffic has not yet become the subject of open public debate in this country. Many people have an interest in not focusing public attention on it too closely: government officials and politicians have the fear of being held responsible for the magnitude of the problem, bankers the need to shore up confidence in the integrity of banking. The cumulative effect of this uncoordinated conspiracy of silence has been to conceal the real dimensions of the problem from public view.

For a number of developing countries, meanwhile, the drug trade forms the most significant source of badly-needed foreign exchange, even though these producer nations as a result suffer from inflation (the economies of Colombia and Bolivia have been seriously distorted in this way), besides contamination from corruption and

321

crime in addition to addiction at home. In at least five Latin American countries drug operators now appear to command as much power as the government. At the same time, both drugs and the anti-drug hysteria are liable to be manipulated for wider political purposes. Drug crops constitute the major economic resource – and means of acquiring arms – of several groups of indigenous people, as well as part of their traditional pharmacopoeia; concurrently, they provide a political excuse for governments to repress them violently, in addition to extracting increased aid from the USA and Europe. The first rule when investigating the global connection is to determine *cui bono* – what is in it, and for whom?

The two main routes for the supply of heroin after the Second World War initially were eastwards from the 'Golden Triangle' of southeast Asia, exported through Bangkok or Hong Kong; and westwards, organized by the 'French Connection' syndicates at Marseilles who refined morphine base out of opium obtained from Turkey. When opium was banned first in Turkey in 1971 (as a result of US pressure and subvention), and subsequently in Iran (following its revolution), Burmese, Thai and Mexican growers increased production to replace these sources of supply. Following the Vietnam War, the Triangle dealers moved to develop new European markets for their heroin, which began to appear in Amsterdam and Frankfurt.[16] Initially distribution in Europe was organized by sectors of the Chinese community in Amsterdam; but when the French Connection was eventually broken, its role was taken over and developed by the Mafia, who moved a number of the Marseilles chemists to Sicily and extended supply routes through their own network in North America as well as Europe. The US government exerted its carrot-and-stick pressure on Mexico to repress its opium growers; but when in the late 1970s a succession of bad harvests hit south-east Asia, the 'Golden Crescent' of south-west Asia expanded both its production and processing so that by 1981 this area had become the world's major source of heroin.

In Pakistan, General Zia's ban on opium shops in 1979 left the barely-policed northern area of the country without a local market for its crop. Pakistan's links with Britain provided one ready alternative outlet for the glut;[17] its heroin now flows to the west by air and sea from Karachi via the Gulf States and Damascus, as well as via India and Lagos. The trafficking of heroin to Europe was facilitated by Pakistani hashish smuggling organizations, a number of which switched to the more lucrative drug. Heroin is relatively easy to refine in simple conditions; by 1981 it was being processed on the spot in Pakistan in twenty-seven laboratories – some of which, despite their lack of sophistication, were capable of producing over 40 kg. of heroin a week: Marseilles and Palermo have ironically now been undercut by the same transfer of skills to the Third World which has devastated Europe's steel, textile and shipbuilding industries. Iranian chemists who fled from the Ayatollah in 1979 took their expertise to the independent tribes of the North-West Frontier, where the main heroin bazaars in Landi Kotal and Bara link the Khyber Pass opium route from Afghanistan to the traders of Peshawar, Lahore and Karachi. Central government has never been able to enforce the laws in this area where, as on the Thai–Burmese border, the local tribes remain fiercely autonomous. The last US Attorney General, William French Smith, had to depart precipitously when he visited there to look at the drug situation. Smuggling runs in the blood of many of the local people, fortified by several generations' experience of playing outside powers off against each other: the Pakistan government is nervous at the prospect of the tribes switching allegiance to Moscow or Kabul if it tried to enforce an overly energetic stance towards drugs, especially since many Pathans as well as Afghan refugees rely on the heroin trade for foreign currency with which to buy modern weapons. Afghanistan has recently become the world's biggest single source of illicit opium, which is being grown in twelve of the country's provinces now under rebel control. Washington, although effectively underwriting Pakistan's economy, is forced to welcome these weapons (though not the resulting heroin) as a means of enabling the Afghan Mujahidin rebels to continue their resistance. The arms, however, in turn make the Pakistan central government even less able to exercise control over the border area. The crops of poppy grown in the rebel-controlled part of Helm and around Musa Qala result in a situation where few of the 3 million Afghan refugees have to rely on international aid, since they provide the cheap labour needed to harvest the opium and process the heroin. 'The war', a rebel commander recently asserted, 'has created its own economic and moral imperatives, since opium is crucial to survival'; and he also claimed that although 'Islamic law bans the taking of opium, there is no prohibition against growing it'. No opium poppy farmer, however, sees much of the huge profits from the trade: a local grower receives $350 for 10 kg. of opium, on which a Pakistani trader will make 100 per cent profit; the Middle Easterners who process it as morphine base then impose a further 700 per cent mark-up, before the Mafia buy it as 1 kg. of 90 per cent pure heroin for $40,000, in order to resell it for $280,000 to a New York distributor. This supplier then markets it to street-dealers in the USA, who dilute and retail it – leaving an average purity of perhaps 6 per cent – to consumers for a total price of some $2 million.

Even if Pakistan were ever able with the help of Western aid to eliminate opium farming within its own borders, this would not stop its heroin industry, since Afghanistan's annual 250 tons of opium supply all that is needed. In addition, corruption remains rife at several levels of Pakistan's administration, police, Customs and airport security; in 1986 ten opium growers in Gadoon-Amazai were killed when they protested that funds for crop-substitution had gone into the pockets of corrupt officials instead of to development projects. Several members of the Pakistan administration privately wash their hands of responsibility for trying to stop drugs, arguing that heroin is a Western problem, the result of atheistic decadence – notwithstanding the rapidly rising addiction in their own country. Several of the limited number of dealers who have been arrested in Pakistan (at the exasperated urging of the USA) have been leniently treated and soon released. Pakistani officials themselves admit that the country's opium production in 1986 will total well over 100 metric tons, compared with 40 tons in 1985. A dozen Western countries have sent their own agents to Karachi in an effort to stem the exports of contraband, only to find that the traffickers have now developed new trading routes through India (via Lahore and Amritsar to Delhi, and especially by night via Jaisalmer and the Rann of Kutch to Bombay).[18]

Another demonstration of how the drug trade defies international control, and also connects with arms-dealing, is to be seen in Lebanon. A senior officer at Interpol drily delivered the verdict: 'The ability of police authorities to arrest drug crime in Lebanon is non-existent.' Lebanon has now supplanted Pakistan as the traditional source of high-quality cannabis resin for much of Europe, because of the amounts being produced in the Bekaa Valley and Hermil Hills: the annual crop of 200 tons prior to the civil war was boosted with the help of mechanical sifters operated under armed protection to a total of nine times that amount in 1981.[19] (Opium also has been harvested there since 1977.) 'Before the war, only a tenth of the land grew hashish, and they planted corn around it to hide it,' said a local Lebanese resident. 'Now it is open and everywhere – even around the police station . . . It is not in the religion, but they said that it was all right because the hashish was going to our enemies.' Because the former export routes from Tyre and Sidon to Cyprus were interrupted by the fighting, the Syrians have organized routes northwards which they can exploit and control. Freighters openly load cargoes of both hashish and opium at the Lebanese ports of Ableh and El Minie, while Syrian military convoys and helicopters transport hashish, and now also refined heroin, from Baalbek to Damascus via the Rayaq air-base for distribution throughout Europe. Dealers who wish to send drug consignments to Jounieh must first make an advance payment to regional Syrian commanders; business is so profitable that Syrians have even persuaded farmers across the border, in the south of Turkey, to revive cultivation of the opium poppy. New heroin laboratories have been started in Aleppo, and Larnaca in Cyprus has also become an international trading centre for the drug trade. Not only is Lebanon's fractured national economy now principally underpinned by profits from the drugs, but the rival militia and terrorist groups there are also dependent on the trade as a source of funding for their supplies and weapons. Drugs have become an accepted international currency for the financing of unofficial arms-deals throughout the entire Middle East: Afghans trade heroin with Saudi Arabian arms-merchants; extreme right-wing groups from Italy and Spain bid against the Phalange, some Palestinian groups, the Turkish Grey Wolves, the Basque ETA and Tamil guerrillas to exchange drugs for weapons in Lebanon and Syria. An investigating Italian judge uncovered the existence of an extensive illegal arms ring in Milan which was using Syrian and Turkish intermediaries to supply weapons – including Leopard tanks and Cobra helicopters – to several Middle Eastern factions in exchange for bulk quantities of heroin and other drugs.[20] In 1985 sixty Tamils were arrested in Rome, Barcelona, Tunis and Paris, accused of smuggling and selling heroin to raise money for their secessionist guerrillas in Sri Lanka; during 1984 an extensive Tamil network was responsible for selling more than 1,500 kg. of heroin in Europe.[21] Some of the Kurdish separatists fighting on the borders of Turkey, Iraq and Iran are reputed to be similarly financed. Iranian opium continues to reach Europe through Turkey, being regularly transported across the mountainous border on horses and mules. The Turkish right-wing Grey Wolves terrorist movement raises funds through a network of several hundred *Gastarbeiter* Turks who help supply the heroin market in West Germany. The Turkish government has recently ended the state monopoly of opium, and allowed production to rise from 3,500 tons in 1985 to 15,000 tons in 1986. US agents frequently accuse Bulgaria of officially acting as a kind of merchant bank for the illicit drugs-for-arms trade, but Western narcotics experts at the UN deny the truth of this suspicion, and believe that most of such arms in fact originate from Czechoslovakia and Belgium. An experienced senior British official at the UN Narcotics Control HQ said that there was no evidence of any communist conspiracy involving drugs, and the Soviet Union and other East European countries were – aside from occasional individuals' corruption – more co-operative in international control than many other countries.

The Western hemisphere's heroin refining and traffic between the mid-1950s and 1970s had been principally organized from Marseilles – a port usefully equipoised between the Levant, Europe and the Atlantic. Here a major ring of professionals flourished, protected partly by political corruption (extending to several members of the Gaullist Service d'Action Civique and SDECE, the French secret intelligence service), and partly because of an official French attitude that heroin was a problem only for the USA – a stance that altered when quantities of the drug began to be sold in Paris, allegedly due to action taken by enraged American CIA agents. The 'French Connection' – founded on the close clan loyalties of a group of Corsicans – specialized in refining Turkish morphine base procured from Lebanese middlemen, using a raw acetic anhydride which they obtained from the famous *parfumeries* in the south of France.[22] The resulting heroin was, from motives of both political prudence and profitability, sold to North America rather than Europe – not only in New York but also through French Canadian allies in Montreal. As the trade's profits grew, however, it received a take-over offer which it was unable to refuse from the Mafia, who, through their uniquely wide network of contacts, set their sights on seizing control of the distribution market in America. Between 1970 and 1975 the skilled heroin chemists who had supplied Jean Jehan –

the French mastermind who was portrayed in the film *French Connection* – were transferred to continue their work in the Palermo area (where the largest heroin laboratory in Europe was set up at Trabia with a production capacity of 50 kg. a day). By the 1980s, more than 5 tons of pure heroin was being refined in Sicily each year. The modern Mafia, however, does not restrict itself to Sicily and Calabria: it has also established offshoot laboratories to meet the increasing demand for heroin on the Italian mainland. Some members of the former French Connection decamped to Uruguay and Bolivia; others as recently as 1985 tried to restart the trade from laboratories in Fribourg (Switzerland) as well as once more in Marseilles, but the attempts collapsed in killings from which the Mafia's fingerprints may not have been entirely absent.

The Mafia

In order to understand the part the Mafia plays in the organized drug-trafficking of the USA and Europe, it is first necessary to strip away the layers of myth. Today the Mafia[23] exercises a conspiratorial system of criminal power, but it likes to claim that its origins lie rooted in the historical oppression of the population of Sicily who – having been conquered and exploited in turn by the Phoenicians, Greeks, Carthaginians, Romans, Vandals, Byzantines, Arabs, Normans, Teutons, Angevins, Spaniards, Savoyards, Austrians and Bourbons – maintain a permanent suspicion towards all governments. In this situation, members of the Mafia have performed different extra-legal roles: originally as bandits with the popular appeal of a secret resistance movement; next, being co-opted by absentee feudal landlords to extract rents, resist tax-collectors, kill and kidnap labour leaders, and deliver election results;[24] most recently, as extortionate profiteers operating protection rackets and monopolies to control markets and drug-trafficking. Behind a façade of 'honour', their area of exploitation gradually spread from western Sicily to permeate other parts of Italy as well. Two other secret organizations, the Neapolitan-based Camorra and the 'Ndrangheta of Calabria, are similar though less powerful. The Mafia's character derives more from a certain attitude within its members than from any formal structure. Amoeba-like, it has always been formed from the cells of separate 'family' fraternities rather than stemming from a single hierarchy. Like the IRA, its morality is intrinsically conservative, combining without any apparent feeling of anomaly a censoriousness towards petty crime (as disturbing the order of things) with a psychopathic indifference to the brutality of its own activities; and an overall ethos which, besides embracing bare-knuckled capitalism, is sentimental, vain and male-oriented – no woman has ever played a role in the Mafia other than as a decoy, housekeeper, or sexual object. Until the Second World War, on the other hand, the 'Old Mafia' leaders had – at least in public – boycotted dealing in hard drugs; Frank Costello had ordered his New York members to stay out of the heroin traffic, because he considered that whereas many members of the public closed their eyes to gambling, prostitution or bootlegging, heroin might give La Cosa Nostra – as the Mafia calls itself in the USA – a bad name.[25] In fact, Capone – together with Costello's lieutenant Luciano, and Buchalter (the Head of Murder Incorporated) – was secretly involved in heroin trafficking in the USA, and when the outbreak of war closed heroin routes from overseas, Luciano from inside his US prison helped to organize new supplies of the drug from Mexico.

A watershed for the Mafia occurred in the 1940s when the USA released 'Lucky' Luciano from jail and helped him to return – like an infected bacillus – to his birthplace of Sicily.[26] Luciano, although the epitome of the traditional gangster, was modern: a stylish entrepreneur who cared nothing for the Mafia's pseudo-romantic tradition. He had first climbed to wealth through controlling 1,500 prostitutes in New York City, introducing many of his hookers to heroin so as to make them subserviently dependent on their only means of earning enough to support their habit. In 1936 he had been jailed for a term of between thirty and fifty years on sixty-two counts of forced prostitution. Re-established with the help of the US army in Sicily and Naples, before his enigmatic death in 1962 at Naples Airport, Luciano built up a multi-billion-dollar-a-year heroin export business in partnership with Meyer Lansky, using his own Cosa Nostra contacts who stretched from the USA to pre-revolutionary Cuba. The famous convention of sixty-one *mafiosi capi* held in November 1957 at Apalachin (in upstate New York) was summoned by Vito Genovese – the head of the New York family previously run by Luciano – in order to organize the demarcation of the expanding drug market throughout the whole of the USA. It was – and continues to be – the huge profits from heroin which enabled the 'New Mafia', with the tacit protection of political allies in the Christian Democratic party and some right-wing churchmen, to make a seemingly irresistible comeback in the face of every effort of the Anti-Mafia Commission, and which also provided it with ready accumulations of capital to finance property development together with other businesses throughout the USA as well as Italy. When some Mafia leaders were banished to other parts of Italy, they spread their operations, like cancer cells, to colonize these new areas. In the 1950s, open war broke out between the Old Mafia and the New for control of Palermo's fruit market, which the New Mafia wanted in order to send heroin to the USA in hollowed-out citrus fruit. In the shoot-out the Old Mafia's sawn-off shot-guns proved no match for the New's sub-machine-guns. Italian author-ities estimate that the Mafia's international drug trade by 1979 commanded a turnover of 800,000 billion lire – twice the gross national product of Italy itself. The courageous and honest new Prefect of Palermo, General Dalla Chiesa, who was dedicated to the eradiction of the Mafia, exposed its links with some of Sicily's most successful businessmen and property developers. However, shortly after he issued the warning: 'I am even more interested in the network that controls the Mafia, which may be in hands above suspicion and which, having placed itself in key positions, controls political power', he and his wife in September 1982 were shot to death in Palermo with a Kalashnikov.[27] His family subsequently publicly accused certain Christian Democrat leaders of manipulat-ing, as well as being manipulated by, *mafiosi*. Recently, among the leaders of the Mafia was discovered to be numbered a sociable Franciscan friar who was the head of a Palermo monastery.

Corroboration of the Mafia's links with Italy's establishment came in the 3,000-page statement Tomasso Buscetta made to the police in 1984, motivated by a wish to revenge himself on Mafia rivals who had killed his two sons, brother, son-in-law and three nephews together with eight of his other relatives. From Brazil, where he acted as the plenipotentiary of both the Palermitan and New York Mafia, Buscetta used to organize a narcotics syndicate which was equipped with 200 aircraft, and whose tentacles stretched from his birthplace of Palermo to chains of American pizza par-lours. The FBI believe, from the evidence given to them by Buscetta

329

and Valachi, that the Cosa Nostra now consists of twenty-five families, each of which controls the organized crime in a different major city (other than in New York which is carved up between five families); each family being ruled by a 'Godfather' boss (or *capo*), who from time to time sits on the overall national 'commission' or cabinet. The total core membership comprises some 4,000 sworn 'men of honour' or 'soldiers', who are supported by some ten times that number of other criminal auxiliaries.[28] The Mafia, besides also having a powerful family in Canada, controls banks and casinos throughout the Caribbean, and now possesses financial interests reaching from all parts of Italy to London and Germany. The key financial figure who channelled the Mafia's profits into legitimate investments was, prior to his recent sudden death in jail, the banker Michele Sindona. The largest family of the Cosa Nostra, which has now profitably expanded into the British drugs market, numbers some 250 full members and 550 associates. The Sicilian Mafia, which has a separate 'cupola' or supreme council, maintains its own representatives in the USA to liaise over the drug traffic. 'Today the Mafia is a non-tax-paying conglomerate as powerful as any of the world's major companies,' according to the investigator Martin Short. 'Organized crime acts like a multinational corporation in the way it develops markets, exploits consumer demand, shuts out competition and eliminates opposition.'[29] A 'Mafia premium' – normally 15 per cent – is levied in the costs of construction or other mob-controlled goods and services in several parts of the eastern USA and Italy. Although *mafiosi* like to think of themselves sentimentally as forming part of the mythical tradition of Sicilian nationalist resistance to Rome, in reality their network of secret mutual support operates more like a self-interested freemasonry.

The cocaine boom, however, is now altering the balance of power amongst the USA's organized criminal leaders in a radical way. Miami has supplanted New York as the New World's financial centre for trafficking; and the new narco-millionaires (sometimes known as the narcokleptocracy) tend no longer to be Italian-American, but Colombians, Chinese and Cubans, even more ruthlessly violent than the Cosa Nostra; while in the USA's prosperous west and south-west much of the heroin market has been taken over by Mexicans who are bringing supplies in over the border. By comparison, the 'Mob' appears old-fashioned, living too much off its past reputation and run by ageing men who often seem preoccupied by the ritual killing of one another. It certainly retains its hunger for respect and influence – and its vanity about publicity; but, as it has grown transnational, the old close-knit Sicilian family ties have frayed and unravelled. The Mafia today is forced to do its drug business with Asian and Latin American dealers whom it does not trust and is unable to control. The number of *penitenti* informers has risen as *mafiosi* have had to expand outside their own trusted *cosca*. The Church authorities in Italy have finally broken their long silence against the Mafia; electronic surveillance has penetrated its vows of secrecy; arrests in the USA have multiplied as its former political patronage has waned – and have been accompanied by some unprecedented 'singing'.

The response of the 'New New' Mafia, the most intelligent *mafiosi*, has been to adapt by diversifying into white collar crime; it is investing its heroin profits in legitimate businesses, having been taught by Meyer Lansky – who himself bought a Geneva bank – the art of sanitizing funds by laundering through offshore havens. (As Brecht's Macheath asked in *The Threepenny Opera*, 'What is robbing a bank compared to founding one?') The 'honoured society's' investments now range from pizza chains in New Jersey together with ski-resorts and olive farms in Italy to a casino and restaurant in London and *haciendas* in Brazil. (The 1-billion lire ransom the Mafia received in 1973 for the release of Paul Getty was used to establish a successful enterprise in Calabria.) In New York, the *capi* cabinet has, in the best tradition of business, allocated the spheres of spoil so that families do not compete with each other. One Cosa Nostra family has concentrated on the docks and waste disposal; a second family on food – including pizza parlours – and entertainment as well as loan-sharking and gambling in Las Vegas; a third, (appropriately) cement and funeral parlours, besides liquor shops, car dealerships, estate agencies and vending franchises; while a fourth specializes in restaurants in addition to pornographic films and magazines, leaving the fifth family with the lucrative construction and garment industries. Mafia-backed enterprises flourish because they scarcely need to compete or advertise (threats or dynamite scare off rivals), while they are also able to intimidate their employees into accepting low wages and eschewing trade unions. In Naples the 'New Organized Camorra' alone has the temerity to vie with the 'New Family' for cocaine profits; while Palermo's Mafia, now controlled by the Corleone family, has in recent years killed – staging its assassinations, like the Red Brigades, for maximum public effect – those who investigate and threaten its business, including judges and the President of the Regional Government himself, besides deputies, a general, journalists and police chiefs.[30] The state has ceded that 'monopoly of violence' which Max Weber describes as its distinguishing safeguard. Some of the bodies of the victims of Mafia executions are – literally – liquidated in tubs of acid; one investigating journalist was entombed in the concrete strut of a motorway bridge, and another fed to pigs. The Mafia's power extends inside prisons, where those thought likely to confess are eliminated, often by poison. (It is ironic that the only Italian who comprehensively defeated the Sicilian Mafia was Mussolini, whose draconian Prefect, Mori, during the 1920s dispensed with jury-trials – as well as ordering that walls on the island should be reduced to no more than a metre's height to prevent ambushes, and that only small short knives would be allowed for any purpose. As a result many Mafia *capi* migrated to the USA, and it was not until the Americans allowed Luciano and other Mafia hoodlums to return to Sicily that the newly 'honoured society' retained its former hegemony: the USA has had cause to rue several times over its short-sighted decision to co-opt the Mafia in the struggle against the Italian communists which allowed it to infiltrate positions of power in post-war Italy.)[31] The Mafia – like other criminal organizations involved in drugs, such as the Japanese Yakuza – constitutes an alternative society, within but opposed to the wider community, and is armed with its own rules and justice: those citizens whom it controls pay protection money as its tax, giving it rather than the nation their allegiance.

The Golden Triangle

Apart from the Golden Crescent, the other major source of opium is the 'Golden Triangle' of south-east Asia, lying between north-eastern Burma, northern Thailand and Laos. The area produces up to 60 tons of heroin annually, of which, after the increasing local demand has been met, about 20 tons each year are sent to North America, Hong Kong, Australia and Europe. (The fact that the USA's total annual consumption at present is 5 tons shows the scope of new markets.) The Triangle's opium crops are grown in virtually unpoliced mountainous border areas that extend for 125,000 square miles.[32] Burma produces 500 metric tons of illegal opium a year: some of which is grown in districts controlled by remnants of Chinese Nationalist (formerly Chiang Kai-Shek) Kuomintang forces; some is grown by Burmese Communist Party army units, in order to finance their armed struggle; but the principal growers are Sua and Shan guerrilla separatist groups. The Shan leader – possibly the world's biggest known drug-dealer – is the 60-year-old warlord Chang Chi-fu (better known as Khun Sa), whose headquarters at Ban Hin Taek has its own hospital and swimming pools, and whose ten heroin refineries on the Thai-Lao border are guarded by an army of 4,500 men. He himself straddles the different heroin-producing groups, his father being a Kuomintang colonel and his mother a Shan, while he also maintains good relations with the Lao and Burmese communists – although his eight children have been educated in the USA and Britain. Another 90 metric tons of illicit opium are produced in each of Laos and Thailand (where it is grown by the Hmong, Lahu, Lisu, Yao and Akha hill-tribes, centred round Chiang Mai).

The genesis of the growth in this area's traffic is an irony for the US government as bitter as the results of its part in the Mafia's resurgence. Earlier, the French when they ruled Indo-China had resisted international pressure against opium trading, selling monopoly franchises to pay for their colonies of Vietnam, Laos and Cambodia, and encouraging the Meo in Laos to expand opium production from 7.5 tons in 1940 to more than 60 tons in 1944. Pre-revolutionary Laos was one of the few countries in the world to have no law against opium. By the late 1950s the Golden Triangle was growing half the world's illicit supplies: a total of 700 tons of raw opium.[33] During the First Indo-China War of 1946 to 1954, French intelligence had used the opium trade to persuade the Meo hill-tribes to take their side as mercenaries against the Viet Minh and Pathet Lao, and had flown their opium in French Air Force planes to Saigon, where it was sold to Corsican underworld dealers. During the Second Indo-China War the CIA employed the same tactics, and in addition the CIA-backed Chinese Nationalist Kuomintang Army increased the Burmese hill-tribes' opium production ten-fold – from 40 to 400 tons per annum by 1962. The opium from the Shan and Kachin states was loaded from mule caravans on to unmarked CIA Air America and Sea Supply Corporation aircraft, whence it was flown to be refined and exported from Bangkok and Hong Kong.[34]

From 1969 onwards, to the Golden Triangle's expanding opium production was added the threat from the area's new heroin processing laboratories, which amongst the American GIs in Vietnam generated an increase in heroin addiction from 7 per cent in 1970 to double that the following year. This contagion not only seriously sapped their fighting capacity (the nightmare that continues to haunt the commanders of both the Soviet forces in Afghanistan and the US forces in Germany today), but also – although most of the conscripts were to recover from their addiction on demobilization – broke the American middle-class's previous taboo against heroin, and also persuaded some of them of the easy profits to be made from drug-dealing. Predictably, at first the finger of blame was pointed at the Vietcong, but this alibi was rebutted by the US army's own Provost Marshal in an embarrassingly frank report that accused senior members of the South Vietnamese police, army and government of protecting and promoting the heroin traffic for personal profit.[35] The Mafia and Corsican syndicates successfully established links with corrupt officials in Saigon (some of whom exculpated themselves by averring 'anyone who uses heroin deserves all he gets') in order to organize the export of surplus heroin to Miami, Los Angeles and Canada via Hong Kong, Tokyo and Paraguay. Heroin used to be flown to the USA from Vietnam even in the coffins of dead servicemen. By 1971, Washington experts estimated that 71 per cent of illicit opium was originating from south-east Asia (compared with 4 per cent from Turkey and 22 per cent from south-west Asia), yet the Nixon Administration still continued to blame the French Connection rather than its own corrupt allies and mercenaries in south-east Asia.[36] Four years later, the rebel Shan leaders sent Washington an offer[37] to destroy their opium poppy crop in return for $12 million, but – after hesitating – the Administration declined to pay such Danegeld for fear of alienating the Burmese government against whom the Shan were fighting. Discord persists even today between the CIA and the US Drug Enforcement Administration concerning certain operations in south-east Asia. However, since the end of the Vietnam War a series of droughts in the area – in addition to armed rivalry between the Shan United Army, Burmese Communists and KMT

(Kuomintang) soldiers – has caused opium production from the Crescent to overtake that of the Triangle.

Only when a political settlement is achieved so that law can be established in the no man's land of the Burmese border areas, and when the Kuomintang army is removed (perhaps to Taiwan), will there be a chance of bringing the Triangle's traffic under control. Meanwhile surplus Asian production has resulted in the wholesale price of heroin in Hong Kong – to where many Chinese underworld drug-dealers moved after the revolution – plummeting from HK $46,000 in 1979 to HK$ 28,700 in 1984. A sophisticated financial system (devised in Hong Kong by a Chinese immigrant) is used to launder several million dollars of drug profits a week through a network of gold and currency dealers linked by telexed trading operations. The criminal involvement of the Chinese Triad syndicates there makes an interesting contrast to the gangs' original aims, when they formed a brotherhood to help the grievances of the poor against their Manchu rulers.

The Latin American sources

The country producing illegal heroin which has had least attention – and the only one also to export significant amounts of cocaine and marijuana – is Mexico. Some 10,000 tons of marijuana (carrying a street value of US $10 billion) were found in November 1984, in Chihuahua on the Mexican-Texan border: this single seizure – the largest anywhere to date – embarrassingly exceeded by a factor of seven the DEA's official figure for Mexico's total production. Experts now estimate that Mexico's marijuana crop is in fact double that of the country hitherto regarded as the world's largest producer, Colombia.

The US government has consistently chosen to underestimate the growth of Mexico's drug trade, partly for political reasons, partly from a wish to believe that the country's Washington-financed policy of spraying drug crops had succeeded.[38] However, some Mexican eradication workers whose costs were being paid by the Americans only sprayed the drug crops with water; and other local farmers quickly learnt how to scrape any poppies sprayed by paraquat-based herbicides so as to collect the opium gum before the plants died. Drug production has recently expanded from the areas of Sinaloa and Chihuahua to Hidalgo, Guerrero, Sonora, Nuevo Leon, Madera, Veracruz and Baja California, and farmers in Sinatoa and Sonora are now themselves processing black tar heroin from their crops. It is indicative that the price of Mexico's characteristic brown and black heroin has fallen in recent years at the same time as its purity has improved; the DEA estimate that 38 per cent of the heroin and 32 per cent of the marijuana consumed in the USA is now produced in Mexico, and also that one-third of America's cocaine is arriving via there. The cheap and potent black heroin produced by Mexico is currently popular in the USA, being difficult for dealers to dilute because it is almost solid; its 70 to 90 per cent purity (compared to the 5 per cent of traditional heroin in the USA) renders it correspondingly dangerous. Mexican opium growers receive a better price than most of those elsewhere in the world, because of the nearness of the US border – although, as happens everywhere else, it is not the peasant farmers but the organizers and corrupt officials who reap the lion's share of the profits. On the remote Chihuahua plantation on the road to El Paso where the record 1984 seizure of marijuana was made, five concentration camps were also discovered where 6,500 slaves – impoverished peasants, some as young as thirteen – were being forced by armed guards to work without pay: treated as serfs, they were compelled to pick and process the marijuana from 4 in the morning to 10 at night, and any captives trying to escape were killed.[39] On average, fifteen 30-ton trucks laden with consignments of marijuana were leaving the plantation for export to the north every day, and experts deduced from the healthy size of the plants that the farm – only forty miles from the state capital – had been in operation for at least two years. The eventual raid took place as a result of US, not Mexican, intelligence; none of the principal organizers was arrested – although among the armed men guarding the plantation were found to be three employees of the state Security Office.

In February 1985 the US DEA expert Enrique Camarena Salazar was kidnapped outside the US Consulate in Guadalajara by Mexican drug-traffickers, and subsequently tortured slowly to death together with the pilot of his aircraft. Among the main suspects for the murder are several former Mexican federal police agents; a tape-recording identified a senior official in the federal Judicial Police as the man supervising the torture. A state judge, however, mysteriously ordered the destruction of the evidence connected with the murders. An angry US State Department threatened to warn tourists not to go to Mexico by telling American travellers that it might no longer be safe – to which a Mexican federal judge responded by issuing an injunction which protected twelve suspected drug-traffickers from being arrested. Heroin millionaires live in impunity protected by armed guards in fortified mansions in the hills around the Mexican border town of Tijuana; one of the country's two main 'Godfathers' is estimated to have made more than \$3,000 million from drugs, and also to have 800 policemen on his payroll. In Mexico many policemen earn less than \$400 a month, and a disturbing number of traffickers carry police credentials. Over a period of eight years, the Mexican police failed to arrest a single major drug-dealer. Francis Mullen (head of the DEA until 1985) stated that Mexican law enforcement officials attempted to thwart his investigations; the shrugged explanation they give is that the real source of the problem – drug abuse – is situated to the north, not the south, of the easily-penetrated 1,800-mile border. As a result of American pressure, several hundred members of Mexico's two principal national police forces (the federal Security Directorate and the federal Judicial Police) in 1985 were dismissed or resigned; however, in September of the same year US customs and DEA officials again complained to President Reagan that Mexican federal policemen were still providing armed protection for traffickers taking consignments of heroin, cocaine and marijuana across the border into Texas.[40] An endless army of impoverished backpackers are ready to transport drugs across the Rio Grande from La Isla to Fabens. Deposits in local banks of the Lower Rio Grande Valley, one of the poorest areas of the nation, rose by \$720 million in a mere twelve months of 1984. To compound the difficulties, the 1985 earthquake flattened the headquarters of Mexico's Prosecutor General, destroying the country's main criminal files, including those of most of the drug-racketeers. However, that did not save a Mexican police commander and twenty-one of his men from being tied up and massacred in cold blood by marijuana traffickers in November 1985 at Veracruz. The following year a further seventeen police officers were castrated and had their tongues and eyes pulled out by drug-dealers before being killed. Mullen confirms: 'The traffickers are virtually untouchable in many areas. I think it's out of control.' Some Mexicans today believe that the threat to the country's political stability from the drug-traffic is now as great as in Bolivia and Colombia.

In Bolivia, the authorities failed to destroy the coca trade until the USA intervened. The extensive cocaine enterprises there have been protected not only by officers of the so-called 'anti-drug squad', but for many years also by paramilitary Nazi mercenaries. Until recently organized by the former Gestapo leader Klaus Barbie and calling themselves 'The Fiancés of Death', these men fly the coca paste under armed escort to Colombia, and launch attacks on any lesser smugglers who try to compete. The richest plantations are centred round Santa Cruz and Chaparé in Cochabamba province, and as much as 90 per cent of the country's production of 160,000 metric tons of coca are now exported. The reputed *Numero Uno* among Bolivia's cocaine millionaires, Roberto Suarez Sen., maintained in power by means of his wealth a sympathetic military government. In a country whose inhabitants are the poorest in America, Suarez has his own fleet of aircraft and exercises more authority in La Paz than most of the nation's presidents; drug analysts in Washington estimate that he is personally responsible for 25 of the 45 tons of cocaine that enter the USA each year, the profits from which provide him with an annual income of at least $600,000,000 – believed to be banked mainly in numbered accounts in Switzerland.[41] By contrast, the impoverished Bolivian government possesses only three helicopters suitable for surveillance. President Paz Estenssoro recently warned that the profits of the cocaine traffickers are so vast they are capable of buying elections and are a threat to democracy itself. Interpol estimates that, of the 180 metric tons of finished cocaine now being produced annually, the North American authorities are managing to seize barely 10 metric tons – and the whole of Europe less than 1 ton. Many Latin Americans, however, take pride in the cocaine trade's success: as one Bolivian explained, 'It's not just about money, it's also about pride. We were the slaves of the Spanish for centuries; and then slaves of Western money. Now, for the first time since the Incas, we have power.'

The fulcrum of the cocaine trade is Colombia, where some three-fifths of South America's cocaine exports are refined, and the police – as in Bolivia – too often seem either disinclined or unable to touch the huge traffickers. They contrive to arrest for the most part only small freelance peasant farmers who venture to compete with the major barons. The immensely wealthy and well-armed 'narcomillionaires' operate a cartel, organized in twelve 'families' and maintaining a permanent tap on the telephone communications between the US Embassy and the Ministry of Justice in Bogota. Mafia-style, they publicly killed the Minister of Justice who denounced them, and in December 1984 their threats caused the US ambassador and 2,000 other Americans hurriedly to depart the country. In a unique reversal of the usual situation, black market dollars in Colombia are worth less than official ones, because so much money is made illegally. Although many banks have made huge profits from the drug trade, one well-known Bogota bank recently collapsed when a single *narcotraficante* withdrew his deposits. The $4 billion annual narco-profits are not only Colombia's biggest source of income, but have bought allies among the armed forces and in politics ranging from right-wing extremists to leftist guerrillas – as well as enabling the traffickers to purchase huge amounts of real estate in Florida and Panama City. The last Justice Minister, Enrique Parejo Gonzales, reported: 'There is hardly an area of political activity or institutional life that in some way has not been affected by drug corruption.' Each year more than 40 tons of cocaine are channelled through Medellín to the USA; many parts of Colombia, where M-19 and FARC guerrillas protect coca and marijuana plantations, are beyond government control. The nineteen well-equipped illegal laboratories found with their airstrip at Tranquilandia (only 400 miles south-east of Bogota) had a capacity of processing some 300 tons of cocaine a year – and thus of more than doubling the world's supply.

Washington has responded to this state of affairs by deploying a record total of sixteen anti-narcotics agents in Colombia – but against them the personal army of one of the principal cocaine tycoons alone numbers more than 2,000 men and is backed by his own fortune of $2.25 billion.[42] Several of the narco-millionaires have political ambitions. They have managed to acquire gratitude and backing from the local people by donating schools and swimming pools to the community as well as buying sports teams and journalists. One leading figure, who has launched his own political party and newspaper, declared on television: 'Cocaine and marijuana have become an arm of struggle against American imperialism. We have the same responsibility in this – he who takes up a rifle, he who plants coca, he who goes to the public plaza and denounces imperialism.'

The 1984 assassination of the young Justice Minister Lara Bonilla, who identified the connections between rich Bogota politicians and the drug trade, was stated in court to have been planned at a house of Lara's own brother-in-law, where a plenary session of the traffickers' cartel had donated 50 million pesos (about £380,000) to pay for the Minister's contract killing. The murder had the effect of arousing the former President, Belisario Betancur, to furious and hitherto unprecedented action: for the first time he agreed to allow a number of suspected drug-traffickers to be extradited to the USA, thereby breaking a long nationalist tradition. In return for badly needed US economic assistance, the Bogota government also banned the sale of acetone, ether and hydrochloric acid – the chemicals used to process cocaine from coca base. However, replacements for these were quickly supplied in Panama and in the USA itself: the 1984 discovery at Miami International Airport of 2,700 lb. of base led to the realization that there are now a number of cocaine-refining laboratories in south Florida.[43] One well organized syndicate has also lately begun exporting coca paste to Europe, where the necessary chemicals are readily available and processing laboratories now also operate.

Besides Bolivia, the countries which are supplying Colombia with coca in bulk for processing into cocaine are Peru, Ecuador and – increasingly – Brazil. Peru's production today almost equals that of Bolivia: the land round Tingo Maria can produce six harvests a year – the most fertile area for cocaine that has yet been discovered. On the Andean slopes of eastern Peru the Maoist *Sendero Luminoso* ('Shining Path') guerrillas have cemented a partnership with coca producers based on anti-Yanqui mutual self-interest, exploiting a situation where trafficking established itself under the former government due to the corrupt rivalry of police and politicians. Despite Peru's new President, Alan García's, commitment to reform, the raw material is still being flown out from 250 clandestine airstrips in the hinterland (some of them disguised with collapsible huts to make them resemble villages); cocaine processing has now spread to Lima itself, to meet the rising demand of young addicts there. The expansion of the drug trade – although ostensibly bringing dividends to the backward economies of Latin America – has sucked increasing numbers of people into corruption and violence. The Indian peasants, lacking political or economic power, inevitably bear the brunt, especially in the Amazon basin valleys of Peru and Brazil which provide an unpoliceable open gateway to supply the Colombian drug syndicates' laboratories. The basic dilemma is that, for many Latin American peasants, coca is at present their only livelihood. 'How can you tell some starving farmer in Peru that he has to give up the money he makes from growing coca,' asks one US diplomat, 'when back home the drug culture is glorified by glittering head-shops on Hollywood Boulevard?'[44] Peruvian towns such as Uchiza and Tocache on the River Huallaga – surrounded by 150,000 fertile hectares planted with coca – are virtually under *narco* control.[45] Drug syndicates offer local coca farmers credit and fertilizers, although the ultimate controller of the Peruvian cocaine trade is a man leading a closely protected existence in Miami. The traffickers' opponents suffer from low morale as well as fear of assassination: 'To be assigned to the State Department's Narcotic Assistance Unit is like getting leprosy,' another American diplomat reflected bitterly. 'You don't quickly get to be ambassador through the NAU.' Enrique Elias Laroza, a former Minister of Justice in Peru, said many people are asking 'how a poor country can win the fight against narcotics trafficking when much more powerful rich countries have failed'; and in 1986 a Mexican diplomat complained, 'It is deeply unfair and even ridiculous for certain officers of a country like the USA, who have been unable to solve their own internal drug-trafficking problem despite almost unlimited resources, to ask a poor country like Mexico to solve not only its own problem but the USA's problem as well.'

As in Peru, the expanding indigenous market for cocaine in Brazil has led to domestic processing in addition to the export of coca base. Whereas traditionally coca has always been grown at certain altitudes on open mountain slopes, an adaptable strain of the plant known as *epadu* is now being successfully cultivated in the lowlands of the Amazon basin, where plantations are easily hidden amongst the rain forest. Laboratories have been discovered near Manaus. An increasing number of Amazonian Indians have, like those in the Andes, lately come to regard coca as a cash crop. A group of Xingu Indians are reported to have been persuaded by one particular criminal syndicate to start growing harvests of coca, although in other cases Indians have been unfairly blamed as scapegoats by corrupt officials and police officers. Many Brazilians, like other South Americans, remain ambivalent about drug control laws –

certainly as regards coca and marijuana. Brazil has attracted more than its share of foreign drug-dealers because under that country's law they are liable only to expulsion, not imprisonment, if they are caught. Escadinha, a young Brazilian cocaine and marijuana millionaire who relishes his Robin Hood reputation among the slum dwellers of Rio, found no difficulty in escaping together with his wife by helicopter from Brazil's top-security island prison of Ilha Grande on New Year's Eve 1985. The previous year the US DEA had discovered that ether, acetone and hydrochloric acid – in such substantial quantities that they could only be intended for manufacturing cocaine – were being purchased in Europe by a Paraguayan general for importation to Paraguay. It was high officials in Stroessner's Paraguay who earlier had sheltered Auguste Joseph Ricord, *El commandante* of the Latin American–French Connection, who organized a ring to send heroin to the USA (with £650,000 of Gestapo funds he had taken from France to Argentina) and whose contribution to human suffering Judge Cannella of New York termed 'equal to the recent figures for the Vietnam War casualties'.

An increasing circle of other Latin American and Caribbean countries also have key roles in the drug business, primarily in trans-shipment or financial dealings. With their help, long-range aircraft take processed cocaine and marijuana from Colombia and Mexico not only to Florida and Texas in the USA, but to Louisiana, Tennessee, Mississippi, Georgia, the Carolinas and California as well – generally avoiding detection by flying in low under the radar screen. US Customs officers believe at least 7,500 smuggling flights a year penetrate the southern border of the USA, being carried out by more than 1,000 aircraft – 'Removing a handful of aircraft isn't going to deter anyone.' In the 1980s, cocaine consignments have been discovered on aircraft belonging to Colombia's own national airline Avianca on more than thirty-four occasions; and an airbus operated by Jamaica's national airline was impounded at Miami in 1985 when 3 tons of ganja were found on board. The smaller Piper Cubs, Aztecs and Cessnas, which when loaded cannot reach North America non-stop, are refuelled at private airstrips in Mexico and on the Turks and Caicos and Bahamas cays, from where Cigarette boats – capable of speeds much faster than coastguard cutters – also deliver shipments to Key West and Miami. At stopovers in the Caribbean, trafficking syndicates switch the 'mules' carrying their drugs on commercial flights, so that US Customs officials will not identify them as originating from South America. Drug wealth is increasingly involved in the politics of the area. A recent plot to assassinate the Honduran President was financed by a massive cocaine deal. Washington has accused – besides the Duvaliers when they ruled Haiti – some Cuban and Nicaraguan officials of playing a part in trans-shipment; at the same time there is clear evidence that CIA-backed Contra guerrillas fighting the Nicaraguan government have been helping cocaine traffickers.

The Bahamas has over seventy airfields – the majority of them unpoliced – spread over its 661 cays and twenty-nine islands which lie scattered across 3,000 square miles of the Atlantic. Grumman Mallard sea-planes from Cartagena and Santa Marta in Colombia ferry drugs via the largely deserted Andros Island to small airstrips in Dade County, often making three round trips from the Bahamas within twenty-four hours.[46] One favourite technique is for a dozen Piper Cubs, amongst which perhaps only three carry drugs, to take off together and scatter on different routes so as to confuse radar or pursuing aircraft. The wreckage of over a dozen DC-3 and DC-6 planes in the sand and shallow water around South Bimini testify to the carelessness of night-time smugglers – some of them over-confident from cocaine; for their employers, however, the cost of aircraft is scarcely an important consideration. In the summer of 1986, at least six more drug planes (one flown by the son of a Bahamian MP) crashed in the islands. Robert Vesco, the fugitive American financier, had a headquarters on a Bahamian cay, complete with large hangars and a 6,000-ft. private airstrip.[47] A key Colombian too recently maintained a formidable armed base on his own island called Norman's Cay; and a businessman from Georgia has recently been arrested on a charge of heading a drug ring which had purchased five Caribbean islands for use as staging-posts for smuggling. At the UN International Narcotics Control Board meeting in 1984, the Bahamian delegation conspicuously spoke out against any proposal to investigate offshore financial systems established by drug-traffickers. However, following the findings of a Bahamian commission of inquiry into drug corruption the same year, a number of government ministers (including the deputy Prime Minister and Finance Minister) resigned or were dismissed. The next year, Norman Saunders, the Chief Minister of the neighbouring Turks and Caicos Islands, was arrested and convicted in

Florida together with another Cabinet minister on charges of accepting huge bribes (in fact offered by the DEA) to permit traffickers to use his country for the trans-shipment of drugs from Latin America to the USA; in March 1986 a military leader of Surinam was arrested in Miami on charges of offering to sell safe passage through the former Dutch colony to cocaine smugglers for $1 million a shipment.

More than three-quarters of all the illegal cocaine and marijuana brought into the USA still enters through south Florida – making drug-smuggling that state's biggest business. One shipment alone impounded at Miami Airport in 1982 comprised 3,906 lb. of cocaine, grossing a market value of $1,300,000,000 (£742,000,000): but even a seizure of this size failed to affect street prices. The narco-dollars – estimated at between 7 and 10 billion annually – awash in the area offer too much temptation for several men in the police force, which has doubled in size since 1980. A number of officers are unable to resist the chance of gaining in a few minutes a sum which will exceed by several times their life earnings: several members of Miami's finest, organizing themselves into a gang known as 'The Enterprise', regularly hijacked shipments of cocaine which they then proceeded to transport in their police cars and sell. At the end of 1985, three police officers were charged with triple murder, carried out whilst they were allegedly stealing from some smugglers 350 kg. (or 'keys' as they are known in Florida) of cocaine. Shortly before that, two other officers who had previously received commendations for making the largest cocaine seizure in Miami's history, were charged with retaining 150 lb. of it (worth almost $2 million) for themselves. As a result, confidence in the whole police system has been undermined: witnesses to police corruption – as in Mexico and Colombia – are frightened to speak out because they fear lest the investigating officers may be in league with their criminal brethren. As a result of the number of threats which have been directed against it, the DEA's Miami office now has no identifying sign outside; in the street a van is parked, with armed guards inside watching from behind darkened windows, permanently blocking the building's front entrance to deter car-bomb attacks. In 1985 the agency received warnings that Colombian traffickers had offered a price of $350,000 for the lives of its top officers. Several of the organized crime syndicates in Miami have been able to rely upon a degree of official indulgence, because they lead a double existence as anti-Castro guerrilla groups. The Florida banking system nets an annual surplus of some 7 billion dollars – more than double the surplus of the other forty-nine states of the USA combined. In 1981 banks in Florida failed to report $3.2 billion in cash deposits: absent-mindedness on this scale, the US Customs Commissioner charged, must point to direct collusion by many banks themselves in the drug-traffic. Some of them offer a service of wiring drug profits to a select list of offshore banks, in conjunction with providing letters of credit to purchase legitimate businesses; due to the extraordinary boom, a number of Florida banks are now charging negative interest on deposits. One Dade County police-man said, 'Florida crooks don't rob banks, they buy them'; in the words of a Florida senator, his state is now addicted to drug money.

In 1986, the police discovered there was the sum of $5,836,000 (£4.05 million) in cash in one small unguarded Long Island house where heroin was being cut. But money – like drugs – can be refined. The longer a trafficker stays in the chain to supply the consumer, the greater the risk and consequently the higher his profit will be. (On landing, one Quaalude fetches 70 cents, while its street price is $3.50; and 1 kg. of cocaine, whose price on landing is $60,000, can after dilution be sold to users for $640,000.) The top organizers, who remain immune by never going near drugs them-selves, have now modernized their financial methods – compared with earlier days, when the Mob's couriers used to fly to the Bahamas and Caymans, staggering under suitcases crammed with 'hot' dollar bills to be deposited in discreet banks on the islands for transfer to numbered Swiss accounts. (Such anonymous numbered accounts were originally introduced fifty years ago, partly to help German Jews to put their fortunes beyond the reach of Hitler.) The UK's ending of exchange controls in 1979 made the task of tracing fugitive capital much harder. Drug money now is 'cleaned' through a maze of tentacular transactions, which stretch from offshore banks in tax-havens situated outside government regulation and exchange controls, to reappear in respectable trusts which purchase real-estate in the Hamptons, Tokyo, Gstaad or London. In 1985 the First National Bank of Boston was fined $500,000 for failing to report $1.22 billion in cash transactions (some of which were of the 'paper bag' variety); since June of that year, ten more banks have been fined amounts of up to $2.5 million. The US government for a long time hesitated before intruding on the sacred territory of private enterprise's secrets: there is a certain irony in the fact that it is just those countries which are the champions of the unfettered market place who in this field are having to take the lead in government intervention. When the US Internal Revenue Service eventually instituted a special audit of all Miami financial transactions larger than $10,000, the traffickers hired college students and old-age pensioners to carry cocaine money to banks elsewhere in the country, where it was changed into cheques with a value of slightly under $10,000. The so-called 'Grandma Mafia' in California successfully laundered over $25 million of such cocaine profits. In Colombia many banks thoughtfully offer the facility of a *ventanilla sinistra* (side window) where no questions are asked about deposits in any currency. As fast as the US government brings pressure on one Caribbean haven such as the Caymans, a dozen others solve their budgetary problems by encouraging 'brass-plate' private banks to dangle the bait of guaranteeing confidentiality to attract depositors. International banking now provides more than a quarter of the Bahamas' GNP; Panama is at present attractive because of the anonymity it offers company owners, while the Netherlands' Antilles are popular with tax-evaders of all kinds as well as traffickers. The police are currently trying to unravel drug-money laundering operations stretching from the Virgin Islands to the Channel Islands and the Isle of Man. In Europe, the small west Sicilian town of Trapani (with a population of less than 72,000) boasts more banks than Italy's financial capital, Milan. Sicily's regional status has served to shield its banks and financial institutions from the scrutiny and surveillance of the authorities in Rome.[48] The Italian police estimate that more than 30,000 of the inhabitants of Palermo live in one way or another off the heroin trade, and that 'at least a quarter of the money spent in this city cannot be accounted for because it is criminal'.

Enforcement officials have become convinced that the best – if not the only – hope of trying to staunch drug-trafficking lies in concentrating on tracing and seizing the financial profits of the main organizers. International agreement, world-wide and enforceable, that would ensure this is long overdue.

15

Hope in Hell:
The Lessons and the Future

'With pleasure drugged, he almost longed for woe.'

Byron

'Reality is for those who cannot handle drugs.'
Graffito on Seurat's grave in Père Lachaise cemetery, Paris

'The question is not how to get cured, the question is how to
live.'

Joseph Conrad

What, overall then, should we do? The first essential is to remove
hysteria from public attitudes about drug abuse, and also to break
out of the present pessimism which surrounds the problem ('Have
you ever tried to hold mercury in your fist? That's what it's like
trying to deal with drugs,' said one government expert.) Similar to
some medieval plague, illicit drugs have been stigmatized as retribution for immorality, materialism or the loss of religion. To demonize
addicts is easier than to shed stereotypes and tackle the underlying
issues; for that will require real political courage, backed by communal help and support.

Too often past policies have instead been the product, and the
handmaid, of emotions. It is hard to surrender addiction to myths,
because these provide us with scapegoats: as long as we have heroin
to blame for the world's evil, we feel we can postpone action about
more difficult issues of which drug misuse is only a symptom.

347

Kenneth Leech has said that the public's response to drug abuse is comparable to the life of an ostrich: first burying its head in sand, then a panicky flapping of wings, and finally the laying of an egg. The starting point must be to demystify the whole subject; as Michael Davies suggests, 'We've got to educate parents, who often know less about heroin than their children. A few parents are familiar with cannabis because they used to use it themselves, but then they may be under the illusion their children are showing a similar independence by using heroin.'[1] Bearing in mind that the key to any solution lies not in the drugs themselves but in people's attitudes towards them, we should remember that drug dependency expresses only one facet of a whole range of human behaviour. Mankind's nature is likely to have similar problems – with only the actual drugs changing – permanently, which makes it all the more important that our policy in response should be coolly and clearly thought out. The beginning of wisdom must be that there is no easy answer, no magical exorcism. It is the classic area for remembering Mencken's warning: 'There is a solution to every problem: quick, simple and wrong.' For more than two decades US presidents have been declaring 'wars on drugs', but simplistic remedies only lead to disillusionment and defeat.

Of the three main strategic options for trying to sever the global connection – first, where drugs are grown; second, at the point of entry into each country; and third, by reducing the consumer demand – enough may have been seen in the last chapters of the limitations of attempting to stop supplies and entry. Drug crop eradication efforts have foundered because they have been under-financed and failed to implement crop substitution as part of a coherent development strategy. As one expert in the Home Office said, 'If the demand exists, even if we nuked both the Golden Triangle and Crescent, drugs would only be grown in dozens of other places. And even if we had Customs officers shoulder to shoulder round the beaches of Britain, supplies would still be dropped by aircraft.'[2] The overall problem is not a supply-side equation, as the USA has for so long believed. *The Economist* recently pointed out: 'The gap between an evening getting stoned on cannabis for £4 and mildly drunk on beer for £8 is widening, which should worry holders of brewery shares. The gap between the price of beer and that of heroin has narrowed fast in recent months, which should worry everyone.'[3] Certainly to date, it appears impossible to prevent supplies increasing, let alone to tourniquet them. As President Carter's adviser Dr Peter Bourne concludes:

> All of the basic hypotheses on which the old strategy was based are wrong . . . The fundamental fallacy has been the assumption that opium would only be grown in those places where it has traditionally been cultivated, and that by controlling it in these areas we could control the world heroin supply. It is now clear that opium has only been grown in a tiny fraction of the places in the world where it could be grown, and that as long as there is a market in the world and immense profits to be made, traffickers will always be able to find sites for cultivation despite our most vigorous efforts to suppress it.

Hard economic laws determine that ineffectual import controls can in fact only boost drug profits, increasing other crimes by consumers as a consequence. Neither would closing down the present illegal drug-processing laboratories – however desirable, though hardly feasible – be a decisive way to break the chain: kitchens and huts from Pakistan and Sicily to Mexico and California are already taking their place.

Although in public Customs and police forces maintain their claim that they intercept some 5 to 10 per cent of smuggled drugs, in private experienced officers say they fear the real figure amounts to only a fraction of that. Yet, judging by evidence from efforts in the last century to suppress the slave trade, a success rate of at least 33 per cent is needed to deter smugglers. The 1984 Rand Corporation study concluded:

> The prospects for directly affecting the retail market in the USA are equally dismal . . . We estimate that to increase the price of all drugs by, say, 15 per cent, investigative resources would have to be tripled at least. The cost increase would be perhaps $800 million, a large figure even for the federal government. That amount is, for example, as large as the total budget of the FBI. Such an expansion is unlikely, especially in view of the marginal change it would make in the price of drugs. Intensified law enforcement does not appear to be the best recourse . . . it is certainly true in this case that an ounce of prevention is worth a pound of cure.[4]

349

Although there are many steps which could and should be taken to improve control – such as forming a UN police service, since the drug-traffic itself (like terrorism) is already internationalized – other dangerous synthetic drugs are bound to multiply, even were it ever feasible (or desirable) to extirpate heroin. We can no more hope to end drug abuse by eliminating heroin and cocaine than we could alter the suicide rate by outlawing high buildings or the sale of rope. Before any alternative policy can be planned, however, it is first necessary to examine what, if any, is the moral justification for intervention.[5]

Is Addiction Freedom? – The Arguments For and Against Legalization

Should the law intervene to prevent addiction or self-destruction? John Stuart Mill's answer in 1859 was very clear:

> . . . the sole end for which mankind are warranted, individually or collectively, in interfering with the liberty of action of any of their number, is self-protection. That the only purpose for which power can be rightfully exercised over any member of a civilized community, against his will, is to prevent harm to others. His own good, either physical or moral, is not a sufficient warrant. He cannot rightfully be compelled to do or forbear because it will be better for him to do so, because it will make him happier, because in the opinions of others, to do so would be wise, or even right. These are good reasons for remonstrating with him, or reasoning with him, or persuading him, or entreating him, but not for compelling him or visiting him with any evil in case he do otherwise . . . The only part of the conduct of anyone, for which he is amenable to society, is that which concerns others. In the part which merely concerns himself, his independence is, of right, absolute. Over himself, over his own body and mind, the individual is sovereign.[6]

Mill, it should be noted, applied this only to those 'in the maturity of their faculties' – not to children, those delirious or 'in some state of excitement'. None the less, in the case of dangerous drugs he specifically said he would not countenance prohibition or any 'material impediment to obtaining the article' that would violate freedom; the most he would allow would be the provision of information: 'labelling the drug with some word expressive of its dangerous character may be enforced without violation of liberty: the buyer cannot wish not to know that the thing he possesses has poisonous qualities'.[7] In our own time Gore Vidal has advocated that controlled drugs should be sold by chemists, with the fatal ones bearing the skull and crossbones that other recognized poisons – apart from alcohol and nicotine are required to display.

Mill was living in a different situation regarding drugs from the present (and in a pre-National Health Service era, before the public underwrote the bill for the consequences of others' self indulgence), but today his libertarianism on this issue has eloquent advocates from across the political spectrum. Geoffrey Wheatcroft has recently argued in the *Spectator* that those who dislike 'permissive' legislation ought to recognize that the state only comparatively recently encroached on areas of individual decision, and that neither the possession nor use of narcotic drugs was a criminal offence before the late nineteenth century: 'These were not necessarily approved, but in a saner age they were left in the realm of private moral judgment . . . Once we concede that the state has the right to protect people from the consequences of their own folly, then there is no limiting it.' Christopher Dunkley in the *Listener* goes on to remind us: 'Attempting suicide is not illegal, mountaineering without a helmet is not illegal, imposing undue demands on the National Health Service by persistent overeating to obesity is not illegal.' (He might have added that the law also allows us to drink and smoke ourselves to death.) Recalling the claim of advocates of the free market that it is the best available mechanism for answering human need, Peter Kellner subtly added in *The Times*: 'Mrs Thatcher wants people to take responsibility for their own decisions without the state telling them what is good for them. Where more appropriate than with heroin? It does not even have the disadvantage of tobacco: if I am in the same room as a smoker, I am forced to inhale carcinogenic fumes, but someone near me consuming a dose of heroin does me no harm at all.' Enoch Powell avers the most precious of all liberties is 'the right to go to the devil in one's own way'. In the USA, the liberty of one's own body is viewed as an inherent constitutional right; Dr Thomas Szasz claims, 'The very idea that the government should lend its police powers to deprive the people of the free choice to ingest certain substances would have seemed absurd to the drafters of the constitution,'[8] and his allies have argued that it is as dangerously abhorrent to allow the government to dictate our diet as it was for the medieval state to claim control of minds and souls: 'No social authority can successfully arrogate to itself the right to dictate and fix the levels of consciousness to which man may aspire, whether these states are induced pharmacologically or otherwise.'[9] Can the law be used to compel people to be 'good'? Many people, who urge the enforcement of authoritarian laws against drugs, say 'You can't legislate morality' over other issues such as racial prejudice. Is it right ever to use legislation to 'save a person from himself'?

In any event, where exactly does drug 'abuse' start: if a person is not addicted, on what grounds do we interfere? A large number of drug-users are not addicts: why should they be condemned for the dependency of others? Michael Schofield says, 'It is hard to believe that the millions of people who want to use these drugs are anti-social, mental or inadequate.'[10] You or I may decide to refuse drugs for ourselves, but that is entirely different from removing other people's right so to choose. Leary today claims he has never recommended the taking of LSD or any other drug, but, 'I do, however, advocate the option of the American citizen to make an intelligent decision about who and what to put into his/her body.' St Thomas Aquinas taught that it is not the function of the law to make men saints; and the nineteenth-century Archbishop Magee of York said he would rather see England free than England sober. (Liberalization of the drug laws has been opposed by the tobacco and alcohol industries.) The Wootton Committee's report argued that personal freedom is more precious than ever today:

> Added weight is, moreover, given to this argument by the multiplicity of restrictions on individual liberty which in any complex modern society are incontestably necessary for the common good. The greater the number and variety of unavoidable limitations on personal freedom, the more pressing, it may be said, is the urgency of preserving freedom of choice in what are matters of purely individual concern.

Regarding personal liberty, most modern democratic countries today incline towards the views of Mill rather than Lord Devlin's contention that the law must enforce morals as a prerequisite for social continuity.[11] Good government views part of its function as being to protect unpopular minorities from the tyranny of the majority. Too rigid an application of the Devlin approach would prevent society from evolving out of burning witches or persecuting homosexuals. (An earlier distinguished jurist, Justinian, believed homosexuality to be the cause of earthquakes.) The UK government's acceptance of the Wolfenden Committee's recommendation that private homosexual acts between two consenting adults should no longer be criminal was part of a growing contemporary acceptance that the morality of a minority is not the law's concern.

Other experienced voices – though still a dissenting minority – call for the law to be changed on practical pragmatic grounds, and often cite the lessons of Prohibition. Sir Geoffrey Wilson wrote to *The Times*: 'Society is paying a heavy price for a policy which manifestly is not working. What reason is there to suppose that the measures now contemplated will virtually eliminate the supply? For if they merely reduce the supply, little or nothing would be gained . . . But its enforcement could only be achieved at great social cost and the resulting scarcity would be likely to increase the profits of the traffickers and the incidence of street crime.' Dr David Marjot, who runs the St Bernards Drug Unit in Ealing, says, 'I am not in favour of legalizing heroin, but I am less in favour of the present situation because I think we have lost control of it. If we really want to pursue prohibition, we should also cut the number of places selling alcohol and tobacco.' And in the USA recently, Judge William Bryant declared when refusing to jail a woman drug addict, 'The only answer is that she be able to get what she's addicted to without resorting to crime.'

The onus must lie on those who want to ban, not those who want to legalize, anything. Why then are laws against drug enjoyment so entrenched – and internationally universal? (Such public attitudes provide a stark contrast with those adopted towards deliriously infatuated lovers, let alone alcoholics or chain-smokers.) A person's deviancy inevitably is defined by others; anybody alleging that another individual is harming himself cannot avoid exercising a comparative value judgment. However – except in the armed forces – harming onself, like 'self-abuse' and even self-destruction, is not illegal. (On occasions – at Masada or in Japanese society – indeed it has been admired.) Why should authorities feel so selectively strongly that they legislate against people who harm themselves only in the case of those using certain chemical drugs?[12] Many young people resent illogical drug laws being directed against them by their gin-swilling elders; libertarian psychologists suggest that it is the users' hedonism and self-induced pleasure – a prospect of visionary happiness untied to a person's social or material status – which attracts the dour disapproval of envious non-users. Certainly drugs constitute a threat to the puritan values of the work ethic. Marshall McLuhan warned Leary: 'You're not going to overthrow the Protestant Ethic in a couple of years. This culture knows how to sell fear and pain.' Supporters of legalization, however, draw consolation from another dictum of J. S. Mill: 'All great movements go through three stages: ridicule, discussion, acceptance.'

Advocates of decriminalization argue that present policies are not only failing palpably, but in fact compound the problems. Unenforceable criminal sanctions against consensual activity weaken the authority of the law in general, and also encourage deviancy by imprinting a wider criminal identity amongst members of society. Such measures 'cut off those who engage in [the activity] from the values of the parent value system. The individuals thus segregated and marked as deviant may come to perceive of themselves as deviant, to develop their own system of values [and sub-cultural society] and to behave in an increasingly deviant fashion. To this, the community may well respond with further repressive measures . . . '[13] Dr Jock Young argues, 'At a minimum it creates a "cops-and-robbers" atmosphere which romanticizes heroin use; at worst it intensifies the feelings of alienation which led to heroin use in the first place.'[14] One of the most powerful arguments of those in favour of decriminalization is that cumulatively draconian laws (such as the reversal of the onus of proof recently enacted in the UK) – often passed in a state of panic or xenophobic emotion against illicit drugs – can open the door for authorities to use similar powers to erode other civil liberties.

In addition, the advocates of legalization deploy a strong economic argument: the present drug laws make a tax-free gift to traffickers of monopolist profits, similar to those Prohibition presented to bootleggers. The current huge mark-up, of several thousand per cent as they pass from grower to consumer, is a direct function of drugs being illegal. Such premium profits are increasingly attracting, again as Prohibition did, the skills of organized crime – whereas after Prohibition's repeal, criminal involvement in the making or trading of alcohol disappeared. The present policy therefore not only results in the extensive psychotropic drug trade making no financial contribution to society (which it would do, were it ultimately realizable), but imposes the spiralling cost of policing on both developed and developing countries.[15] Richard Emery of the New York Civil Liberties Union argues that the current expenditure on attempts at control (which police chiefs themselves characterize at best as only a holding operation) merely exacts a further toll of frenzied crime being committed by addicts to pay for their supplies – besides the fact that each person held unnecessarily in jail incurs a cost to the law-abiding of more than $26,000 a year. If instead of outlawing drug use we licensed it, the money currently enriching this extensive underground economy could be channelled towards constructive public use; the courts, prison and police services would be relieved of a thankless burden; users would not be deterred from seeking official help; the current criminal links would be severed; and quality control would minimize the health hazards from drugs. As a final point, the proponents of reform hopefully point to the experience of the Netherlands, where decriminalization of cannabis has not resulted in its increased use.

'Drugs are with us to stay,' suggests Dr Andrew Weil. 'Fight them and they will grow ever more destructive. Accept them and they can be turned into non-harmful, even beneficial, forces.' Another doctor argues that to outlaw drugs such as heroin needlessly discriminates against and condemns those people who use particular substances, since any 'problem' lies in them, not the drugs. Release workers add: 'To discuss the "problem" more rationally, we must attempt to define the stage when a drug-user becomes a danger to other people, to the extent that the power of the state should be brought against him.' Michael Schofield defends recreational drug use against allegations of abnormality: 'Why do I like wine with my dinner? Not because I am looking for kicks or escape, but because it gives a pleasant feeling and is unlikely to do me much harm unless I lose all sense of proportion. Perhaps that is true of all recreational drugs.'[16] While it is obviously preferable not to be addicted to anything, among people who become dependent on drugs, it is those placed on the other side of the law who are in the most danger. 'It is unsupervised addiction which leads to deaths,' according to Dr Ann Dally. 'Used under medical supervision, heroin can be less harmful than tobacco or alcohol.' Although not all such patients –

who include businessmen, lawyers and civil servants continuing to do responsible work – will come off drugs completely, many are nevertheless able to lead honest lives and to remain united with their families, through being enabled to regulate their habit thereby avoiding sliding into destitution or criminality. Dr Dally cites the example of one woman who recently died at the age of ninety-five having taken heroin daily for the last sixty years of her life.

The overall aim of any realistic drug policy must be the limitation of damage to the individual and to society. Most users and non-users alike will prefer social policies that, balancing costs and benefits, minimize the known ill-effects of drug use. A number of advocates believe that the legalization of cannabis would provide a safer alternative to the dangerous attractions of heroin. Alternatively, prosecution is not the only way a government can intervene: it can regulate and tax (as it does in the case of alcohol and tobacco); it can exercise control and maintain standards of purity by making itself the monopoly supplier; it can press addicts to undergo treatment; or it can permit personal use but prohibit commercial exploitation (in the same way as, after the recommendations of the Wolfenden Committee, it is legal to be a prostitute but illegal to be a pimp). However, a policy which permitted drug use without legalizing any means of supply would be a hypocritical half-measure – just as it is an anomaly at present to allow cannabis use *de facto*, and then to prosecute its suppliers. To legalize the use of drugs without legalizing trade in them would leave consumers in the hands of criminal pushers who have (like tobacco companies) an interest in promoting addiction. (From the viewpoint of containing addiction, it is also illogical – as at present – to ban the sale of drugs while not also banning gifts of drugs. Equally, it would be an evasion to decriminalize drugs while shrinking from actually legalizing them: either something is legal or it is not.)

The compromise policy of giving drug prescriptions for maintenance, although at first glance of humane benefit to addicts, has in practice serious disadvantages. While those users who are dependent would receive their supplies from doctors, Dr John Strang points out:

> Recreational users would have to pay for their heroin on the black market. It does not take much imagination to see that this system would actively encourage recreational users to become

daily dependent users in order to save money! The proposal to extend maintenance prescription as a way of eliminating the black market is as dangerous as it is foolish. What is more, a glaring contradiction lurks beneath this muddled libertarianism . . . How bizarre it is at a time when the medical profession is rightly under criticism for its prescribing practices with drugs such as Valium, that there should also be criticism about their failure to prescribe other mood-changing drugs.[17]

It is true that maintenance supplies would keep the price of drugs down – but is this in fact really desirable? Perhaps instead, drugs should be heavily taxed and made an expensive luxury like cognac brandy (If so, would doing this be more unfair on the rich or the poor?) The Vera Institute of New York advocated that clinics should supply cheap legal heroin as a way of trying to coax addicts to attend for treatment. However, the policy of prescribing narcotics to addicts, after several years' trial, is now being phased out in most treatment centres. The experience at Sheffield, for example, was that addicts frequently used their drug prescriptions to supplement their black market supply, with the result that their total consumption increased. Proponents of maintenance, however, are rarely clear about whether they would equally include young addicts; and if not, why not. Maintenance also totally fails to address the problem of the growing number of polydrug abusers. And furthermore, alcoholics and heavy smokers might demand why they equally should not be entitled to maintenance supplies of their drug on prescription – a social policy that has few advocates. Dr Maurice Lipsedge, consultant psychiatrist at Guy's Hospital in London, says:

> You cannot cure a drug-addict with another drug. Addicts are best helped by confrontation, by being encouraged to face reality and by having their self-deception challenged. The answer to the problem lies ultimately in the personality of the addict . . . Far too many NHS clinics still prescribe substitute drugs to help addicts give up heroin, for example. It's like trying to cure an alcoholic by giving him vodka instead of gin. It only encourages addicts to go on feeling there is a chemical solution to their problems.

Those who oppose the legalization of drug use deploy their case on three levels: the well-being, first of society as a whole; secondly, of drug-users; and thirdly, of those people who do not use drugs. They argue that every society, reluctantly or otherwise, has to protect itself from destruction – including self-destruction – and cannot afford to tolerate, for example, violent revolutionaries. A few people taking drugs may be a private matter for the individual, but if decriminalization runs the risk of a surging increase in numbers, few in society – user or non-user – would escape from the consequent effects. 'No man is an island' implies reciprocal responsibility: every individual is also a member of the whole – if not a social contractor, as Rousseau argued. Those people who remove themselves into self-indulgent nihilism increase the burdens of life for the rest of society. Burke wrote of the 'partnership not only between those who are living, but between those who are dead, and those who are to be born'.[18] Stokely Carmichael takes the view that if we are not part of the solution, we are part of the problem.

In a democracy, social policy is – in theory at least – determined by the wish of the majority (although popular intolerance may be mitigated by government, as for instance over capital punishment; the alternative of dictatorship is generally even less tolerant as well as less easy to remove). There is no doubt that an overwhelming majority of the public strongly oppose the recreational use of heroin, although attitudes towards cannabis are more ambivalent. No major political leader today would think it feasible publicly to advocate legalizing all drugs. The present drugs laws, even if – like speed limits – less than wholly effective, at least discourage some people from the risk of possible addiction. Professor Nigel Walker has suggested that the criminal law should be determined on grounds of cost-benefit, not morality; among the material consequences of drug abuse's social and economic cost to society are addicts' demands on the health and social services, which in any welfare state cause an unnecessary and increasing drain on limited public resources. (Drug overdose cases account for a quarter of the emergencies admitted to British hospitals, and 90 per cent of all deliberate self-injuries.) Why should scarce medical facilities be diverted to the merely self-indulgent, when there are long queues of other people who are involuntarily sick? Choosing oneself to go to pieces is one matter; it is arguably different when others have to cope with the results. Society may be said to have a right to try to limit the damage, because it is society which has to carry much of the cost of drug-dependency's consequences.

Co-existent with or separately from reasons of social defence, the community may express caring concern by protecting drug misusers from ignorance or 'weakness' (as with the trusteeship society adopts – or should adopt – for mental patients or children).[19] Many of those who have become dependent on drugs (including alcohol) prefer not to recognize or admit their condition. It is not only addicts who suffer; there is also the incidence of cases of overdose, intoxication, bad trips and accidents due to drugs. Finally there is the damage to innocent non-users: the emotional havoc wrought on the families and friends of addicts, plus the risk of 'contagion' by addicts proselytizing and pushing drugs on new users to pay for their habit.

Almost every social policy helps some people at the expense of others; it is rational to protect the innocent at the price of controlling drug abusers. Professor Sir Martin Roth believes that, compared with today, society in Mill's time was more stable and that he did not realize how contagious drug abuse can be. Roth himself is so concerned by the danger of this spread that he believes it will be necessary for us to isolate or compulsorily hospitalize addicts within the next five years.[20] Dr George De Leon of New York's Phoenix House argues that most disadvantaged youths are in reality scarcely well enough informed to exercise the free choice advocated by Mill; and he also believes that it is less well-off people who are most vulnerable because they are the least likely to seek treatment to counter drugs' negative effects.[21] The view of the experienced and tolerant Dr Martin Mitcheson is: 'My personal feeling is that heroin is far too powerful a drug ever to be left to normal social controls. I'm perfectly able to accept the idea that, to a heroin addict, heroin is such a rewarding drug that he is prepared to ruin every aspect of his life to get it.' Claims that drugs never hurt anyone are as false as the charge that they are responsible for most of the ills of youth today: no drug is free from danger if it is used wrongly or to excess. Whereas long experience of drug use in traditional cultures bred informal controls, these are absent in modern urban life. No longer can it be contended that the attraction of drugs is due to their being forbidden fruit: nobody seriously expects that the use of heroin or cocaine would diminish if they were made more easily accessible. Alcohol and tobacco have already taken their toll in terms of drunken violence, car accidents and cancer wards, and it would scarcely help the quality of life to add further addiction from other substances; society's future will inevitably be vulnerable to risks from new drugs, whose dangers may only be realized too late and when the drugs have become established – like tobacco today. Weaknesses in the present policy are not a reason for abandoning it, but for making improvements: nobody suggests that because the incidence of rape or burglary is rising this is an argument for legalizing these.

The liberal rejection of legalization is based on a further, wider view. Most addicts themselves want to abandon their habit. Drugs are a flight from, if not an abdication of, life – as well as being destructive of social communication. Addiction not only results in the waste of human potential, but in making people besottedly self-centred and predatorily uncaring about others in society.[22] 'Aversion to drug-taking is part of a liking for life,' says Barbara Wootton. Chemical attempts to put our bodies into overdrive or to take shortcuts to spiritual visionary feelings are an ersatz delusion. Rather, the human ideal should be to dispense with unnecessary drugs of any kind, because we are unlikely to live responsibly unless we have the courage to face reality, helped by the fullest awareness of our body and senses. Enslavement to any drug deprives the individual of the potential of his full faculties, and reduces him to being an appendage to, rather than a positive participant in, society. George Orwell as well as Aldous Huxley has warned us of the potential dangers of the chemical road, including the psychological conditioning of people through the manipulation of their suggestibility. Life is too important – too serious as well as too precious – to opt out of through drugs. The overriding need today is for people to communicate more clearly and honestly, not to isolate and immolate themselves in befuddlement. Recreational drugs are, for the most part, evasion: a running away from reality, when today's world all too obviously cries out for concerned involvement. And legalization would, ultimately, only prolong the problem by postponing any eventual solution.

Future generations would certainly never forgive us were we to bury our heads in the sand, or despair at the challenge of the drugs crisis – however complex the problem may be. For nearly a century anti-drug exertions have concentrated, without avail, on attempting to stop supplies. More realistic – indeed perhaps the only – hope lies in a united effort to cut the demand, at the same time as trying to rectify those aspects of the social environment which produce the problem in the first place. This requires the whole-hearted involvement of the entire community: neither politicians, doctors, nor police by themselves have any chance of success. The difficulties are only too obvious, but they should be faced frankly. Drugs cannot ever be disinvented – any more than any other potentially threatening discovery made by mankind. 'No human society', warns Don Aitken, 'has ever been without its intoxicants . . . Hence to label the use of psychoactive drugs in terms of individual or social psychopathology is futile.'[23] Yet the fact that something has happened in the past does not *ipso facto* make it desirable to encourage or increase that practice – if this were the case human civilization would never have made the limited progress it has to date. If nicotine and alcohol were newly discovered today together with the full knowledge of their detrimental effects, they would be put under firm control: but their uncontrolled spread is no recommendation or argument for compounding them with other problems.

Up until now the public and drug-users alike have shrunk from confronting the true reality of the drug issue. Political will to tackle the problem is insufficient, because many parents are still not aware of the extent of the danger. Even when the children of political leaders have become addicted, they have almost invariably been able to have private treatment, so there is still no proper public provision or policy. Oscillating between hysteria, voyeurism and apathy, popular opinion has taken refuge in a shocked reaction as an alibi for inaction. Drugs have been made into a scapegoat for, and a diversion from, the deeper social anomie of which drug abuse (like much depression and mental illness today) is often only a tracer symptom. It is a tragic condemnation of our contemporary society that it cannot offer increasing numbers of people any preferable satisfaction.[24] At the same time it is important not to sensationalize the pervasiveness of illegal drugs: the majority of people, young or old, do not take them; and of those who do only a minority become addicted, of whom only a very few die as a consequence. Both the pleasure and the terrors of drugs have been made the subject of emotive hype as a result of rival fears and fantasies. The real danger to civilization of drug abuse lies in the problem's future growth – because we have not yet found the answer. Without a major preventive effort, the spiral of abuse will widen, as more and more suppliers are attracted to the profits from a rising number of addicts, who will in turn sell more drugs to raise money to finance their dependency.

A government such as that of the UK, which is benefiting by £4,500 million a year in revenue from alcohol and nicotine, has no excuse at all not to provide comprehensive and positive health education. At present such teaching receives only a grudgingly minute fraction of the budgets at the disposal of tobacco, drink and patent drug-peddlers for their counter-promotions. Instead the main burden of coping with the effects of drugs' currently falls on over-worked volunteers and financially precarious non-governmental bodies. The tiny unit at the UK Department of Health and Social Security that is responsible for drug problems has a mere handful of staff – who have to cope with other major workloads, while the Home Office musters only six people full-time on the policy.[25] Moreover, many local authorities, under pressure over rates, entirely avert their eyes from the problem, refusing to establish a drug clinic for fear that it will (like Amsterdam's project) attract addicts from outside their area. This is why only a nation-wide approach can succeed. In Britain the present fragmentation of responsibility between the Home Office, the DHSS, the Treasury (who control Customs) and the Department of Education should be replaced by a single national agency; in the USA equally, the long-awaited overall drug co-ordinator should be appointed forth-with. The staff of the UN Narcotics Division likewise should be strengthened in number from its present absurdly inadequate thirty-four; it should also be backed by the resources to enable it to carry out research into the reasons for the spread of drug use and to evaluate the best response, both at national and international level. Now on a global scale, the problem must be tackled globally. The inevitable costs would be defrayed many times over by the benefits.

Next, it is necessary to change the public perception of drug-addicts in order to support the policy programmes. Instead of using them as scapegoats – which only increases the anti-social resent-ment of a sub-group's members, as well as strengthening their defences – we should learn to see them as neighbours with a temporary problem who need help. Some moral crusaders are guilty of dehumanizing addicts by referring to them as 'junkies' or 'the living dead'; the myth in the USA that all addicts are criminals is in danger of becoming a self-fulfilling prophesy. Griffith Edwards says:

People who have become entrammelled in drug-addiction are of us – we share their humanity and they ours. It is intolerable that they should be alienated, discarded, treated as rubbish, forced by our rejection into an amplification of hopelessness. The process of recovery is not an imposed treatment but the offering of an alternative to being a drug-addict, and an invitation of growth, freedom and self-responsibility.[26]

Far from being a race apart, users form a spectrum, with most of them taking a variety of drugs controlledly and moderately, though a minority harm themselves – just as do the consumers of legal drugs. The majority of drug abusers are not incurable or doomed, any more than every non-teetotaller is fated to become a drunkard.[27] Many would give up drugs if they could be offered rehabilitation, hope and work; but at present young people who have been detoxified are unlikely to be offered jobs or training places.

Nobody at present, however, has been given the key responsibility to co-ordinate drug prevention, which is more crucial as well as easier than attempting cures. (In 1984 for the first time the US government said that prevention, not enforcement of the law, was its highest priority; yet in the previous two years it had cut spending on education and prevention by 5 per cent, while increasing spending on enforcement by 70 per cent.) The most common reason for drug-taking is dissatisfaction with life, leading to a desire to distort or escape reality. Many young people think our contemporary society a moral and spiritual desert. We should concentrate on giving them the opportunity of a more meaningful life than that offered by drugs, while involving them as much as possible in positive health and anti-drug campaigns. Our policy should have the twin aims of discouraging anybody new from starting drug use, while helping those who want to stop. The current situation of there being no drug training available for GPs should be rectified immediately; every doctor should be trained about drug abuse, and given the resources to cope. No doctor, however, should be allowed to profit from supplying any addictive drug. The present tribunals for doctors who prescribe irresponsibly are too cumbersome and slow (often taking months before a case is heard), and should be replaced by a fail-safe system of licensing. The UK government meanwhile must reverse its short-sighted rejection of the Commons

Home Affairs Select Committee's recommendation that a National Drugs Advisory Service be set up: this would co-ordinate all the agencies in the field, whether National Health Service, voluntary or private; have them share insights and data; and train people to an acceptable standard. Equally mistaken was the government's decision to reject the committee's call for a twenty-four-hour emergency telephone service (neither need nor motivation work to timetable). At the same time, drug abusers, once rehabilitated, might be asked whenever possible to contribute towards the cost of their treatment and certainly, tobacco and alcohol manufacturers should be made to pay for the medical consequences which they bring about through their profitable products. Meanwhile there should be a co-ordinated campaign directed at both the public and doctors to cut to a minimum the prescription of all dependency-producing drugs, including tranquillizers.

The present British government should be given credit for at last publicly admitting that there is a drug problem. However, even if the total of £12 million offered for treatment centres (spread over three years) were concentrated solely on the UK's officially estimated 60,000 heroin users, this would provide each of them with less than £6 a month – whereas the lowest treatment costs start at £1,000 a year. Money alone, however, cannot buy a solution – as the $1.4 billion a year being thrown by the USA at enforcement shows. The growth of self-help groups is a response to the absence of official provision, and at the same time evidence of the essential value of communal support. At present the frequency of failure makes rehabilitative casework less than attractive. Most non-users' primitive reaction of fear and loathing towards drug-dependants at present decreases the chances of rehabilitation.[28]

History has shown that attempts to prohibit people using one substance after another have failed. Instead we should use education and the media to teach self-defence through knowledge and the sharing of responsibility. The drug problem will never be contained, let alone reduced, without enlisting the understanding and involvement of society as a whole. By mobilizing the support of its population, China alone has succeeded in almost totally eradicating its inherited problem of addiction, because a community will concern itself with the cure of a drug-dependant and help to find him a job. By contrast, any proposal to start a new drug treatment centre in a Western country is almost invariably opposed by a barrage of hostile objections from local citizens.

Preventive efforts can be pursued at several levels simultaneously. Education about drugs should be treated, as it is in Sweden, as an integral part of comprehensive teaching about general health.[29] Drug abuse should not be emphasized dramatically through being highlighted as an isolated topic. The ideal aim for us all should be to experience life as fully and clearly as possible (even though this entails pain as well as happiness): the antithesis of addiction is to achieve a true relationship with the world. Yet positive health teaching today is almost non-existent. Everybody should learn that we can achieve mood alteration and 'highs' without resorting to drugs. As Jeanne Henny says:

> Stimulating chemical change can be safely recreated by natural means. Craving for stimuli is caused by an imbalance in our chemistry – itself often due to stress, boredom or feelings of inadequacy; the body's chemistry can be rebalanced by increased blood circulation – i.e. more oxygen – as well as the right food. Most sports people have experienced how their bodies release opiates when they exercise at a certain level; a similar 'high' can occur for example in dancing, full-throated singing, mountaineering, etc. (Encouragement could lay emphasis on such activities in a social context, in order to help also with today's increasing problem of isolation which is being exacerbated by unemployment.) The campaign should begin in schools to help people appreciate the human body . . . It is time we started to realize the mind is not the only key to success and happiness . . . A similar balance may be achieved by acupuncture, but it is better to heal oneself. Our society at present does not encourage us to respect nature: when human beings begin to destroy their lives or themselves it is because they have not been made aware of what it is to be a living part of nature.[30]

Before the UK government launched its current media campaign against heroin, its expert Drug Misuse Advisory Council had unanimously advised against any such form of publicity,[31] warning that it might do more harm than good by generating interest in non-users and despair among users. Nevertheless, most young

365

people today – whether or not authority likes it – are exposed to drugs, so the sensible policy is to give them reliable information to dispel any mystic aura and to help them guard against harmful consequences, since the unofficial sources of information more often describe the pleasures than the risks involved in drugs. Every person, at any age, has a right to the correct facts which will enable them to make decisions affecting their own life. Education about drugs should not be restricted to young people, but given as well to parents, doctors, teachers, social workers, politicians, journalists and the police: many young drug fanciers today are better informed than those who are expected to guide them. Children's own knowledge ranges from worldly-wise street-lore to fantastic misapprehensions: some are not even aware that the 'skag' and 'smack' they experiment with is heroin, while many teachers and social workers themselves suffer confusion, and doctors also disagree with each other. Until now the most usual rule has been 'the least said, the better'; a number of teachers hesitate to raise the subject lest theirs will be branded a 'druggy school'. At present 70 per cent of schools in Britain have no drug education whatsoever, and amongst those which do, the occasional 'fire-brigade' visit has only a very limited value.

Most of us become aware from our own lives how difficult it is to change a strongly-held pattern of behaviour. Research could help by studying the recent turn of opinion against smoking to learn which lessons might be applied in the case of other drug use. Crude propaganda, it should be remembered, itself can become something against which to rebel. Information about drugs has to be 'street-cred' honest if it is to be trusted; young people, sceptical towards lectures from adults in authority, are wary of being preached at or patronized. Although former addicts may be listened to with more respect, moral lectures are especially resisted when delivered by adults who smoke and drink. Young people have criticized the UK government's present heroin campaign as being 'too middle class: working-class people can't relate to it'. Others, cynical beyond their years, say, 'It's not really aimed at us, is it? It's political window-dressing aimed to be for the benefit of all those concerned parent voters, so that the government can pretend it's doing something.'[32] The original plan for this campaign was that it should aim to frighten – 'Heroin is a death sentence sooner or later' being one of the original slogans; this, however, was dropped on the advice of experts, since it was felt first, that this would lack credibility among people who personally know heroin users who are able to handle their habit; secondly, that it risked enhancing the dangerously romantic image of heroin; and thirdly, that the effect of death as a deterrent is questionable, already overworked as it has been in drink–driving and other campaigns. It was decided instead to stress the physical and mental deterioration that heroin can cause. (Although at least one critical young viewer rejoined, 'The lesson of all those ill junkies they show us is that heroin should be given pure and unadulterated'; and the effect of concentrating exclusively on heroin has been to turn some drug abusers on to crack and amphetamine sulphate.) 'Education should stress the silliness of drug-taking, rather than the forbidden excitement of its danger. Show that drugs are a poor, second-rate substitute for living,' was the advice of one former addict. 'The facts don't need any hyperbole; they're sufficiently devastating to speak for themselves.' 'It's crucial to have at least one teacher who's a specialist in drug education in every school and college which has teenagers,' counselled a New York doctor. His son added: 'But don't preach in the way some adults do against sex. You should realize kids want to learn about their feelings more than about the mechanics.' Six million British people visit chemists' shops every day: this opportunity should be used for health education. Brian Arbery of Turning Point concludes: 'Not having drug education is as sensible as having no sex education and hoping young people will never have sex. Instead, we should try to get the young thinking why people make wrong moral choices. We should start at the end of primary school, when they're eleven and twelve, before they begin in a large older school – and we should educate their parents too.'[33]

In the USA, comic books dealing with drug education are being given to nine-year-olds in the fourth grade. By contrast, their parents generally read only sensationalist reports about the subject in the media – not infrequently produced by journalists marinated in alcohol and wracked with smokers' coughs. Parents, like other adult authorities, have the capacity to be part of the solution, or at other times part of the problem. 'Communities seldom examine what they are communicating to youth,' warns Dr Helen Nowlis, 'they seldom assess the adequacy with which their institutions are serving the needs of youth. But they are often all too ready to mobilize to deplore and repress the symptoms of neglect.'[34]

An important fact which needs to be remembered is that decisions to use drugs are most often taken on impulse, influenced by social pressures more than by any premeditated calculation. Consequently, drug education is best tackled similarly in a group – through discussions and role-playing simulated situations – so as to present the issue in a context of social responsibility rather than as a repressive confrontation which is all too likely to invite resistance. Such a three-dimensional approach is both more realistic and more meaningful to participants than the slick connotations which advertising campaigns have for passively detached viewers. None the less some experts, like Dr David Morris of the Middlesex Hospital, believe that people should not be shielded from harrowing sights such as addicts bleeding in lavatories: 'It's difficult to convey the horrors in a lecture when the speaker looks as healthy as the audience.' And other authorities are convinced that a campaign should recognize the fact that many contemporary adolescents will only watch television videos or films and never read even the briefest leaflet. Drug education films in the 1970s (such as *Better Dead*) were gruesome, aiming to shock and scare – but a large proportion of today's young viewers have learnt from horror and SF films to discount exaggeration. Recent US films concentrate instead on how to resist peer pressure at parties and 'Just say No'. *Chasing the Bandwagon*, one of the most imaginative new British films, made by the YMCA with the black comedian Lenny Henry, uses the powerful weapon of humour to hold teenagers' attention at the same time as demolishing drug myths.

As a first priority, emergency training courses are overdue to spread informed drug teaching throughout all schools, colleges and youth centres. But any education will be swamped in the wider sea of life in the world outside unless the efforts of the whole community are also enlisted – just as the effect of even the best treatment centres can be reversed by a person's home environment. The problem of drug abuse can no more be solved without the co-option of the society in which it occurs, than guerrillas can be defeated if they enjoy the support of the population amongst which they operate. At present, the growth in the number of new users of heroin and cocaine is fast outstripping any counter-provision such as clinic facilities. The solution, which David Steel MP has rightly urged, is to mobilize more community concern rather than to increase state intervention. The first essential is to link up the different people – parents, doctors, teachers, councillors and MPs, ex-addicts, police officers, social, church and youth workers, NA, FA, the media and others who are trying to help. 'Instead of getting angry, we should get organized,' urges a Glasgow mother. Parents, who have the most to lose and the most to gain, can start by learning the facts about drugs and thus help the general public – including, crucially, employers – to change their attitudes. Organizations formed by parents in order to counter drug abuse are expanding in Poland and Sweden as well as throughout the USA. At the same time, a police officer pointed to one of the main problems of modern metropolitan life: 'People used to care about other people in their road. Everyone was known to each other, and residents took an interest in the children of their neighbours. Now families move much further and more often, whole households are out all day, and many people don't know who their next-door neighbours are.'

Some districts containing the worst social and drugs problems possess no form of neighbourhood community network at all: these areas could be helped by service from outreach teams linked to the nearest treatment centre. Community involvement can best be won by decentralized initiatives which recruit local people to gain rapport with the neighbourhood as well as the trust of drug users.[35]

Lay participation to date has taken varied forms. Some of the most useful initiatives concentrate on offering employment opportunities to help the rehabilitation of former addicts. For example, Channel One at Gloucester (Massachusetts) specializes in jobs restoring buildings and the countryside which also have a high community visibility, so as to win the interest of the public: it offers drug-free young people, besides those with problems, opportunities to practise a variety of skills capable of leading to income-producing jobs. Similarly, the Wildcat Service Corporation of New York trains and finds jobs for ex-addicts who are not easy to employ, using close supervision and peer-group support. As at Channel One, these trainees progress from subsidized to competitive employment; the help they are given includes interview technique and teaching in skills such as basic English, maths, typing and computers, as well as in the 'life skills' of how to communicate and to find and retain jobs. It aims, besides providing work experience and references, to give ex-addicts the equally important self-confidence in their own capability as successful employees.

As an opposite form of lay participation, some ex-addicts in north

London have formed themselves into a group called the Heroin Hit Squad, with the aim of using their inside knowledge of the drugs scene to sabotage the heroin dealing network. One of their members explained: 'The whole existence of a black market in anything depends on the buyers not turning the sellers over to the authorities. What we're saying is that people who sell heroin are killing other people, so whatever reservations we may have about the police, we're prepared to use them against heroin dealers.' Part of the problem, however, one policeman confided unattributably, is that 'most coppers see junkies as scum, so they're not too bothered about getting rid of their dealers'. Westminster Council has started to offer rewards for information about local dealers. But so frustrated are the parents of addicted children in Birkenhead and Rugby that they have taken matters into their own hands by offering their own rewards and have put up posters to publicize the names of local pushers.

On Edinburgh housing-estates – where one in twelve young people were using heroin in 1983 – residents have joined together to form a pioneering example of self-help. In deprived parts of Dublin, the drug incidence is even worse: in 1980 the official number of heroin addicts was 100; four years later there were 6,000. Here, vigilante groups of neighbours have organized round-the-clock patrols and physically attack dealers to drive them away. Residents who had gathered at a public meeting marched to the homes of three dealers and evicted them; other suspected pushers were given a warning to desist or leave the neighbourhood. By 1985 local anti-drug groups were active in eleven different working-class areas of Dublin, and a city-wide 'Concerned Parents Central Committee' had been formed, without the involvement of the police. (When the drug wholesalers retaliated by ambushing and shooting one of the community leaders in St Teresa's Gardens, the IRA counter-attacked by kidnapping one of the men reported to be responsible for the shooting, and a woman alleged to be involved with drugs was tarred and feathered.) Some forty Dublin thieves and burglars were so worried by the police attention being aroused that they formed a body calling itself 'Concerned Criminals against Drug Abuse'. By contrast, in Toxteth, some pushers have taken covert advantage of vigilantes' anger to eliminate rival dealers. However, one lasting result in areas of Edinburgh and Dublin has been to bring the local community together for the first time, unifying people with a sense of purpose and self-help to take the place of the isolated despair they had felt previously.

One litmus test to distinguish whether or not a government is serious in its commitment against the harm caused by drugs is its attitude towards the two most widely harmful drugs of all.[36] Alcohol and nicotine surpass every other drug in terms of the human waste, family devastation and medical demands they cause society. By any objective criteria, tobacco and alcohol do greater damage to several times more people than do cannabis, heroin, cocaine, LSD and glue sniffing combined. Cigarettes kill 100,000 people and alcohol at least 6,500 (some estimate 25,000) a year in Britain alone, compared with less than 300 as a result of the aggregate of all the illegal drugs including heroin and cocaine. Each week people in the UK spend some £9 million on illicit drugs – but £111 million on tobacco and £275 million on alcohol.[37] The current response by the UK government, however, is to devote £35 for each premature death caused by smoking, and £344 for each death from alcohol abuse; but £1.7 million for each death resulting from illegal drugs. More than 60 per cent of all murders and 50 per cent of all rapes, for example, are claimed to be committed under the influence of alcohol. A new Congressional study puts tobacco's annual cost to the USA in health and lost productivity at $38–95 billion, while the revenues of all tobacco sales total only $30 billion. Yet the UK government is at present spending an annual total of only £6 million to combat alcohol and tobacco abuse, compared with £411 million against illegal drug abuse. The same pattern is being repeated in other countries: in China, which is virtually free of heroin, tobacco smoking is widespread and growing with remarkable rapidity. Throughout the world, more resources are probably devoted to controlling cannabis than any other drug; yet it is not cannabis (or even heroin) users who wreak violence at football matches and kill thousands each year on the roads. Whereas abusers of heroin are liable to injure themselves, many abusers of alcohol are likely to injure others as well.[38] Where is the morality of a society that imprisons cannabis dealers while according peerages and fortunes to nicotine and alcohol pushers?

Laws about harmful substances are themselves irrationally capricious: drinking meths, for example, is highly dangerous yet perfectly legal. Public attitudes are not formed as a result of scientific research, but frequently are moulded by powerful interests: the tobacco, pharmaceutical and alcohol lobbies are wealthy and powerful (with not a few law-makers and journalists who fulminate against illicit drugs themselves being addicted to their products). 'Problem' drinkers and smokers in society far outnumber users of narcotic drugs as voters, even though this is no argument for increasing the ranks of the latter. Pete Townshend strongly opposes legalizing heroin even though it 'is no worse than alcohol in many respects', arguing that heroin should be prevented from becoming as great a social menace as booze: 'If heroin addicts become as numerous as problem alcoholics are today, life would become intolerable for GPs, social workers, probation officers, parents and teachers.' It is an eloquent view of social responsibilities that the drink industry chooses to spend more on sponsoring horse racing than it does on the victims of its alcohol. However, a matter of more serious concern is the addiction of governments to revenues from tobacco and alcohol. Yet each extra penny of tax placed on a packet of cigarettes could, besides saving smokers' lives, produce £50 million annually in Britain, which would be more than enough to double the whole amount the government is devoting to the drug problem.

In the future, will illicit substances ever be unwanted? There is no sign of this happening, even though exactly what role drugs will have is likely to be determined by our civilization's future values:

> the place accorded to the individual in society, in every sense; the value put on freedom and rights to pleasure-seeking; the importance and essential meaning given to health . . . In a world experiencing upheaval and breakdown in old structures and values, much of the long-standing equilibrium between societies and their use of drugs will break down too. In the immediate future the world is likely to experience an intensification of drug-related harm.[39]

A variety of culprits have been blamed for this apparently unstoppable trend. The rise in the use of drugs is, it is claimed, due to desire for a less-censorious substitute for religion as an antidote to our materialist society; or to a longing for metaphysical and numinous experience, because of alienation from nature as a result of our increasing mechanization and urbanization. Loneliness can generate drug-taking, as family structures continue to fracture: more than twice as many people now live alone in so-called developed countries as did in the previous generation. Stress is often cited as an explanation; but previous generations were threatened certainly no less by wars, illness and poverty. Dr Martin Mitcheson believes that 'heroin addiction is an inevitable by-product of a drug-orientated culture'. People today are bombarded by advertising campaigns which imply their lives are boring, but can be transformed by the purchase of a certain product, and that a person is deficient and unattractive (if not downright defective) unless he or she buys such a key to swift success and happiness. In addition, several countries' populations now contain the highest-ever percentage of males in their late teens – the demographic group most prone to anti-social conduct including drug abuse, and whose problems are being exacerbated by increasing unemployment. Aldous Huxley's nephew Francis comments, 'My pessimism tells me that the industrial world is doing its unconscious best to turn the population into battery-chicken people, institutionalized from birth as much by the medical as by any other professions; and that the drug problem is at least half embedded in the circumstances of the human battery-farm.'[40] T. S. Eliot wrote that humankind cannot bear very much reality. For some, on one hand, recreational drug-taking heralds the dawn of the leisure society; whereas other young people accuse governments of not taking the drugs problem seriously because 'if we're high on them, we won't be causing trouble'. In the future the financial costs of trying to control drugs will rise indefinitely, because no government will want to be seen to do less than its predecessor. Some experts at present detect a correlation between the heroin addiction rate and countries where the capitalist ethos's religion of the market place is at its strongest: for example, the USA, Hong Kong, Thailand, Pakistan and Western Europe. Nevertheless, it was in communist Poland that an addict said, 'There comes a time when one prefers one's own lies to those inanely repeated *ad nauseam* by others.' In fact, neither drugs nor traffickers are respecters of political boundaries; although any country is a prime candidate for drugs if it combines liberal social attitudes with a competitive ethic where the unsuccessful feel they are failures. A number of intelligent authorities in the USA and in other countries believe that the problem of drug abuse is the single most serious threat to the future, and has overtaken communism and terrorism as the principal concern they face. Perhaps the gravest danger of all may be that if the more tolerant countries do not quickly work out better solutions to deal with addictive drug use, it is likely to be only the totalitarian nations that will survive, and the world's political future will then pass to those countries where control is most ruthless and whose armed forces are least undermined by drugs.

If civilization is to survive, it cannot be beyond human intelligence to find a solution to this crisis. The task is daunting, but the penalty for failure would be even more so. Michael Davies of the UN urges that it is first necessary to change the attitude that the only way to solve a problem is to escape from it:[41] and that this applies to policy makers as much as to drug misusers. Most of us contrive to damage ourselves during our lives by some means or another. Aldous Huxley's counsel was: 'The only reasonable policy is to open other, better doors in the hope of inducing men and women to exchange their old bad habits for new and less harmful ones.'[42] The typical drug-user, in Dr Martin Mitcheson's experience, is 'mostly an inadequate personality, who lacks the confidence and basic resources to cope with the demands made of him by society'; however, the previous policy of treating drug abusers as aberrant and highly exceptional cases has been undermined by the fact that forms of drug-taking are now widely accepted amongst many young people. The most recent survey in the USA found that between 75 and 80 per cent of young adults have tried an illegal drug, and that more than half have tried one other than marijuana. This trend is more likely to continue than to contract in the immediate and foreseeable future (drugs often produce a missionary effect on their takers – most marked in the case of LSD, many of whose users became proselyters for its experience). Gone for good is the scenario of discounting a few deviant and mainly apologetic addicts, for whom the Rolleston and Brain Committees prescribed their medical model of treatment. The most urgent need is for detoxification units to be available twenty-four hours a day, for everybody who wants to 'kick the habit'. But a 'cure' is only likely to be feasible where a drug abuser is suitably motivated; the vast majority of heroin and cocaine users at present, however, do not even contact clinics or doctors for help or advice. Meanwhile, Valium and amphetamines ('speed') remain the UK's most serious addiction problems after alcohol and nicotine, but receive hardly any attention. Speed is only one-fifth of the price of cocaine, while its effect lasts longer, and the police report that it is now being manufactured by O-level chemists.

It seems probable that the whole issue of drugs will have to be reassessed in terms of damage and dependency rather than usage. Professor Griffith Edwards and Dr Awni Arif, however, warn:

> But at the same time, care must be taken that the extension of facilities does not mean the cruder extension of the medical model, which conditions the individual to learned helplessness and the community to surrendering its responsibilities. The helping professions must not expect or be expected to take responsibilities for all problems. A response planned in terms of medical care alone would be not only beyond the economic resources of any country, but also likely to be largely ineffective. What is needed rather is the further development of a model that would see treatment as a partnership between the individual, the community and the helping professions, with the helping professions in an assistant role.[43]

Dr Mahler, the Director General of the WHO, suggested to a conference of health ministers in 1986 that it is society itself that will have to change its values if the young are to gain protection from drug abuse. He warned that in a shallow and materialist society where the norm is to demand more of everything:

> it is not surprising if the 'more' includes more narcotic and psychotropic drugs . . . If our social values make drug-taking an acceptable norm amongst peer groups of youngsters, then it is those values that have to be reconsidered . . . Perhaps it is not the youngsters we have to change; perhaps it is some of our social values . . . Youngsters have to have self-esteem, and if that is shattered some turn to crime, others to drugs.

Why is twentieth-century society so much more afraid of drug-addicts than people were in the eighteenth and nineteenth century? Each age's attitude projects the values of its own times. Today's concept of a more cohesive society has replaced earlier laissez-faire individualism; but contemporary society's unease about drugs may be in danger of becoming so great that it may abandon hard-won traditions of liberty. Populations and governments are likely to become increasingly frightened in the future as drug habits spread.

It is also in some governments' interests to keep their populations scared, in order to exercise control over them. Let us hope that we remember the common humanity we share with drug-users.

In *Inventing the Future* the scientist Dennis Gabor forecast 'Till now man has been up against nature; from now on he will be up against his own nature.' Research will help us to learn more about the body's health and own natural peptide endorphins. Jasper Woodcock, however, hypothesizes: 'Suppose for example you manage by some magic to find a bug which ate all the opium plants in the world, which I know the researchers are looking for. What effect would it have? The schedules to the international conventions on narcotic drugs provide a shopping list of alternative synthetic drugs, some of them very much more potent than heroin. It's only because opium and heroin are cheap that hardly anybody has so far bothered to take up the question of how to produce such drugs illicitly.' Inevitably, progressively potent new drugs (of which crack and 'designer' drugs are only forerunners) are going to be developed as a result of research stimulated by similarly expanding profits. (A drug to stop or postpone ageing will gain the greatest prize.) When chemists eventually perfect a non-addictive narcotic, what right would society then have to interfere?[44]

Can (*pace* Jeremy Bentham) anything be justified if it adds to the sum of human happiness: since drugs are acceptable to relieve physical pain, their users ask why they should not be enlisted for mental comfort too? Perhaps, on the other hand, human nature needs a psycho-drama of the struggle between Good and Evil, in which it can wage war against the Devil in the shape of drugs and traffickers – even if this is likely to involve a war without end.[45] Society will always seek scapegoats: it is after all easier to blame our ills on a god or on an alien plague such as drugs than to grapple with what really causes the ills in the first place. Most non-users read into the complexity of drug issues only those moral, political and psychological patterns they prefer to find. Hence it is not so surprising that they find it difficult to agree on solutions – or even whether there are or should be any. Drug abuse generates alternating myopia and hysteria partly because it can easily be seen to support the nostrum which generations of adults have clung to: that things aren't what they used to be and the younger generation is going to the dogs. In reality the rise in the use of drugs owes less to their intrinsic appeal than to many people's dislike of present-day existence. Our starting-point should be to ask ourselves what is so wrong with our society that more and more of our contemporaries should be driven to embrace and abuse drugs.

The present increase in drug abuse is frightening in precisely the same way as AIDS: because society as yet has no answer to it. Fear about the potential future implications, especially regarding the consequences for the tolerant liberal countries of the Western world, is already producing panic reactions. Currently an unfortunate combination of emotional hyperbole with ineffectual policies is beginning to prompt a political auction in the USA and elsewhere – with demands for censorship and capital punishment and the jettisoning of the presumption of innocence as the first bids – which could corrode values of our society permanently. Among the harmful consequences is the erosion of social trust, with children denouncing their parents and vice versa.

The global connection presents a threat to every nation's social fabric. Perhaps some good will eventually result out of the drug crisis if because of it more parents concern themselves with their children and learn to communicate better with them; if it persuades adults to give younger people greater hope for their future lives; and if tackling the problem regenerates a sense of community in our society by showing the essential human dependency on mutual support and responsibility.

We can no longer disregard the extent of the challenge, or the part we must all play if we are to overcome it. This book is written in the hope that it may help kindle the public involvement needed to succeed.

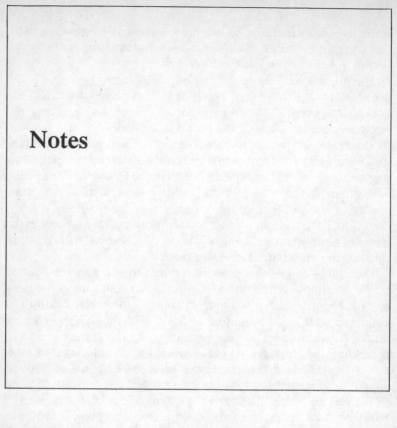

Notes

Introduction: The Crisis Today

[1] Chatto & Windus, 1959.
[2] Report of the House of Commons Social Services Committee (HMSO, 1985).

1 A Mazy Road: The Historical Perspective

[1] 'And he drank of the wine, and was drunken; and he was uncovered within his tent' (Genesis, 9: 21).
[2] In Book X of the *Odyssey*, Circe supposedly employed henbane (which contains hyoscyamine scopolamine, and was later used by Dr Crippen to murder his wife) to put a spell on Odysseus.
[3] '*Humida mella soporiferumque papaver.*' The Romans also called borage the 'herb of courage' because it raised the spirits of a depressed person.

4 See Brian Inglis's fascinating history *The Forbidden Game* (Hodder & Stoughton, 1975) and Dr S. Cohen's *Drugs of Hallucination* (Paladin, 1970). The ancient Zoroastrian religion used the intoxicant hayyuma in its sacrificial rites.

5 Richard T. Martin, 'The Role of Coca in the History, Religion and Medicine of South American Indians', *Economic Botany*, 24 (1970).

6 William G. Mortimer, *History of Coca* (J. Vail, 1901). For further details, see G. Andrews and D. Solomon (eds), *The Coca Leaf and Cocaine Papers* (Harcourt Brace Jovanovich, 1975), and Antonil, *Mama Coca* (Hassle Free Press, 1978). When Dr Robert Christison (1797–1882) climbed Ben Vorlich in the Scottish Highlands at the age of seventy-nine, he chewed coca.

7 R. Whitaker, *Drugs and the Law* (Methuen, Toronto, 1969). Chocolate by contrast was recommended in the seventeenth century as a medicine as well as an aphrodisiac. See J. Jacob, *Henry Stubbe* (Cambridge University Press, 1983).

8 Whitlock, *A History of Non-Medical Drug Use*. Until the nineteenth century, sugar was also prescribed as medicine.

9 *Cottage Economy* (London, 1822).

10 B. Griggs, *Green Pharmacy* (J. Norman and Hobhouse, 1981). M. J. Harner, *Hallucinogens and Shamanism* (Oxford University Press, 1973), records the origin of the legend of witches who flew on broomsticks: some women in the Middle Ages would rub belladonna (deadly nightshade) on to broomsticks and straddle them when naked; ingesting the drug through their labia, they experienced soaring hallucinations. It has been suggested that part of the motive for witch-hunts was male attempts to wrest the power of the healing role away from 'medicine women'.

11 *Coffin's Botanical Journal*, III (May 1962).

12 'I banish . . . brandy . . . Barbados waters . . . but for cowslip wine, poppy waters and all dormitives, these I allow' – William Congreve, *The Way of the World*. See also V. Berridge, 'Opiate use and legislative control', *Social Science and Medicine*, 13a, and 'Morality and medical science: concepts of narcotic addiction in Britain 1820–1926', *Annals of Science*, 36; V. Berridge and G. Edwards, *Opium and the People* (Allen Lane, 1981), and also T. Parssinen, *Secret Passions, Secret Remedies: Narcotic Drugs in British Society 1820–1930* (Manchester University Press, 1983).

13 *The Doors of Perception* and *Heaven and Hell* (Penguin, 1959).

14 *Confessions of an English Opium Eater* (Cresset Press, 1950, first published in the *London Magazine*, 1821). De Quincey's purported cure at the end of the book was untrue – see G. Lindop, *The Opium Eater* (Dent, 1981).

15 J. L. Lowes, *The Road to Xanadu* (Houghton Mifflin, 1964). The sacred river Alph and its caverns are not far from the River Axe and the caves at Wookey.

[16] *A Season in Hell* (1873). See also Alethea Hayter, *Opium and the Romantic Imagination* (Faber, 1968). John Calder, the publisher of, amongst others, Trocchi, says (in a personal communication): 'In my experience drugs are an absolute evil that destroy the creativity of creative people, even though it excites their brain.' Cf. J. B. S. Haldane, who said, 'I have tried morphine, heroin and hemp. The alteration of my consciousness due to those drugs was trivial compared with those produced in the course of my work.' On cannabis, see also John Julius Norwich's introduction to Suomi La Valle, *Hashish* (Quartet, 1984).

[17] G. Stimson and E. Oppenheimer, *Heroin Addiction: Treatment and Control in Britain* (Tavistock, 1982).

[18] The historian I. C. Y. Hsu believes that opium was 'the immediate, but not the ultimate, cause of the war' (*The Rise of Modern China*, New York, 1970), though Hsin-Pao Chang argues that it might as easily have been the Molasses War if molasses had been what the British merchants had wanted to sell (*Commissioner Lin and the Opium War*, Harvard University Press, 1964). Alasdair Clayre questions this: 'Britain wanted tea and silk from China, but the Chinese traders required nothing from Britain except payment in silver. To improve the balance of trade it was important for the British to find a product which the Chinese lacked. This proved to be opium from India.' (*The Heart of the Dragon*, Collins-Harvill, 1984.)

[19] J. Rowntree, *The Imperial Drug Trade* (Methuen, 1905). Mervyn Manby, however (in a personal communication), points out that although William Jardine and his fellow Scot James Matheson were motivated in the war by opium profits, London was also interested in free trade and diplomatic relations, and Manchester (probably the strongest influence on London) was seeking a market for its cotton goods.

[20] P. Lowes, *The Genesis of International Narcotics Control* (Librairie Droz, 1966, thesis at the University of Geneva, from which the author has kindly allowed me to quote). See also S. O'Callaghan, *The Drug Traffic* (New English Library, 1969).

[21] Prince Kung said to Sir Robert Alcock on his departure from Peking in 1869: 'Take away your opium and your missionaries and you will be welcome.'

[22] *Hansard*, vol. 144, p. 2043.

[23] *Journal of South-east Asian History*, March 1961.

[24] *Saturday Evening Post*, 20 September 1924.

[25] Heinrich Dreser of Dusseldorf, who in 1898 named the compound, in the next year also synthesized acetylsalicylic acid for Bayer, and gave it the brand name of 'aspirin', today probably the most widely used drug of all after alcohol and nicotine.

[26] D. Courtwright, *Dark Paradise: Opiate Addiction in America Before 1940* (Harvard University Press, 1981). He quotes one iatrogenic patient

impatiently asking her physician: 'Oh doctor, shoot me quick!': an example of the ballistic slant to much heroin slang.

27 E. Carlson and M. Simpson, *American Journal of Psychiatry*, 120 (1963).

28 An indication of the addictive character of some opiate medicines is shown by an analysis of 10,000 prescriptions made up by Boston drug-stores in that same year of 1888: 25 per cent of those renewed once contained opiates, but opiates were also present in 61 per cent of those renewed twice and 78 per cent of those renewed three times (A. Lindesmith, *Opiate Addiction*, Principia Press, 1947).

29 S. Freud, *Über Coca* (Vienna, 1884), which he described as 'a song of praise'; Ernest Jones, *The Life and Work of Sigmund Freud* (Basic Books, 1953). In *Letters to Wilhelm Fliess* Freud wrote, 'The condition of the heart depends upon the condition of the nose' (Harvard University Press, 1985).

2   The Struggle to Control

1 The 1930 Simon Report (vol. 1, pp. 360–1) shows that the bulk of this revenue was derived from exports, which the administration of India undertook to cease by 1935. The government of Burma – then part of India – told the Simon Commission that its annual revenue from internal sales of opium in 1927 was about £30,000: about half the total of taxes on liquor. In the Indian army during the Second World War, addicted soldiers, including a Naik corporal, were still allowed to draw a weekly issue of opium (Prof. Hugh Tinker, personal communication).

2 'He is the most ghastly menace to our present civilization which has appeared since Attila the Hun' (*The Mask of Fu Manchu*, 1932) 'Sax Rohmer' was in fact A. H. Ward, a Birmingham-born Irishman. The British Press similarly made a 'Yellow Peril' scapegoat of the Chinese – of whom there were less than 1,000 in Britain: see, for example, the contemporary *Daily Express* and *Evening News* reports of 'dancedope dens' where 'the same sickening crowd of undersized aliens' mingled with 'pretty, underdressed' English maidenhood.

3 In the 1922 case of US v. Behrman, the Supreme Court held that, regardless of medical intent, clinics supplying maintenance narcotics were acting illegally. The case of Hawkins v. US deterred doctors from prescribing heroin even to terminal patients.

4 *The Case Against Heroin* (Foreign Policy Association, New York, 1924).

5 *The Heroin Solution* (Yale University Press, 1982).

6 G. Stimson and E. Oppenheimer, *Heroin Addiction: Treatment and Control in Britain* (Tavistock, 1982): a particularly intelligent and objective survey.

7 Report of the Ministry of Health Departmental Committee on Morphine and Heroin Addiction (HMSO, 1926). The Committee was

appointed by John Wheatley who was Minister of Health in 1924, but reported to his successor, Neville Chamberlain.

8 H. B. Spear, 'The British Experience' (*John Marshall Journal*, 9, 1975), and personal interviews.

9 D. Courtwright, *Dark Paradise: Opiate Addiction in America Before 1940* (Harvard University Press, 1982).

10 D. Musto, *The American Disease: Origins of Narcotic Control* (Yale University Press, 1973); T. Parssinen, *Secret Passions, Secret Remedies* (Manchester University Press, 1983).

11 (G. P. Putnam, New York, 1977): 'Rockefeller played the politics of fear so adroitly in the national media that President Nixon borrowed from him many rhetorical images and the statistical hyperbole linking heroin and crime in the public's mind. Rockefeller succeeded in making the heroin vampire a national issue and himself vice-president, even if in the next two years the laws themselves proved unworkable.' Cf. Alfred McCoy, who in his *The Politics of Heroin in South-east Asia* (Harper and Row, 1972), blames a major growth of addiction on CIA policies, or C. Lamour and M. Lambert's *The Second Opium War* (Allen Lane, 1972) who attribute it to racist capitalism.

12 The Committee was composed in December 1970 of representatives from the Department of Labor, the Defense Department, the Federal Bureau of Narcotics and Dangerous Drugs, the Department of Housing and Urban Development, the Office of Economic Opportunity, the Veterans Administration, and the National Institute of Mental Health.

13 *Problems of Drug Abuse in Britain*, ed. D. J. West (Cambridge Institute of Criminology, 1978).

14 Second Report of the Inter-departmental Committee on Morphine and Heroin Addiction (HMSO, 1965). Whereas the first Report had said addiction was 'an expression of mental disorder', the second stated that 'the addict is a sick person, provided he does not resort to criminal acts'.

15 *Keep the Faith, Baby: A Close-up of London's Drop-outs* (SPCK, 1973). In 1984 the police told a House of Commons Committee that the Chinese community is extremely law-abiding, and that there was now no evidence of any groups in Britain having links with the Triads in Hong Kong or elsewhere.

16 'British Experience in the Management of Opiate Dependence', *The Dependence Phenomenon*, ed. M. Glass (MIT Press, 1982). See also Spear's prescient 1969 article, 'The Growth of Heroin Addiction in the United Kingdom', *British Journal of Addiction*, 64, and A. H. Godse, 'Treatment of Drug Addiction in London' (*Lancet*, 19 March 1983). By 1974 Dr F. Fish also found warning signs of a rapid increase amongst young people in Glasgow: 'Prevalence of Drug Misuse Among Young People in Glasgow 1970–72', *British Journal of Addiction*, 69.

17 *New Statesman*, 4 January 1985.

3 International Solidarity: The Present Situation Across the World

1 When the police in helicopter raids seized 100,000 *Papaver somniferum* plants (from which opium is extracted) at Raddusa, Sicily in May 1985, the local growers protested to the Italian President that for centuries they had used poppy seeds to garnish loaves for religious occasions; the police, however, suspected that some of the crop also fed the nearby heroin refineries in Palermo. Similar poppy crops are being grown for seeds on bread near Bury St Edmunds in England.

2 '*Diffusione della Tossicodipendenze quantita e qualita degli interventi pubblici e privati in Italia*' (Ministero dell'Interno, Rome, 1983).

3 U. Avico, 'Prevalence of opiate use among young men in Italy' (*Bulletin on Narcotics*, XXXV, no. 3).

4 L. Wever, *Drug Problems and Drug Policy in the Netherlands* (Ministry of Welfare and Health, The Hague, 1983). See also, Report of the Narcotics Working Party: *Background and Risks of Drug Use* (Government Publishing Office, The Hague, 1972). The Dutch 1976 Opium Act, which reduced the penalty for cannabis use, tripled the penalty for trafficking in hard drugs to twelve years' jail.

5 The Finance Ministry has agreed to allow a Dutch father who pays for his son's heroin supply to deduct the cost from his tax.

6 Personal interview, The Hague, February 1985.

7 Survey by J. C. Hoekstra of Groningen University (*Economisch Statistische Berichten*, 21 December 1984).

8 In 1982 the figures were as follows: Amsterdam 0.29, Los Angeles 0.28, New York 0.24, Chicago 0.23, Paris 0.10, London 0.02 and Tokyo 0.01 – all per 1,000 of population.

9 Personal interview, February 1985.

10 Such an approach was successfully pioneered by the Projetto Uomo at the Centro Italiano di Solidarieta in Rome.

11 *Soviet Life*, no. 6, 1985. Accurate data is hard to obtain, but delegates to one recent medical conference in Moscow were puzzled to be categorically informed that neither prostitutes nor drugs existed in the USSR, when several of them had had first-hand experience of both the previous night.

12 Originally it was only obtainable from the Tsar's Bar, on the site of what is now the Gum department store in Red Square.

13 Martin Walker of the *Guardian* reports that several Soviet authorities believe that alcohol is a greater threat to Slav survival than a nuclear war.

14 *Rzeczpospolita*.

15 B. Freemantle, *The Fix* (Michael Joseph, 1985), quoted by kind permission of the author.

16 The 1982 prices in Canada were 25 per cent lower than the previous year.

[17] *South*, February 1984.

[18] *Washington Post*, 16 November 1980.

[19] *International Herald Tribune*, 23 May 1984.

[20] R. Vere, 'Peru, an unnatural disaster' in *RRDC Bulletin*, October 1984.

[21] *Catha edulis Forsk.*

[22] Dr T. Baasher in *Courier* (UNESCO, January 1982). A WHO study found that 86 per cent of Djibouti's men, but only 13 per cent of the women, regularly chew kat.

[23] Dr S. Acuda of Nairobi University also points out: 'Educated or professional people may have to adjust to a different type of problem: that of working to rigid schedules in competitive situations. In the country, life was relatively simple and unstructured, and the amount of work done depended on the individual's capacity and on natural conditions like rain, the sun and darkness.'

[24] Sporadic attempts have been made to control opium in Thailand since the fourteenth century. See, Dr K. Edmundson and others, *National Drug Abuse Policy in Thailand* (WHO, 1982), and Serin Punnahritanond, *Survey of Attitudes of Thai Youth Toward Drugs* (Chulalongkorn University, undated).

[25] *New Scientist*, 16 February 1984.

[26] J. Westermeyer, *Poppies, Pipes and People: Opium and its Use in Laos* (University of California Press, 1982).

[27] For an excellent analysis of what should be done, see *Aliran Monthly* (Penang, P.O. Box 1049, Malaysia), February 1985.

[28] See, their documentary film *Changing the Needle*.

[29] A leading article in the *South China Morning Post* noted that some important Hong Kong entrepreneurs owed their first steps up the financial ladder to drug-dealing. A number operate from Taiwan, with which Hong Kong does not have an extradition treaty.

[30] M. Heikal, *The Cairo Documents* (Doubleday, 1973).

[31] Dr I. Khan and Prof. Cai Zhi-Ji, *Drug Abuse Control in the People's Republic of China* (WHO, 1982).

[32] Patrick Hughes, *Beyond the Wall of Respect* (University of Chicago Press, 1977).

[33] Three times as much illicit opium – 1,334 kg. – was seized in the first nine months of 1983 as in the whole of 1980.

[34] Derived from *Khemar* (veil): hence anything which veils the mind. See Dr T. Baasher, 'The Use of Drugs in the Islamic World' in *Drug Use and Misuse*, ed. G. Edwards, A. Arif and J. Jaffe (Croom Helm, 1983); and also M. Ruthven, *Islam in the World* (Penguin, 1984).

[35] Cf. the folklore Tales of the Arabian Nights.

[36] A. W. McCoy, *Drug Traffic* (Harper and Row, Sydney, 1980).

[37] D. Hirst, *Heroin in Australia* (Quartet, Melbourne, 1979). The author saw ten of his friends die from heroin while he was at the Australian National University.

[38] Australian Senate Welfare Committee report, 1977; New South Wales

Parliament's Joint Committee on Drugs Progress Report, 1978; US Congress Select Committee on Narcotics Study Mission, 1978.

39 Australian Government Publishing Service, Canberra, 1983. See also R. Hall, *Greed* (Pan, 1981).

4 For Good or Ill: A Survey of Drugs in General

1 Dr Wilner and G. Kassebaum (eds.), 'Problems in the Social Psychology of Addiction', *Narcotics*, 1965.

2 A British professor recalled that using speed – the name derived from the syndrome for twentieth-century living – was 'Simplicity itself. Just lick your finger, dip it in the packet, suck off the powder as though it were childhood sherbet, and you were guaranteed to be awake and buzzing for the next eight hours.'

3 H. van Praag, *Psychotropic Drugs: A Guide for the Practitioner* (Macmillan, 1978); see also *Drug Misuse* (Institute for the Study of Drug Dependence, 1985); Nicholas Saunders, *Alternative London* (Saunders, 1971) and P. Taberner, *Aphrodisiacs: the Science and the Myth* (Croom Helm, 1985). The detrimental effects of drugs on sexual performance almost invariably occur in males, because the male requires a fully functioning nervous system for success in sexual activity.

4 Martindale's *Extra Pharmacopoeia* (28th edition, Pharmaceutical Press, 1982), and P. Turner and G. Volans, *Drugs Handbook 1984–5* (Macmillan, 1984). Regarding caffeine, see M. Kenny and A. Darragh (*Psychiatry in Practice*, October 1985).

5 Hunter S. Thompson describes one experience of ether as follows. ' . . . total loss of all basic motor skills: blurred vision, no balance, numb tongue – severance of all connection between the body and the brain. Which is interesting, because the brain continues to function more or less normally . . . you can actually watch yourself behave in this terrible way, but you can't control it.' (*Fear and Loathing in Las Vegas*, Paladin, 1972.)

6 See Peter Sperryn, *Sport and Medicine* (Butterworth); Charles Burgess, 'Drugs: Use and Abuse' (*Guardian*, 17 September 1983); and T. F. Burks, 'Drugs used by athletes' in G. Nahas and H. C. Frick II (eds), *Drug Abuse in the Modern World* (Pergamon, 1981). By contrast, in 1984 a north Italian soccer team was accused of putting Valium in their opponents' tea at half-time.

7 *Beyond the Pleasure Principle, Collected Papers* (International Psychoanalytic Press, 1950).

8 H. Isbell, *Medical Clinics of North America* (1950).

9 R. Smart *et al.*, *Journal of Safety Research* (1.2, 1969).

10 B. Cromie, *Journal of the Royal Society of Medicine* (73, 1980).

[11] Report on the Work of the Prison Department 1983 (HMSO, Cmd. 9306); see also *New Statesman*, 2 December 1983. In 1983, 47,866 doses of anti-depressants, sedatives and tranquillizers were given to female inmates of Holloway, compared with only 5,177 to the men of Leicester Prison, which has approximately the same number of inmates.

[12] 'Some observations on the use of tranquillizing drugs', *Archives of Neurological Psychiatry*, 1957.

[13] 'Drugs and Social Values', *International Journal of Addiction*, 1970.

[14] Peter Laurie, *Drugs* (Penguin, 1981, 2nd edition). For useful advice for lay people: see, MIND's *Tranquillizers, Hard Facts, Hard Choices*, and Release's *Trouble with Tranquillizers* (1982). An association to help tranquillizer users in Britain is TRANX, 2 St John's Road, Harrow, Middlesex.

[15] M. B. Balter, 'Coping with Illness' in R. Helms (ed.), *Drug Development and Marketing* (American Enterprise Institute for Public Policy Research, Washington, 1975). See also Prof. M. Smith, 'Drugs and the Right to Happiness', *Drug Intelligence and Clinical Pharmacy* (14, 1980).

[16] For some case histories see, for example, Celia Haddon, *Women and Tranquillizers* (Sheldon Press, 1984); and Joy Melville, *The Tranquillizer Trap* (Fontana, 1984).

[17] Five people died out of 212 cases who had taken it – J. Gowdy, *Journal of American Medical Association*, 1972. Algonquin Indians used to feed adolescents Datura during puberty rites so that they would forget childhood because of amnesia from the drug. See also G. Mendelson, 'Abuse of Thorn-apple' in *Medical Journal of Australia* 1, 1973; Dr R. Julien, *A Primer of Drug Action* (W. H. Freeman, 1978); and W. Embolen, *Narcotic Plants* (Macmillan, New York, 1979).

[18] Cf. the sixteenth-century Franciscan B. de Sahagun's *Historia de las cosas de Neuva Espana* (Santa Fé, 1961): 'When [the Aztecs] ate peyote, [they] esteemed it above wine or mushrooms. They assembled together somewhere in the desert; they came together; there they danced, they sang all night, all day. And on the morrow, once more they assembled together. They wept, they wept exceedingly. They said eyes were washed; thus they cleansed their eyes.'

[19] The leading British cases are R. v. Goodchild (House of Lords, 1978) and R. v. Stevens (Court of Appeal, 1981). For those who want more certainty about which mushrooms are safe, see Roger Phillips, *Mushrooms and other Fungi* (Ward Lock, 1983) for a useful guide.

[20] Dr M. Gossop, *Living with Drugs* (Temple Smith, 1982).

[21] *Othello*, 3.iii. Mandragora is the mandrake plant.

[22] Napp Pharmaceuticals of Cambridge's patented controlled release system tablet uses the selective hydration of a polymer called Hydroxyalkyl cellulose. Dr Richard Lamerton describes it as 'the most important step forward in drug control of pain since morphine itself'.

[23] 'Cancer ward', *World Medicine* 15(12), 1980. A majority of terminal

cancer patients in one research survey were judged to have been denied proper relief of their pain (C. M. Parkes, *Journal of the Royal College of General Practitioners* 29, 1978).

24 *New Scientist*, 18 February 1984.

25 *British Medical Journal*, 22 January 1966.

26 Dr Lloyd Johnston *et al.*, 'Drugs and the nation's high school students' in *Drug Abuse and the Modern World* edited by G. Nahas and H. Clay Frick II (Pergamon, 1981).

27 Personal communications, 1984.

28 The *Journal of the American Medical Association* advised in an editorial article, 'When withdrawing a placebo on which a patient has become dependent it will not help him to be told it was only a placebo.'

29 Khint received a maximum fifteen-year prison sentence (*Sunday Times*, 13 May 1984).

30 Rev. Gordon Moody, personal communication, 8 October 1984.

31 *The Times*, 16 November 1983.

32 Personal communication, 2 August 1984.

33 Jane Fonda was one surprising example of this in her earlier years, recounting that she was eating food fifteen to twenty times a day.

34 T. Szasz, *Ceremonial Chemistry* (Routledge, 1975); T. Du Quesne and J. Reeves, *A Handbook of Psychoactive Medicines* (Quartet, 1982).

35 D. Lawrence and J. Black, *The Medicine You Take* (Croom Helm, 1978).

36 *Cured to Death: the effect of prescription drugs* (Secker and Warburg, 1982). As long ago as 1970 Dr Donald Brodie, of the US National Center for Health Services Research and Development, stated that the annual cost of adverse reactions in the US was over $1 billion (*Drug Utilization*, 1970).

37 *British Journal of Clinical Pharmacology*, 1981, 12: Dr Griffin was at that time senior officer at the Department of Health's medicines division. See also Dr R. Mann, *Modern Drug Use* (MIT Press, 1984).

38 C. Medawar, *The Wrong Kind of Medicine?* (Hodder & Stoughton and the Consumers' Association, 1984) and *Drug Diplomacy* (Social Audit, London). *Which?* magazine pointed out in its first issue that aspirin BP was identical with, but cost only one-fifth of the price of, some branded versions. In 1973 the UK Monopolies Commission found that in 1970 Hoffmann-La Roche were selling Valium in Britain for £1,962 per kilo, when the raw materials' cost to the company was £20 a kilo. See also S. Adams, *Roche versus Adams* (Cape, 1984). In 1986 US drug firms were told by the UK Department of Health to repay £25 million excess profits on sales to the National Health Service.

39 See Derek Cooper, 'Health on your doorstep' and 'Magic products' in the *Listener*, 1984 and 9 May 1985. Dr Pickles of the DHSS found in 1984 that forty-two out of seventy-four drugs advertisements did not comply with their own code of practice. Prof. Michael Rawlins wrote in the *Lancet* in July 1984: 'The charge against us is that in many of our dealings

with the industry we have become corrupt; that in return for needlessly and sometimes recklessly prescribing their expensive products we accept or even demand reward on a breath-taking scale . . . In the meeting between doctor and rep little is left to chance. Most major companies maintain a computerized register of doctors that includes not just name, address and age, but also principal interests, both medical and non-medical, as well as details of individual prescribing habits.'

[40] Dr Mahler (Director-General of the WHO), *World Health Forum* (1981). See also Dr Norman Myers, 'Shamanism without sham' (*Guardian*, 16 May 1985).

[41] For evaluations of the policy's success, see *World Health* (WHO, July 1984), and F. Rolt, *Pills, Policies and Profits* (War on Want, 1985).

[42] D. Melrose, *Bitter Pills* (Oxfam, 1982).

[43] UK Association of Public Analysts, 1984 Annual Report. One public analyst found non-pharmacy outlets in his area selling 30 tons of sub-standard aspirins that had become unstable and had an excess of salicylic acid over the amount permitted by the *British Pharmacopoeia*.

[44] Personal interview.

[45] See D. Bull, *A Growing Problem* (Oxfam, 1982).

[46] G. Tindall, 'Living with Risk', *New Society*, 15 November 1984. See also C. Faulder, *Whose body is it?* (Virago, 1985). In addition, over 2 million experiments take place in Britain annually to test and develop new drugs and products. The majority of such new chemical items offer either only a marginal or no advantage over existing products, and Dr R. Mann, Principal Medical Officer at the DHSS, says that discouraging the development of such 'me-too' drugs 'would save many animal lives'.

[47] A full list of harmful additives is given in the UK Ministry of Agriculture's booklet *Look at the Label*. See also D. Raynor, 'Labels on medicines: do patients understand them?' (*Self Health*, 1985).

[48] See Milton Silverman, *The Drugging of the Americas* (University of California Press, 1976).

5 'Some More Poison?' – 'I Don't Mind If I Do': Alcohol

[1] Methylated spirits are alcohol with 5–10 per cent wood naphtha. Eau de Cologne is 90 per cent alcohol with a sweet-smelling oil such as bergamot added, and was a recognized tipple in the nineteenth century. Today there is a disastrous vogue amongst Canadian Indians for drinking disinfectant which is 85 per cent alcohol and much cheaper than whisky.

[2] In its natural form a tasteless alcoholic distillate, gin can be fermented from many carbohydrates, including potatoes, sugar-cane juice and

molasses as well as grain; its flavour is added by juniper berries. Vodka is similar, but without the flavouring. Purified sulphur and small quantities of asbestos are considered safe additives in wine.

3 'It provokes the desire, but it takes away the performance' (*Macbeth*).

4 R. Boycott, *A Nice Girl Like Me* (Chatto and Windus, 1984).

5 Dr M. Gossop, *Living with Drugs* (Temple Smith, 1982).

6 *Medicine on Trial* (Aldus, 1967). By contrast, Jung said of a patient: 'His craving for alcohol was equivalent, on a low level, to the spiritual thirst of our being for wholeness . . . Alcohol in Latin is *"spiritus"* and you use the word for the highest religious experience as well as for the most depraving poison.' He told this to Bill Wilson, the co-founder of Alcoholics Anonymous, who believed alcoholics could only be rescued by a 'spiritual approach since alcoholism is partly a spiritual search'.

7 G. Vaillant, *The Natural History of Alcoholism* (Harvard University Press, 1983). In the USA, Washington DC's consumption rate of 5.22 gallons per head a year reaches almost twice the national average.

8 J. Davies and B. Stacey, *Teenagers and Alcohol* (Office of Population Censuses and Surveys, HMSO, 1972). In Britain, it is a criminal offence to give alcohol to any child under five.

9 M. Grant and P. Guinner (eds), *Alcoholism in Perspective* (Croom Helm, 1979).

10 *Understanding Alcohol and Alcoholism in Scotland* (Scottish Health Education Group, 1982). A recent Scottish survey found that three-quarters of alcoholic liver patients continued to drink alcohol.

11 Formerly President of the Royal College of Physicians in Edinburgh. In 1981 coroners' courts in England and Wales recorded over four times as many deaths from chronic alcoholism as in 1971 – a far greater increase than for deaths from other drug addictions. See also Prof. A. Maynard and P. Kennan, 'The Economics of Alcohol Abuse', *British Journal of Addiction* (76, 1981). *An Agenda for Action on Alcohol* (Action on Alcohol Abuse 1986) estimates that more than 25,000 people a year are dying in Britain as a result of alcohol abuse.

12 Personal communication, August 1984. See also 'Alcohol a Cause for Concern', M. Meacher *et al.*, *Cold Comfort* (1985). A number of senior police officers believe that drivers should not drink any alcohol at all if they wish to remain safe. The effects of a heavy evening's drinking can last well into the following day.

13 'Dread delightable drink and thou shalt do the better. Measure is medicine, though thou much yearn. All is not good for the ghost [spirit] that the gut asketh, nor is livelihood to the body what is life to the soul.' William Langland, *Will's Vision of Piers Plowman*.

14 Dr T. Baasher, 'The Use of Drugs in the Islamic World' in G. Edwards, A. Arif and J. Jaffe (eds), *Drug Use and Misuse* (Croom Helm, 1983). See also M. Ruthven, *Islam in the World* (Penguin, 1984). Cf. the 'Drink, for tomorrow we die' hedonism of Hafiz of Shiraz:

> Let us get drunk with a cup of the rose-red wine –
> Before this transient world has itself passed out.
> Since one day we'll be clay for Fate to make pitchers of,
> Let my skull be a cup kept sweet, being filled with wine.

15 *Characters* (1688).

16 B. Inglis, *The Forbidden Game* (Hodder and Stoughton, 1975).

17 See S. Whipple, *Noble Experiment* (1964), A. Sinclair, *Prohibition* (1962); and M. Short, *Crime Inc.* (Thames Methuen, 1984). Bootleggers fight similar Prohibition wars today in the 'dry' Indian state of Gujarat.

18 In 1981 Swedes drank an average of 5.08 litres of spirits a year, compared to 3.16 in Iceland, 4.15 in Norway, 6.40 in Finland, 9.60 in Denmark, 9.70 in Britain and 10.12 in Greenland. Those EEC countries with virtually no controls on alcohol (Italy, Austria, France, Spain) have much greater rates of death from cirrhosis of the liver than a country such as Eire, which has controls.

19 *Listener*, 27 September 1984.

20 *The Disease Concept of Alcoholism* (Hillhouse Press, 1960). Jellinek concluded that alcoholism can be of at least five different forms, and that drunkenness is by no means synonymous with alcoholism; see M. Glatt, *The Alcoholic* (Priory, 1972).

21 Robert Julien, *A Primer of Drug Action* (Freeman, 1978); *Alcohol and Health* (US Department of Health, 1974). See also Dr Colin Brewer, 'The Cost of Drying Out' (*Self Health*, the College of Health, 1986).

22 Breathlessness, throbbing headaches, nausea, vomiting, and sometimes convulsions. This is due to the accumulation of acetaldehyde in the body, and may be precipitated by even a small amount of alcohol.

23 Another offspring is Analysands Anonymous, open to anyone who has been in psychoanalysis for twelve or more years and who needs help to terminate the analysis.

24 David Robinson, 'The Growth of Alcoholics Anonymous', *Alcohol and Alcoholism* (18.2, 1983). For a critical counter-view, see N. Heather and I. Robertson, *Problem Drinking* (Pelican, 1986).

25 The Los Angeles-Hollywood membership is one of the biggest, with over 100,000 joining in 1985. In the Middle East, most of the members are employees of foreign firms.

26 AA's contact address in the UK is P.O. Box 514, 11 Redcliffe Gardens, London SW10 8BQ (telephone 01-834-8202), and Al-Anon Family Groups can be contacted at 61 Great Dover Street, London SE1 4YF (telephone 01-430-0888).

27 *The Economist*, 15 June 1985.

28 The publicly-funded UK charity Alcohol Concern receives only £400,000 a year from the Department of Health, from which it can spend a mere £12,000 on promotion; while the Department of Transport, whose 'drink/drive' campaign saves many lives, has had its advertising budget cut from £5.4 million in 1983–4 to £3.9 million in 1986–7. See also

P. Tether and D. Robinson, *Preventing Health Problems* (Tavistock, 1986).

6 The Fatal Habit: Tobacco

[1] Snuff is tobacco which has been washed and then sometimes coloured and flavoured. In eighteenth-century England it became more fashionable than smoking, so much so that in 1773 Dr Johnson wrote, 'Smoking is dying out.'

[2] W. Hale-White, *Textbook of Pharmacology and Therapeutics* (Pentland Young, Edinburgh, 1901).

[3] *Smoking and Health* (Pitman Medical Publishing Co., 1962).

[4] *Smoking and Health* (US Department of Health, Education and Welfare, 1964).

[5] *Smoking and Health Now* (Pitman, 1971).

[6] 'Deaths from coronary heart disease are responsible for about half of the total excess deaths among cigarette smokers and are numerically greater than the excess deaths from either lung cancer or chronic bronchitis . . .' *Smoking or Health* (Pitman, 1977).

[7] *Smoking and Health* (US Department of Health, Education and Welfare, 1979).

[8] *The Health Consequences of Smoking: Cancer* (US Department of Health, Education and Welfare, 1982). In literature, the smoker's *Under the Volcano* is Italo Svevo's *Confessions of Zeno* (Penguin, 1964).

[9] L. Breslow, 'Control of Cigarette Smoking from a Public Policy Perspective', *Annual Review of Public Health* (1982–3), and WHO annual statistics.

[10] *Living with Drugs* (Temple Smith, 1982).

[11] *New England Journal of Medicine*, 8 November 1984.

[12] R. Stepney, 'Why do people smoke?', *New Society*, 28 July 1983. J. Bynner in *The Young Smoker* (HMSO, 1969) wrote that head-teachers' smoking habits in particular have a strong effect on school-children.

[13] A. Starke, *International Journal of Psychoanalysis*, 1921.

[14] Smokers with beards and moustaches inhale even more toxic chemicals, since these are trapped in their hair.

[15] *New England Journal of Medicine*, 27 September 1984. See also H. Ashton and R. Stepney, *Smoking: Psychology and Pharmacology* (Tavistock, 1982).

[16] James Repace, *Working Paper RC-4* (Center for Philosophy and Public Policy, Maryland, 1983).

[17] Between 1972 and 1982 the proportion of adult British males who smoke fell from 52 per cent to 38 per cent, while among women the percentage dropped from 41 to 33. *Population Trends*, 37 (HMSO). There are wide

regional variations: Scots spend most on cigarettes with an average of £4.82 a week, compared with £2.75 in East Anglia. In the 1985 Budget, for the third successive year, duty on pipe tobacco was not increased – thus lowering its cost against inflation.

[18] Documents recently released under the thirty-year rule at the Public Record Office.

[19] Peter Taylor, *Smoke Ring: The Politics of Tobacco* (Bodley Head, 1984). See also *The Big Kill* (UK Health Education Council, 1985).

[20] Minnesota, Montana, Nebraska, Utah and Connecticut have also passed laws limiting smoking at work, and thirty-one US states restrict it in public places. Czechoslovakia now gives every worker the right to a work-place where smoking is banned. On an Air Canada flight recently it was announced that 'Anyone caught smoking in the toilets will be asked to leave the plane immediately'.

[21] Since tobacco thrives in semi-arid land, its production leads to the increase of deserts (J. Madeley, 'Tobacco: A Ruinous Crop', *Ecologist*, 1986).

[22] *Smoking Among Secondary School Children* (HMSO, 1983 and 1986). In 1985 the UK Office of Population Censuses and Surveys found that 13 per cent of teenagers under the age of sixteen now regularly smoke fifty or more cigarettes per week, compared with 11 per cent in 1982. A recent survey among tobacconists in Hampstead found that one-third did not know it is illegal to sell cigarettes to those under the age of sixteen.

[23] The film is obtainable from Project Icarus, 4 Clarence Parade, Southsea, Hants. The Institute of Psychiatry in London suggests that a new way to help give up smoking might be to take vasopressin, a hormone that aids concentration and is released by the body when a person smokes.

[24] 'The Biggest Kill', 28 November 1985. David Steel has suggested that smoking should be restricted to consenting adults in private.

7 The Faustian Pact: Heroin

[1] It was not ever thus. The British nineteenth-century Royal Commission on Opium in India found little evidence of harm or abuse, and reported that opium was a reasonable aid for most people in their life's work. Sir George Birdwood, a medical professor in Bombay, in 1881 described opium smoking in a letter to *The Times* as 'almost as harmless an indulgence as twiddling the thumbs, and other silly-looking methods of concentrating the jaded mind.' However, in 1713 the agent at the British trading station in Sumatra wrote that it produces 'very different effects on different constitutions. Some are laid by it into so profound a sleep that the noise of a drum, a cannon or even a scolding woman cannot wake them. Others are reduced to a perfect state of indolence, insensible of pain and possessed with such a kind of negative pleasure as renders them regardless of everything. A third sort are downright delirious,

sleep with their eyes wide open, and talk a great deal without any design or connection.' Quoted in B. Inglis, *The Opium War* (Hodder and Stoughton, 1976).

2   After tests on sixty unwitting patients, Henrich Dreser of Bayer and Co. pronounced it excellent for treating asthma, tuberculosis, bronchitis and coughs – and it lacked morphine's disadvantages of being emetic and habit-forming.

3   A. S. Trebach, *The Heroin Solution* (Yale University Press, 1982); see also G. Stimson, *Heroin and Behaviour* (Irish University Press, 1973).

4   D. L. Gerard compared the two in *Drinking and Intoxication*: 'The addict is comfortable and functions well as long as he receives large enough quantities of drugs to stave off his abstinence syndrome. The chronically intoxicated alcoholic, on the other hand, cannot function normally as long as he maintains his intoxicating intake of alcohol.' The deadly snakes in the famous Snake Temple of Penang are supposed to owe their docility to a diet of gum opium.

5   Its restriction on respiration can also be dangerous for asthmatics.

6   Recent tests at the larger prisons in France revealed that 57 per cent of male and female drug-addict inmates who had used syringes are infected with the AIDS virus. Such addicts represent 10 to 30 per cent of the prison population.

7   W. McAuliffe and R. Gordon, 'A Test of Lindesmith's Theory of Addiction', *American Journal of Sociology*, 79.4 (1974). Dr Norman Zinberg, of Harvard Medical School, studied some users who had been taking heroin for twenty-five years.

8   Anyone with a suspected overdose should be taken quickly to hospital. A close check should be kept on pulse rate and breathing, and artificial respiration given if needed. There are antidotes to a heroin or morphine overdose (such as Naxolene, Naline or Narcon) but these have to be given under medical supervision lest they start an instant withdrawal which could be fatal.

9   *The Continuum Concept* (Penguin, 1986). Timothy Leary condemns heroin as 'a euphoric downer that has no appeal to me or to any other active person who wishes to maintain freedom or independence . . . Opiates, which lower intelligence, have the opposite effect from psychedelic drugs which increase sensitivity to and understanding of the broad spectrum of human realities.'

10   Dr Ian Oswald, *British Medical Journal*, 1, 1969.

11   *Confessions of an English Opium-Eater* (Cresset Press, 1950). But cf. Baudelaire's *Le Poison*:

> Le vin sait revêtir le plus sordide bouge
>   D'un luxe miraculeux
> Et fait surgir plus d'un portique fabuleux
>   Dans l'or de sa vapeur rouge:
> Comme un soleil couchant dans un ciel nébuleux

> L'opium agrandit ce qui n'a pas de bornes,
>   Allonge l'illimité
> Approfondit le temps, creuse la volupté,
>   Et de plaisirs noirs et mornes
> Remplit l'âme au-delà de sa capacité.
>
> Tout cela ne vaut pas le poison, qui découle
>   De tes yeux, de tes yeux verts . . .

[12] 'Real Lives: Pushers', *Listener*, January 1985.

[13] Calder, 1963: 'I say it is impertinent, insolent, and presumptuous of any person or group of persons to impose their unexamined moral prohibitions upon me.'

[14] *Junky* (Penguin, 1977).

[15] Vol. 53, no. 2.

[16] *The Naked Lunch* (Calder, 1982).

[17] Dr Jerome Jaffe's study of Chicago addicts found that some 40 per cent supported themselves by theft. He discovered that there were about twenty separate 'copping' communities, each of some one hundred addicts in a geographical area, and each with its wholesale dealer (sometimes a non-addict), retail street-dealers, 'bag followers' (hookers), touts and hustlers.

[18] G. Stimson and E. Oppenheimer, *Heroin Addiction* (Tavistock, 1982).

[19] J. Kaplan, *The Hardest Drug* (Chicago University Press, 1983).

[20] For example, John Maher, organizer of the Delancey Street drug-free community project in San Francisco, suggests the answer is to organize people 'to get them working for things that are worthwhile'.

8   The Land of Cocaine

[1] Personal communication, 1984.

[2] *British Journal of Addiction*, vol. 53, no. 2. Also, 'Coke is pure kick. It lifts you straight up; a mechanical lift that starts leaving you as soon as you feel it. I don't know anything like C for a lift, but the lift only lasts ten minutes or so. Then you want another shot.' W. Burroughs, *Junky* (Penguin, 1977).

[3] Coca paste is formed by soaking the plant's dried leaves in water and kerosene, and then mixing it with sulphuric acid, potassium permanganate and lime to make coca base, which is refined with ether and acetone. The detritus is known as 'bazuka'.

[4] J. Jaffe, 'Drug Addiction and Drug Abuse', in L. Goodman and A. Gilman (eds), *The Pharmacological Basis of Therapeutics* (Macmillan, 1975).

[5] Pure cocaine is 5–15 per cent hydrochloride; without this it would be insoluble in water and unable to be sniffed.

6 G. Andrews and D. Solomon (eds), *The Coca Leaf and Cocaine Papers* (Harcourt, Brace, 1975). Advertisements for coca tea in Peru say, 'Hot or cold, it's a different kind of drink, good for the stomach. It reduces weight.' Hermann Goering lost 85 lb. by dieting on cocaine.

7 Using cocaine through or on the genitals is called 'balling'.

8 Antonil, *Mama Coca* (Hassle Free Press, 1978).

9 General Conclusions of the 4th Congress of CRIC, Toez, August 1975.

10 See Brian Moser's excellent 'Frontier' trilogy of films on cocaine in Colombia, Bolivia and the USA, shown by Central TV in September, 1983.

11 Royal Canadian Mounted Police (NDIE, 1982).

12 Gabriel García Márquez wrote in *El Espectador* (Bogota, 31 August 1983): 'The violence in Magdalena [Colombia] is much worse than in Central America . . . down the river the corpses float; the authorities have decided not to collect them because they are numerous . . . The perpetrators are paid gangs, killing in broad daylight; everybody knows them, but no one dares to denounce them . . . The corpses abandoned on the roads have been skinned with knives and have the genitals cut off and sometimes stuffed into the mouth, and are without tongue and ears.'

13 In 1985, the West German police seized 363 lb. of cocaine, compared with less than 6 lb. ten years before. According to American officials, the surplus coca leaf is grown in Bolivia (52,000,000 kg.), eastern Peru (50,000,000 kg.), Colombia (2,500,000 kg.), with a small amount also in Brazil, Ecuador and northern Chile.

9 Routes to Paradise: LSD

1 LSD's initials abbreviate its original German name *Lysergsaure Diathylamid*; '-25' identifies that it was the twenty-fifth synthesis in a series of amides prepared from lysergic acid in trial attempts to derive a new analeptic stimulant drug. Lysergic acid itself is not hallucinogenic.

2 W. Stoll, 'LSD 25' (*Swiss Archives of Neurology*, 60, 1974).

3 *Loporophora williamsii*, which also grows wild in parts of southern and western USA.

4 See Dr M. Gossop's excellent *Living with Drugs* (Temple Smith, 1982); E. Lieberman, 'Psychochemicals as weapons' (*Bulletin of Atomic Scientists*, January 1962); and J. Marks, *The Search for the Manchurian Candidate: the CIA and Mind Control* (Allen Lane, 1970).

5 In March 1985 he said, 'I took LSD once a week in 1964. I became happier for it and it dispelled a great many of the fears I had prior to that time. It's a shame it was damned by the Press and by people who knew nothing about it. Like anything that's good for you, they will probably take it away and use it for warfare.'

6 Research of Dr Pahnke, a doctor of divinity and a psychiatrist at Spring Grove Hospital, Maryland.

[7] 23 February 1978.

[8] *LSD in Britain: a review and assessment* (ISDD, 1978). See also Dr S. Cohen's thoughtful *Drugs of Hallucination* (Paladin, 1970), still probably the most detailed balanced study. Sidney Cohen's survey of 5,000 inhabitants who had been given LSD or mescalin found that the attempted suicide rate was nil amongst volunteer experimenters, and 1.2 per 1,000 amongst patients undergoing psychotherapy at the time.

[9] *The Doors of Perception* (Chatto & Windus, 1954) and *Heaven and Hell* (Chatto & Windus, 1956). For an alleged Mexican Yaqui Indian guru's relationship with peyote and Datura, see C. Castaneda, *The Teachings of Don Juan* (Penguin, 1970).

[10] The word 'psychedelic', from the Greek *psyche* (mind) and *delos* (visible), was coined by the psychiatrist Humphrey Osmond who introduced Aldous Huxley to mescalin.

[11] From his article 'A Journey to Paradise'. Cf. Hunter S. Thompson's description of the effects of taking acid in his laconically hilarious account of two junkies attending a District Attorneys' Drugs Convention, *Fear and Loathing in Las Vegas* (Paladin, 1972): 'Suddenly there was a terrible roar all around us: the sky was full of what looked like huge bats, all swooping and screeching and diving . . .' together with 'your dead grandmother crawling up your leg with a knife in her teeth.'

[12] Havelock Ellis, 'Mescal, a new artificial paradise' (*Contemporary Review*, January 1898).

[13] T. Leary, *Flashbacks* (Heinemann, 1983).

[14] In December 1962 Aldous Huxley wrote, 'Yes, what about Tim Leary. I spent an evening with him a few weeks ago and he talked such nonsense.' Huxley appreciated the need for intellectual honesty and extreme caution.

[15] *Flashbacks*, op.cit. 'It has been twenty years since that first LSD trip with Michael Hollingshead. I have never forgotten it. Nor has it been possible for me to return to the life I was leading before that session. I have never recovered from that ontological confrontation. I have never been able to take myself, my mind, or the social world quite so seriously. Since that time I have been acutely aware that everything I perceive, everything within and around me, is a creation of my own consciousness. And that everyone lives in a neural cocoon of private reality. From that day I have never lost the sense that I am an actor surrounded by characters, props, and sets for the comic drama being written in my brain.'

[16] See S. Tendler and D. May, *The Brotherhood of Eternal Love* (Panther, 1984).

[17] D. Lee and C. Pratt, *Operation Julie* (W. H. Allen, 1978). The millionaire manufacturers transferred their profits to Swiss banks to avoid tax, like other capitalists; and under the UK law of that time the police were unable to seize such assets.

[18] See Troy Duster, *The Legislation of Morality* (Free Press, 1970).

[19] A. Hofmann, *LSD: My Problem Child* (Tarcher, 1983).

[20] T. Du Quesne and J. Reeves, *Handbook of Psychoactive Medicine* (Quartet, 1982).

10 Glue Sniffing and Solvent Abuse

[1] *Drug Misuse* (Institute for the Study of Drug Dependence, 1985).

[2] This 1985 incidence, in a survey of 5,223 fourth-year secondary school-children by the UK National Campaign Against Solvent Abuse, compares with 7.6 per cent in a similar survey in 1984. The Campaign's advice and help telephone line (01 733 7330) is manned by counsellors who include former solvent abusers.

[3] House of Commons debate, 19 April 1985.

[4] See D. O'Connor, *Glue Sniffing and Volatile Substance Abuse* (Gower, 1983); *Human Toxicology* (vol. 1, 1982); and O. Sattaur, 'How glue sniffers become unstuck' (*New Scientist*, 1 March 1984).

[5] One American attempt to add an adversely smelling substance had to be abandoned when it was discovered that this particular additive could cause cancer. Dunlop, for example, has recently developed a heavy-duty glue (trade-named Powerfix) which does not contain the solvent toluene. And, after a number of teenagers died in the USA from sniffing typewriter correction fluid, the makers of Liquid Paper have stated that they are reformulating their product with mustard oil to discourage abuse.

[6] Investigation by Clements and Simpson in 1978, referred to in S. Eysenck, 'Solvent Abuse and the Law' (*Magistrate*, May 1984).

[7] This states: '1 (1) It is an offence for a person to supply or offer to supply a substance other than a controlled drug: (a) to a person under the age of eighteen whom he knows, or has reasonable cause to believe, to be under that age; or (b) to a person: (i) who is acting on behalf of a person under that age; and (ii) whom he knows, or has reasonable cause to believe, to be so acting, if he knows or has reasonable cause to believe that the substance is, or its fumes are, likely to be inhaled by the person under the age of eighteen for the purpose of causing intoxication.'

[8] R. v. Ahmed and Khaliq Raja (1983). The appeal court's ruling, that 'If substances were supplied to another person in the full knowledge that the person would use the substance to the danger of his health and life, the supplier had acted criminally', would seem also to give cause for worry to tobacco vendors and many publicans in Scotland.

[9] Under Section 28 of the 1969 Children and Young Persons Act, the English and Welsh police are empowered to detain a juvenile at risk by taking him to a place of safety. Scotland has the more explicit Solvent Abuse (Scotland) Act of 1983, which provides that a child caught abusing solvents in Scotland can be referred to a children's panel (a non-judicial alternative to juvenile court which Scotland alone possesses), and if necessary taken into compulsory care. More than 300

children were referred to a panel for glue sniffing in the first few months of the Act being in force.

[10] Bradford v. Wilson, Queen's Bench Divisional Court, 29 March 1983.

11   Pot or Not?

[1] A 1980 UK government chemist's report on the THC content of seized supplies found Zimbabwe cannabis had 3 per cent, Thai sticks 1–3 per cent, Indian hashish 10 per cent, and Pakistani hash oil 13.25 per cent. *Alternative London* (6th edition, ed. Georganne Downes, 1982) advises: 'Always try before you buy – it's normal practice.'

[2] See M. Schofield, *The Strange Case of Pot* (Penguin, 1971).

[3] N. Saunders, *Alternative London* (N. Saunders, 1971).

[4] Monkeys, given cannabis by Professor Giono at Dakar University, Senegal, lost their sense of balance, and reduced their social contacts, sexual and play activity. (Unesco, *Courier*, May 1973.) Hemp seeds have no noticeable ill-effect on pet birds. In humans, however, cannabis can be dangerous for car drivers, who, for instance, may stare at a tree, thinking it so beautiful that they forget they are driving.

[5] 'No drug is completely safe. In sufficient quantities, common salt can be lethal . . . but . . . with cannabis it would be virtually impossible to ingest enough of the drug for it to have a lethal effect. It has been estimated that the lethal dose could be as high as 40,000 times that of the effective dose. Cannabis is one of the least toxic drugs known to man, and there is no evidence that anyone has ever died as a direct result of taking an overdose of it.' Dr M. Gossop, *Living with Drugs* (Temple Smith, 1982). On dependence, see J. Griffith Edwards in the Advisory Council's *Report on Cannabis* (UK Home Office, 1982).

[6] H. J. Anslinger, 'Enforcement of the Narcotic Drug Laws of the USA', 14 May 1938. The Egyptian delegate at the Second Opium Conference, 1924, said, 'Hashish in large doses . . . predisposes to acts of violence and produces a characteristic strident laugh . . . the countenance of the addict becomes gloomy, his eye is wild and the expression of his face is stupid . . . the whole organism decays. The addict very frequently becomes neurasthenic and eventually insane . . . The illicit use of hashish is the principal cause of most of the cases of insanity occurring in Egypt. In support of this contention, it may be observed that there are three times as many cases of mental alienation among men as among women, and it is an established fact that men are much more addicted to hashish than [are] women. (In Europe, on the contrary, it is significant that a greater proportion of cases of insanity occur among women than among men.)'

[7] *Bulldog Drummond at Bay* (Hodder and Stoughton, 1935).

[8] UN document E/CN.7/SR.727.

⁹ *Cannabis: Report of the Commission of Inquiry into the Non-medical use of Drugs* (Ottawa, 1972).

¹⁰ Article 36.

¹¹ *Cannabis: Report by the Advisory Committee on Drug Dependence* (HMSO, 1968). One member, Michael Schofield, dissented and proposed that possession of up to 30 g. should be punished not by prison but by a fine of £50.

¹² Lady Wootton, who received a great deal of unfair and abusive mail when her Report appeared, observed in the House of Lords on 27 March 1969: 'The causes [of the hysteria] are familiar to students of social psychology. They occur in other connections as well, particularly in relation to sexual crimes, and they are always liable to recur when the public senses that some critical and objective study threatens to block an outlet for indulgence in the pleasures of moral indignation.'

¹³ *Report of the Expert Group on the Effects of Cannabis Use* (UK Home Office, 1982). The report on psychiatric effects was contributed by Prof. Griffith Edwards.

¹⁴ T. Malyon, in A. Henman, R. Lewis *et al.*'s *Big Deal* (Pluto, 1985).

¹⁵ Marijuana in the USA today is reported to be significantly more potent than previously. *Ninth Annual Report* to the US Congress from the Secretary of Health, Education and Welfare (Washington DC, 1982). Professor Gabriel Nahas, a UN consultant on narcotics, considers that cannabis can also impair female ovulation and male fertility.

¹⁶ Travellers at London Heathrow Airport are now given the option of confiscation plus an automatic 'compound' penalty of £50 as an alternative to prosecution if they are found in possession of only a small amount (less than half an ounce) of cannabis.

¹⁷ In 1982, 1,738 people were jailed for cannabis offences in the UK. In Louisiana, mere possession recently carried a minimum sentence of five to fifteen years' hard labour. In the USSR, Professor Konstantin Azadovsky was given two years' hard labour in Siberia for possession of 5 g. of cannabis (allegedly planted on him) in 1981. The law which appears to stand on the statute book as 'a mere convenience to be applied from time to time, on a very selective and discriminatory basis, to "make an example" of someone, is bound to create a strong sense of injustice, and a corresponding disrespect for law and law-enforcement. It is also bound to have adverse effects on the morale of law-enforcement authorities. Moreover, it is doubtful if its deterrent effect justifies the injury inflicted upon the individuals who have the misfortune to be prosecuted under it.' (Interim Report of the Le Dain Commission.)

¹⁸ Frank Logan (ed.), *Cannabis: Options for Control* (Quartermaine, 1979). The US state of Oregon decriminalized marijuana in 1973; contrary to the Dutch experience, four years later known adult use had risen by 6 per cent, and that of young adults by 16 per cent.

¹⁹ Federal Judge Edward Gignoux ruled that the First Amendment's

protection of religious beliefs is abrogated when these pose a substantial threat to public health and welfare.

12 Drug Misusers: Who? Why? and Treatment

[1] United Nations, *Development Forum*, June 1985.

[2] UK Advisory Council on the Misuse of Drugs, *Prevention* (HMSO, 1984). Earlier, the Advisory Council had warned, 'There is no evidence of any uniform personality characteristic or type of person who becomes either an addict or an individual with drug problems.'

[3] N. Dorn and A. Thompson, *Comparison of Levels of Mid-Teenage Experimentation with Illegal Drugs in Some Schools in England* (ISDD, 1975).

[4] In the UK, 34 per cent of females, compared with 18 per cent of males, have taken sleeping pills or tranquillizers on prescription (MORI, 1979). At present 8 per cent of all adults are being treated with psychotropic drugs in the UK, and the position is similar in the USA, Belgium, Denmark, France, West Germany, Italy, the Netherlands, Spain and Sweden. (See J. Marks, *The Benzodiazepines*, MTP, Lancaster, 1978.)

[5] *Junky* (Penguin, 1977).

[6] *Confessions of an English Opium-Eater* (Cresset Press, 1950).

[7] G. Lindop, *The Opium-Eater* (Dent, 1981). For the effect of opium-taking on Coleridge and his wife, see M. Lefebure, *Samuel Taylor Coleridge, the Bondage of Opium* (Gollancz, 1974) and *The Bondage of Love* (Gollancz, 1986).

[8] People who do not take alcohol or tobacco are very unlikely to use cannabis, and if they do not use cannabis are most unlikely to use heroin. (Only a tiny proportion of cannabis users progress to heroin, but almost all heroin users have tried cannabis first.) But Dr David Smith, Director of the Haight-Ashbury Free Medical Clinic, believes that the child of an alcoholic parent has thirty-five times the average chance of becoming dependent, and with two alcoholic parents, 400 times the probability.

[9] Papers presented at the American Medical Association's 6th National Conference on the Impaired Physician, September 1984.

[10] Dr Lawrence Prescott, *British Medical Journal*, 30 May 1985.

[11] *New Statesman*, 4 March 1966.

[12] G. V. Stimson, *Heroin and Behaviour* (Irish University Press, London, 1973).

[13] To the despair of his doctor, who advised him to rest and open his window (G. Painter, *Marcel Proust*, Chatto and Windus, 1965).

[14] In an experiment in which two successive doses of morphine were given to 150 healthy young males, only three were willing to allow the injection again and none would have requested it. (I. Chein *et al.*, *Narcotics, Delinquency and Social Policy*, Tavistock, 1964.)

[15] M. Nyswander, *The Drug Addict as a Patient* (Grune & Stratton, 1956).

See also P. Laurie, *Drugs* (Penguin, 1967). Some drug-taking and alcoholism may also be viewed as a 'game' – i.e. transactions to gain an interpersonal advantage: see Anthony Clare on the subject in M. Grant and P. Gwinner, *Alcoholism in Perspective* (Croom Helm, 1979).

16 *The Drugtakers* (MacGibbon & Kee, 1971). The Wootton Committee suggested that the recent increase in mood-altering drugs 'could not unreasonably be ascribed to growing disenchantment with the highly competitive and threatening nature of contemporary society, or to the destruction of the natural environment'.

17 Personal interviews, 1985.

18 'Suffering from the awareness of his powerless and separateness, man can try to overcome his existential burden by achieving a trance-like state of ecstasy . . . [by] the sexual act . . . religious cults, ecstatic dance, the use of drugs, frenzied sexual orgies, or self-induced states of trance.' Erich Fromm, *The Anatomy of Human Destructiveness* (Penguin, 1977).

19 'Our belief in technology . . . presupposes that man can contrive substances that will easily relieve and better his condition. Whatever the reason, Americans have conventionally sought relief from pills. Generations of young people have been brought up with the notion that there is a chemical solution for any unpleasantness: physical, social or psychological.' D. Holmes, L. Appignanesi and M. Holmes, *The Language of Trust* (Science House, USA, 1971).

20 'They hate those whom they love since they cannot get from them what they really need, and since they dare not show this hate for fear of losing even that which they have, they turn it inwards in self-torment and despair.' Anthony Storr, *Human Aggression* (Pelican, 1970).

21 Stanton Peele with A. Brodsky, *Love and Addiction* (Abacus, 1977). See also Erich Fromm, *The Art of Loving* (Harper & Row, 1956).

22 *Drugs Demystified* (UNESCO, 1975).

23 If 'drug dependence' is defined as a continued reliance on chemicals, then women drug dependants outnumber men in industrialized Western societies, although most of them are using prescribed drugs. At the same time the organization DAWN (Drugs, Alcohol and Women Nationally) points out the hypocrisy of a society where women are encouraged to be dependent on men and on therapeutic drugs, but are then vehemently condemned if they are publicly seen to be influenced by drugs in a socially accepted form.

24 Roy Wallis, *The Elementary Forms of the New Religious Life* (Routledge & Kegan Paul, 1984). The new cults are almost invariably formed by leaders whom their followers find charismatic: Scientology's L. Ron Hubbard, EST's Werner Erhard, Synanon's Charles Dederich, the Sannyasins' Bhagwan Shree Rajneesh, the Divine Light Mission of Maharaj Ji, the Process's Robert de Grimston, David Berg of the Children of God (or Family of Love), Jim Jones of the People's Temple, the Family of Charles Manson, Transcendental Meditation's

Maharishi Yogi, the Unification Church's Sun Moon – similar to the earlier Christian Science's Mary Baker Eddy and the Mormons' Joseph Smith.

25 'The Narcissistic Society' (*New York Review of Books*, 30 September 1976).

26 The 1985 study of heroin misuse carried out for the UK Central Office of Information by Andrew Irving Associates concluded: 'Most parents knew little about the relative dangers of different drugs . . . The majority of parents seem confused and ill-equipped either to recognize or handle drug misuse by their children . . . They were generally uncertain about what resources were available. When they did look for help they often found a lack of sympathy and helpful guidance especially from GPs.'

27 Nora Sayre reports from New York of some cases where mothers welcomed the fact that their drug-addicted sons were so dependent on their help, and sabotaged their treatment.

28 FA (like AA, Narcotics Anonymous and Gamblers Anonymous) started in the USA. Al-Anon similarly helps the families of alcoholics, and Gam-Anon the families of gamblers. For contact addresses, see the list at the end of the book. The USA also now has a growing National Federation of Parents for Drug-free Youth, and Cocaine Anonymous.

29 'In view of the gravity of the drug epidemic, I believe every parent should assume that his child is using or possibly dealing in drugs until proven otherwise.' Dr H. M. Voth, 'Drugs and the Family', in G. Nahas and H. Frick (eds), *Drug Abuse in the Modern World* (Pergamon, 1981).

30 The relationship is not always one-way: In the USA a young teenage daughter recently turned over to the police the cocaine she found her parents using. See also, Bill Rice, *Young People and Drugs: Guidelines for Parents* (Teachers' Advisory Council on Alcohol and Drug Education, 1980).

31 D. Holmes, L. Appignanesi and M. Holmes, *The Languge of Trust* (Science House, 1971).

32 Including Enfield, Ealing, Brent, Waltham Forest, Greenwich, Haringey, Hackney, Redbridge, Sutton and Merton.

33 *Misuse of Drugs, with special reference to the Treatment and Rehabilitation of Misuers of Hard Drugs* (HMSO, 1985). This report stated that there were only thirty-five specialist drug-dependency units, mostly concentrated in and around London, and that 'a few dozen doctors, primarily psychiatrists, are striving to provide a service for 10,000 notified addicts which was designed briefly for 1,000'. It also alleged that jailed addicts have little incentive to give up drugs because supplies are easily obtained inside: 'Our greatest concern is that the time so many addicts spend in custody represents a wasted opportunity for tackling the problem of their addiction.'

34 'Methadone is just substituting a cheap habit for an expensive one,' said Dr Eric Comstock of Baylor University in the USA. Even short-term

maintenance suffers from the weakness that addicts, having dropped out, may continually revert for further periods.

[35] 'This provides a framework for the addict and, perhaps more important, means that the GP doesn't see himself endlessly involved with the patient.' in London. Dr Martin Mitcheson, however, also warns about the power of control the ability to prescribe gives a doctor. Some 'junkie doctors' are ambivalent: needing the junkie patients as much as vice versa, and feeling guilty about this.

[36] *GP*, 22 February 1985. Cf. 'Because of his personality defects, an addict needs a strong, stable one-to-one relationship with a wise adult who will be able to play the role of the deficient father.' H. Dale Beckett, *Transactions of the Medical Society of London*, 11 December 1967.

[37] Lecture in Geneva, 20 March 1985.

[38] See L. N. Robins in D. Kandel (ed.), *Longitudinal Research on Drug Use* (Halstead–Wiley, 1978); and also M. Patterson, *Hooked?* (Faber, 1986).

[39] Naltrexone cannot be taken by people with damaged livers. Marketed by Du Pont under the brand name Trexan, it received the approval of the US FDA in November 1984.

[40] Dr Mitchell Rosenthal of Phoenix House, New York, said: 'In a Phoenix House the teaching of socialization and its consequent morality is made both explicit and emphatic . . . We regard anti-social, anti-military [*sic*], amoral and acting-out behaviour as "stupid".' H. Steinberg (ed.), *Scientific Basis of Drug Dependence* (Churchill, 1969). At one time (though not now) the London Phoenix House's inmates who lapsed back on to drugs were humiliated by having their heads shaved, so that as their hair grew again they could measure how long they had stayed 'clear' or drug free.

[41] Wealthy godparents are reported to wonder whether to put children's names down at birth for expensive fashionable clinics such as Broadway Lodge, which are almost as hard to get a place in as Eton.

[42] Marmottan currently claims a 31 per cent rate of cure.

[43] Prison costs some £200 a head a week; a residential rehabilitation centre around half that. For histories and accounts of some drug agencies see especially R. Yates, *Out of the Shadows* (NACRO, 1981), N. Dorn and N. South, *Helping Drugs Users* (Gower, 1985) and J. Picardie and D. Wade, *Heroin* (Penguin, 1985). Rowdy Yates of Lifeline blames the persistence of the medical model of addiction for failure to develop sufficient skills in social work. For a summary of treating alcoholics see P. Gwinner, 'Treatment approaches' in M. Grant and P. Gwinner (eds), *Alcoholism in Perspective* (Croom Helm, 1979).

[44] Christiane F. in *H: Autobiography of a Child Prostitute and Heroin Addict* (Corgi, 1981) recounted that she went into a West German mental hospital where she was made to sign an agreement to remain for three months under the threat that, if she did not, she would be compulsorily hospitalized for six months. She absconded. She preferred

one drugs advice centre where, instead of being talked at as by her parents, she herself was encouraged to speak about her problems; however, she repeatedly returned to her heroin friends round the Zoo Station in Berlin. She eventually broke free from drugs when she went to live with her grandmother in the country, where she found a reliable substitute family, work and new friends.

45 Compulsory powers for removal to hospital exist under the Mental Health Act 1959 in cases of mental disorder, and under Section 47 of the National Assistance Act 1948 where persons are unable to look after themselves.

46 W. Deedes, *The Drugs Epidemic* (Stacey, 1970).

47 50th Annual Report of the Magistrates' Association, 1969–70.

48 E. Vallance (ed.), *The State, Society and Self-destruction* (Allen & Unwin, 1975).

49 D. J. West (ed.), *Problems of Drug Abuse in Britain* (Cambridge, 1978).

50 The authorities at the 1986 Wimbledon tennis tournament equally attracted controversy when they announced that any player found after tests to have taken drugs would not be censured or named, but told to undergo treatment with a psychiatrist: 'If any player is guilty, we want to help, not punish, him.'

13 Trying to Stem the Rising Tide

1 Mr Ronald Broome, Chief Constable of Avon and Somerset who heads the British Association of Chief Police Officers' working group on drugs, rightly points to the need for clearer data concerning the size of the problem, since much of the present research is client-orientated and fails to measure illicit drug use. (Personal communication, 1985.)

2 Speech to the London Diplomatic Association, 1984.

3 *Sunday Times*, 19 August 1984.

4 The US General Accounting Office in 1983 reported that the price of a milligram of heroin had fallen from $2.25 in 1979 to $1.66; during the same period the price of cocaine fell from 65 to 52 cents, and that of marijuana from $1.38 a gram to $1.32.

5 Representative Glenn English (Oklahoma). Senator DeConcini (Arizona) says, 'We have never had a war on drugs. It's all talk. The effort, at least in the interdiction area, has been limited to photo opportunities for the President and the Vice President.' In addition, Francis Mullen of the FBI had to wait Senate confirmation as Head of DEA from July 1981 until November 1983.

6 Personal interviews, New York, 1984.

7 Selwyn Rabb (*New York Times*, 27 May 1984). For the UK, see R. Taylor, 'Criminal Convictions of drug addicts', *Home Office Research Bulletin* (20/1986).

8 Survey by Andrew Irvine Associates for Central Office of Information,

1985. See also Detective Superintendent T. Jones, *Drugs and the Police* (Butterworth, 1968).

9 A senior Scotland Yard officer said in the summer of 1985: 'It's embarrassing to admit we have so few men. It means there are some jobs we just have to let pass by, because we just don't have the resources to take them on.' Later, plans were announced to increase the number to fifty-seven.

10 *Much Ado About Nothing* (III. 3). See B. Cox, J. Shirley and M. Short, *The Fall of Scotland Yard* (Penguin, 1977), and even perhaps B. Whitaker, *The Police in Society* (Sinclair Browne, 1982).

11 The Royal Canadian Mounted Police are now giving their undercover operators special psychological tests because of concern at the problems encountered when they stay undercover for long. In Canada the use of gerbils to sniff out drugs in prisons has recently also had to be stopped because the rodents are too sensitive.

12 Rochin v. California, 342 U.S. 165.

13 Lucien Conein, a CIA colonel of Corsican extraction, acknowledged that he had been sent to the Bureau to superintend a special unit which would have the capacity to assassinate selected targets amongst narcotics dealers (*Washington Post*, 13 June 1976).

14 The London telephone number is (01) 230 2121. It was not set up until December 1984, being adapted from Ulster (where it is used against terrorists). On average, it has resulted in one arrest for every nine calls.

15 The ruling on schoolchildren was given by a New Jersey court on 11 December 1985. In the Chicago Transit Authority ten years ago some 40 per cent of disciplinary offences were due to alcohol; today about 10 per cent are due to alcohol and 30 per cent to drugs.

16 David Leigh, *Observer*. (In 1927 the Privy Council upheld a Canadian government attempt to tax an Ontario bootlegger.) The Inland Revenue eventually recovered almost £500,000 from participants in the Operation Julie case.

17 N. Liverpool, 'The seizure and forfeiture of property associated with criminal activity' (*Bulletin on Narcotics*, XXXV.2, 1983).

18 These proposals go much further than the recommendations of the Howard League Committee under Mr Justice Hodgson that was set up following the Operation Julie case's judgment (R. v. Cuthbertson, 1981 A.C. 470).

19 P. Bucknell, 'Developments in Drug Abuse' (*Justice of the Peace*, 5 November 1983).

20 R. v. Shiupuri, Court of Appeal, 5 November 1984.

21 J. Kaplan, *The Hardest Drug* (Chicago University Press, 1983). But in the case of Lanham v. Rickwood (4 May 1984) the British Divisional Court ruled that the offence of being drunk in a public place applied to intoxication only from alcohol and not from glue.

22 'Interpol is not a police force that carries out operational work, and the

officers are not international policemen who travel anywhere to make arrests.' W. Leamy (Head of the Interpol Drugs Sub-division, *Bulletin on Narcotics*, XXXV.4, 1983).

23 Personal interview, 1984.

24 There is now one in Pakistan and one in the Netherlands. The USA's DEA has eleven men in Pakistan.

25 'The benzodiazepines represent an enormous market in which there is intense competition; and the pharmaceutical industry had last year and earlier fought hard and successfully to prevent their scheduling by the UN Commission on Narcotic Drugs . . . The UK, [the] Federal Republic of Germany, Switzerland, Belgium, [the] Netherlands and Brazil were among countries opposed to scheduling almost all benzodiazepines.' *Lancet*, 17 March 1984.

26 K. Bruun *et al.*, *The Gentlemen's Club* (University of Chicago Press, 1975).

27 J. Kaplan, *op. cit.*

28 House of Commons debate, 13 July 1984.

29 'The person seated in a soft and comfortable chair in an office or conference room may tend to believe that "the easiest way of stopping the illicit drug traffic is to declare cultivation of the opium poppy illegal and, because it is illegal, to destroy the plantations". Such reasoning, applied to the "Golden Triangle", is quite utopian. It is impossible to control a territory larger than some European countries, mountainous, inaccessible, without roads or any means of communication. In order to destroy the plantations declared illegal, whole battalions of troops would have to be committed, who would certainly be met with bullets from people who would totally fail to understand why their livelihood should be taken from them when hardly out of the ground. What, after all, would be the reaction of the vine-growers of France, Italy or California, if troops arrived, and, without more ado, began to cut down their vines where they stood, on the grounds that the products obtained from them were injurious to human health? Or, in more practical terms, how is it possible to apply the law in a region lacking an administrative infrastructure? In the case of the "Golden Triangle" the entire population and social context clearly precludes any policy of destruction of plantations, even if they are declared illegal.' J. Nepote (former Secretary-General of Interpol), 'In the Golden Triangle with a Handful of Dollars', *Bulletin on Narcotics*, Vol. 28, No. 1, 1976.

30 US State Department annual report on world narcotics production, February 1986.

31 A. McNicoll, *Drug Trafficking* (North-South Institute, Ottawa, 1983). Dr J. Ashton of Liverpool also comments: 'Had the excess of supplies been of milk or butter within Europe, by now we would have adopted an interventionist policy to buy up the supplies from the producers in Afghanistan and Pakistan, in order to maintain the standard of living of the farmers in those countries.'

32 J. M. Polich, P. L. Ellickson, P. Reuter, J. Kahan, *Strategies for Controlling Adolescent Drug Use* (Rand Corporation, 1984).

14: The Global Connection: Smugglers, Multinational Trafficking and the Mafia

1 This is not solely a modern phenomenon. In the 1920s cocaine was smuggled into Britain in hollowed walking-sticks, as well as in sausages, opera hats and even models of the Whitehall Cenotaph. (The *Evening News* of 29 March 1922 commented about the latter, 'only the German mind could have sunk to this level'.)

2 Russell Pasha in 1930 bribed informers to reveal how heroin was being brought into Egypt inside the soles and heels of shoes, and in stoves with false bases, as well as in tubes inside people's orifices.

3 See David Leigh, *Hard Times* (Heinemann, 1984).

4 A witness told the Stewart Royal Commission: 'The toys would take the attention of the Customs officer in Australia, and make him feel sorry and let the courier through. The courier felt relaxed by saying to the Customs officer, "Oh, no, it's got broken." '

5 Smugglers were recently caught in Testa-Grigia near the Matterhorn, having skied from Cervinia in Italy. Miniature submarines have operated in Lake Lugano and Lake Maggiore.

6 In 1983 a waterproof storehouse, lined with fibreglass and containing radar and radio equipment, together with outboard motors, inflatable boats and hauling gear, ready for the landing of several tons of cannabis, was by chance found to have been constructed under a beach on the west Wales coast. Local fishermen's suspicions had been aroused by the life-style of strangers seen nearby (one of whom took £760,000 in cash to deposit in the Isle of Man) – but these visitors claimed to be filming seals. While the police watched at night, a boat approached and transmitted the message, 'I am ready to get rid of the dirt,' but since the police did not know the answering code sign, the boat sped off – and was never caught, because the police had no means of intercepting it.

7 One Customs officer said, 'At present people have almost no expectation or fear of being caught. We've even found people carrying heroin in shoulder bags without any attempt to hide it.' Michael Hancock MP told the Commons that when he flew from Morocco – where he'd been offered every variety of drug – to Gatwick, there was not a single Customs officer to be seen. (*Hansard*, 13 July 1984.)

8 Brian Spiller, a Customs officer at Plymouth, points out how easily drugs can be landed from private yachts in his area: 'There are hundreds of little creeks and inlets where smugglers can sail four or five miles inland at high tide.' On Britain's south coast are moored several thousand boats

(6,000 in Chichester harbour and 4,000 in the Hamble), many of which are capable of sailing to international ports.

9 Personal interviews in New York, May 1984.

10 One British Airways baggage supervisor at Heathrow, recently convicted of running a cocaine smuggling scheme, aroused suspicion through possessing a country mansion with stables and sending his children to Millfield public school. The *Sunday Times* (24 March 1985) reported that a doctor in Pakistan stated that out of forty airport security staff sent to him for screening, thirty were heroin addicts.

11 Some policemen find it ironic that one of the most luxurious scents sold at airports is named Opium; and that a board game called Dealer McDope, about making multi-million-dollar drug deals, is now being marketed in the USA.

12 Dr Philippe Bargain, of the Paris airports medical authority, says diagnosis is sometimes all too easy: 'They're so skinny, I just need to palpate them.' A Dutch police expert comments: 'We have a special way of picking them out of the flights or trains. Most of them carry the same money, $1,000. They have new suits and underneath very old things. They do not know what they are doing in our country.'

13 Sergeant J. Burnett's advice concerning body-searching for drugs in the *Police Review* (1976) shows the difficulties for law enforcement agents: he stated that it is necessary to make a thorough examination of each suspect's ears, nostrils, anus, vagina, folds of foreskin, faeces, any open wounds, and teeth. ('Drug-takers frequently have bad teeth with cavities. A few microdots wrapped in silver paper . . . remarkably resemble a filling, so check.') But in December 1985 a couple were awarded £3,750 damages for assault and being strip-searched by police looking for drugs.

14 For example, Frank Fiala, a 37-year-old machinist murdered in Brooklyn in 1981, bought with his drug-smuggling dividends a disco (paid for with $1.5 million in cash, reportedly because he did not like the service he had received when he had visited it), a $300,000 helicopter and two twin-engined Cessna aircraft, besides a Rolls Royce, a Mercedes convertible, another 22-foot stretch limousine and a 41-foot yacht. By contrast, a young Dutch woman arrested for running a $400 million international heroin ring had acquired a Goya masterpiece and was negotiating to buy a New York bank (Nicholas Pileggi, 'Drug Business', *New York*, 13 December 1982). Sometimes both legitimate and illegal businesses coalesce: Oxford's most stylish cannabis dealer had his headquarters for several years in the building of an ultra-fashionable dress boutique.

15 Two sociologists who were able to study some upper-echelon cannabis dealers in California found that after the initial exhilaration, disenchantment and 'burnout' often set in, but that the attraction of the danger and the money generally drew them back to dealing (*Social Problems*, 31:2). At street level, some dealers say that they obtain 'satisfaction from

helping people' (as well as using pyramid selling to support their own habit), though others abuse the power they wield over female addicts.

16 The UN reported: 'In 1979 . . . Western Europe clearly replaced parts of the Americas as the main target for traffickers dealing in illicit opiates. More heroin was seized in Europe than in any other single region. There were no indications that this heroin was in transit to North America.'

17 The UK Customs' seizures of heroin coming from Pakistan rose from 11.6 kg. in 1980 to 54.9 kg. in 1981 and 158.2 kg. in 1982 (in addition to 12.1 kg. coming from India). In 1986 the Chairman of the Karachi High Court Bar Association said, 'There are so many cases where people are known, but are not arrested. They are enjoying some sort of immunity.'

18 In 1983 the Indian authorities discovered the country's first-known heroin factories, in Lucknow and Varanasi.

19 Other principal countries exporting cannabis include Nigeria, Ghana, Congo, Benin, Zaire, Morocco, Kenya, South Africa, Nepal, Jamaica and Mexico.

20 The ring offered, *inter alia*, twenty Exocet missiles to the Argentine military government for 42 billion lire (about £20 million) though this particular deal was discovered and forestalled by British intelligence.

21 *Le Monde*, 31 July 1985.

22 Roger Lewis *et al.*, *Big Deal* (Pluto, 1985). The town of Calenzana in Corsica traditionally has given birth to many Marseilles gangsters. In the sixteenth century the majority of renegade Europeans helping the pirates in Algiers were from that harshly beautiful though impoverished island.

23 In his beautifully written book, *The Honoured Society* (Collins, 1964), Norman Lewis traces the word *mafia* to an Arabic word meaning 'place of refuge', used in the eleventh century when the Normans conquered Sicily's relatively civilized Saracen inhabitants. Others have suggested that it originates from the Ma'afir, an Arab family in Palermo, or – less convincingly – from the initials of 'Morte Alla Francia Italia Anela', a password during the Sicilian Vespers revolt. *Omerta* means, not as sometimes supposed 'silence', but 'being a man'. The Calabrian *'Ndrangheta* derives its name from a Greek word meaning 'superiority'.

24 When it organized the plebiscite in Lampedusa's Donnafugata (which he portrayed in *The Leopard*), the result was: voters, 515; voting, 512; in favour 512; against, none.

25 Joe Valachi, the first *mafioso* informer, quoted in G. Servadio's excellent *Mafioso* (Secker and Warburg, 1976). See also James Walston, *The Mafia in Calabria* (forthcoming); H. Hess, *Mafia* (Bari, 1973); Pino Arlacchi, *Mafia, Peasants and Great Estates* (Cambridge University Press, 1983), and *Mafia Business* (Verso, 1986).

26 The motive for this may have been the hope that *mafiosi* would assist the Allied landings in Sicily, or help to organize the Italian-American New York dock-workers for the war effort; on the other hand many people now believe it was a self-interested political move by the Republican

Thomas Dewey to win over the Italian–American vote which traditionally goes to the Democrats. The Allied forces, in any event, joined with *mafiosi* to defeat the Italian Communist resistance, and in return accepted them into the post-war establishment of Italy. The notorious Mafia leader Vito Genovese, despite having supported the Fascists and being wanted by the New York police for murder, was appointed to be a key interpreter-liaison officer at the US Army HQ in Naples, where he organized a profitable black market before ultimately being jailed for heroin trafficking in New York. D. Mack Smith, *A History of Sicily* vol. 3 (Chatto and Windus, 1968) and N. Lewis, *Naples '44* (Eland, 1983). Luciano's real name was Salvatore Luciana, although when he held court at the Waldorf-Astoria Hotel he called himself Charles Ross.

27 The killing took place near his headquarters at Villa Whitaker, the former house of the author's great-aunt. The assassination is reported to have been carried out by the Catania Mafia on behalf of the Corleone Mafia.

28 Joe Colombo Jnr suggested that an 'Italian-American Civil Rights League' should counter-attack against the FBI by persuading law-abiding Italian-Americans that any criticism of the Mafia defamed them. As a result the producer of the film *The Godfather* was reported to have been compelled to remove from the script all references to the Mafia or Cosa Nostra.

29 See Martin Short's well-informed *Crime Inc.* (Methuen, 1984). Anslinger infiltrated Italian informers into the Cosa Nostra at a time when J. Edgar Hoover was still denying its existence. Short states that later the CIA contracted the Cosa Nostra's boss in Tampa to kill Fidel Castro with poison, through John Rosselli of the Chicago family. When Rosselli revealed this, he himself was killed in an oil drum thrown into a creek.

30 Sometimes it hardly needs to: the Mafia boss Michele Zaza, charged with being a smuggler of heroin and cocaine, escaped from prison in Rome when a judge remarkably gave him permission to attend a New Year's Eve Ball on 31 December 1983.

31 In 1985, a Euro-MP was jailed for ten years, but later freed, on charges of drug-trafficking links with the Camorra. On the rebirth of the Camorra after the last war, see Norman Lewis, *Naples '44* (Eland, 1983).

32 In tropical zones, the opium poppy flourishes in temperate hill areas over 1,000 metres above sea-level, preferring alkaline soil, especially limestone.

33 US Bureau of Narcotics, *The World Opium Situation* (Washington, DC, 1970). No evidence was found to back Anslinger's allegation that the Chinese People's Republic exported opium from either political or commercial motives. See the US Strategic Intelligence Office's *Special Report: China and Drugs* (Washington, DC, 1972).

34 The details of this were first uncovered in Alfred McCoy's brilliantly-

researched and courageous book *The Politics of Heroin in South-east Asia* (Harper and Row, New York, 1973), which the CIA helped to authenticate by trying to prevent its publication: Cord Meyer, the CIA's Deputy Director for Plans (the covert action department) paid a personal visit to Cass Canfield, the President Emeritus of Harper and Row, who to his credit refused to censor the book. In August 1971 McCoy (who now teaches history at the University of New South Wales) narrowly escaped assassination by CIA mercenaries in Laos (personal communication to the present author from McCoy, July 1984).

[35] US Military Assistance Command Vietnam, Report of the Office of the Provost Marshal, *The Drug Abuse Problem in Vietnam* (Saigon, 1971). Three years earlier, US Senator Albert Gruening had accused Air Vice-Marshal Ky of smuggling opium, and in 1971 US congressman Robert Steele informed a Congressional Sub-Committee of evidence that General Ngo Dzu was 'one of the chief traffickers'.

[36] In 1972 Richard Helms, the Director of the CIA, was reported to have offered to spend an hour a day in meditation for the rest of his life if Allen Ginsberg could prove the CIA's involvement in the transport of heroin in south-east Asia.

[37] The offer was made via the British documentary film-makers Adrian Cowell and Chris Menges.

[38] The US assistance in the last decade is estimated to have cost $140 million, and included forty-nine American helicopters and twenty-two spotter-aircraft (a number of which mount a special camera claimed to be capable of identifying opium and marijuana crops covering areas of 1,200 square kilometres a day).

[39] The Anti-Slavery Society, *Reporter* (1985); *International Herald Tribune*, 19 November 1984.

[40] Armed with machine-guns, they are reported to have provided an escort for consignments of drugs across the border near Laredo, and then to have established 'perimeter defence' on Texan soil while the drugs were unloaded. *International Herald Tribune*, 26 September 1985.

[41] B. Freemantle, *The Fix* (Michael Joseph, 1985). One former Bolivian Minister of the Interior was also stated in court to have seized cocaine from smaller traffickers who would not pay protection money, and then to have stored it for safe-keeping in the nation's empty bank vaults. Many Bolivians, however, regard Suarez as an anti-Yanqui folk-hero and public benefactor: see Amado Canelas Orellana and Juan Carlos Canelas Zannier's *Bolivia: Coca Cocaina* (Los Amigos del Libro, Cochabamba, 1983).

[42] Colombia's greatest writer, Gabriel García Márquez, said about his own works, 'What Europeans insist on calling surrealism is merely a reflection of our reality in Latin America.' Medellín (Colombia's second city, where there are an average of more than six murders a day) is the cocaine centre; Barranquilla (where the British consul was murdered in 1986)

and Cartagena in Guajira province on the north coast are the main ports which export marijuana.

43 The Colombian drug syndicates' brutality excels even that of the Mafia: their shooting in Brooklyn in April 1984 of Virginia Lopez (five months pregnant), her four children, her cousin with her two children and two other young members of her family, was unprecedented even by New York standards. Violent black drug syndicates are also becoming powerful: the Barnes Harlem heroin ring who were sentenced in 1984 specialized in chainsaw executions; and a man applying to join the syndicate was made to prove himself by murdering a randomly-selected passer-by. Another of its members was acquitted at a drug trial where he arranged to have poison put in the court water-jug from which a key government witness and the judge were drinking; a $50,000 bribe he paid to a juror resulted in his obtaining a hung jury.

44 *Newsweek*, 25 February 1985.

45 Hugh O'Shaughnessy (*Observer*, 10 November 1985). The UK has recently offered £1 million to Peru to help reduce the coca being grown in the Huallaga valley. See also *Cultural Survival Quarterly* (vol. 9, no. 4, 1985).

46 More than 2,000 illegal immigrants a month enter southern Florida. A steady flow of Haitian refugees are smuggled from Haiti and the Bahamas to the docks along Miami's river; it is far easier to conceal a bag of cocaine. The same route to south Florida was used by gun-runners to beat the blockade in the American Civil War, and later to import rum in Prohibition days.

47 Freemantle, *op. cit.* See also the excellent piece of investigative journalism by the Insight team in the *Sunday Times* (29 September 1985) magazine.

48 Michele Sindona, the jailed Sicilian financier who died mysteriously in prison, owned the largest chain of banks on Long Island, the Franklin National. 'As a good Sicilian he knew there was no such thing as the Mafia, and that his customers . . . just happened to want to make huge payments in Ankara or transfer even huger payments from Jersey City.' Jonathan Steinberg (*London Review of Books*, 7 October 1982).

15: Hope in Hell: The Lessons and the Future

1 Personal interview, UN, Vienna, 1984.

2 Personal interview, 1985.

3 2 March 1985.

4 J. M. Polich, P. Ellickson, P. Renter and J. Kahan, *Strategies for Controlling Adolescent Drug Use* (Rand, Santa Monica, 1984).

5 Mervyn Manby, a former senior UN drug enforcement official, points out: 'The original agitation against opium and the opiates in the UK, USA and China was unequivocally based on the view that drug-taking

was a moral evil, a vice. Now the Western world hardly recognizes vice at all, while drug abusers are claimed for psychiatrists, sociologists and educationalists. Yet still the drug laws are based on a moral view. It is not very surprising that they are unenforceable. My own personal attitude is that a law which is for any reason unenforceable is bad in itself, and bad for the rest of the law and ought to be repealed.' (Personal letter, 1984.)

6 J. S. Mill, *On Liberty* (Pelican, 1974; first published in 1859). Later in the same essay he also wrote: 'It is important to give the freest scope possible to uncustomary things, in order that it may in time appear which of these are fit to be converted into customs.'

7 *ibid.* Cf. attitudes to smoking and laws requiring health warnings on cigarette publicity today.

8 *Reason* (January 1978).

9 D. Solomon, *LSD* (Putnam, New York, 1966).

10 Personal letter, 1984.

11 P. Devlin, *The Enforcement of Morals* (Oxford University Press, 1968).

12 'It might be suggested that it would be helpful to view drug behaviour in the same way as other forms of human behaviour, rather than as something *sui genesis* which automatically requires extraordinary measures . . . No one requires of such presumptively dangerous activities as climbing mountains . . . or swimming that they should be "proved" to be "harmless" before society can "allow" them to occur; indeed the very suggestion is self-evidently ludicrous as soon as stated.' Don Aitken, 'The Criminal Law in the Control of Drugs' in E. Vallance (ed.), *The State, Society and Self-destruction* (Acton Society Study, Allen & Unwin, 1975).

13 W. G. Carson, 'Criminal Law and Self-destructive Action' in E. Vallance (ed.), *ibid.*

14 'One of the most unfortunate aspects of the drug laws is that the people at whom these laws are directed are just those people who are most in need of careful absorption into society rather than alienation from it . . . When the social environment in which one is brought up is so repressive and highly competitive, it is easy to lose faith in oneself and in doing so lose faith in society as well.' C. Coon and R. Harris, *The Release Report on Drug Offenders and the Law* (Sphere, 1969).

15 This is a view widely and strongly felt in developing countries. Bholanath Shankar of Katmandu argues: 'Legalized and judiciously controlled, recreational drugs such as cannabis and cocaine could generate much revenue that could be used for social programmes in America and help pay off the debt burden of many developing countries. Now they become the source of antisocial behaviour, swelling the coffers of cops, crooks and corrupt politicians with billions of dollars.'

16 Personal letter, 1984. William Deedes has also written: 'I am ready to admit uneasiness about moralizing on the use of mood-changing drugs. We know quite well that most of us find social occasions assisted by the

gentle stimulus of alcohol . . . A man, after all, can drink himself insensible in his own home if he chooses.' (*The Drugs Epidemic*, Stacey, 1970.)

17 J. Strang and L. Kay (of the Prestwick Drug Unit, Manchester), *New Scientist*, 18 October 1984. See also J. and J. Ditzler, *Coming Off Drugs* (Papermac, 1986) and I. Mothner and A. Weitz, *How to get off Drugs* (Penguin, 1986).

18 *Reflections on the Revolution in France* (1790).

19 The Wolfenden Committee suggested that the functions of the criminal law included: 'to provide sufficient safeguards against exploitation and corruption of others, particularly those who are specially vulnerable because they are young, weak in body or mind, inexperienced, or in a state of special physical, official or economic dependence'.

20 Personal interview, 1984.

21 Personal interview, New York, 1984; see also his article 'The Decriminalization Issue Revisited' in *Social Policy*, Fall 1982.

22 See Jock Young, *The Drugtakers* (MacGibbon & Kee, 1971).

23 'It is essential in regard to any control measure to prepare a balance-sheet of the observed or likely undesired consequences of the measure itself as against those of the behaviour it is sought to control.' E. Vallance, *op.cit*. See also T. Duster, *The Legislation of Morality* (Macmillan Free Press, 1970).

24 T. S. Eliot described in *The Wasteland*, 'Decent, godless people, their only monument the asphalt road and a thousand lost golf-balls.'

25 An inter-ministerial group on the misuse of drugs in the UK is chaired by a junior Home Office minister. A senior civil servant said: 'Junkies have a very low priority. If you look at it from a crime point of view, the victims of rape, murder, arson, who are all totally innocent, rate much higher. If you think of it as a health issue, a junkie rates lower than a heart patient or a kidney patient because a junkie's problem is self-inflicted. There are clearly very strong arguments for adopting an entirely new approach. But it seems unlikely that this government will be willing to fight the political battle that would be necessary.' But see *Tackling Drug Misuse* (UK Home Office, 2nd edition, 1986), and S. Caplin and S. Woodward, *Drugwatch* (Corgi, 1986).

26 Remarks made at the AGM of Phoenix's Featherstone Lodge project (*Druglink*, No. 14, summer 1980).

27 One worker at Release adds: 'In the current climate of moral outrage and hysteria, hard information has gone out of the window. The "Heroin Screws You Up" adverts, with their image of the teenage drug-user totally isolated, sinking through torpor into half-life, reinforce already ingrained attitudes to drug-users: that they are a hopeless category whose world is quite separate from the rest of us. This damaging view colours the way the problem is dealt with at all levels.'

28 Michael Davies of the UN suggests that drug hauls should be expressed not as street values (often over-estimates, not allowing for the discounts

given to friends or old customers), but in terms of the cost of consequent detoxification and rehabilitation.

[29] B. Shahandeh, *Rehabilitation Approaches to Drug and Alcohol Dependence* (ILO, 1985).

[30] 'The present counter-measures such as clamping down on the traffickers can only succeed if the punishment is as extreme as the Ayatollah's, so it is best to deal with the craving itself – whose existence has to be recognized.' (Personal letter, November 1985.)

[31] The Advisory Council on the Misuse of Drugs specifically advised against media campaigns, warning that 'ill-chosen educational methods attach disproportionate importance to drug misuse and arouse in some people an interest which they would not otherwise have felt'. *Prevention* (HMSO, 1984). Janet Fookes MP, who was a teacher, remembers, 'Children love to do what they are forbidden to do.'

[32] It is true that one of the specific objects of the mass media campaign was to 'reassure the public that the government is taking effective action'. (Report of a study carried out by Andrew Irving Associates for the UK Central Office of Information, 1985.) It was decided to concentrate the campaign on heroin, despite the risk that this might implicitly exonerate other dangerous drugs. Sammy Harari, the Director of Yellowhammer, the advertising agency running the UK campaign, said, 'Kids are very sophisticated, but they are illiterate and inarticulate. Long words like "Heroin will make you impotent" don't work: they don't know the word.' Evaluative research in 1986, after one year of the campaign, however, also found that parents were as ignorant and confused as before the campaign began; and that family doctors had, if anything, become even more hostile to addicts.

[33] Personal interviews, 1985.

[34] See her excellent introduction to drug education, *Drugs Demystified* (UNESCO Press, Paris, 1975). Cf. 'To teach or not to teach?' (*Courier*, UNESCO, May 1973). The UK Department of Education warned in *Health Education from 5 to 16* (HMSO, 1986): 'Work in schools aimed specifically at preventing drug or solvent misuse should be approached with caution because of the danger that it may promote experiment by pupils. However it is handled, it should form part of a broad health or personal and social education course . . . ' Booklists of further recommended resources are published by the UK Health Education Council (78 New Oxford Street, London W1), by the ISDD (1 Hatton Place, London EC1) and by TACADE (2 Mount Street, Manchester).

[35] See the Chicago experience of Dr Patrick Hughes, *Behind the Wall of Respect* (University of Chicago Press, 1977).

[36] 'Their pushers enjoy vast profits, making some of their most lucrative deals at carefully chosen locations at Heathrow often under the very eyes of Customs officials.' – Peter Kellner.

[37] J. Collier and H. Ghodse, *The Times*, 20 September 1985.

[38] Dr Avram Goldstein of the Addiction Research Foundation, Stanford

University, terms heroin 'a soft drug because whoever heard of a person under the influence of heroin doing anything of any great harm to anybody else, whereas alcohol is a hard drug, so often leading to actions which directly damage others.'

[39] G. Edwards and A. Arif, 'A problem in constant evolution' (*Courier*, UNESCO, January 1982).

[40] Personal letter, 1984.

[41] Personal interview, 1985.

[42] *The Doors of Perception* (Penguin, 1959).

[43] G. Edwards and A. Arif, note 39 *supra*.

[44] Norman Macrae's vision of the future includes: 'During the 1990s, the advance of elementary genetic engineering made possible the commercial production of B-endorphin. So heroin addiction (and its worst pains) could be effectively counteracted. Sensibly, governments then replaced bans with taxation systems – with the highest taxes on the addictive substances that did most harm (opium, gin, tobacco, and some of the drugs which were given free by state health services in the early 1980s) and no taxes on endogenous morphines.' *The 2024 Report* (Sidgwick & Jackson, 1984). Cf. F. Pohl and C. Kornbluth's novel *The Space Merchants*, in which a company gives away free samples of its drink, which contains a safe but habit-forming drug, to customers who become hooked on the product for life.

[45] See the interview with Dr Wisotsky in Brian Moser's Central TV film *Frontier USA*; and also C. Brazier, 'Dealing with Dreams' (*New Internationalist*, October 1984).

Useful Addresses

UK Organizations concerned with Alcohol Problems

ACTION ON ALCOHOL ABUSE, Livingstone House, 11 Carteret Street,
   London SW1H 9DL   (01) 222 3454
AL-ANON FAMILY GROUPS, 61 Great Dover Street, London SE1 4YF
   (01) 403 0888
ALCOHOL CONCERN, 3 Grosvenor Crescent, London SW1 6LD
   (01) 235 4182
ALCOHOLICS ANONYMOUS, PO Box 514, 11 Redcliffe Gardens,
   London SW10 8BQ   Greater London (01) 834 8202;   rest
   of country (01) 352 9779
NORTHERN IRELAND COUNCIL ON ALCOHOL, 41 University Street,
   Belfast   (0232) 238173 & 238202

SCOTTISH COUNCIL ON ALCOHOLISM, 147 Blythswood Street, Glasgow G2 4EN   (041) 333 9677

UK Anti-Smoking Organization

ACTION ON SMOKING AND HEALTH LTD (ASH), 5/11 Mortimer Street, London W1N 7RH   (01) 637 9843

UK Organizations concerned with Drug Abuse

ADFAM, St Georges, Aubrey Walk, London W8 7JY
    (01) 727 3595
FAMILIES ANONYMOUS, 88 Caledonian Road, London N1 9DN
    (01) 278 8805
HEALTH EDUCATION COUNCIL, 78 New Oxford Street, London
    WC1 1AH   (01) 631 0930
INSTITUTE OF PSYCHIATRY ADDICTION RESEARCH UNIT, 101 Denmark
    Hill, London SE5 8AF   (01) 703 5411
INSTITUTE FOR THE STUDY OF DRUG DEPENDENCE (ISDD),
    1 Hatton Place, London EC1N 8ND   (01) 430 1991
NARCOTICS ANONYMOUS, PO Box 246, 47 Milman Street, London
    SW10 ODP   (01) 351 6794
NATIONAL CAMPAIGN AGAINST SOLVENT ABUSE, Box S13, 245a
    Coldharbour Lane, London SW9 8RR   (01) 733 7330
RELEASE, 347a Upper Street, London N1 OPD   (01) 603 8654
THE STANDING CONFERENCE ON DRUG ABUSE (SCODA), 1 Hatton
    Place, London EC1N 8ND   (01) 430 2341
TEACHERS' ADVISORY COUNCIL ON ALCOHOL AND DRUG EDUCATION
    (TACADE), 2 Mount Street, Manchester M2 5NG
    (061) 834 7210
TRANX, 2 St Johns Road, Harrow, Middlesex   (01) 427 2065

Some Local Drug Help and Advice Centres

BLENHEIM PROJECT, 7 Thorpe Close, London W10 5XL
    (01) 960 5599
DRUGLINE, 28 Ballina Street, London SE23 1DR   (01) 291 2341

DRUGS AND NARCOTICS ANONYMOUS, 52 Queen Street, Edinburgh,
Scotland   (031) 225 6028
HUNGERFORD PROJECT, 26 Craven Street, London WC2N 5NT
(01) 930 4688
INFORMATION AND RESOURCE UNIT ON ADDICTION, 82 West Regent
Street, Glasgow G2   (041) 332 0062
LIFELINE PROJECT, Joddrell Street, Manchester M3 3HE
(061) 832 6353
MERSEYSIDE DRUGS COUNCIL, 25 Hope Street, Liverpool
L1 9BQ   (051) 709 0074
MIDLANDS DRUGLINE, Dale House, New Meeting Street,
Birmingham 4   (021) 632 6363
SUPPORT HELP AND ADVICE ON DRUG ADDICTION (SHADA), Unit 15,
Muirhouse Shopping Centre, Edinburgh   (031) 332 2314

Outside the UK

FAMILIES ANONYMOUS US, PO Box 528, Van Nuys, California 91408
JELLINEK CENTRUM, PO Box 3907, 1001 AS Amsterdam
(020) 220261
NARCOTICS ANONYMOUS US, PO Box 622, Sun Valley, California
91352
UN DIVISION OF NARCOTIC DRUGS, UN International Centre, PO Box
500, A-1400 Vienna, Austria   26310

Index